MINERAL RESOURCES

MINERAL

RESOURCES

Geology · Engineering ·

Economics · Politics · Law

by PETER T. FLAWN
Director, Bureau of Economic Geology
The University of Texas

JOHN WILEY & SONS, INC.
NEW YORK · LONDON · SYDNEY · TORONTO

CONTENTS

Preface

I. Minerals, Mineral Deposits, Reserves, and Resources   1

    Minerals and Mineral Deposits   1
    Water As a Mineral   7
    Mineral Reserves and Mineral Resources   9
    The Orebody Concept and the Cost Concept of
        Mineral Resources   17
    Exploration and Discovery   22
    Extraction of Minerals from the Earth   30
    Processing, Beneficiation, Refining, and
        Manufacturing   31
    Valuation of Mineral Deposits   33
    REFERENCES   36

II. Formation of Mineral Deposits   39

    HISTORY OF IDEAS   39
    SURFICIAL PROCESSES   43
        Physical (mechanical) processes   43
        Chemical and biological processes   45
    INTERNAL PROCESSES   48
    PROBLEMS OF CLASSIFICATION   52
    REFERENCES   53

III. Classification of Minerals and Mineral Deposits   54

    General Statement   54
    Classification of Mineral Deposits   59
    REFERENCES   72

IV. Lessons and Laws from Ancient History   73

    Introduction   73
    The Minerals of Prehistoric Man   81

Minerals in the Ancient World of the
Mediterranean   85
MINERALS IN THE WORLD OF ROME   96
The Far East   100
Dark or Middle Ages   103
CONCLUSIONS   109
REFERENCES   109

V. Renaissance, New Worlds, New Mines, and the
Dawn of Industrialization   112
Introduction   112
The New World   121
Britain and Northern Europe   124
REFERENCES   125

VI. Modern Mineral History   127
Introduction   127
The United States   130
Canada   135
Mexico   137
South America   137
Europe, Scandinavia, U.S.S.R., and the Balkans   139
Africa   140
Australia   141
India and Burma   143
Far East   145
Other 19th and 20th Century Developments   145
REFERENCES   146

VII. Ownership of Mineral Deposits   148
Introduction   148
Systems of Mineral Ownership   150
Regalian Theory   157
Mineral Law in the United States   160
The Need for Modernization of United States
Mineral Law   174
Canadian Mineral Law   178
Mineral Law in the U.S.S.R.   180
REFERENCES   180

VIII. Minerals and Government   182
Introduction   182

GEOLOGY AND MINERALS IN THE NEW CONSERVATION
    MOVEMENT   183
STOCKPILES AND OTHER ASPECTS OF A NATIONAL
    MINERAL POLICY   195
TAXATION   204
    Percentage depletion provisions of the U.S.
    Internal Revenue Code   205
MINERALS AND MONEY   210
    Introduction   210
    The nature of money   212
    Gold, silver, and the gold standard   213
    International Monetary Fund, international
    currency reserves, and international
    liquitdity   216
MINERALS IN THE DEVELOPING NATIONS   218
    Introduction   218
    The Alliance for Progress   227
    Zambia (Northern Rhodesia), a case history   229
    World Bank   232
    A First Step   234
MINERALS AND CITIES   235
THE ROLE OF MINERALS IN THE ECONOMY OF THE
    UNITED STATES   243
REFERENCES   247

IX. Minerals, Mining, and Ecology   251
    Introduction   251
    Mining   253
    Water Resource Projects   258
    Concentration, Beneficiation, and Refining   259
    Redistribution   261
    Conclusion   262
    REFERENCES   262

X. Occurrence, Distribution, and Outlook   264
    Introduction   264
    Reserve Index   271
    MINERAL FUELS   273
    Coal   273
    Crude oil   287
    Natural gas   289
    Uranium   290

IRON AND FERRO-ALLOY METALS   293
    Iron   293
    Manganese   295
    Chromium   297
    Nickel   299
    Molybdenum   300
    Tungsten   302
    Cobalt   303
    Vanadium   305
NONFERROUS INDUSTRIAL METALS   306
    Copper   306
    Lead   309
    Zinc   310
    Tin   311
    Aluminum and bauxite   316
PRECIOUS METALS   320
    Gold   320
    Silver   323
    Platinum group metals   327
MINOR METALS   327
    Beryllium   328
    Magnesium   329
    Mercury   330
    Titanium   332
SELECTED NONMETALLIC INDUSTRIAL MINERALS   334
    Asbestos   334
    Flourine   335
    Industrial diamonds   337
    Mica   338
    Phosphate rock   339
    Potash   345
    Sulfur   346
OTHER MINERAL COMMODITIES   350
CONCLUSION   352
REFERENCES   353

XI. *Future Supplies of Minerals*   **356**
    Introduction   356
    Discovery of New Deposits   358
    Development of Deposits Containing Lower
        Concentrations Than Are Now
        Exploitable   365

Development of Different Kinds of Deposits   368
Increased Recovery from Scrap and Waste   374
Synthesis and Substitution   378
Utilization of Minerals or Elements Not
   Now Used by Society   380
Extra-Terrestrial Sources   381
Imminent Problems—Silver and Mercury   382
Conclusion   385
REFERENCES   386

Index   389

LIST OF ILLUSTRATIONS

Tables—

I.1   Classes of Mineral Resources Estimates (after McKelvey, in preparation)   12

I.2   Concentration Clarkes for Orebodies of the Commoner Metals (after Mason, 1952)   21

I.3   Costs of Modern Mineral Exploration (after Bailly, Plates 11–14, 1964   24

I.4   Probability of Success in Mineral Exploration (modified from Bailly, 1964)   28

I.5   Gambler's Ruin (modified from Arps, 1961, and Bailly, 1964)   29

II.1   Processes of Formation of Mineral Deposits   50

III.1   The Metals   55

III.2   Grouping of Metals and Nonmetals (after McDivitt, 1965)   56

III.3   The Nonmetals   57

III.4   Classification of Nonmetallic Industrial Rocks and Minerals by Bates (1960)   58

III.5   Classification of Industrial Rocks and Minerals by Fisher (in press)   60

III.6   Classification by Niggli (1929)   62

III.7   Classification by Lindgren (1933)   63

III.8   Classification of Epigenetic Ore Deposits by Schneiderhöhn (1941)   64

III.9   Classification by Bateman (1950)   65

III.10 Classification of Nonmetals by Bateman (1950)   68

IV.1 Chronological List of Mining and Metallurgical Inventions (after Hoover, 1912)   77

IV.2 Evolution of Early Fire-using Mineral Industries (after Wertime, 1964)   78

IV.3 Highlights of Chinese Mineral History from the Detailed Chronicle of Collins (1918)   101

IV.4 Outline of the Evolution of Mining and Processing of Ores (after Forbes, 1963)   105

VII.1 Chronology of Major United States Mineral Legislation (from American Law of Mining, Vol. I, Chapters II, III, V)   171

VIII.1 Inventories of Mineral Commodities in U.S. Stockpiles (U.S. Bureau of Mines, Mineral Facts and Problems, 1965 edition, and Chemical Week, August 21, 1965) 198

VIII.2 Composition and Distribution of gross international monetary reserves, 1913–1962 (after Triffin, 1964)   218

VIII.3 Role of Minerals in the Economy of the United States— Salient Statistics, 1963 (U.S. Bureau of Mines Minerals Yearbook)   244

VIII.4 Trends in Consumption of Minerals and Other Natural Resources (after Romney, 1965)   246

X.1 Approximate Percentage Distribution of World Mineral Production in 1963 (U.S. Bureau of Mines Minerals Yearbook)   267

X.2 World Distribution of Minerals in Terms of 1963–64 Production, Reserves, and Resources (modified from U.S. Bureau of Mines Commodity Data Summaries)   274

X.3   Degree of Concentration (Grade) in Currently Exploited
       Mineral Deposits, Average Price of Commodity as
       Quoted in the United States in 1964, range of aver-
       age price 1960–1964   313

X.4   Reserves and Potential Reserves of Bauxite (Williams,
       1965a)   318

X.5   Silver Supply and Demand (Merrill et al., 1965)   324

X.6   World Productive Capacity of Phosphate Rock 1960–63
       (Chemical Week, October 24, 1964)   340

X.7   Phosphate Rock in the United States—Productive Capac-
       ity in 1965 (Chemical Week, October 24, 1964)   343

X.8   Production and Shipments of Sulfur in 1963 and 1964
       (excluding Sino-Soviet Bloc) (Chemical Week Report
       —Sulfur—September 12, 1964)   349

XI.1   Classification of Undiscovered Mineral Deposits   359

XI.2   Post-World War II revolution in mining technology
       (Knoerr, 1964)   366

XI.3   Scrap Metal in the United States   375

Figures—

I.1   Relation between investment and acreage during various
       stages of appraisal, reconnaissance, investigation and
       development of mineral property (after Bailly, 1964)   23

I.2   Value added by processing industrial minerals (after
       Fisher, 1965)   33

IV.1   The ancient gold mines at Fawa Khir in eastern Egypt
       (after Murray, 1925)   81

IV.2   Ancient Egyptian turquoise mines in Sinai (after Petrie,
       1906)   82

IV.3   Sites where bronze and iron were first exploited (3500–
       2000 B.C.) (after Wertime, 1964)   84

IV.4   Sites where metals were discovered in the sixth and fifth
       millenia, B.C. (after Wertime, 1964)   87

IV.5   The Sinai Peninsula (after Petrie, 1906)   88

IV.6   The Roman roads of the eastern desert of Egypt showing
       mines and quarries (after Murray, 1925)   97

V.1   Fire-setting to break the rock in a 16th century mine
       (after Agricola, 1556)   118

V.2   Mine surveying in the 16th century (after Agricola, 1556) 120

VI.1   The Comstock lode in the late 1870s (Nevada Historical
       Society)   131

VI.2   The Cane Creek (Utah) potash mine of Texas Gulf Sul-
       phur in 1962 (Texas Gulf Sulphur Annual Report,
       1962)   132

VI.3   Mining with a dredge—North Carolina phosphate (Texas
       Gulf Sulphur Annual Report, 1963)   133

VI.4   Mining phosphate with a dragline in North Carolina
       (Texas Gulf Sulfur Company)   134

VII.1   Ownership of the North Sea (after Eng. and Mining
            Jour., 1964a)   151

VII.2   A lode claim under United States mining law   165

VII.3   Lindley's exposition of the apex law (Lindley, 1914)   169

VIII.1   The government stockpile and the aluminum price crisis
            of November, 1965 (after Pendergast, 1965, p. 5)   200

VIII.2   A modern mining community in an undeveloped land:
            Oranjemund, built by Consolidated Diamond Mines
            of South-West Africa (Anglo American Corporation
            of South Africa, Limited, Johannesburg)   224

VIII.3   A quarry in the parth of urban expansion (after Bauer,
            1965)   236

VIII.4   Haulage costs of selected rock materials (after Fisher,
            1965)   238

VIII.5   Delivered costs (per cubic yard) of common aggregate
            materials in central and coastal Texas (after Fisher,
            1965)   239

VIII.6   A sound-proofed drilling rig on a one-acre site in the Los
            Angeles area (after Spaulding, 1965)   241

IX.1   Utah Copper's great pit in Bingham Canyon (Kennecott
            Copper Corporation)   256

X.1   Sources of United States iron ore supply 1940–63 and
            predicted sources 1964–80 (Reno, 1965)   293

X.2   Projected production and consumption of molybdenum
            in the United States (Holliday, 1965b)   302

X.3   Free world silver production and consumption 1955–63,
            with projections to 1967 (not including the United
            States) (Merrill et al., 1965)   325

X.4   U.S. silver production and consumption 1955–63, with projections to 1967 (Merrill et al., 1965)   326

X.5   The price history of mercury (E & MJ Market Guide, Mercury, January 25, 1965)   331

XI.1   Concealed mineral deposits related to the present (or Recent) surface   361

XI.2   Concealed subjacent mineral deposits   363

XI.3   Increase in the variety of minerals used by society (U.S. Geological Survey Long Range Plan, 1964)   381

PREFACE

THIS BOOK ATTEMPTS to relate geology, engineering, economics, politics, and law to mineral resources. Volumes have been written on each of these several disciplines—on economic geology, mineral engineering, mineral economics, various aspects of government mineral policy, and mineral law—and they are studied by geologists, engineers, economists, political scientists, and lawyers. But it is rare for these specialists to attend each other's professional meetings or listen to each other's papers. Much is to be gained by breaching the walls of the traditional disciplines so that students of mineral resources can pass through; although it would be difficult to find a better example of a transdisciplinary subject, the field of inquiry is occupied by many specialists and only a few generalists.

This book is for those seeking a broad background in mineral resources, for the generalist, but throughout the text there are many points of departure for those who would pursue a special interest. Both specialists and generalists have a contribution to make but the generalist is perhaps better able to perceive and understand relationships between his field of inquiry and the problems of human society. That this is of considerable importance in the complex modern world was clearly shown in the discussion provoked by C. P. Snow's "two cultures." A group within society but distinct from it by training, profession, and way of thinking—the scientific community, for example—cannot develop an 'apartheid' culture without arousing antagonisms. If science cannot be effectively related to society, the result will be a less vital science and a less well informed nonscientific society inclined to be belligerent toward science. It is up to science to build the bridge.

This book was inspired by T. S. Lovering's *Minerals and World Affairs* published in 1943, a delightful book brought out in the war years which related mineral resources to the world of that era and presented fundamental principles for students of mineral resources. Now, almost a quarter of a century later, the world has changed to such a degree that a new look at the subject is in order. This writer, a geologist attempting to cross fences into other fields, in many places found himself on unfamiliar ground and called upon colleagues for counsel and criticism. The helpful comments of M. K. Woodward of The University of Texas School of Law, and J. C. Dolley of The University of Texas Department of Finance are gratefully acknowledged. Parts of several chapters were read by J. Hoover Mackin. V. E. McKelvey and Paul A. Bailly undertook a review of the entire text. If this book has merit, it is due in no small way to the thoughtful suggestions and comments of these colleagues.

Peter T. Flawn

Austin, Texas
April, 1966

CHAPTER I

MINERALS, MINERAL DEPOSITS, RESERVES AND RESOURCES

Minerals and mineral deposits.

To many people, the term 'mineral' brings to mind a popular game entitled "Twenty Questions" where an unknown is identified simply as 'animal,' 'mineral,' or 'vegetable.' To them the word conveys the idea of a nonliving substance; it is in this context a useful general term. However, the fledgling scientist or engineer in his freshman year is faced with the necessity for precise definition and in an early course memorizes the standard definition of 'mineral' that can be found in most geology, mineralogy, and crystallography texts, and in the dictionary—to wit: A mineral is a naturally occurring inorganic solid crystalline substance with a definite chemical composition and a characteristic crystal structure. In first discussions of the matter the professor points out that ranges in composition due to solid solution series and substitutions of elements, ions, or ion complexes for others do not really prejudice the definition.

However, while the budding scientist studies the crystal lattices of minerals, his opposite in law school is also learning about mineral substances. He learns that in American jurisprudence a wide variety of inorganic and organic substances are legally classed as minerals, including substances in the liquid or gaseous state, and that, in fact, some man-made products have been held by the courts to be minerals or have been declared minerals through legislation or decision of the U.S. Department of Interior (American Law of Mining, vol. 1, pp. 166–167). A commonly cited legal definition of a mineral is "any substance occurring in the earth having sufficient value separated from its situs to be mined, quarried or dug for its own sake or for its own specific use" (Pruitt, 1966, p. 12). This definition is based on value whereas the scientific definition is based on the chemical and physical properties of the substance itself.

The result of these two different approaches to minerals is a courtroom dialogue as follows:

ATTORNEY: Mr. Roe, you have qualified as an expert witness; tell us, please, just what is a mineral?

WITNESS: A mineral is a naturally occurring inorganic solid crystalline substance with a definite chemical composition and a characteristic crystal shape.

ATTORNEY: Thank you. Is coal a mineral?

WITNESS: Coal? Well . . . ah . . . no, not under the definition I just gave.

JUDGE: (Opens his eyes and raises his eyebrows.)

ATTORNEY: What about oil and gas, Mr. Roe, are they minerals?

WITNESS: Well . . . no . . . not exactly, not under the scientific definition. Oil is a liquid mixture of hydrocarbons . . .

JUDGE: (Leans over the bench and interrupts.) You say oil is not a mineral? (The judge, who has heard nearly a hundred cases involving mineral interests in oil and gas leases, looks rather startled.)

WITNESS: Not . . . ah . . . scientifically speaking, your Honor.

JUDGE: Hummmmmppphh!

ATTORNEY: Well, Mr. Roe, is water a mineral?

WITNESS: Well, sir, of course water isn't solid and it doesn't have a definite crystalline structure, and its chemical composition varies according to the dissolved salts . . . so . . . scientifically speaking, of course, water isn't a mineral. (His face lights up.) But ice is! It fits the definition.

ATTORNEY: You mean if you melt a mineral it stops being a mineral? Why isn't it just a melted mineral?

WITNESS: (Shifts in the chair.) Well . . . . . .

ATTORNEY: Is sulfur a mineral, Mr. Roe?

WITNESS: Yes, sir.

ATTORNEY: Isn't it true that when sulfur is mined by the Frasch method the solid mineral is melted in the ground and pumped out?

WITNESS: That's true.

ATTORNEY: Well, then, according to your definition, if I have a mineral lease on a sulfur deposit it's only good as long as the sulfur is solid, because when I melt it to pump it out of the ground the sulfur stops being a mineral?

WITNESS: Hummmmmmmm. Well. . . . (Looks at his attorney.)

OPPOSING
COUNSEL: Objection. That's not a proper question.

JUDGE: Sustained. (Crazy scientists, he says to himself, oil and gas have been minerals for all the 42 years I've been on the bench.)

ATTORNEY: Thank you, Mr. Roe, that will be all.

Of course, experienced economic geologists and mineral lawyers recognize that there is a difference between the scientific and legal approach to minerals and that there is a need for both. However, the above dialogue is not entirely fanciful—it is, in fact, a composite of several the writer has heard in courtrooms. It is common for expert witnesses to feel frustrated in attempts to communicate with attorneys and judges and it is difficult for them to maintain the proper professional detachment when they hear extraordinary statements from opposing expert witnesses. Such experience arouses partisan feelings and a desire to cross-examine the other witness so as to expose his errors. Such desire is usually expressed by a series of notes written to the friendly attorney—but the attorney ignores the notes and later explains that he could not ask the technical questions because he had no way of evaluating the witness's answers.

In the vast limbo between sciences and the law there is room for a large number of well-prepared 'interpreters,' and in the future there will be room for legions. The reason is clear. As society becomes more complex, science and engineering affect the lives of people more directly with each passing year. The operation of vast urban complexes, conservation and management of resources, and control of the toxicity of the environment—so-called environmental science and engineering—are bound up with the very existence of our culture. Scientific data and concepts associated with and emerging from these endeavors find their way into courtrooms almost as soon as they issue from the laboratory. In the U.S. District Court for the Northern District of Texas, Lubbock Division, for example, there was a contest in 1962 to determine whether or not the government should allow cost depletion for ground water which was being extracted at a rate so much greater than the recharge rate that it was to all practical purposes being 'mined.' Testimony introduced included model studies of the aquifer by analog computer and analyses of the amount of the isotope tritium present in the water. Tritium analyses were the basis of attempts to establish the age of the water. The first scientific papers on the occurrence and significance of tritium antedated the trial by only a very few years.

A mineral, then, is different things to different people, and no one is *wrong* in his own context. Dapples (1959, p. 54), writing a geological textbook for engineers, attempted to rationalize the problem as follows:

Use of the word 'mineral' has not met with uniform application. Economists have generally applied it to include any nonliving material which is extracted from the earth. Until recently mineralogists have restricted the term to designate a naturally occurring, inorganic, crystalline substance. A more flexible definition such as the following is suggested: Minerals are both inorganic and organic substances which normally occur in the crystalline state, which for specific species have well-defined physical properties varying between narrowly restricted limits, a chemical composition that can be represented by either a precise formula or a variation within specifically defined ranges, and are both naturally occurring and synthetically produced.

This definition attempts to broaden the conventional scientific definition to include organic materials but does not depart far enough from it to include substances such as coal which is solid but not crystalline or the naturally occurring fluids which are 'mineral' fluids in the nonscientific world. Orderly people who like pigeonholes just big enough but not too big will have to make two compartments for 'mineral'—one might be labeled 'scientific definition' and the other 'economic and legal definition.'

It is a short step from mineral to mineral deposit—or is it? Asked to define a mineral deposit, the geologist shrugs and says—an accumulation of minerals. Perhaps he hesitates and says, 'naturally occurring,' or perhaps he thinks of accumulations such as mill tailings formed as a result of human activities and omits this restriction. However, the attorney dealing with the realities of the Internal Revenue Code who must establish the legal existence of a mineral deposit for depletion purposes finds he must satisfy three legal requirements: (1) It must be a natural accumulation of minerals of economic value; (2) It must be subject to depletion; (3) It must be subject to exploitation. Thus, under the present law, a concentration of minerals produced by human activity would not qualify, nor would a deposit which was being naturally replenished, nor would a deposit which could not be exploited under current economics and technology. In 1954 the depletion allowance sections of the Internal Revenue Code were amended so as to allow mine owners or operators to claim depletion on the waste or residue of prior mining (mine dumps, tailings) which are not natural deposits. The reworking of dumps and tailings was considered an integrated step in the mining process. However, *purchasers* of such waste or residues were not granted the right to claim depletion. Purchaser in this sense was strictly defined.

On the public lands a valuable mineral deposit, whether the subject of a lode claim or a placer claim, is one which will justify the locator, as a person of ordinary prudence, in the further expenditure of his time and money, in the expectation of developing a paying mine (American Law of Mining, vol. 1, p. 163). The Supreme Court of Utah remarked as follows (American Law of Mining, vol. 1, p. 164):

It must be appreciated that under the common generality (which is almost but not quite universally true) that matter is divided ino three categories: animal, vegetable and mineral, a very high proportion of the substances of the earth are in that sense "mineral." For instance, compounds of sodium, carbon, the silicons and other such commonly occurring minerals are widely distributed over the earth's crust. The discovery necessary under the mine location statutes is not satisfied by the discovery of 'mineral' in that very broad sense. If it were, there would be justification for making mine locations on virtually every part of the earth's surface. That is the very thing the statutory requirement is aimed at: to prevent the 'appropriation of presumed mineral ground for speculation purposes'; to hold it on the chance that it may prove to have valuable minerals, but without any bona fide intent to develop the property. Accordingly, the terms are construed to refer to metals and to other minerals of some actual or potential commercial value and the requirement of their discovery is usually referred to in mining parlance as the discovery of 'mineral in place.'

Although ownership of minerals is the subject of a subsequent chapter, it is in order here to define 'mineral rights' and distinguish them from 'surface rights.' In the United States and some other countries, the owner in fee simple of a tract of land is the proprietor of the surface and the earth within the boundaries of the tract as projected to the center of the earth. He may undertake to sell the mineral part of his real estate and retain the surface. From the time of the sale, then, the mineral estate is severed from the surface estate. Conflicts between the two users may commonly arise and must be resolved. In many other countries, title to the mineral estate is vested in the government and owner of the surface has never had rights to the minerals (pp. 150–160).

As long as the valuable mineral estate is deep beneath the surface and is extracted through a shaft or well which occupies a relatively small surface area, the owners of surface and mineral estates can hold, work, and enjoy their separate proprietorships in a compatible manner. The two estates become one in a very practical way, however, when the mineral material constitutes the surface of the land and extraction of it destroys or consumes the surface. Mining of surface deposits of sand and gravel or stone, for example, removes soil and vegetation. Because mining of these common materials consumes the surface, they are considered part of the surface estate rather than the mineral estate. Thus, they do not pass with the mineral estate unless specifically conveyed. Common clay, sand, gravel, limestone, other common varieties of stone, and volcanic ash have not been considered as mineral by the courts unless it can be shown that they possess some unique value.

The lawyers' approach to mineral deposits, and their concern with them as wasting or depletable assets, prompts consideration of those mineral deposits which are growing. According to geological theory, it is not reasonable to suppose that the natural processes which gave rise to accumulations of minerals—mineral deposits in the broad sense—have all ceased to operate. It can, in fact, be proved that the same processes that created mineral deposits in the past are still operating in and on the earth's crust, and that in some areas mineral deposits are now being formed. It is true, of course, that rates of exploitation are so much greater than the rates of formation that few if any deposits are being replenished in the economic sense.

For convenience in this discussion, mineral deposits can be classified as (1) deposits formed in the past and preserved in a steady state without additions or losses, (2) deposits formed in the past and now being destroyed by natural processes, such as erosion or leaching, and (3) deposits still being formed. The kinds of deposits at or near the present surface which can be demonstrated to be growing deposits include brine deposits in desert valleys, kaolin or bauxite being formed by alteration of subjacent source rocks, cave phosphate being formed by active leaching of guano deposits, and some stream and beach placer deposits. Quantitative data on the rate of growth of such deposits are extremely scarce. Gale (1915, p. 263) presented data on the amount of salts added to Owens Lake by the Los Angeles River. More recently, Hahl and Langford (1964) reported on the dissolved-mineral inflow to Great Salt Lake in Utah. Deposition of metals by hot springs and around fumaroles suggests that metalliferous deposits are being formed today in deeper parts of the crust in active volcanic areas. Sea-floor manganese nodules and continental shelf phosphorite nodules are probably live growing deposits in their present environment. Weed (1912, p. 164) believed that in the deeper levels of the Butte district, copper sulfides were being deposited in fractures at the time the rocks were drained by new drifts and stopes.

Probably metals are moving in the oxidized zones of sulfide deposits where production of acids through oxidation is still taking place. The first convincing example of an ore-forming fluid was recently encountered in a well drilled in southern California on the southeast shore of the Salton Sea to prospect for steam (White et al., 1963; White, 1963). The well produced hot chlorine-rich brine carrying as much as 30 percent dissolved solids (>300,000 ppm), including metals such as iron, manganese, strontium, zinc, barium, lead, copper, and silver. Another living example of hydrothermal solutions in the form of hot brines depositing zinc and iron in sediments on the floor of the Red Sea was reported by Manheim and others (1965).

Rarely, however, is the known rate of growth of a mineral deposit sufficient to produce a commercial deposit in the lifetime of the operator, unless movement of large masses of sand and gravel in rivers during floods, whereby a sand and gravel deposit is moved from upstream to a new downstream location, is considered as 'growth' of a deposit. Other exceptions are ground water deposits which are harvested and then replenished by natural inflow, some salt (including borax and trona) and brine deposits where natural processes of inflow and concentration renew the deposit, and some organic deposits such as guano where the biological processes of deposition are not disturbed by the harvesting. It should be emphasized that, apart from some ground water basins, there is very little data on rates of deposition or growth. These are very clearly rare exceptions which prove the rule that individual mineral deposits are a one-crop harvest and therefore are distinct from those renewable natural resources such as timber, pasture and wildlife.

Water as a mineral.

That the foregoing lengthy analysis of the nature of a mineral is not just so much dialetic is shown by the case of water. Farmers in the High Plains of Texas have for years been extracting ground water for irrigation from the Ogalalla Formation. The Ogalalla is unique in that it is an aquifer whose limits are rather precisely known and because a series of observation wells maintained over many years by the U.S. Geological Survey have provided a continuing flow of data on the performance of the aquifer. Geologic evidence indicates that the natural recharge is insignificant in comparison to the withdrawal so that in the High Plains area the ground water is being mined. Realizing that the value of irrigated lands was declining as the water level in the aquifer fell, the High Plains Water Conservation District proposed to the U.S. Internal Revenue Department that farmers in the area be allowed to claim cost depletion because of their capital investment in a wasting asset, and that the cost depletion be calculated on the decline of the water level as compared with its level when the land was purchased or otherwise acquired. The test case, already referred to (p. 3), was styled *Marvin Shurbet et ux.* v. *U.S. Internal Revenue Department.* Inasmuch as percentage depletion is not allowed for water in the Internal Revenue Code, the plaintiff claimed cost depletion. In order to substantiate his claim, the plaintiff was required to establish and prove that: (1) water is a mineral; (2) ground water is a natural deposit, in the legal sense, and (3) the deposit in question is a wasting asset. These propositions were attacked by the defendant on the ground that the liquid and mobile nature of the deposit, together with the small amount of natural recharge, prejudiced the mineral character of the deposit and its status as a natural deposit subject to exhaustion. The plaintiff substantiated his position by drawing a strong analogy with oil and gas deposits recognized by the courts as 'mineral' in character and for which depletion allowances are granted but which are mobile or subject to small-scale natural replenishment during the economic life of the deposit. The plaintiff called attention to deposits of brines, tars, and asphalt and to placer deposits which are in steady or intermittent motion and which are or have been replenished or increased by small increments through natural processes. The trial court found for the plaintiff. In 1965 the Fifth Circuit Court of Appeals sustained the trial court's verdict. One of the most important results of this litigation was the court's recognition that although surface water deposits and some ground water deposits are replenished relatively rapidly by natural processes, other ground water deposits are not being replenished at significant rates. Some water deposits are exhausted by withdrawal of the water, whereas some are not. The logical conclusion is that different kinds of water deposits require different legal treatment.

The idea that water is a mineral is confused by the common use of such terms as 'mineral water' or 'mineralized water' which, of course, refer to water which contains a quantity of dissolved solids. The fact that one mineral in its liquid state may not be a pure substance, and may contain amounts of other mineral matter in solution as ions, or as colloids or fine particles, does not of itself prejudice the mineral character of the liquid host. Such impurities are common in water, which is a better solvent than most other melted naturally occurring minerals. However, the crystalline record of other natural mineral melts wherein one crystal contains a myriad of inclusions of other minerals proves that purity in nature is rather rare. In its crystalline state—ice—water is really an ordinary mineral. It is the oxide of a common element—hydrogen—and has many of the crystalline properties of halite (rock salt).

Because water remains in the liquid state over a large part of the range of temperatures which prevail at the earth's surface, and because water is essential to viable systems, it is a very special mineral and occupies a special resource category. For example, water law, like oil and gas law, is a distinct body of jurisprudence. More attention is given to water management than to management of all other mineral resources together. Government—city, county, state, federal, as well as specially constituted authorities, districts, and boards—is in the water business in a big way. The lion's share of government money spent on conservation, reclamation, and resource development is spent on water projects. In the field of mineral exploration, however, which is mostly prosecuted by private interests, much more money is spent searching for deposits of oil and gas and valuable metals than for water. The reasons are obvious. Water, although necessary to sustain life, is a low-value mineral (30 cents per thousand gallons is a common municipal price in the United States, and irrigation water generally costs 3 to 5 cents per thousand gallons) with only a local market. Except in extraordinary circumstances water does not move in international trade. It cannot be manufactured into a higher value salable product except through ranching and farming. An historical example of an extraordinary circumstance is shipment of block ice for long distances; British colonies in India and the Far East paid high prices for ice delivered by sailing ships.

Mineral reserves and mineral resources.

Although the terms 'reserves' and 'resources' are commonly used interchangeably in casual conversations, it is useful to define them rather precisely so as to separate two quite different things. Reserves are quantities of minerals measured in tons, cubic yards, cubic feet, or barrels that can be reasonably assumed to exist and which are producible with existing technology and under present economic conditions. If not exactly in the bank they are analogous to a well-secured loan. Various systems have been employed to express the degree of reliability of these quantities. Leith (1933, pp. 47–48) presented the miner's geometrical definitions of reserves as follows:

Proved or assured ore:—Ore blocked out in three dimensions by actual underground mining operations or by drilling, but it includes in addition minor extensions beyond actual openings and drill holes, where the geological factors that limit the ore body are definitely known and where the chance of failure of the ore to reach these limits is so remote as not to be a factor in the practical planning of mine operations.

Probable or semiproven ore covers extensions near at hand, where the conditions are such that ore will probably be found but where the extent and limiting conditions cannot be so precisely defined as for proved ore. Semiproven may also mean ore that has been cut by scattered drill holes, but too widely spaced to assure continuity.

Possible ore: Ore is classed as possible or prospective where the relations of the land to adjacent ore bodies and to geologic structures warrant some presumption that ore will be found but where the lack of exploration and development data precludes anything like the certainty of its actual location or extent. Often it is not desirable to assign figures to "possible" tonnages, but they may be designated by terms like "small" or "large."

Blondel and Lasky (1956, p. 694) pointed out the need for a broader set of terms for use in regional or national appraisals and suggested the use of the classification adopted by the U.S. Geological Survey and Bureau of Mines as follows:

Measured reserves are those for which tonnage is computed from dimensions revealed in outcrops, trenches, workings, and drill holes and for which the grade is computed from the results of detailed sampling. The sites for inspection, sampling, and measurement are spaced so closely and the geologic character is so well defined that size, shape, and mineral content are well established. The computed tonnage and grade are judged to be accurate within limits which are stated, and no such limit is judged to be different from the computed tonnage or grade by more than 20 percent.

Indicated reserves are those for which tonnage and grade are computed partly from specific measurements, samples, or production data and partly from projection for a reasonable distance on geologic evidence. The sites available for inspection, measurement, and sampling are too widely or otherwise inappropriately spaced to permit the mineral bodies to be outlined completely or the grade established throughout.

Inferred reserves are those for which quantitative estimates are based largely on broad knowledge of the geologic character of the deposit and for which there are few, if any, samples or measurements. The estimates are based on an assumed continuity or repetition, of which there is geologic evidence; this evidence may include comparison with deposits of similar type. Bodies that are completely concealed may be included if there is specific geologic evidence of their presence. Estimates of inferred reserves should include a statement of the specific limits within which the inferred materials may lie.

The threefold divisions of the two classifications cannot be equated because the *Inferred* reserves of the broader classification go far beyond the *Possible* ore of the miner. McKelvey (in preparation) presented various classes of mineral resource estimates in tabular form and this table is reproduced here as Table I.1.

Blondel and Lasky (1956, p. 692) defined as *potential ores* those materials which might become available under future economic conditions and technology but which are not now available because of high costs due to remote location or inaccessibility due to other factors, difficult extraction conditions resulting from excessive depth or the nature of the ground, small size or low grade of the mineral concentration, or problems of beneficiation and treatment. Because of limiting connotations of the word *ore*,[1] the writer prefers the term *potential reserves*. These materials go beyond the inferred reserves and include a wide variety of marginal, submarginal, or latent mineral materials. *Mineral resources*, then, as used by this writer, are *reserves* (of various categories expressing degree of surety) plus *potential reserves*. This usage differs slightly from McKelvey's (Table I.1) in that known quantities which are marginal are termed "potential reserves" rather than "known marginal resources." Whatever definitions are used, the important distinctions are (1) between known deposits and deposits yet to be discovered and (2) between deposits which are of a grade or quality that can be produced in the prevailing economic and technologic structure and those which cannot and

---

[1] Ore in the classic sense is a mineral aggregate from which one or more metals can be economically produced. In actual usage, however, the economic limitation is applied rather loosely to include mineralized rock that perhaps could not be economically produced at today's price from a particular mine but which contains enough values to be of commercial interest. The term has also been broadened to include some nonmetallic substances such as fluorite or barite that occur as epigenetic deposits, that is in bodies emplaced in a host rock subsequent to formation of the host. However, the term is not applied to industrial rock deposits such as gypsum, salt, or limestone.

TABLE 1.1

CLASSES OF MINERAL RESOURCE ESTIMATES
(after McKelvey, in preparation)

	In known deposits or districts				In undiscovered districts	Total
	Known recoverable reserves					
	Measured reserves* (Proved reserves / Developed reserves)	Indicated reserves — Probable reserves	Indicated reserves — Possible reserves	Inferred reserves		
Recoverable under current economic and technologic conditions					Undiscovered recoverable resources	Potential resources
Recoverable at prices as much as 1.5 times those prevailing now or with comparable advance in technology	Known marginal resources				Undiscovered marginal resources	Potential marginal resources
Recoverable at greater than 1.5 times those prevailing now or with comparable advance in technology	Known submarginal resources				Undiscovered submarginal resources	Potential submarginal resources
Total	Known resources				Undiscovered resources	Potential resources

* The terms *measured*, *proved*, etc., may also be applied to known marginal and submarginal resources where knowledge of them is sufficiently detailed to warrant differentiation in the degree of certainty of the estimates.

are thus in some degree, marginal. Application of modern mathematical statistical techniques to problems of reserves to establish confidence levels for various categories is now widespread in the mineral industry and makes it possible to arrive at a more uniform and reliable evaluation of tonnage and grade figures. New recovery techniques also have a way of increasing proved reserves by large increment.

A group of mineral economists in an organization called Resources for the Future, Inc., have developed a slightly different terminology which makes similar distinctions and employs the terms "reserves," "resources," and "resource base" (Schurr et al., 1960, p. 298; Netschert and Landsberg, 1961, p. 3). In this classification, reserves are those known quantities which can be extracted in the existing economic and technologic structure; resources are quantities which can be expected to become reserves through predictable technologic improvements, and resource base refers to total amount of mineral in the earth's crust. Schurr et al. (1960, pp. 295–301) defined resource base as follows:

The "resource base" is conceived to include the sum total of mineral raw material present in the earth's crust within a given geographic area. If reserves are denoted by A, the resource base C, equals A plus B, where B comprehends all of the stock not included in A, whether its existence is known or unknown and regardless of cost considerations and of technologic feasibility of extraction. The resource-base concept is thus absolute in that it includes all the occurrences within the geographic area specified.

They vigorously defended the usefulness of the concept while recognizing the difficulty of specific application in a quantitative way and argued that it emphasizes the possibilities awaiting realization through technology. The difficulty, indeed the danger, in attempting a quantitative application of the resource base concept needs to be underscored and re-underscored. The inquiring student should consider how amounts of a particular element or mineral in a large volume of the earth's crust have been determined. The basic data are from Clarke and Washington (1924) and Goldschmidt (1954). First, on the basis of thousands of rock analyses from over the world the composition of various average rocks, such as the average granite, were calculated. Then the relative amounts of these average rocks in the crust were estimated. From these data the relative abundances of various elements in the earth's crust were calculated. Mason (1952, p. 39) summed up the objections to averaging of analyses as follows:

· 1. The uneven geographic distribution of analyses.
2. Their non-statistical distribution over the different rock types.
3. The lack of allowance for the actual amounts of the rocks represented by the analyses.

Nevertheless, these averages and "abundances" derived from them are widely used. It should be clear that the significance of a quantitative expression of resource base is dubious at best. For example, the amount of element x in the average rock of the crust was determined by averaging rocks varying in their content of x by many orders of magnitude (p. 13). Average rock will never be mined. In any foreseeable economic situation concentrations of elements or minerals will be exploited and rocks containing 10 parts per million of x will be used before rocks containing 1 part per million of x. It is the distribution of values that is important. Area A might have a higher average content of x than area B but no concentrations; area B with a low average content might be a major producer or potential producer of x because of significant higher concentrations. A quantitatively significant resource base could be calculated if there were enough data on the composition of crustal rocks to determine in a particular region the volumes of rocks containing more 10 ppm, more than 100 ppm, more than 1,000 ppm, and more than 10,000 ppm of x. Such a reconnaissance inventory of rocks containing elements or minerals in amounts far less than modern economical concentrations remains to be realized. It would be a great contribution.

It is important that the student of mineral resources understand and fully appreciate the degree of judgment that goes into calculations of reserves and resources. Measured or proved reserves are calculated on sound engineering and geological data and should be subject to only small errors. Indicated and inferred reserves are progressively less reliable as the judgment of the geologist is applied to the probabilities of continuation of mineralization beyond the measured limits. The student should be aware that as numerical data decrease and geologic projections become more important, calculation or estimation of reserves passes from the province of the engineer to the province of the geologist. The economist comes into the picture of mineral *resources* where there is, added to the problems of reserve estimations, uncertainty about future economic conditions and future technological developments. At this point, prognostications about mineral resources became predictions based more on philosophy or concepts than on any real numerical data. A good case in point is the current predictions as to domestic oil reserves (resources) in the United States.

Estimates of reserves of petroleum are traditionally reported by the industry as 'proved reserves.' These are quantities of petroleum in explored fields that can be economically produced. Thus, each year exploration and development work increases the nation's petroleum reserves by a certain increment, and each year the reserves are diminished by the amount of that year's production. For some reason, a good deal of significance is attached to whether or not the reserves proved in the course of a year balance production in that year. Such a relationship between discovery and depletion is, of course, significant over a period of years to establish a trend. Withdrawal is directly related to demand for crude and is therefore predictable within rather narrow limits. However, discovery follows no such smooth curve and, in fact, history shows success in discovery to be cyclic. Although the tempo of exploration picks up as demand rises and stocks run low, success depends on more than the number of drilling rigs operating. Success depends on concepts or models and tools to test them (Owen, 1964). Thus a period of 5 years of successful exploration might prove reserves equal to those withdrawn over a 10- or 20-year period.

In order for the nation to formulate a sound petroleum policy, it is necessary to look beyond proved reserves and consider the quantity of petroleum which might ultimately be recovered from domestic fields, both known and as yet undiscovered. This would include indicated, inferred, and potential reserves. Two such estimates have been made recently and the extent of the disparity between them illustrates difference in philosophy rather than differences in basic data. Hubbert (1962, pp. 42–43), using a mathematical approach based on rates of discovery, concluded that the United States (excluding Alaska) was originally endowed with 175 billion barrels of *recoverable* petroleum and that, after the 67 billion barrels already produced up to 1962 is subtracted, 108 billion barrels remained in 1962. Hubbert also concluded that of 460 major fields predicted to exist in the United States, 401 have already been discovered. These estimates, of course, do not include petroleum in oil shales and tar sands.

Another estimate of petroleum reserves in the United States was made by Zapp (1961, 1962) who arrived at total reserves of about 590 billion barrels including (1) 48 billion barrels of proved reserves, (2) 40 billion barrels of proved marginal reserves, (3) undiscovered recoverable reserves of 200 billion barrels, and (4) undiscovered marginal reserves of 300 billion barrels.[2] Zapp's calculations assume that

---

[2] Zapp's total includes an estimated 30 billion barrels for Alaska.

petroleum is just as abundant in unexplored ground as it is in explored acreage.

Because of the spread between these two estimates, they have been labeled casually as the 'pessimistic' and 'optimistic' viewpoints and each has its advocates. Hubbert's analysis has been criticized because it does not allow for the human factor—ingenuity—which will develop new models and technology to find more and more oil. Zapp's has been attacked as not valid because his basic assumption is not weighted to account for the fact that the *most* favorable ground for exploration has already been prospected. To accept these two estimates as limits with the corollary that the truth lies somewhere in between is to apply the doctrine of compromise, which permeates American thought, to analysis of an aspect of a natural phenomenon—the occurrence of petroleum. Although not popular in the social or even in the judicial world, it is common in science and engineering for one party to be 100 per cent right and the other 100 per cent wrong.

Thus, it cannot be assumed that the correct amount of recoverable petroleum in the United States lies between 108 and 590 billion barrels simply because there is such a wide spread between the estimates. Each estimate must be evaluated by analysis of the assumptions on which it was based; each carefully made estimate means something once the base on which it rests is thoroughly understood. Hendricks (1965) discussed the various petroleum resource estimates and their rationale in some detail.

The making of mineral resource estimates is far from a mere exercise in analysis of data; indeed, it is difficult to overemphasize their importance. From the point of view of industry, such estimates, combined with demand forecasts, guide exploration and development programs, and construction of beneficiating and refining facilities. Thus they indirectly control the employment and deployment of vast amounts of private capital. This is not the place to explain the importance of capital beyond calling attention to the plight of nations without it. From the point of view of government, mineral resource estimates directly effect economic and political policy and are reflected in import-export policies, domestic mineral industry tax policies, stockpiling programs, industry support programs (subsidies) and expenditures by federal agencies such as the Bureau of Mines and Geological Survey. More covertly, these resource estimates influence U.S. foreign policy toward other mineral-producing and mineral-consuming nations. In short, mineral resource estimates are a quantitative expression of that part of national economic and military security based on minerals.

The field of mineral resources is a true interdisciplinary area, or, perhaps more correctly stated, it is transdisciplinary and goes beyond any one discipline. Geology, mineral engineering, economics, politics and law all are tributary to the area; mastery of the subject requires, if not a competence in all of the contributing disciplines, at least an understanding of their interrelationships:

Geology   Mineral Engineering

Mineral Resources

Economics   Politics and Law

The orebody concept and the cost concept of mineral resources[3]

The problem of population growth has been called the second most important problem of our time—the first being 'peace.' The high population growth rates and the prospects of a population of 6 or 7 billion by the year 2000, and, with the same growth rate projected, of 25 billion by 2070 are clearly a matter of grave concern. It is argued that highly valued institutions of our culture cannot survive in a world of teeming multitudes, and that the rate of population growth is out of all proportion to any realistic rate of economic development. It is alleged by some that the waste products of such a population and the industry necessary to sustain it will pollute earth and atmosphere so that the human race, like some fast-reproducing bacterial cultures, will ultimately render its environment too toxic to sustain the culture. But most often, concern is expressed that the earth's resources will prove inadequate to meet the demands of the population, both in regard to food resources and mineral resources. The predicted ultimate inadequacy of the earth's resources is a direct consequence of the forecasters' consideration of population growth as an independent variable, or in other words, their assumption that population cannot be stabilized. The converse of the philosophy which holds that resources must be supplied on the basis of a growing population's need for them is that population must be held to a level commensurate with resources available. There is nothing new in the latter view—Polynesian island dwellers held it centuries ago.

---

[3] Previously published in slightly different form as "Minerals: Final Harvest or Endless Crop": Engineering and Mining Journal, vol. 166, no. 5, pp. 106–108.

Recently, a number of reassuring articles and books have appeared which express the view that mineral resources are practically unlimited and are in fact defined by costs rather than boundaries of a physical nature, and that through human ingenuity and new technology we can extract minerals from the sea and we can mine 'ordinary' rock.

This cost concept which holds that mineral resources are not really finite in the sense of ultimate exhaustion is now widely held by those who deal with national inventories of mineral resources over a long term. On the other hand, those in the extractive industries working with a mine or an oil well generally think of their small piece of the resource as an orebody or an oil field which is finite in volume and subject to relatively rapid exhaustion. Both are correct in their own context. An analogy can be drawn with the calculus wherein a continuous volume is approximated by integration of a very large number of small finite volumes. *It is in the important area of mineral exploration that the advocates of the long-term cost concept and the short-term orebody concept come into conflict.* When the advocate of the cost concept insists that for every economic situation there exists an orebody, the proponent of the orebody concept who is concerned with putting rock in the box or oil in the tank asks the practical question, 'Yes, but where?'

The known reserves—the measured, indicated, and inferred volumes of mineralized rock—which form the base of mineral resource estimates in the United States were developed by private companies engaged in mineral exploration. The part of those reserves classified as marginal or potential reserves, volumes of rock not subject to exploitation in the current cost structure and with present technology, were developed in the search for exploitable reserves, or ore in the economic sense, and were not developed as the result of a program designed to find, measure, and inventory marginal mineral deposits. One important result of mineral exploration in the past, whether intentional or not, has been the discovery of marginal mineral accumulations. These have been further explored and developed as changing economics and technological improvements have converted them to 'ore.' The trend has been toward working of lower and lower grade ores on a larger and larger scale, although new sources of supply resulting from successful exploration can shut down fringe operations and return very low-grade ores to a marginal status. Since 1900, cut-off limits in copper mines generally have declined from about 3 per cent copper (60 pounds per ton) to 2 per cent copper down through 1 per cent copper to less than 1 per cent and even to 0.5 per cent or

10 pounds per ton in some mines. Of course, cut-offs during this period have varied up and down with changes in cost-price structure and from mine to mine. The exploration which created this bank account of marginal ore, this private company inventory of domestic mineral resources, has cost a great deal of money. The investment has been possible because of policies of the United States Government designed to encourage the mineral industry. That these policies are not as effective today as they have been is suggested by the increasing activities of U.S. mineral companies in Canada and Australia which are as much a result of an encouraging mineral policy as of good prospects of discovery.

These generally encouraging U.S. policies have been maintained not because everyone loves the mineral industry, but because of a series of hot and cold war strategic needs and official and unofficial reports which indicated a relatively short life for domestic production of most mineral commodities and exhaustion of reserves within a matter of decades. These gloomy prognostications considered the nation's resources as a multi-pieced orebody defined conservatively by then prevailing economics. Considering the exigencies of the times, a conservative approach was clearly justified. Application of this orebody concept to the nation's mineral resources, while not strictly defensible because of failure to take into account the impact of technology and changing cost structures, and despite the fact that they were wrong, had a salubrious effect in making government policy makers sympathetic to the problems of the mineral industry. The results, extensive exploration and development of the nation's resources, has been in the public interest whether or not it was prompted by incorrect pessimistic forecasts.

Now, as a result of so many old prognostications proved wrong, and with more and better data, advocates of the cost concept have explained why the orebody concept of finite tonnages, yards, or barrels cannot be applied to national resource problems, and they have pointed to ordinary rocks of the earth's crust and to waters of the seas as ultimate orebodies. The corollary, seized upon happily by professionals and nonprofessionals alike, by business leaders and by legislators, is that we are in no danger of running out of this or that mineral commodity. We can, after all, stick a pipe in the sea!

Curiously enough, while such ideas are appearing in sophisticated publications, the prosaic trade journals are talking about shortages of a number of metals, including mercury, silver, and tin. Advocates of the cost concept regard such shortages as short term and insist that the problem will be solved by bringing marginal properties into production and developing substitutes.

We can consider three groupings of minerals: minerals for materials, minerals for energy, minerals to sustain life. Least critical in terms of eventual exhaustion are minerals for materials because as the limit is approached there are substitutions, such as ceramics, glass, and plastics for metals, although modern culture would certainly be drastically affected by a metal shortage. Energy minerals consist of fossil fuel minerals and nuclear energy minerals. The breeding process, wherein fertile isotopes are converted to fissile isotopes, makes available for use as nuclear fuel a very large reserve of uranium and thorium minerals. The ultimate substitute for the energy minerals is continuous energy sources including solar, tidal, and geothermal energy, but a shortage of energy minerals would also profoundly change modern society. There is no practical substitute for the life-sustaining minerals such as water, salt, and food-producing minerals (soils and crop nutrients).

Our concern, therefore, is on several different levels. We can live with substitutes on the materials and energy levels but not on the life-sustaining level. Within our present social and economic structure, technology cannot *create* water economically on a large-volume basis. It can make potable water out of sea water, but if we were suddenly forced to turn to the sea for large volumes of water, the distribution systems required to move it to the continental interior would revolutionize living patterns.

One proper function of government is to promulgate policies which will minimize disruptions in the supply of mineral raw materials and maintain a steady flow of needed commodities to United States industry. One way to prevent disruptions—indeed, the only way—is to maintain a reserve of a known quantity of mineral commodities, either in the ground or in the form of a stockpile. Minerals in the present stockpile, accumulated in the interests of national security to supply essential mineral raw materials in the event of war, are now being sold to ease shortages and prevent disruptions in the supply (p. 195).

Fortunately, exploration efforts by private companies continue to add to the inventory of marginal reserves as a consequence of the search for immediately exploitable ores. Because of this effort, when copper ores containing 12 pounds of copper per ton are exhausted, it will be possible to turn without chaos to known orebodies containing 10 pounds per ton with only minor, or perhaps without any, increase in costs. But consider the chaos if, when our 12-pound-per-ton ores are exhausted, we are forced to mine 'ordinary rock' containing four ounces or less or go to extracting copper from sea water. Of course, the laws of economics do not permit this. Corrective actions would occur short of chaos. The point is, to prevent disruptions and maintain a steady flow of mineral materials, it is essential that the effort of finding and measuring marginal ores lower in grade than those now exploited must be continued, either by private companies or by government agencies, such as the Geological Survey and Bureau of Mines. The inventory must precede the demand because of the many months or years required to prosecute an exploration program, locate targets, prospect them, and develop the discovery to prepare it for extraction. For the foreseeable future, we must continue to explore these parts of the earth's crust where natural processes have done part of the job and enriched a volume of rock in a particular constituent or constituents. These volumes of rock are finite and exhaustible. A comparison of the relative abundance of various elements in the earth's crust with the grade of ore currently being mined (Table I.2) shows the extent we depend on natural concentrations

TABLE I.2

CONCENTRATION CLARKES FOR OREBODIES OF THE COMMONER METALS
(after Mason, 1952, p. 43)

Metal	Clarkes (average % in earth's crust)	Minimum per-cent profitably extracted	Concentration clarke necessary for an orebody
Al	8.13	30	4
Fe	5.00	30	6
Mn	0.10	35	350
Cr	0.02	30	1500
Cu	0.007	1	140
Ni	0.008	1.5	175
Zn	0.013	4	300
Sn	0.004	1	250
Pb	0.0016	4	2500

or orebodies. This table is a 1952 vintage and needs minor modification but its significance is clear.

It should be emphasized that although potential reserves of a marginal nature most surely will constitute the domestic mineral sources of tomorrow, they will not come easily to the bin or tank. They must be found and measured. It will require drive, imagination, and financial investment to develop sophisticated earth models and exploration tools to find the deposits and expanded engineering research to permit economic extraction and conversion to products.

The world in which Granite Mountain is exploited for base metals, or a pipe in the sea produces quicksilver, is a more distant world with different economics and a different technology. We may be approaching it, but we are not there yet.

Exploration and discovery.

Many people outside of the mineral industry hold the mistaken idea that mineral discovery is wholly fortuitous—that the discoverer is just lucky. They are brought to this view by romances of the Old West where the burro prospector struck it rich, by the image of Texas oil millionaires who struck oil while drilling for water or digging postholes, or by the tales of a weekend uranium prospector sitting down to rest on a sandstone ledge and having his geiger counter suddenly stutter the news of massive uranium mineralization. What all of these popular versions of mineral discovery convey is acquisition of huge wealth by sheer accident without any work; the reward is a treasure that comes to a lucky individual who did not work for it. There is just enough truth in modern mineral history to give substance to the image. However, modern mineral exploration bears little resemblance to this image. It is high capital investment, long, painstaking investigation, and a shrewd evaluation of risks. It is a scientific appraisal of probabilities rather than casual good fortune. One successful Texas oil man used to say "I didn't find any oil . . . I just got in the way." Behind the fact that this operator held acreage in advance of developing oil plays lies a great deal of work in evaluating trends in exploration and development. Even the successful amateur uranium prospector who sat down in the right place spent many a hard, hot, thirsty day just covering the ground. Staking claims in itself is hard work. The mineral wealth being found and developed today and that which will be found in the future is the product of combined scientific and engineering effort by teams of specialists. Stages in this exploration effort include: (1) appraisal of geologic provinces—large regions containing tens of thousands of square miles; (2) geologic and geophysical reconnaissance; (3) land acquisition—options to explore, to spend more money; (4) focus on targets within the prospective area—concealed or blind deposits for the most part, covered by rock or soil; (5) following a potential discovery, evaluation of the economic feasibility of extracting and recovering the desired minerals from the aggregate and making a marketable product; (6) detailed exploration of the potential discovery—follow-up on geologic projections, geophysical and geochemical anomalies by drilling programs. Fortescue (1965) described the several stages of the mineral search as "exploration architecture." Significant new discoveries will not be made without regional programs of this kind; they are necessary to supply mineral resources for the future. A regional exploration program might require five or six years from the first appraisal to testing of a target. Exploration costs alone—without including costs of acquiring land and costs of preparing the deposit for mining—may be in the millions of dollars. Bailly (1964) tabulated costs of various methods of exploration and illustrated relations between investment and acreage during various stages of appraisal and development of mineral property (Table I.3; Figure I.1). Clearly no agency can make investments of this magnitude without security of land tenure and

FIGURE I.1

Relation between investment and acreage during various stages of appraisal, reconnaissance, investigation, and development of mineral property (after Bailly, 1964).

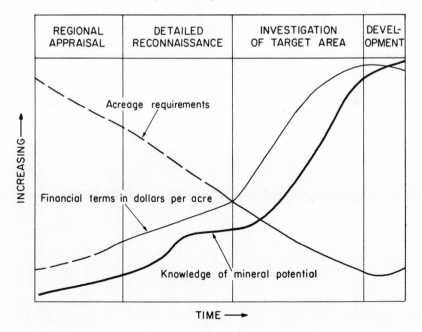

TABLE 1.3

COSTS OF MODERN MINERAL EXPLORATION
(after Bailly, 1964, Plates 11–14)

EXPLORATION COSTS BY METHODS	Regional	Detailed Recon	Target	Cost per Square Mile (in dollars)	Square Miles per Day (1 machine per man)
AIR PHOTO BASE MAPS					
New black and white photos, large area contract	X				
New black and white photos, small area contract		X	X		
New color photos, small area contract			X		
Planimetric map from photos, small scale	X	X			
Planimetric map from photos, large scale		X	X		
Topographic map from photos, large scale			X		
GEOLOGIC METHODS					
Office compilations, small scale	X	X			
Office compilations, large scale			X		

Cost per Square Mile (in dollars) scale: 0.1, 1, 10, 100, 1,000, 10,000

Square Miles per Day (1 machine per man) scale: 0.1, 1, 10, 100, 1,000

Photo geology, small scale

Photo geology, large scale

Geologic observations from air

Geologic field mapping, small scale

Geologic field mapping, large scale

Mineralogic & petrologic studies

Boulder tracking

AIRBORNE GEOPHYSICS

Fixed wing plane—radioactivity

Fixed wing plane—magnetic

Fixed wing plane—electromagnetic

Fixed wing plane—e.m. + magnetic + radioactivity

Helicopter—electromagnetic + magnetic

GROUND GEOPHYSICS

Car—radioactivity

Radioactivity

Car—magnetic

Magnetic

(Continued on following page)

TABLE 1.3 (Continued)

Costs of Modern Mineral Exploration
(after Bailly, 1964, Plates 11–14)

Exploration Costs by Methods	Regional	Detailed Recon	Target	Cost per Square Mile (in dollars)	Square Miles per Day (1 machine per man)
GROUND GEOPHYSICS (Continued)					
Self–potential		X	X	100–1,000	0.1–1
Gravity	X	X	X	10–1,000	0.1–10
Resistivity			X	1,000	1
Electromagnetic			X	1,000–10,000	0.1
Induced potential		X	X	1,000–10,000	0.1–1
Seismic–shallow		X	X	1,000–10,000	0.1–1
GEOCHEMICAL					
Chemical provinces	X			100	1–10
Drainage reconnaissance	X	X		100	1–10

STAGES

Area soil sampling	X		
Local soil sampling	X	X	
Biogeochemical sampling	X	X	
Geobotanical observation	X	X	
Dispersion pattern in bedrock	X		

Drilling	Cost per Foot (in dollars)		
	to 1000 ft.	1000–2000 ft.	2000–3500 ft.
Wagon drill	0.50— 1.25		
Churn drill	2.00— 8.00		
Rotary/diamond non-coring	0.75— 7.00	1.50— 9.00	3.00—12.00
Diamond coring	2.50—10.00	3.50—12.00	5.00—20.00
Rotary coring	3.00— 8.00	4.00—10.00	5.00—15.00
Casing	2.50— 4.00	2.50— 5.00	2.50— 6.00

	Cost (in dollars)	Per
Pitting	3–50	Cubic yard
Trenching	2–25	Cubic yard
Shaft sinking	200–1000	Foot

the right to manage the venture. No private agency can risk and lose sums of this kind without assurance that they can recover exploration costs from income earned as a result of a successful venture.

What are the possibilities for success? This matter has recently been discussed by Bailly (1964):

What are the chances of finding new ore bodies? This subject has been on the minds of many for a number of years. In recent years, we have had a flurry of more or less theoretical papers by Nolan, Blondel, Allais, Slichter, Koulomzine, attempting to define such chances in various environments. More practically J. D. Bateman wrote in 1963 that in Canada about 1,000 prospecting teams have taken to the woods each summer in recent years; each season only 5 significant discoveries were made and some of them did not turn out to be profitable. Thus on the average the single prospector or prospecting team in the Canadian bush should work 200 years to have one chance of a significant discovery; and yet this is by no means assured.

Plate 8 [Table I.4] will illustrate this point. If we assume that we have at hand

TABLE I.4

PROBABILITY OF SUCCESS IN MINERAL EXPLORATION
(modified from Bailly, 1964, Plate 8, and Arps, 1961, Table 1)

Assumption: 5 prospects, each with a 20 per cent chance of being an exploitable mineral deposit.

Possibilities:	*Probability*
5 failures	32.77%
4 failures, 1 success	41.00%
3 failures, 2 successes	20.50%
2 failures, 3 successes	5.10%
1 failure, 4 successes	0.60%
5 successes	0.03%

Conclusion: Operator has a 32.77 per cent chance of realizing nothing from expenditure of exploration capital in these 5 prospects.

5 equally good prospects, each with 20% chance of being an ore deposit, the alternative outcomes are that we may have 5 failures, or 4 failures and one ore body, etc., or, finally 5 ore bodies. The probability of these events happening are shown on the right side column. The chances of finding 5 ore bodies is three in 10,000 whereas the chances of five failures are one in three. This means that if all our exploration funds are used on exploring these five prospects

we have 33% chance, one in three, of ending up in complete state of ruin. Well, the situation is not bad when you have 20% chances of being successful at each single exploration spot. However, as shown in Plate 9 [Table I.5]

TABLE I.5

GAMBLER'S RUIN
NUMBER OF TIMES A VENTURE MUST BE REPEATED
TO REDUCE THE RISK OF GAMBLER'S RUIN
(modified from Arps, 1961, Table 2, and Bailly, 1964, Plate 9)

Probability of success	Probability of ruin through a run of bad luck		
	10%	5%	1%
1%	229	298	461
2%	114	148	228
5%	45	58	90
10%	22	28	44
20%	11	14	21
50%	4	5	7

Example: If each prospect has a 20 percent chance of being an exploitable deposit (Table I.4), at least 11 prospects must be tested before the chance of 11 failures is less than 10 per cent. To reduce chances of complete failure to less than 1 per cent, 21 such prospects must be explored.

our chances of reaching gambler's ruin are much worse, if the probability of a prospect being an ore deposit is much lower. For instance if each prospect has only 1% chance of being an ore deposit, which is quite a realistic percentage, we find that we must go successively through 461 consecutive failures, assuming these prospects are all equal, to reduce to 1% the probability of going broke through a run of bad luck. Even when the probability of a prospect being an ore deposit is one in 20 (5%) we must explore consecutively 45 shows without success before the probability of going broke through gambler's ruin is reduced to 10%. Exploring large numbers of prospects will give a greater assurance of success; and we can improve this chance of success by limiting our exploration endeavors to those prospects which have a very high chance of becoming an ore deposit.

The conclusion is that in exploration the magnitude of available capital resources improves immunity to gambler's ruin, however, this obviously does not mean that the 'independent' or the small firm cannot prospect profitably anymore; they certainly can by working only on prospects which have a very high chance of being ore. The larger exploration concern can perhaps take greater risks; but it should beware that taking too many high risks, too often, can lead to losses or ruin. All of us in exploration must spend as little money as possible on those prospects which turn out to have little chance of being an ore deposit, in Slichter's words we must practice 'skimming,' and we must spend most of our funds on those shows with the highest chance of being ore deposits.

Extraction of minerals from the earth.

After a mineral deposit is found and evaluated, there is the problem of extracting the desired material—of separating it from its natural habitat and reducing it to possession. The practical problems involve getting to the deposit as cheaply as possible and making as effective a separation as possible of the mineral matter so that the expense of extracting undesired material or waste is kept at a minimum.

One of the cheapest methods of extracting subsurface minerals is through wells or boreholes but unfortunately only naturally mobile mineral matter (gases or liquids) or minerals that can be rendered mobile by melting or leaching (solution) can be captured and brought to the surface through boreholes.

Mineral deposits at or near the surface (down to depths as much as 800 to 1,000 feet for very large and valuable deposits) are mined in quarries or open pits. The method involves stripping of the overburden and design of an excavation to permit orderly removal of the mineral matter. Generally the excavation proceeds from the center of the deposit outward and from the surface downward in a series of benches with material blasted loose from more or less vertical faces and removed by a truck or rail transportation system (Fig. IX.1). In placer deposits, unconsolidated mineral matter is mined by dredge or dragline. With the dredge, the wet sediment is loosened by a cutting head and pumped to a floating mineral factory for separation of the desired minerals (Fig. VI.3). The dragline (Fig. VI.4), able to reach out with a long boom and work below the level of its tracks, excavates the unconsolidated material and conveys it by bucket to trucks, cars, or conveyor. Underground mines are a system of workings variously called shafts, inclines, adits, drifts, galleries, cross-cuts, raises, winzes and stopes designed to reach the underground deposit, extract the mineral matter, and convey it to the surface. The mining method employed depends on the size and shape of the orebody, the distribution of values within it, and the nature of ore and of the enveloping host rock. A stope is an excavation from which ore has been extracted and a stoping method is the system of extraction. There are many methods, each tailored to a particular kind of orebody. Mitke (1930, pp. 23–25) proposed a two-fold classification of methods, distinguishing between (1) supported stopes and (2) caved stopes. In his classification, supported stopes are either open (naturally supported) or filled (square set, cut and fill, or shrinkage methods). Caved stopes are utilized in a variety of mining methods. Flat lying tabular deposits are commonly mined by a room and pillar method, narrow steeply-dipping deposits by shrinkage, or sublevel stoping, and large low-grade homogeneous masses by caving methods. Methods such as square set stoping are expensive and can only be justified where ores are high grade.

Nuclear explosives hold out promise for a revolution in mining. The increased rock breaking capabilities of nuclear explosives can be applied to removal of overburden. Costs of mining by caving methods might be substantially reduced by using nuclear explosives underground to shatter large rock masses. Shattering by nuclear explosives might be employed to prepare ground for leaching or other chemical mining. Controlled nuclear explosions in oil and gas reservoirs are expected to improve recoveries. Nuclear explosions might also be used to 'retort-in-place' deposits of oil shale and tar sands.

Processing, beneficiation, refining, and manufacturing.

Most mineral commodities are not saleable products as they come out of the ground. In the modern mineral industry nearly all producers engage in some form of mineral processing to convert a crude mine, quarry, or well product into something that can be sold. Exceptions are few. Certain kinds of natural gas are piped directly from well to consumer. Irrigation water from the well is applied to the field but water for domestic and even industrial use is commonly treated. Traditionally, only very high grade ores or 'direct shipping ores' are sold to smelters by the hard-rock miner and such ores are very rare today; nearly all metalliferous ores are concentrated before smelting and refining.

Mineral processing operations designed to separate or concentrate the desirable minerals or elements at the expense of the waste material, to clean and size the desirable minerals, or to convert them into more usable form cost money. At each step in the operation dollars are put into the product in the form of work done on it, the labor of transporting and handling it, and the capital costs of the equipment. It is clear that these costs must be paid for out of the price received for the finished mineral product. The processing is not always done by the miner. Some mining operations produce a crude material which is sold to a company in the business of processing mineral material from a number of mines or quarries. The processing operations are commonly referred to as 'custom mills.' They buy from the miner and sell a final product or perhaps in turn sell a concentrate to a smelter and refinery. However, most large mining companies have an integrated operation which includes all of the necessary stages between raw mineral product and marketable mineral or metal.

The simplest form of the upgrading or improving process is mine or pit control where the operator takes care to avoid inclusion of deleterious rock in the mining and loading of mine-run material. This simple selection is carried one step further in some operations where either ore or waste is picked by hand, commonly from a moving belt. This elementary concentration process is known as hand cobbing; it is commonly used in pegmatite mining operations where beryl, mica, spodumene, or other coarsely crystalline and easily identified minerals are separated from quartz and feldspar in comparatively small volumes. Some mineral commodities, sand and gravel for example, are saleable after only washing and screening to separate the undesirable fines and size the material to meet specifications. Silica sand is commonly scrubbed in addition to further reduce impurities in the clay size fraction. In other simple processing, crushing and grinding may be added as in crushed stone operations and in production of ground talc and barite. Some commodities require sintering or other kiln treatment; Portland cement, lime, and lightweight aggregate are examples. Mills that process metalliferous ores are commonly more complex. Depending on the nature of the ore, they may utilize a variety of mineral properties to effect separations—specific gravity, magnetic permeability, specific conductance, surface chemistry, and solubility are some of the properties which milling systems are designed to exploit through jigs, shaking tables, heavy media tanks, flotation cells, magnetic and electrical separators, and leaching tanks. The concentrates resulting from milling are sent to smelters and in some cases from the smelter to refineries using electrolytic methods.

Fisher (1965, Fig. 4) showed how processing adds to the value of some industrial minerals (Fig. I.2). The largest increase in price is for common clay. In the pit, the brick clay may be nominally valued as low as 50 cents per ton with no market for it. However, after mining, hauling, grinding, blending, screening, pugging, forming, trim-

Figure I.2

Value added by processing industrial minerals
(after Fisher, 1965, Fig. 4).

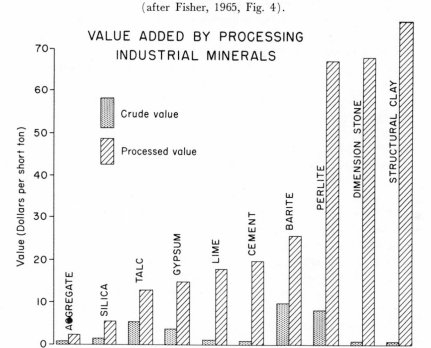

VALUE ADDED BY PROCESSING
INDUSTRIAL MINERALS

ming, drying, perhaps glazing and careful sizing, and firing, the value
is increased to as much as 80 dollars per ton or more. Since common
clay is widespread, it is clear that the developed mineral resource is
the result of the capital investment and engineering skill of the
operator combined with the existence of a market for brick or tile.

Valuation of mineral deposits.

Consideration of the large capital investment necessary to develop
mineral property and bring it to the stage of production makes it
clear that determination of the value or worth of the property is a
most important and practical step in the progression from prospect
to producing property and in fact determines whether or not the
deposit will be exploited at any particular time. The purpose of valuation under the capitalist or free market system is, of course, to answer
the question—Is there a dollar in it? Or, perhaps more properly, is

there a margin of profit in a certain cost-price structure? Under a socialist or communist system the same basic question must be faced but it is expressed differently—is this deposit one which can contribute to the needs of the economy with minimum investment and minimum operation costs?

The engineer or geologist concerned with valuation must be a very broadly trained specialist. He must examine data from many sources to reach a final judgment on the value of the property and answer the question raised in the first paragraph. He must obviously know the size of the deposit—how many tons or yards or barrels—and the quality of the mineral material which can be produced from it. He must know costs of acquiring the property and the investment requirements for such exploration and development as remains to be done. The capital costs of plant and equipment must be calculated. He must know the costs and efficiencies of the appropriate extraction methods. He must know the costs and efficiencies of the appropriate methods of beneficiating the raw mineral product and bringing to the stage of a marketable product. He must know the many factors of the market place. Transportation costs commonly are critical. There are political factors which must be evaluated—taxes and tariffs, conservation laws, labor laws, subsidies. He must peer into the future and anticipate changes in economic, political, and technological factors. He must estimate the productive life of the deposit under a variety of circumstances and determine the present value of the future income. There is always legal question of secure title; other legal and business questions are concerned with the conveyance, with performance requirements, with royalties, taxes, insurance. It is not surprising, therefore, that valuation of large properties where large sums of money are involved commonly involves a team of specialists rather than one man. In most cases complete data needed for the analysis are not available and must be developed. This in itself can be a costly process if the physical parameters of the deposit are not adequately known. Where it is necessary to learn more about the deposit, the purchasing or investing group usually obtains an option on the property which gives them a period of time in which to complete the valuation, but also, in the seller's interest, requires them to perform certain operations to develop information about the deposit. If prospective buyer and seller are acting in good faith, both are interested in knowing as much as possible about the deposit.

Investors, developers, and operators are not the only ones interested in knowing the value of mineral deposits and consequently not the only ones concerned with valuation of mineral property. Various branches of the government—state, county, and local school districts, for example—derive revenue from taxes on real estate and the taxes levied are related to the value of the real estate. Appraisal of mineral property for tax purposes, therefore, is a valid concern to agencies with the power to tax. For the most part at the state level, the responsibility lies with boards of equalization and assessment. A curious paradox is involved in appraisal of mineral property for tax purposes, where the tax base is the market or cash value of the property. If the owner of the mineral property has followed good mineral-industry practice and developed reserves well in advance of extraction, and if these reserves are disclosed to the tax assessor, then the good and prudent operator will be penalized through higher taxes for having proved in advance the existence of the reserves. Any forward-looking equalization board should develop methods of assessment which do not penalize the efficient and prudent operator.

An interesting and realistic concept is applied by the California State Board of Equalization for appraisal for tax purposes of sand and gravel deposits. Land containing sand and gravel is appraised as raw land up to the time when the deposit is brought into production. This is a practical recognition that many low-unit-value mineral deposits such as sand and gravel are made valuable assets only through development of a market and that without a market they are common earth materials. Sand and gravel deposits may be known to underlie a tract of land but may not yield any income for decades, if ever. After production begins and a royalty income accrues to the land owner, the tax is levied by capitalizing the royalty income because the value of the minerals to the landowner lies in the royalties paid by the lessee. Where the fee owner is the operator, an equitable tax assessment is developed by imputing a royalty rate consistent with general economic data for the industry (R. A. Paschall, personal communication, 1966). Probably the best known state mine valuation procedures are those developed by the State of Michigan and described by Pardee (1957). Minnesota's system was described by Weaton (1965). The field of state taxation of metallic deposits was covered in a book by that title by Roberts (1944).

There are many different methods of mineral property evaluation. Pioneers in the field were Herbert Hoover (1909) and J. K. Finlay (1909). The best known 'valuation formula' among engineers is the Hoskold formula, a rather complex mathematical approach involving two interest rates and a sinking fund in which the original investment is returned during the life of the mine. Under the Hoskold premise, the original investment is not recovered until it is returned in full by liquidation of the sinking fund. Under the simpler straight discount method, future income is discounted to present worth. Valuation short cuts such as break-even formulas (Callaway, 1954) and graphical methods (Evans, 1960; Shoemaker, 1963) have been devised. Summaries of valuation methods are presented by Just and others (1959, 1960) and by Raymond (1964).

REFERENCES

American Law of Mining (1964) Vol. 1, Public Domain, Rocky Mountain Mineral Law Foundation: Matthew Bender and Co., New York, 906 pp.

Arps, J. J. (1961) The profitability of exploratory ventures, in Economics of petroleum exploration, development and property evaluation: Prentice-Hall, Englewood Cliffs, N.J., for Southwestern Legal Foundation, Dallas, Texas, pp. 153–173.

Bailly, P. A. (1964) Methods, costs, land requirements, and organization in regional exploration for base metals: Paper presented at meeting of Alaska Section, American Institute of Mining, Metallurgical, and Petroleum Engineers, March 18–21, 1964.

Blondel, F., and Lasky, S. G. (1956) Mineral reserves and mineral resources: Econ. Geol., vol. 51, no. 7, pp. 686–697.

Brooks, D. B. (1964) Between economics and geology: Geotimes, vol. 8, no. 7, pp. 10–12.

Callaway, H. M. (1965) Basic break-even formulas devised to simplify mine evaluation: Eng. and Mining Jour., vol. 166, no. 11, pp. 90–92.

Clarke, F. W., and Washington, H. S. (1924) The composition of the earth's crust: U.S. Geol. Survey Prof. Paper 127, 117 pp.

Dapples, E. C. (1959) Basic geology for science and engineering: Wiley, New York, 609 pp.

Evans, J. B. (1960) The evaluation of mining properties—a graphical approach: Canadian Mining and Metallurgical Bull., vol. 53, no. 582, pp. 797–803; and Canadian Institute Mining and Metallurgy Trans., vol. 63, pp. 547–553.

Finlay, J. R. (1909) Cost of mining, 3rd ed. (1920): McGraw-Hill, New York, 415 pp.

Fisher, W. L. (1965) The search for nonfuel minerals: Bull. South Texas Geol. Soc., vol. 5, no. 2, pp. 6–12.

Flawn, P. T. (1964–65) Orebody concept versus cost concept: Geotimes, vol. 9, no. 5, pp. 17–18.

——— (1965) Minerals: final harvest or endless crop?: Eng. and Mining Jour., vol. 166, no. 5, pp. 106–108.

Fortescue, J. (1965) Exploration architecture, *in* Some guides to mineral exploration: Geol. Survey of Canada, Paper 65–6, pp. 4–14.

Gale, H. S. (1915) Salines in the Owens, Searles and Panamint Basins, southeastern California: U.S. Geol. Survey Bull. 5802, pp. 251–323.

Gonzales, R. J. (1964) Production depends on economics—not physical existence: Oil and Gas Jour., vol. 62, no. 13, pp. 59–64.

Goldschmidt, V. M. (1954) Geochemistry, edited by Alex Muir: Clarendon Press, Oxford, 730 pp.

Hahl, D. C., and Langford, R. H. (1964) Dissolved-mineral inflow to Great Salt Lake and chemical characteristics of the Salt Lake brine, Part II, Technical Report: Utah Geol. and Min. Surv. Water Resources Bull. No. 3, Part II, 40 pp.

Hendricks, T. A. (1965) Resources of oil, gas, and natural-gas liquids in the United States and the world: U.S. Geol. Survey Circ. 522, 20 pp.

Hoover, Herbert (1909) Principles of mining: Hill Publishing Co., New York, 199 pp.

Hubbert, M. K. (1962) Energy resources a report to the Committee on Natural Resources of the National Academy of Sciences–National Research Council: NAS-NRC Pub. 1000-D, pp. 42–73.

Just, Evan, Chandler, J. W., Jurden, W., Matthews, A. B., and Riddle, J. A. (1959, 1960) Economic valuation of proposed mining ventures: Mining Congress Jour., vol. 45, no. 11, pp. 43–51; no. 12, pp. 26–33; vol. 46, no. 1, pp. 33–38.

Leith, C. K. (1933) Mineral valuations of the future, *in* Elements of a national mineral policy, prepared by The Mineral Inquiry, C. K. Leith, Chairman: American Institute of Mining and Metallurgical Engineers, New York, 162 pp.

Manheim, F. T., Hathaway, J. C., Degens, E. T., McFarlin, P. F., and Jokela, A. (1965) Geochemistry of recent iron deposits in the Red Sea (abstract): Geol. Soc. Amer. Program, 1965 annual meetings, p. 100.

Mason, Brian (1952) Principles of geochemistry: Wiley, New York.

McKelvey, V. E. (in preparation) Meaning and preparation of mineral resource estimates.

Mitke, C. A. (1930) Mining methods: McGraw-Hill, New York, 195 pp.

Netschert, B. C., and Landsberg, H. H. (1961) The future supply of the major metals: Resources for the Future, Inc., Washington, 65 pp.

Owen, E. W. (1964) Some facies of regional history: Trans. Gulf Coast Assoc. Geol. Soc., vol. 14, p. 1.

Pardee, F. G. (1957) The Michigan mine appraisal system, *in* Examination and valuation of mineral property by C. H. Baxter and R. D. Parks, 4th ed. by R. D. Parks: Addison-Wesley, Cambridge, pp. 447–465.

Pruitt, R. G. Jr. (1966) Mineral terms—some problems in their use and definition, *in* Eleventh Annual Rocky Mountain Mineral Law Institute, Matthew Bender and Co., New York, pp. 1–34.

Raymond, L. C. (1964) Valuation of mineral property, *in* Economics of the mineral industries, 2nd ed.: American Institute of Mining, Metallurgical and Petroleum Engineers, New York, pp. 131–165.

Roberts, W. A. (1944) State taxation of metallic deposits: Harvard Economic Studies, vol. 77, 400 pp.

Schurr, S. H., Netschert, B. C., et al. (1960) Energy in the American economy, 1850–1975: Resources for the Future, Inc., Johns Hopkins Press, Baltimore, 774 pp.

Shoemaker, R. P. (1963) A graphical short-cut for rate of return determinations: World Oil, vol. 157, no. 1, pp. 73–84; no. 2, pp. 69–73; no. 4, pp. 64–68.

Weaton, G. F., Jr. (1965) Estimating Minnesota's natural iron ore reserves: Mining Eng., vol. 17, no. 7, pp. 38–41.

Weed, W. H. (1912) Geology and ore deposits of the Butte district, Montana: U.S. Geol. Survey Prof. Paper 74, 262 pp.

White, D. E. (1963) The Salton Sea geothermal brine, an ore-transporting fluid (abstract): Mining Eng., vol. 15, no. 11, p. 60.

———, Anderson, E. T., and Grubbs, D. K. (1963) Geothermal brine well: Science, vol. 39, pp. 919–922.

Zapp, A. D. (1961) World petroleum resources, *in* Domestic and world resources of fossil fuels, radioactive minerals, and geothermal energy: Preliminary reports prepared by members of the U.S. Geological Survey for the Natural Resources Subcommittee of the Federal Science Council, 9 pp.

——— (1962) Future petroleum producing capacity of the United States: U.S. Geol. Survey Bull. 1142-H, 36 pp.

CHAPTER II

FORMATION
OF MINERAL
DEPOSITS

HISTORY OF IDEAS

In the absence of any record on the earliest functioning of man's imagination and ability to develop concepts, it is not possible to know when some curious individual first wondered about the origin of natural phenomena such as accumulations of minerals. However, we can reason that the development of techniques of chipping and flaking by stone-using cultures cannot be separated from the empirically derived knowledge that certain kinds of stone—namely, flint and some volcanic glasses—can be worked by chipping and flaking whereas others cannot. Likewise, the knowledge that such desirable stones occur in some places but not in others was a matter of practical experience. The 'why' of their unequal distribution was probably treated by primitive religions which undertook to explain the whole of nature in animistic terms; for example, flint nodules in chalk might have been interpreted as eggs laid in the ground by the spirit of the mountain.

At a higher cultural level and after the inception of a written his-torical record, Greek philosophers tried to fit the various aspects of nature into a coherent and logical philosophy. The early Ionian philosophy that began with Thales (ca. 640–ca. 550 B.C.) was con-cerned principally with 'substance' and the origin of natural phenom-ena. The more practical working engineers of the period who were concerned with finding ores and extracting metals began to develop a body of knowledge on the occurrence of ores, and this new knowl-edge was in part chronicled by the philosopher-historians, such as Herodotus (ca. 484–ca. 425 B.C.), who described the association of gold and quartz veins. But the wonderful tradition of first deductive and then inductive reasoning, pioneered by the Greek culture and carried on by the best Roman minds, withered and was almost buried by mysticism in the Dark and Middle Ages; the origin of mineral deposits was explained by alchemists who invoked fantastic theories and strange forces derived not from observation and the scientific method but from their own introspection.

However, by the 15th century the body of knowledge about mineral deposits had grown to the point where theories of origin that did not fit the facts were unacceptable to rational men. It was in the first half of the 16th century that a rational thinker and keen observer named Georgius Agricola formulated the first theory of ore genesis based on field observations; in his book *De Re Metallica* (1556) he de-scribed the circulation of ground waters, showed that ores in fissures and fractures were formed subsequently to the host rocks, and con-cluded that the ores were deposited from circulating waters. He thus laid the foundation for modern ideas of epigenetic ore deposits. Although subsequently proved wrong in some parts, Agricola's thesis stood without improvement or modification for two hundred years.

By the 18th century new knowledge about chemistry and physics, together with more and more data from the German and to a lesser extent Swedish mining districts, spawned a number of ideas and hypotheses about the genesis of ores, and many of these were tested in long and heated controversies. The result was a general 18th century acceptance of the idea earlier proposed by Steno and Descartes that ore-forming elements ascended as exhalations from a hot interior and were deposited as lodes in the fissures of the surficial crust. An-other important idea was generated in this century by Delius, Ger-hard, and Lassius—that ascending solutions dissolved disseminated metals in the rocks through which they passed and subsequently deposited them in concentrated form. The period of the late 18th and early 19th centuries was the temporal battlefield of the Hutton-Werner controversy. Abraham Gottlob Werner of Freiberg Mining Academy (1749–1807) and his many disciples rejected the previously conceived theories and proposed that mineral lodes had been deposited by the descending waters of a primeval ocean. For this view Werner has been termed a 'Neptunist.' His adversary, James Hutton, a Scot, carried on development of the rising exhalation theory by correct interpretation of igneous rocks as the crystallized products of rock melts or magmas. However, in his desire to present a comprehensive theory, Hutton failed to distinguish between high temperature igneous injections (dikes) and the products of lower temperature aqueous solutions (veins). He regarded ore veins as crystallized material injected into fissures in an original molten state.

Over a period of many years the concepts of Hutton and Werner were debated by disciples of both, but what is more important they were tested in the field and laboratory and tried and retried in the scientific courtroom as new evidence was brought to bear; eventually, the sound principles were winnowed from the erroneous ones. Hutton has clearly had the best of it from the vantage point of the 20th century, even though he has been proved wrong in his concepts of vein formation since it has been proved that metals are transported in and deposited from aqueous solutions. Werner's idea that crystalline rocks are precipitates from a primeval ocean rather than crystallized from melts or in the solid state under high temperatures and pressures was wrong, but a form of his idea survives today and is endorsed by syngeneticists—those who believe that the metals in some kinds of deposits, the great stratiform or stratabound copper, gold, and uranium deposits—originated at the same time as the host rock, as detrital grains or contemporaneous precipitates. Epigeneticists, on the other hand, believe that the metals in these deposits were introduced by solutions subsequent to the formation of the strata.

During the first half of the 19th century, many new mining properties were opened and developed and there were significant advances in mining engineering. Although new ideas on the origin of mineral deposits were few, many observations on the mineralogy and geometry of the deposits became part of the record. It was recognized that in some areas certain kinds of deposits are associated with certain kinds of rocks and that some deposits are characterized by a mineralogical symmetry or zonation. During the last half of the 19th century, the growing body of data provided the base for a series of original contributions. The role of hot-water solutions was reemphasized. The physical and temporal association between ore deposits and igneous intrusions was demonstrated. The importance of the structure of the host rock in controlling the emplacement of ore bodies was clearly set forth. The fact that some minerals, including ore minerals, have selectively replaced earlier-formed minerals in the host rocks was proved, although the process was not and is still not clearly understood.

After the turn of the century modern comprehensive genetic classifications of ore deposits began to appear (Chapter III). Mineral deposits were classified according to the process of formation. These classifications had the usual difficulties of classifications of natural phenomena which attempt to be all inclusive but which must deal with transitions. Although generally sound, many mistakes were made in placing specific deposits in the classifications. The deposit is the fact and the process of formation is inferred from it. In recent decades, the mechanisms invoked to explain the origin of different kinds of deposits have been reviewed in the light of new geochemical and geophysical data and with knowledge about the limits of systems as determined in laboratories through increased capabilities to achieve, reproduce, and control high temperatures and high pressures. Amstutz (1964, pp. 1–2, Table I) pointed out the relationship between general cultural trends and changing patterns of thought about ore genesis from classical times to the present and compared the cultures which sought causes from within to those which sought causes from without.

In considering the natural processes which effect an accumulation or concentration of minerals or elements, it is helpful to separate surficial processes which operate at or on the surface of the earth from internal processes which operate within the crust or in the mantle. The surficial processes operate at the range of temperature and pressures which obtain at the lithosphere-atmosphere interface while internal processes operate at higher temperatures and pressures. The surficial processes can be observed and studied directly. The internal processes must be inferred or even deduced from the few direct measurements made in deep boreholes and deep mines, from measurements of gravity, magnetic, seismic, and electric phenomena, and from study of the product of the internal processes—the mineral deposit—which subsequently has been brought to the surface or near surface by tectonism or through erosion of the overlying rocks. It is also convenient for discussion to make distinctions between terrestrial and marine environments and between physical, chemical and biological processes. The distinctions made for discussion, however, are not so clear-cut in nature—many natural processes operate in both terrestrial and marine environments and very commonly physical, chemical, and biological processes operate together. The physical process may indeed make possible, cause, or catalyze the chemical process. In the following discussion, processes are described as physical or chemical and biological according to the principal or characteristic process operating.

SURFICIAL PROCESSES

Physical (mechanical), chemical, and biological processes now operating on the surface of the earth effect concentrations of certain minerals or elements. Most of these operate too slowly to make it possible to farm minerals or raise successive mineral crops but there are a few exceptions where mineral deposits have been formed or are being formed rapidly (p. 6).

Physical (mechanical) processes.

The most common physical processes which concentrate minerals are processes of sedimentation—the transport and deposition of rock and mineral grains. These processes operate on land and in the seas. Perhaps the best known are the fluvial and marine processes which produce placer deposits. The principle that obtains is that when an aggregate of minerals is agitated in a fluid medium, the heavier grains accumulate or are concentrated at the bottom of the system. In nature, the mineral grains are first released from the rock aggregate by weathering processes, and once freed respond according to their specific gravities. Thus, the heavy minerals settle and accumulate along the bottoms of stream courses and along certain beaches according to the laws of sedimentation. Extremely fine silt or clay-size particles of most heavy minerals do not have enough mass to accumulate and very coarse fragments do not move far from their source, so the aggregate also has a size range. Gold with a very high specific gravity occurs in placer deposits in extremely fine grains called 'dust' or 'colors' as fine as 2 microns in thickness (Bateman, 1950, p. 236). Man has utilized this principle of gravity concentration in various ore-dressing techniques with jigs, mechanical tables, and spirals. Crushed, ground, and sized ores are agitated or set in motion in water and the heavy fraction is drawn off by various devices.

The minerals that have accumulated in this way in nature must be stable as well as heavy—that is, they must be ones that resist chemical alteration as well as physical destruction by impact and abrasion. The common minerals which have been concentrated by these mechanical processes in alluvial and beach placers include platinum, diamonds, gold, tin minerals, chromite, native copper, tungsten minerals, phosphate nodules, and suites of so-called heavy minerals including magnetite, ilmenite, rutile, monazite, garnet, columbite-tantalite, and rare-earth minerals. Concentrations have also resulted from mass wasting processes where weathered and disintegrated material moves down hill slopes under gravity stresses. Heavier minerals move more slowly and are thus concentrated. This process is less efficient than mechanical concentration in a more fluid medium such as water where grains have greater freedom to move. Concentrations also take place with air as the fluid medium and wind turbulence as the agitating mechanism. However, because air has lower viscosity and rarely flows in channels, it has less ability to transport and winnow the mineral aggregate.

Fluvial and beach processes also concentrate valuable minerals other than the heavy placer minerals. High-energy currents commonly effect separations of coarse and fine material, thus removing clay from sand and gravel. Sand and gravel concentrations are valuable mineral deposits when located close to population centers because they are basic to the construction industry as aggregates. A gravel bar formed in a particular reach of a river as a result of a violent flood is an example of a rapidly formed mineral deposit. Extremely pure quartz sand deposited in high-energy environments such as prevail on certain beaches is a chemical raw material used for manufacture of glass. Sedimentary processes play a part in the formation of some mineral deposits when geologic conditions are such that only a material of a certain size or composition is transported to a basin of accumulation. Perhaps only one kind of rock is exposed in the source area or perhaps the stream dynamics permit transportation of only clay-size sediment. The resulting mineral deposit might be a stratum of pure clay or an accumulation of plant debris which subsequently is converted into a coal seam. In a very broad sense, the sheets of silty loam spread over the bottom lands of river valleys by floods are a prime agricultural mineral resource. Moving water—a fluid mineral—can, where topography is favorable, be harnessed as a power resource. It is, of course, the most important mineral resource as an indispensable ingredient to support life and as an industrial raw material. The surficial and atmospheric processes which distribute fresh water over the land and fill subsurface reservoirs are well known as the hydrologic cycle.

An interesting example of a rapidly formed fluvial mineral deposit is the scrap mica accumulated behind a dam built on the Nolichucky River in Tennessee. The fine mica came from the tailings of an old mica mining district upstream at Spruce Pine, North Carolina, and was transported by the river until trapped by the dam. At one time the deposit was mined by dredging.

Chemical and biological processes.

The chemical and biological processes operating on the surface of the earth can be conveniently separated into (1) processes of the terrestrial environment including chemical weathering and shallow ground water processes; evaporation; the chemical and biological processes operating in lakes, swamps and lagoons; and hot spring, fumarole and surface volcanic processes, and (2) processes common to the marine environment including selective precipitation and biological concentration.

The weathering process whereby rocks are reduced and changed to soil include a number of very complex processes which can be simply grouped as hydration, oxidation, bacterial action, selective leaching by organic and inorganic acids, and selective deposition or fixation. The relative importance of these factors and how they operate depend on the original composition of the rock mass, the topography, and the climate. Examples of commercial deposits produced by such processes include bauxite where the process has operated to selectively remove iron and silica and leave a high alumina residue, kaolin clays where granitic rocks have been altered to kaolin (potassium aluminum silicate), lateritic iron-nickel-cobalt concentrations resulting from weathering of serpentines and other ultrabasic rocks, residual manganese deposits resulting from weathering of manganiferous rocks, and iron oxide concentrations resulting from weathering of iron silicate and iron carbonate-rich rocks.

The deposit does not always result from concentration of material left behind during the weathering process. The oxidation of sulfide minerals, particularly iron and copper sulfides, mobilizes the copper as a sulfate. Commonly, the copper is reconcentrated just at the water table (below the zone of oxidation) by precipitation on other sulfide minerals, and the result is a deposit richer than the original. If natural solvents are not available to effectively mobilize the copper, it remains in the oxidized zone as an oxide, carbonate, silicate, or native metal; in some places the copper is precipitated in oxide form at some distance from the original sulfide deposit. In some regions silver, copper, zinc, and lead are concentrated in the zone of oxidation either as a chloride mineral (silver) or as carbonate or sulfate minerals (copper, zince, lead) .

Evaporation of salt water in shallow surface depressions—small or large—results in formation of brines and precipitation of salts—sodium, calcium, magnesium, and potassium salts. In the past such salt lakes or pans were important natural sources of salt; today the process is controlled and utilized in some coastal areas to produce salt. In the geologic past vast inland seas precipitated salts which accumulated in 'evaporite' basins and these are exploited today for sodium chloride, sodium carbonate, sodium sulfate, calcium salts, magnesium salts, potassium salts, and lithium salts. There may be some question as to whether the evaporation process should be considered under the heading of terrestrial processes or marine processes, but it is, broadly speaking, a surficial process. Chemical and biological processes combined with general sedimentation processes in lakes, swamps and lagoons have resulted in transformation of accumulated fragmental plant debris to coal and lignite and of plant and animal matter (aquatic organisms, algae, pollen) to oil (kerogen) shale.

Hot springs, fumaroles, and volcanic vents, whether terrestrial or submarine, mark the place where surficial and internal processes come together. Such phenomena are the uppermost manifestations of vast internal igneous and hydrothermal systems. Valuable minerals deposited around such orifices are few. They include sulfur, manganese oxides, tufas, sinters, and travertines, and volcanic ash deposits useful as pozzolanic materials, abrasives, and even building stone (as sillars) . Some pumice is used as an abrasive and both pumice and lava are utilized as building stone (as crushed stone and dimension stone) . Although minor amounts of metals such as mercury are deposited at the surface in hot springs, the main environment of metal deposition is lower in the system, below the surface, at higher temperatures and pressures. Steam itself is a valuable resource produced by superheating of water in contact with hot igneous rocks. In some areas it is used for power generation.

Marine chemical and biological processes which serve to concentrate minerals include selective precipitation and concentration by organisms (including bacteria) . It is difficult to separate logically precipitation caused by evaporation from precipitation caused by other physical, chemical, and biological processes which affect relative ion concentrations. In modern seas, pure lime muds accumulated through precipitation of calcium carbonate indicate that this same mechanism produced the valuable high-calcium limestone deposits utilized today. Phosphatic rocks are also produced by selective precipitation. In the case of calcium, silica, and phosphorous, some organisms selectively extract these elements which then are concentrated by accumulation of the animals' remains in areas where the accumulation is not diluted by other sediments. Concentrations of phosphatic nodules formed probably as a result of agglomeration of colloidal phosphate derived from decaying organisms occur on parts of the continental shelves. Concentrations of manganese nodules consisting of manganese, iron, cobalt, nickel, copper, and lead exist on the sea floor in certain parts of the world and seem to be forming at a relatively rapid rate (Mero, 1965, pp. 176–178). The source of these metals and the mechanism of agglomeration are not fully known (Mero, 1965, pp. 145–151).

Shell reefs are valuable mineral deposits in some areas; they provide calcium carbonate for lime manufacture and other chemical processes, cement raw materials, and are used as aggregate and road base material.

Bacteria operating directly or indirectly have been invoked to explain concentrations of iron, manganese, copper, uranium, and sulfur. Some bacteria act to reduce sulfates, thereby producing hydrogen sulfide gas. This important compound may combine with metal ions to produce metallic sulfide deposits or it may be oxidized to form native sulfur and water. Some bacteria precipitate iron and manganese directly. Bacterial concentration takes place on the surface but probably continues in near-surface environments, long after deposition of the sedimentary host rocks. Some oxidizing bacteria strains have been developed to improve leaching of mine dumps by converting sulfides to sulfates.

The formation of petroleum is generally accepted as primarily a marine process, the raw materials being marine organisms, and the process involving physical, chemical, and bacterial alteration of the organic residue during or soon after entombment. Probably many of the changes that occur are part of what is commonly considered as the diagenetic process, which is defined as the chemical and physical changes that sediments undergo during and after their accumulation but prior to consolidation. Accumulation of petroleum into economically valuable deposits was effected through migration and collection in a trap, a sealed reservoir. Shale oil or, more properly, kerogen is a potentially economical source of petroleum. In these deposits migration and entrapment of a fluid did not occur. The kerogen—a solid bituminous mineraloid—is distributed throughout the rock and must be liberated from it. Some of the largest deposits are in the Green River Formation of Colorado and Wyoming. This formation is a lake deposit so it is clear that lacustrine as well as marine processes can produce petroleum or substances from which petroleum can be extracted.

INTERNAL PROCESSES

Volcanoes, fumaroles, hot springs, and temperature gradients measured in boreholes and mines, all indicate that the interior of the earth is hotter than the surface and, at least in some places, is hot enough to melt silicate rocks. Basaltic lavas which pour out on the earth's surface are at temperatures as high as 1100° C. to 1200° C. Steam and other hot gases emerge from various volcanic vents and are composed of H_2O, CO_2, and sulfur compounds, with minor amounts of other gases containing chlorine, fluorine, hydrogen, and boron at temperatures as high as 650° C. Recently, a well drilled in southern California tapped hot chloride brines containing over 300,000 parts per million (30 per cent) of dissolved solids including Cl, Na, Ca, K, Fe, Mn, Mg, Sr, Li, Ba, Rb, Zn, Pb, Cs, Cu, Ag, at temperatures of 300° C. This evidence indicates clearly that in parts of the earth characterized by igneous activity there are circulating through the rocks hot aqueous solutions charged with mineral matter. In areas where mines have explored concentrations of minerals in fissure and fracture systems and disseminated in adjacent rocks, it is reasonably inferred that the depositing agents were similar hot aqueous solutions. The zonation observed in the deposits indicates that the minerals were selectively deposited under different conditions of temperature and pressure. The locus of the concentrations proves that certain geologic structures and certain kinds of rocks—loci of greatest porosity and permeability and rocks of certain composition and texture—were more favorable sites for accumulations than other structures and rocks. This, briefly and simply, is the evidence on which the hydrothermal or hot water theory of the origin of mineral deposits rests. It is corroborated by geochemical data on the temperature of deposition of certain minerals and by geochronological data on the time of deposition. It carries the corollary that the deposits are younger than the enclosing rocks—i.e., the deposits are epigenetic. The chemical composition of the ore-forming fluids—the mechanism by which relatively insoluble elements are transported—is still not thoroughly understood, but probably such elements are carried as ion complexes.

The concentration of elements in the solution is, of course, not as great as in the deposit because the aqueous solution selectively dumps its load as it passes into a zone where temperature, pressure, and concentration of the solution cause precipitation. The elements are in the solutions because they have been selectively dissolved from other rocks by the migrating solutions or because the elements did not fit into the crystal lattice of the principal rock-forming minerals that crystallized from the melt or magma.

As contrasted to hot aqueous solutions, the other principal internal mechanism of mineral concentration is a magmatic one which involves separation of a melt of particular composition or of crystals in a melt. In some magmatic bodies, particularly stratiform bodies, earlier formed crystals settled to the bottom of the system. The chromite deposits of the Bushveldt complex of South Africa are accumulations of crystals in layers, although perhaps there was some remobilization of the deposits subsequent to the original accumulation. Other mechanisms involve concentration by progressive crystallization—the residual liquid remaining after crystallization of the melt, commonly high in rare and alkali elements, is squeezed off and injected into fissures or fractures. Lithium pegmatite deposits are an example. Of course, some igneous rocks such as granite or trap rock are in themselves mineral deposits valuable as stone.

Through internal earth processes, valuable mineral deposits may result from simply the form of the crystallization; asbestos deposits are valuable not because of the composition of the serpentine or amphibole minerals but because of the long silky crystals. Application of heat alone may convert limestone to marble and produce a valuable stone deposit. Changes in rocks brought about by heat and pressure are included under the general term 'metamorphism.'

Some deposits such as the large lead and zinc deposits of the Mississippi Valley have been interpreted to be the result of deposition from low temperature cold-water solutions which picked up the widely disseminated metals as they percolated through a volume of sedimentary rocks and then concentrated them by precipitation in favorable loci. This explanation, however, is only one of four which purport to account for the metal accumulations. The others invoke

TABLE II.1

PROCESSES OF FORMATION OF MINERAL DEPOSITS

I. Surface processes	EXAMPLES OF DEPOSITS
A. Physical processes	
(1) Terrestrial environment	
General sedimentation processes	clays, worldwide; volcanic ash, worldwide
Fluvial and eolian processes	gold placers, California and Alaska; tin placers, Malaya; eolian gold placers, Australia
Mass-wasting processes	eluvial gold placers, Australia, New Zealand, California
(2) Marine environment	
General sedimentation processes	clays, worldwide; volcanic ash, worldwide
Mechanical processes operating along the strand and on the shelf	diamond beach placers, South-West Africa; gold beach placers, Nome, Alaska; pebble phosphate, Florida; St. Peter sandstone, Illinois and Missouri
B. Chemical and biological processes	
(1) Terrestrial environment	
Weathering and shallow ground water processes	bauxite, Arkansas, Jamaica; lateritic nickel and iron, Cuba, New Caledonia; residual kaolin, southeast U.S.
Evaporation processes	salt, Michigan; potash, New Mexico; lithium, California; gypsum, Texas
Lake, swamp, and lagoon processes	coal and lignite, worldwide; oil shale, Colorado and Wyoming
Hot spring, fumarolic, and surface volcanic processes	tufa, geyserite, sinter, Italy, New Zealand, Iceland, Wyoming; natural steam, California, Italy
(2) Marine environment	
Selective precipitation: accumulation in stratiform bodies or nodules (see evaporation)	phosphate, western U.S.; iron formations, worldwide; manganese, Ukraine; limestone, Texas, Indiana, worldwide
Fixation by organisms; accumulation in stratiform bodies or reefs	diatomite, California; shell reefs, coquina, worldwide

TABLE II.1

PROCESSES OF FORMATION OF MINERAL DEPOSITS (Continued)

II. Internal processes	EXAMPLES OF DEPOSITS
A. Aqueous processes	
(1) Ground water processes (cold)	
Selective precipitation and replacement	uranium, Colorado Plateau, Texas Coastal Plain
(2) Hydrothermal processes (hot)	
Selective precipitation and replacement	copper, Butte, Montana; gold, Cripple Creek, Colorado; molybdenum, Climax, Colorado; copper-gold, Noranda, Quebec
B. Magmatic processes (molten rock)	
(1) Crystal and melt separations	chromite, Rhodesia, South Africa; diamonds in pipes, South Africa; anorthosite, New York; feldspar, New England (pegmatite deposits are transitional between II, A and B)
C. Heat-pressure processes—formation of new minerals in the solid state in response to changes in temperature and pressure (metamorphism)	graphite, Texas, Mexico; anthracite, Pennsylvania; marble, Vermont; kyanite, Virginia; garnet, New York

hydrothermal solutions circulating through the host rock, precipitation of metals in chemically favorable environments at the same time as the carbonate rocks were deposited and submarine volcanic exhalations concurrent with deposition of the carbonate rocks. Whether or not the cold water theory is applicable to specific deposits, concentration by ground water is a mechanism that should be considered, whether it is classified as an internal or surficial process. Whether or not the original concentrations were due to deposition from such low temperature dilute aqueous solutions, there is convincing evidence that some deposits, such as the uranium deposits of the Colorado Plateau and the Texas Coastal Plain, have been reconcentrated or redeposited by such solutions.

Geologists distinguish between epigenetic and syngenetic and between exogenous and endogenous deposits; the former, a temporal distinction, contrasts deposits formed later than the host with deposits formed contemporaneously with the host; the latter is a spatial distinction separating deposits which originated within a body from those originating externally. It is helpful to keep these distinctions in mind when considering the processes of formation of mineral deposits as set forth in Table II.1.

PROBLEMS OF CLASSIFICATION

Table II.1 is an attempt to summarize in logical order the foregoing discussion of the formation of mineral deposits. Like all classifications designed to set complex natural phenomena in a simple framework, it suffers from inconsistencies, repetitions and omissions. If these are repaired to satisfy the exacting geologist, the classification will lose the simplicity which makes it useful for the student of mineral resources who is not a geologist but who nevertheless needs some understanding of the principal kinds of mineral deposits and how they form. Perhaps the best solution is to point out the defects of the classification and the difficulties in achieving perfection within the simple structure.

First, the two-fold division of the classification into Surface Processes and Internal Processes presents the problem of separating these two environments. What magnitude of third dimension does 'surface' include—to the base of operation of weathering and soil-forming processes or to a depth where there is a significant rise in temperature? Specifically, there are difficulties in classifying ground water processes which operate from the surface to considerable depths, particularly in sedimentary basins, and which at the upper limit of their range are surface processes and at the lower limit are internal processes. In the proposed classification (Table II.1) these are listed both as surficial and internal processes. The student should be aware of the reasons for the duplication. It is also difficult to separate for purposes of classification the deposits formed by ground or meteoric water from those formed by far-traveled hydrothermal solutions originally from an internal igneous source but more or less mixed with ground water and reduced in temperature as a result of movement through the upper parts of the crust. Thus, some geologists classify the lead-zinc deposits of the Tri-State district as formed by meteoric waters and others classify them as low-temperature hydrothermal deposits. The changes which sediments undergo prior to consolidation are called diagenesis. They involve both chemical and physical changes; they occur in both terrestrial and marine environments; generally speaking, diagenetic processes are surficial but in rapidly subsiding sedimentary basins they may continue to operate at depths of several hundreds or even thousands of feet. Obviously, it would be difficult to include diagenetic processes operating over such a wide range of conditions as a division of a classification which separates surface processes from internal ones and marine environments from terrestrial ones. Diagenesis plays an important role in formation of petroleum, coal, bauxite, and lateritic nickel-iron deposits. In the proposed classification these are considered under the headings of several chemical and biological processes. Consideration of diagenesis raises the problem of mineral deposits formed by several processes acting together or in sequence. Iron-rich formations resulting from marine sedimentary processes and subsequently further concentrated by weathering processes are a case in point. Coal deposits which result from chemical and physical alteration of plant material accumulated under delicately balanced conditions of sedimentation and crustal subsidence are another example. The sequence necessary for the origin of petroleum deposits has been discussed (p. 47). Such deposits defy simple classification by process. The student should also be aware that the same kinds of sedimentary processes operate in bodies of water on land as obtain in marine environments, and if these bodies of water are large, selective precipitation and fixation by organisms can give rise to significant mineral deposits. One principal difference is, of course, that the chemical composition of the water in land-locked bodies depends on evaporation and replenishment rates so that a greater range in composition prevails than in the seas.

REFERENCES

Amstutz, G. C. (1964) Sedimentology and ore genesis, *in* Developments in sedimentology, Vol. 2: Elsevier, New York, 184 pp.

Bateman, A. M. (1950) Economic mineral deposits, 2nd ed.: Wiley, New York, 916 pp.

Mero, J. L. (1965) The mineral resources of the sea: Elsevier, New York, 312 pp.

CHAPTER III

CLASSIFICATION OF MINERALS AND MINERAL DEPOSITS

General statement.

Classifications can be tested in a number of ways. Does the classification express relationships between the individuals of the series or group in a clear and logical manner? Does it include all of the members of the series? Is it consistent throughout? However, the ultimate test, assuming it meets the elementary requirements, is the test of usefulness. Does the classification further the understanding of relationships between the members of the series or is it in fact an intellectual straight-jacket? Thus the most direct way to evaluate a classification is to ask—does it help?

Most natural phenomena have been classified and reclassified, and minerals, mineral deposits, reserves and resources are no exception. Some broad classifications of minerals and of reserves and resources have been discussed in the first chapter. Inasmuch as this exposition is concerned with minerals in the economic sense, i.e., mineral commodities and mineral deposits, mineralogical classifications are not considered.

In the broadest terminology, mineral commodities are separated into mineral fuels, metals, and nonmetals. Although in common use, even this simple classification is not consistent. The first group is defined on use—as fuel or as a source of energy, the second two groups on the chemical character of the mineral matter. Likewise, the separation of individual commodities is not complete because uranium fits into more than one category, and mineral fuels are also nonmetals. Such inconsistency can be avoided by recognizing a two-part division between metals and nonmetals and further subdividing on the basis of use. The U.S. Bureau of Mines Minerals Yearbook includes one volume devoted to *Fuels* including (1) coal and related products and (2) petroleum and related products, and a second volume on *Metals and Minerals* (except fuels) in which commodities are treated in alphabetical order without regard to their metal or nonmetal character. Nuclear fuel minerals are not treated in the *Fuel* volume but rather in the *Metals and Minerals* volume. Although rarely included in classifications of minerals, natural liquids and gases other than fuels (water, brine, and CO_2 for example) are earth materials of value to man and hence are mineral resources in the broad sense (pp. 2, 8).

Metals are traditionally subdivided into Precious metals, Nonferrous metals, Iron and Ferroalloy metals, and Minor metals (Table III.1). This is a list and not a classification, although some of the

TABLE III.1

THE METALS

I. Precious metals—gold, silver, platinum, and rhenium

II. Nonferrous metals—copper, lead, zinc, tin, and aluminum

III. Iron and the ferroalloy metals—iron, manganese, nickel, chromium, molybdenum, tungsten, vanadium, cobalt

IV. Minor metals—antimony*, arsenic, barium, beryllium, bismuth, cadmium, calcium, magnesium*, lithium, mercury*, radium and uranium**, rare-earth metals, selenium and tellurium, columbium and tantalum, titanium*, zirconium, and other miscellaneous minor metals

---

° Also considered as nonferrous industrial metals in some tabulations.
°° More properly a mineral fuel.

metals in the main groups have similar chemical and physical properties. Another convenient listing or grouping was used by McDivitt (1965, Fig. 1) and is reproduced here as Table III.2. Under Metals

TABLE III.2

GROUPING OF METALS AND NONMETALS
(after McDivitt, 1965, Figure 1)

	Iron	Iron ore
	Iron alloy	Manganese ore Chromite Nickel Molybdenum Cobalt Vanadium
Metals	Base	Copper Lead Zinc Tin
	Light	Aluminum Magnesium Titanium
	Precious	Gold Silver Platinum
	Rare	Uranium Radium Beryllium
Nonmetals	Building	Sand and gravel Limestone Cement materials
	Chemical	Sulfur Salt
	Fertilizer	Phosphate rock Potash Nitrates
	Ceramic	Clay Feldspar
	Refractory and Flux	Clay Magnesia
	Abrasive	Sandstone Industrial diamonds
	Insulant	Asbestos Mica
	Pigment and Filler	Clay Diatomite Barite
	Precious and Gem	Gem diamonds Amethyst

are included iron, iron alloy, base, light, precious, and rare metals; under Nonmetals are building, chemical, fertilizer, ceramic, refractory and flux, abrasive, insulant, pigment and filler, precious and gem groups. The well-known Periodic Table provides a meaningful scientific classification of metals and can be found in any elementary chemistry text.

Nonmetals are separated in various ways, the common larger groups including ceramic materials, construction materials, metallurgical, chemical and refractory materials, fertilizer materials, industrial and manufacturing materials, and gemstones. Water and mineral fuels are either considered separately or as nonmetals (Table III.3). In such a

TABLE III.3

THE NONMETALS

  I. Water

 II. Mineral fuels—coal (lignite and peat) , petroleum, natural gas

III. Construction materials—dimension stone, crushed stone, aggregates, gypsum, lime, cement materials, pigments, insulators, and binders

IV. Ceramic materials—clay, feldspar, talc and pyrophyllite, wollastonite and minor ceramic materials (bauxite, borax, lithium minerals, fluorspar, barite)

 V. Metallurgical, chemical and refractory materials—foundry sands, limestone, dolomite, magnesite, phosphorite, fluorspar, sulfur, salts and brines, fire clays, quartz and quartzite, sillimanite-andalusite-kyanite-dumortierite, brucite, diaspore, bauxite, spinel, chrome, zircon

VI. Industrial and manufacturing minerals—asbestos, mica, talc, barite, diatomite, graphite, zeolites, bentonite, silica sand, abrasives, other mineral fillers and mineral filters

VII. Fertilizer materials—sulfur, potash, phosphate, nitrate, agricultural limestone

VIII. Gemstones

tabulation many nonmetallic substances occur in several groups, depending on specifications and use. For example, sand as a component in concrete is a construction material; as a foundry sand it is a metallurgical material, as a source of silica for silica brick it is a refractory, as a raw material for glass it is an industrial or manufacturing material; a similar case can be made for limestone which serves as aggregate, dimension stone, cement raw material, chemical raw material, metallurgical fluxstone, and soil additive. The common treatments of

TABLE III.4

CLASSIFICATION OF NONMETALLIC INDUSTRIAL ROCKS AND MINERALS BY BATES
(1960, p. 17, Table 2.2, and p. 18, Table 2.3)

CRITERIA FOR TWOFOLD SUBDIVISION OF THE NONMETALLICS		
Aspect	*Group I*	*Group II*
Bulk	Large	Small
Unit Value	Low	High
Place Value	High	Low
Imports and Exports	Few	Many
Distribution	Widespread	Restricted
Geology	Simple	Complex
Processing	Simple	Complex

CLASSIFICATION

Industrial Rocks	*Industrial Minerals*
Igneous Rocks	Igneous Minerals
Granite	Nepheline syenite
Basalt and diabase	Feldspar
Pumice and pumicite	Mica
Perlite	Lithium minerals
Metamorphic Rocks	Beryl
Slate	Vein and Replacement Minerals
Marble	Quartz crystal
Sedimentary Rocks	Fluorspar
Sand and gravel	Barite
Sandstone	Magnesite
Clay	Metamorphic Minerals
Limestone and dolomite	Graphite
Phosphate rock	Asbestos
Gypsum	Talc
Salt	Vermiculite
	Sedimentary Minerals and Sulfur
	Diamond
	Diatomite
	Potash minerals
	Sodium minerals
	Borates
	Nitrates
	Sulfur

these commodities meet few of the tests of classifications and are merely convenient listings rather than classifications. Such listings are adequate for statistical purposes and for commodity reviews but are not really helpful in understanding the scientific or economic relationships between the various commodities.

Bates (1960, pp. 16–17) proposed a classification of nonmetals based on both economic and geologic elements. He analyzed characteristics of each mineral commodity in terms of bulk, unit value, place value, imports-exports, distribution, geology and processing (Bates, 1960, Table 2.2) and proposed a separation into industrial rocks and industrial minerals. Although the resulting classification (Bates, 1960, Table 2.3) contains some contradictions with some rocks included in the Minerals column because of economic considerations, it illustrates economic relationships (Table III.4). Nonmetals can be classified purely on economic grounds on volume of production and unit value, and preparation of such a classification is a beneficial exercise for the student of economic geology. The distance a particular commodity moves in trade, indeed trade and market patterns, can be used as a basis for classification to demonstrate economic relationships. It is also profitable to consider degrees of preparation of a commodity and its effect on the value of the mineral product. For example, granite used as riprap, as crushed stone for ballast, as rough dimension stone, and as dressed dimension stone constitutes a product series of increasing unit value. Minerals such as talc and barite are marketed as crude quarry products and also are ground to meet varying specifications. Mica ground for a mineral filler is a relatively low-value product as compared to sheet mica for electrical applications. Clays range from common clay to clays processed as special purpose catalysts. These 'value series' reflect product quality and the work input required to meet specifications. A recent classification of industrial rocks and minerals by Fisher (in press) effectively portrays relations between various economic aspects (Table III.5).

Classification of mineral deposits.

Classifications of natural phenomena such as mineral deposits are attempts to order very complex natural systems and it is clear that the classification can be no better than the degree of understanding of the system. There have been attempts to classify mineral deposits on the basis of form, texture, mineralogy, and process of formation or environment of formation (Noble, 1955; Park and MacDiarmid, 1964, pp. 206–214). Arguments on the relative merits of genetic as opposed to descriptive classifications reduced to simple terms are as follows: Genetic classifications are more meaningful than descrip-

TABLE III.5
CLASSIFICATION OF INDUSTRIAL ROCKS AND MINERALS
(after Fisher, in press)

Volume: Representative volumes of commercial operations

Unit Value: Determined from average price for common grades (unless grades specified) after treatment and before processing, f.o.b. plant

Note: Values for volume and unit value are order-of-magnitude only

I Concrete Group: Bulk constructional and building materials
- Sand and gravel
- Raw materials for cement
- Raw materials for lightweight aggregate
- Crushed stone aggregate
- Rock asphalt

II Brick and Lime Group: Bulk ceramic raw materials, lime, and commodities of or from diversified industries
- Clay for structural ceramic products
- Limestone for lime
- Agricultural limestone
- Chemical limestone
- Limestone fluxstone
- Industrial specialty sands
- Clay for specialty ceramics (floor and wall tile, pottery)
- Specialty ceramic and metallurgical process raw materials

III Plaster and Refractory Group: Specialty building materials and principal refractories
- Gypsum
- Pumicite (aggregate)
- Low grade mineral fillers
- Fire clay
- Magnesite
- Dolomite for refractories

IV Salt and Sulfur Group: Major industrial, chemical and fertilizer raw materials
- Salt-in-brine
- Rock salt
- Rock phosphate
- Frasch sulfur
- Potash
- Natural soda ash
- Salt cake

V Fluorspar and Talc Group: Industrial rocks and minerals

Aplite	Iron oxides (nonmetallic use)	
Asbestos	Kaolin	
Bauxite (nonmetallic use)	Lithium minerals	
Ball clay	Mica	
Barite	Mineral fillers (special grades)	
Bentonite	Natural nitrogen compounds	
Boron minerals	Natural aluminum minerals	
Celestite	Nepheline syenite	
Corundum	Perlite	
Cryolite	Pumice (abrasive)	
Diatomite	Pyrites	
Epsomite	Pyrophyllite	
Feldspar	Talc	
Fluorspar	Tripoli	
Fullers earth	Vermiculite	
Garnet	Wollastonite	
Kyanite concentrates	Zircon concentrates	
Graphite		

VI Diamond Group: Specialty grade and precious rocks and minerals
- Asbestos (special grade)
- Diatomite (abrasive)
- Gemstones
- Industrial crystals
- Industrial diamonds
- Mica (sheet)
- Mineral pigments
- Rare earths
- Sepiolite (meerschaum)

Value per ton	$1.50	$5.00	$40.00	$100.00	
Unit Value	Lowest	Low	Moderate	High	Highest (prices quoted generally in less than ton units)
Place Value	Highest (except for secondary products)	High	Low	Moderate	Low	Little significance

Representative Volumes of Production (thousand tons per year)

500	Largest
100	Large
50	Moderate
25	Small

tive classifications and present significant relationships between entities being classified. Descriptive classifications may be less meaningful than genetic classifications are *ideally,* but genetic classifications are only as good as the theories or concepts on which they are based; descriptive classifications are based on observable properties or characters of the entities being classified and are not subject to such potential error. Gilmour (1962) proposed a nongenetic classification of copper deposits:

A genetic classification is comparable, say, to a zoological classification derived from some worker's notion of phylogeny rather than from observed anatomical features. Obviously, a classification of ore deposits should be made as objective and as descriptive as possible and with this object descriptive criteria, such as the form and composition of the deposits and the type and setting of the host rocks should be employed.

However, notwithstanding this criticism, the natural processes that effect the separation and concentration of elements or minerals are well enough understood to provide a sound basis for classification without serious risk of major error as far as the structure of the classification is concerned. On the other hand, classification of *a particular deposit* on a genetic basis requires that the mode of origin of that deposit be determined from a study of the deposit. Thus, although we may recognize an earth process as capable of effecting a concentration of minerals or elements, proving that *a particular concentration* was formed by such a process is another matter. Perhaps the danger is not in the formulation and use of genetic classifications but rather in the premature classification of individual deposits within the genetic framework. Historically, a number of genetic classifications of mineral deposits had to be abandoned because they were based on insufficient knowledge of earth processes or on misconceptions as to the meaning of the data. Perhaps in the future some modern genetic classifications will have to be abandoned or drastically modified as more is learned about earth processes, and perhaps it will be demonstrated that existing genetic classifications for a time obstructed a full understanding of the origin of mineral deposits. However, as long as people inquire about the 'how' of things and are curious about the way in which natural phenomena come to be, there will be attempts at genetic classifications and over a period of time such classifications, even unsound ones, have contributed to understanding, albeit inversely, by challenging those who found them inadequate. To the mineral prospector seeking to evaluate exploration possibilities in a region, a classification by geological environment or associations may be most useful. It may be purely descriptive, purely genetic, or a hybrid. With such a classification and a geologic map, the prospector has a guide for exploration.

For the most part propounders of classifications are aware of their weaknesses and of the reservations necessary in their application. It is those who accept ready-made classifications without critical analysis and testing who are thereby intellectually fettered.

The building of classifications or the critical analysis of classifications is a profitable exercise for the student. For example, the material

TABLE III.6

CLASSIFICATION BY NIGGLI
(1929, p. 39)

VOLCANIC OR EXTRUSIVE		
	Native copper	Sub-aquatic-volcanic and at the same time biochemical deposits
Antimony-mercury		
	Gold-silver	
Heavy metals		
	Tin-bismuth (silver)	

PLUTONIC OR INTRUSIVE		
	Carbonates-oxides-sulfides-fluorides	Nickel-cobalt-arsenic (silver)
Hydrothermal		
	Lead-zinc-silver	
	Iron-copper-gold (arsenic)	
	Tourmaline-quartz association	
Pneumatolytic to Pegmatitic	Silicon-alkali-fluorine-boron-tin-molybdenum-tungsten	Heavy metals-alkaline earths-phosphorus-titanium
Ortho-magmatic	Titanium-iron-nickel-copper	
		Diamond, platinum-chromium

of mineral deposits (excepting fluid deposits) is rock, albeit rock of unusual composition, and a classification of mineral deposits can be built from the general genetic classification of rocks. In such an exer-

TABLE III.7

CLASSIFICATION BY LINDGREN
(1933, pp. 211–212)

I. Deposits produced by mechanical processes of concentration (temperature and. pressure moderate)

II. Deposits produced by chemical processes of concentration (temperature and pressure vary between wide limits)

A. In bodies of surface waters

1. By interaction of solutions

a. Inorganic reactions	Temperature, 0° to 70° C ±
b. Organic reactions	Pressure, moderate to strong

B. In bodies of rocks

1. By concentration of substances contained in the geologic body itself

a. Concentration of rock decay and residual weathering near surface	Temperature, 0° to 100° C ± Pressure, moderate
b. Concentration by ground water of deeper circulation	Temperature, 0° to 100° C ± Pressure, moderate
c. Concentration by dynamic and regional metamorphism	Temperature, up to 400° C ± Pressure, high

2. Concentration effected by introduction of substances foreign to the rock

a. Origin independent of igneous activity

By circulating atmospheric waters at moderate or slight depth	Temperature, to 100° C ± Pressure, moderate

b. Origin dependent upon the eruption of igneous rocks

(1) By hot ascending waters of uncertain origin, but charged with igneous emanations

(a) Deposition and concentration at slight depth. Epithermal deposits.	Temperature, 50° to 200° C ± Pressure, moderate
(b) Deposition and concentration at intermediate depths. Mesothermal deposits.	Temperature, 200° to 300° C ± Pressure, high
(c) Deposition and concentration at great depth or at high temperature pressure. Hypothermal deposits.	Temperature, 300° to 500° C ± Pressure, very high

(2) By direct igneous emanations

(a) From intrusive bodies. Contact metamorphic or pyrometasomatic deposits.	Temperature, probably 500° to 800° C ± Pressure, very high
(b) From effusive bodies. Sublimates, fumaroles.	Temperature, 100° to 600° C ± Pressure, atmospheric to moderate

c. In magmas, by processes of differentiation

(1) Magmatic deposits proper	Temperature, 700° to 1500° C ±

TABLE III.7 (Continued)

CLASSIFICATION BY LINDGREN
(1933, pp. 211–212)

	Pressure, very high
(2) Pegmatites	Temperature, about 575° C ±
	Pressure, very high

cise, the questions that arise concerning basic differences between earth processes such as igneous and metamorphic processes are challenging. The diamonds that occur as 'phenocrysts' in kimberlite have long been cited as a primary igneous deposit. Recently it has been suggested that kimberlite is in fact material of the earth's mantle erupted into the crust. Is the mantle igneous or metamorphic rock? Did it pass through a fluid phase? Is kimberlite an igneous rock or a breccia of metamorphic rock fragments containing porphyroblasts?

Most textbooks on economic geology or mineral deposits review the history of classification of mineral deposits and present the classifications of Niggli (1929), Lindgren (1933), and Schneiderhöhn (1941). All are genetic classifications. They are classifications by geologists for geologists and are presented so that they can be compared. Niggli (Table III.6) characterized his system as a "minero-chemical" classification; he made a primary subdivision on the basis of process and a

TABLE III.8

CLASSIFICATION OF EPIGENETIC ORE DEPOSITS BY SCHNEIDERHÖHN
(1941, pp. 314–316)

I. Intrusive and liquid-magmatic deposits

II. Pneumatolytic deposits
    A. Pegmatitic veins
    B. Pneumatolytic veins and impregnations
    C. Contact pneumatolytic replacements

III. Hydrothermal deposits
    A. Gold and silver associations
    B. Pyrite and copper associations
    C. Lead-silver-zinc associations
    D. Silver-cobalt-nickel-bismuth-uranium associations
    E. Tin-silver-tungsten-bismuth associations
    F. Antimony-mercury-arsenic-selenium associations
    G. Nonsulfide associations
    H. Nonmetallic (ore-free) associations

IV. Exhalation deposits

TABLE III.9

CLASSIFICATION BY BATEMAN
(1950, pp. 363–364)

Process	Deposits	Examples
1. Magmatic concentration.	I. Early magmatic:	
	A. Disseminated crystallization.	Diamond pipes.
	B. Segregation.	Chromite deposits.
	C. Injection.	Kiruna magnetite?
	II. Late magmatic:	
	A. Residual liquid segregation.	Taberg magnetite.
	B. Residual liquid injection.	Adirondack magnetite, pegmatites.
	C. Immiscible liquid segregation.	Insizawa sulfides.
	D. Immiscible liquid injection.	Vlackfontein, S. Africa.
2. Sublimation.	Sublimates.	Sulfur.
3. Contact metasomatism.	Contact metasomatic: Iron, copper, gold, etc.	Cornwall magnetite, Morenci (old), etc.
4. Hydrothermal processes.		
A. Cavity filling.	Cavity filling (open space deposits):	
	A. Fissure veins.	Pachuca, Mexico.
	B. Shear-zone deposits.	Otago, New Zealand.
	C. Stockworks.	Quartz Hill, Colo.
	D. Ladder veins.	Morning Star, Australia.
	E. Saddle-reefs.	Bendigo, Australia.
	F. Tension-crack fillings (pitches and flats).	Wisconsin Pb and Zn.
	G. Breccia fillings:	
	a. Volcanic.	Bassick pipe, Colo.
	b. Tectonic.	Mascot, Tenn., Zn.
	c. Collapse.	Bisbee, Ariz.
	H. Solution-cavity fillings.	
	a. Caves and channels.	Wisconsin-Illinois Pb and Zn.
	b. Gash veins.	Upper Mississippi Valley Pb and Zn.
	I. Pore-space fillings.	"Red bed" copper.
	J. Vesicular fillings.	Lake Superior copper.

TABLE III.9 (Continued)

CLASSIFICATION BY BATEMAN
(1950, pp. 363–364)

Process	Deposits	Examples
4. Hydrothermal processes (cont.)		
B. Replacement.	Replacement:	
	A. Massive.	Bisbee copper.
	B. Lode fissure.	Kirkland Lake gold.
	C. Disseminated.	"Porphyry" coppers.
5. Sedimentation (exclusive of evaporation.	Sedimentary: Iron manganese, phosphate, etc.	Clinton iron ores.
6. Evaporation.	Evaporites:	
	A. Marine.	Gypsum, salt, potash.
	B. Lake.	Sodium carbonate, borates.
	C. Ground water.	Chile nitrates.
7. Residual and mechanical concentration.		
A. Residual concentration.	Residual deposits: Iron, manganese, bauxite, etc.	Lake Superior iron ores, Gold Coast manganese, Arkansas bauxite.
B. Mechanical concentration.	Placers:	
	A. Stream.	California placers.
	B. Beach.	Nome, Alaska, gold.
	C. Eluvial.	Dutch East Indies tin.
	D. Eolian.	Australian gold.
8. Surficial oxidation and supergene enrichment.	Oxidize, supergene sulfide.	Chuquicamata, Chile. Ray, Ariz., copper.
9. Metamorphism.	A. Metamorphosed deposits.	Rammelsburg, Germany
	B. Metamorphic deposits.	Graphite, asbestos, talc, soapstone, sillimanite group, garnet.

secondary subdivision on the basis of mineralogy. Lindgren (Table III.7) likewise made a primary separation on the basis of process, but his secondary divisions are environmental rather than mineralogical and defined by depth and temperature. Schneiderhöhn (Table III.8) also classified first by process of formation; his secondary divisions are based on metal and mineral associations. Bateman Table III.9) made a primary separation on process; his second rank divisions labeled "Deposit" are not consistent—some are a further subdivision of process, some are temporal, some are based on form or relationship to host rock, but the classification is a usable one. Those of Niggli and Schneiderhöhn deal only with epigenetic deposits—those formed later than the host rock and introduced into the host (as distinct from syngenetic or deposits formed at the same time as the host rock). Classifications by Lindgren and Bateman include syngenetic deposits. Bateman (Table III.10) also presented a classification of nonmetallic deposits based on process of formation and further divided on use. Genetic classification of nonmetallic deposits, while useful in analysis of the mode of occurrence of the various nonmetals, results in much repetition and confusion because the same product is formed by several processes. Limestone, for example, is formed by common sedimentary processes but it can be also a chemical precipitate or the product of organic processes. Talc is the product of both igneous and metamorphic processes. Clays are formed as sedimentary deposits, hydrothermal deposits, and residual deposits.

A classification of processes of formation of mineral deposits devised by the writer to minimize geological terminology but which is nevertheless in the overall scientifically accurate and comprehensive is presented in Chapter II as Table II.1. It can be read in terms of the product of the process as a simplified genetic classification of mineral deposits. Students of mineral resources who are not geologists should understand the basis for classification and the differences between principal kinds of deposits. Failure to master the jargon of geology and the details of genetic classifications might diminish their ability to communicate with geologists but will not affect their competence in the mineral resource field.

Apart from scientific classifications based on the origin of the mineral accumulation or descriptions of it, other engineering or economic classifications might be designed to do a particular job. For example, a mining company might find it useful to classify its deposits on mining methods (open pit versus underground, and further by engineering procedures employed), by cost per unit volume of rock mined, by capital investment, by shift volumes, by the nature of the mineral tenure (fee ownership versus lease), or by any other of a host of economic and engineering elements. A governmental agency might devise classifications of mineral deposits on the basis of availability of tonnages of ores or barrels of fluids under various conditions.

To summarize, for the geologist and engineer concerned with find-

TABLE III.10

CLASSIFICATION OF NONMETALS BY BATEMAN
(1950, pp. 632–633)

GENETIC AND USE CLASSIFICATION OF IMPORTANT NONMETALLIC MATERIALS

PROCESS OF FORMATION AND IMPORTANT PRODUCTS	Dominant Use Groups									
	Mineral Fuels	Ceramic Materials	Structural-Building Materials	Metallurgy and Refractory Materials	Industrial and Manufacturing Materials	Chemical Minerals	Fertilizer Minerals	Abrasives	Gemstones, Ornamental	Water Supplies
A. Igneous processes:										
I. Rocks:										
Building			⊗						X	
Soapstone			⊗							
Pumice					X			⊗		
Corundum				⊗				⊗	X	
Diamond								X	⊗	
II. Pegmatites:										
Feldspar		⊗								
Quartz (silica)		X		X	X			⊗	X	
Mica			X	X	⊗			X	X	
Cryolite		X		⊗						
Spodumene					⊗					
Gemstones					X			⊗	⊗	

III. Magmatic emanations:
Pyrite (sulfur)
Fluorspar
Barite and witherite
Magnesite

B. Sedimentary processes:
I. Sedimentary Rocks:
Building stones
Lime, dolomite magnesite
Hydraulic cements
Clay, shales
Phosphates
Sand, sand-stones
Bentonite, fuller's earth, diatomite

II. Chemical precipitates:
Rock salt
Gypsum
Potash
Nitrates
Borax and borates
Sodium compounds
Miscellaneous chemicals

(Continued on following page)

TABLE III.10 (Continued)

CLASSIFICATION OF NONMETALS BY BATEMAN
(1950, pp. 632–633)

GENETIC AND USE CLASSIFICATION OF IMPORTANT NONMETALLIC MATERIALS

PROCESS OF FORMATION AND IMPORTANT PRODUCTS	Dominant Use Groups									
	Mineral Fuels	Ceramic Materials	Structural-Building Materials	Metallurgy and Refractory Materials	Industrial and Manufacturing Materials	Chemical Minerals	Fertilizer Minerals	Abrasives	Gemstones, Ornamental	Water Supplies
B. Sedimentary processes (continued)										
III. Organic deposits:										
Coal	⊗									
Oil, gas	⊗									
Sulfur						X ⊗	X			
Bitumens			⊗							
C. Weathering processes:										
I. Residual concentration										
Bauxite		X	X	⊗ X	⊗			X		
Clays		⊗	⊗							

Mineral
    pigments
Tripoli
II. Mechanical
    concentra-
    tion:
    Sands
    Monazite and
      zircon
    Ilmenite
    Phosphates
    Gemstones
D. Metamorphic
    processes:
    Asbestos
    Graphite
    Emery, garnet
    Talc
    Sillimanite
      minerals
    Gemstones
    Roofing stones
E. Ground-water
    processes:
    Water supplies
    Brines (salt)
    Bromine,
      iodine
    Nitrates
    Sulfur
    Gemstones
    Salines (except
      salt)

X Indicates the chief uses.

ing new deposits and evaluating known ones, a sound genetic classification of mineral deposits is helpful in that knowledge of the mode of formation and the geologic environment enables him to assess the probability of discovering extensions of the deposits or other similar deposits. He can also evaluate the likelihood of occurrence of certain kinds of deposits in certain geologic environments. A descriptive classification of mineral deposits is less useful but still helpful in achieving a logical organization of geologic, physical and chemical data. Classification by commodity or mineral product is useful in dealing with mineral production statistics, specifications, and for certain engineering purposes. In evaluations of specific deposits and assessing the value of inventories of mineral commodities in certain regions, classifications which emphasize economic factors are most useful.

REFERENCES

Bateman, A. M. (1950) Economic mineral deposits, 2nd ed.: Wiley, New York, 916 pp.

Bates, R. L. (1960) Geology of the industrial rocks and minerals: Harper, New York, 441 pp.

Fisher, W. L. (in press) Classification of industrial minerals and rocks: Trans. Amer. Inst. Mining, Met. and Petrol. Engrs.

Gilmour, Paul (1962) Notes on a non-genetic classification of copper deposits: Econ. Geol., vol. 57, no. 3, pp. 450–452.

Lindgren, Waldemar (1933) Mineral deposits, 4th ed.: McGraw-Hill, New York, 930 pp.

McDivitt, J. F. (1965) Minerals and men: Resources for the Future, Inc., Johns Hopkins Press, Baltimore, 158 pp.

Niggli, Paul (1929) Ore deposits of magmatic origin, translated by H. C. Boydell: Thomas Murby and Co., London, 93 pp.

Noble, J. A. (1955) The classification of ore deposits: Econ Geol., 50th Anniversary Vol., Part I, pp. 155–169.

Park, C. F., Jr., and MacDiarmid, R. A. (1964) Ore deposits: W. H. Freeman and Co., San Francisco, 475 pp.

Schneiderhöhn, Hans (1941) Lehrbuch der Erzlagerstättenkunde, Vol. I: G. Fischer Verlag, Jena, 858 pp.

CHAPTER IV

LESSONS AND
LAWS FROM
ANCIENT HISTORY

Introduction.

History is a fascinating subject for its own sake and an essential subject for what can be learned from it. The broad pattern of human culture through the ages has been woven by countless historians in chronicles, analyses, and dissertations; the evolution of social, political, and religious institutions, the lives of leaders, and the significance of events have been well documented. Scientists and engineers have become concerned with the history of ideas and ways of doing things and the part science and engineering have played in human history. Today, it is not only the historian who is writing histories but also the specialist preoccupied with the history of his own discipline. It is indeed fascinating to pick a single thread from the broad pattern of history, trace it through the pattern, and evaluate its influence on the pattern. Some single threads influence or control parts of the pattern in an astonishing way; and so it is with minerals.

Historians have rated cultural level in terms of the materials used by the culture and thus the popular labels of Stone Age, Bronze Age, and Iron Age or Age of Metals. These names are usually ascribed to Christian J. Thomsen, Director of the Royal Museum in Copenhagen, who coined them in 1837 following the work of a scientific commission appointed to study artifacts in refuse and shell mounds in Denmark. However, Daniel (1943) and Heizer (1962) noted that the same historical divisions were made during the first century by both a Chinese and a Western historian; Lucretius (98–55 B.C.) in *De Rerum Natura* remarked on the following stages of human development—nails and teeth; stones, wood and fire; copper; and iron (Daniel, 1943, p. 13). Many writers have referred to subdivisions of recent history in terms of the common mineral energy source, hence, Coal Age and Oil Age. Today, frequent reference is made to the Atomic Age or Nuclear Age. Although the name primarily reflects recognition of a new energy source, it is, indirectly, mineral oriented. The term Radioactive Minerals Age might be substituted so as to continue the nomenclature of cultural stages in the traditional form.

The cultural stages named from the characteristic material used in the society correlate rather well with stages of political development. The stone age was the age of tribal units; the bronze age saw the rise of kingdoms; empires and federations marked the age of metals; and our own radioactive minerals age is the age of continental power blocks.

The term Bronze Age is really a misnomer because of the indiscriminate application of the term 'bronze' to copper and a wide variety of natural and man-made mixtures of copper and other metals. According to Wertime (1964, p. 1282), a quantity of metals other than tin were present in bronze until about 3000 B.C. when the superiority of the tin alloy became recognized. There was then a gradual improvement in bronze metallurgy. Knowledge of the manufacture of the closely controlled copper-tin alloy containing 10 percent tin and called bronze in metallurgical terminology was widespread in the eastern Mediterranean by about 2000 B.C.

Rickard (1932, p. 171) pointed out that it is more significant to separate a stone age and an age of metals, leaving out a bronze age and recognizing a premetallurgical transitional period in which metals were used as stone (shaped by hammering or abrasion) and smelting was unknown. Various societies passed through the stone—native metals—smelting cultural stages at various times, depending on their cultural development and the availability of metalliferous ores. Indeed, through contact with more advanced cultures, some cultures, such as those in parts of Africa, passed from stone to iron without an intervening bronze age. Forbes (1963, p. 108) emphasized the overlap in time of stone and metal by citing the use of stone-tipped arrows by Egyptian soldiers as late as the 7th century B.C., more than a thousand years after bronze was known in Egypt.

As cultures advance, the quantity and variety of minerals consumed increase exponentially. Today's measure of a nation's development is its mineral consumption. The industrial nations, of course, have the greatest appetite for mineral raw materials, but in the future, even the dominantly agrarian nations, and those that remain so, will consume great quantities of mineral fertilizers to feed the world's growing population.

Some minerals that were important at the dawn of history now play a relatively less dominant role in society—these include clay, dimension stone, flint, peat, lignite, natural pigments, and some kinds of gems. Other minerals are newly important, as new industrial processes require materials with special properties. These include beryllium, zirconium, hafnium, germanium, selenium and tellurium, silicon, rare-earths, and titanium; they prove that man continues to create resources through his own activities. And, of course, some minerals have been important since the dawn of history and are still important. Water and salt are necessary to sustain life. The six metals recognized by primitive metallurgists prior to the Christian era—gold, silver, copper, iron, lead, and tin—retain their key roles in modern industrial society.

One of the most significant cultural break-throughs in history involves the reduction of ores to metals, the treatment of metals, and the alloying of one metal with another to produce a new metal with desirable properties. There have been many speculations on the manner in which the metallurgical arts were begun—some invoke campfires or hearths accidentally located on outcropping ores, others fragments of ores accidentally dropped into fires. Rickard (1932, p. 113) related various theories including an ignited oil seep in contact with copper ore in the Caucasus, an Egyptian lady dropping some malachite cosmetic into a charcoal brazier, and copper ores dropped into campfires. Some believe that important inventions were made once and spread; others believe that discoveries were made independently at more or less the same time in separated cultures at more or less the same level. Probably copper was melted out of rock in many accidental firings until one man had the wit to perceive the significance of the process. In any case, from production of copper by campfire metallurgy, it was a short step to crude hole-in-the-ground furnaces and thence to clay-lined ground furnaces, to the use of charcoal as a fuel and reductant, and thence to inventions to increase the air blast, and to make alloys. Hoover (1912, p. 354) believed that smelting is a very old technique utilized "prior to recorded history" and presented a chronology of the history of mining and metallurgical inventions (Table IV.1). Wertime (1964, p. 1259, Table 2) (Table IV.2) chronologically tabulated the evolution of early fire-using mineral industries with earliest smelted objects dated about 4000 B.C. Probably the best estimate on the establishment of metallurgy as an art is about 4000 to 3500 B.C. although undoubtedly there were earlier beginnings.

The earlier metallurgical experiments and products utilized copper, tin, gold, silver, and perhaps, by accident, zinc and lead. The next big step forward was the extraction of iron from its ores. The history of iron working is dim, partly because the artifacts oxidize rapidly and are soon gone to rust, and partly because meteoric iron was used as a native metal by the fortunate few who had supplies of it prior to development of smelting capability. According to Rickard (1932, pp. 143, 832-842), the first ore-won iron implements (as opposed to meteoric iron implements) date from about 1350 B.C. and are from Palestine. Iron must have been a true wonder metal in the ancient world, and the superiority of iron weapons and iron tools over those made from bronze or stone gave the possessor a distinct advantage. Many myths and legends grew up around magic swords which by metallurgical design or accident possessed a superior temper. Surely there were wide variations in quality in early smelting operations due to lack of control over techniques, fuels, and raw materials so that outstanding batches won renown as superior products endowed with mystical qualities. Forbes (1963, pp. 116-117, Table VII) outlined the evolution of mining and metallurgy in the eastern Mediterranean region from the Paleolithic to the Roman Empire.

The fuel for metallurgical operations was charcoal until the 18th century. The earliest primitive hearths were improved by the Egyptians who used blow pipes and bellows. Big improvements in furnace technology came at about the beginning of the Christian era, or at least they became a matter of record then, with furnaces designed with high stacks, dust chambers, and bellows. Distillation apparatus to recover quicksilver was described by Pliny and Dioscorides. Fluxes were little known but the list of known mineral products and alloys · indicates considerable sophistication (Hoover, 1912, p. 355). The

TABLE IV.1

CHRONOLOGICAL LIST OF MINING AND METALLURGICAL INVENTIONS
(after Hoover, 1912, p. 354)

Gold washed from alluvial	Prior to recorded civilization
Copper reduced from ores by smelting	Prior to recorded civilization
Bitumen mined and used	Prior to recorded civilization
Tin reduced from ores by smelting	Prior to 3500 B.C.
Bronze made	Prior to 3500 B.C.
Iron reduced from ores by smelting	Prior to 3500 B.C.
Soda mined and used	Prior to 3500 B.C.
Gold reduced from ores by concentration	Prior to 2500 B.C.
Silver reduced from ores by smelting	Prior to 2000 B.C.
Lead reduced from ores by smelting	Prior to 2000 B.C. (perhaps prior to 3500 B.C.)
Silver parted from lead by cupellation	Prior to 2000 B.C.
Bellows used in furnaces	Prior to 1500 B.C.
Steel produced	Prior to 1000 B.C.
Base metals separated from ores by water concentration	Prior to 500 B.C.
Gold refined by cupellation	Prior to 500 B.C.
Sulfide ores smelted for lead	Prior to 500 B.C.
Mercury reduced from ores by (?)	Prior to 400 B.C.
White-lead made with vinegar	Prior to 300 B.C.
Touchstone known for determining gold and silver fineness	Prior to 300 B.C.
Quicksilver reduced from ore by distillation	Prior to Christian Era
Silver parted from gold by cementation with salt	Prior to Christian Era
Brass made by cementation of copper and calamine	Prior to Christian Era
Zinc oxides obtained from furnace fumes by construction of dust chambers	Prior to Christian Era
Antimony reduced from ores by smelting (accidental)	Prior to Christian Era
Gold recovered by amalgamation	Prior to Christian Era
Refining of copper by repeated fusion	Prior to Christian Era
Sulfide ores smelted for copper	Prior to Christian Era
Vitriol (blue and green) made	Prior to Christian Era
Alum made	Prior to Christian Era
Copper refined by oxidation and poling	Prior to 1200 A.D.
Gold parted from copper by cupelling with lead	Prior to 1200 A.D.
Gold parted from silver by fusion with sulfur	Prior to 1200 A.D.
Manufacture of nitric acid and *aqua regia*	Prior to 1400 A.D.
Gold parted from silver by nitric acid	Prior to 1400 A.D.
Gold parted from silver with antimony sulfide	Prior to 1500 A.D.
Gold parted from copper with sulfur	Prior to 1500 A.D.

TABLE IV.1 (Continued)

CHRONOLOGICAL LIST OF MINING AND METALLURGICAL INVENTIONS
(after Hoover, 1912, p. 354)

Silver parted from iron with antimony sulfide	Prior to 1500 A.D.
First text book on assaying	Prior to 1500 A.D.
Silver recovered from ores by amalgamation	Prior to 1500 A.D.
Separation of silver from copper by liquidation	Prior to 1540 A.D.
Cobalt and manganese used for pigments	Prior to 1540 A.D.
Roasting copper ores prior to smelting	Prior to 1550 A.D.
Stamp-mill used	Prior to 1550 A.D.
Bismuth reduced from ore	Prior to 1550 A.D.
Zinc reduced from ore (accidental)	Prior to 1550 A.D.

TABLE IV.2

EVOLUTION OF EARLY FIRE-USING MINERAL INDUSTRIES
(after Wertime, 1964, p. 1259, Table 2)

Pottery	Metals	Glazes, paints, and glass
Before 6000 B.C.		
		Ochre used in funerary practices; cave painters employed crushed oxides. Finds of rouge and eye shadow show crushing of hematite, galena, malachite.
6000–5500 B.C.		
Catal Hüyük pottery shows phases of pottery evolution.	Copper tubes, Catal Hüyük.	
5000–4500 B.C.		
First Jarmo pottery. Sialk red wares use iron oxide slip.	First metal hoards in Anatolia and Iran suggest hammered-annealed copper.	
4000 B.C.		
Closed kilns at Sialk III. Halaf polychrome wares follow metallic forms.	Cast Halaf and Sialk objects indicate melting of copper, smelting of lead, silver, and possibly copper. Extensive metal finds in Iran, Badarian Egypt shows first evidence of copper.	Badarian glazes in Egypt bring together crushed ore and alkali in closed chambers at temperatures not exceeding 850° C.

TABLE IV.2 (Continued)

3500 B.C.

Ubaid wares show achievement of higher temperatures, first reducing conditions.	Widespread casting of copper on Near Eastern plateau involves many impurities, particularly arsenic, lead, nickel, and tin. Meteoric iron objects found at Gerzeh. New metallurgy gradually spreads to Egypt, along with other influences from Mesopotamia.	Slags begin to suggest nature of glazes. Egyptian blue comes into vogue.

3000 B.C.

Potter's wheel comes into use at Amouq and elsewhere.	Age of metals begins great flourishing expansion in Mesopotamia as bronze first tentatively appears, then gradually asserts industrial strength. Lead bronze castings of Uruk give way to purer tin bronzes of Ur. Similar developments in Syria, Azerbaijan, and elsewhere. Silver is medium of exchange, gold appears in statuary and jewelry. Bronze and lead dominate castings. Metal tools for cutting, digging, and shaping are common by Jemdet Nasr phase.	Glass beads first appear in Egypt, soon appear also in Mesopotamia.

2500 B.C.

		Glassmaking, employing metallic colors, begins to flourish in Egypt.

2000 B.C.

	Trade in metals is widespread in mid-East. Bellows depicted ca. 1500.	

process of cupellation whereby lead is separated from silver by heating, conversion of the lead to oxide, absorption of the oxide by bone ash, and reduction of the separated oxide with charcoal was utilized by the Greeks at Laurium around 500 B.C., but was surely known earlier.

Although the art of metallurgy had its inception in accidental firings of easily smelted natural ores, it must have been early realized that if the metalliferous minerals could be separated from the rock, the smelting operation would be more efficient. Therefore, the earliest attempts at concentration of ores had as the object the reduction of the bulk of the mine-run ore by separation of the barren rock. Two elements were involved and are indeed involved today: (1) crushing of the ore fine enough to liberate the ore minerals, and (2) removal of the waste or separation of the ore minerals from the undesired gangue. The first application of this principle was to ores wherein natural processes of weathering had liberated the ore minerals—the gold-bearing sands and gravels—so that only the separation process remained to be effected. This, of course, was done by simple washing. Washing in this sense, of course, refers not to cleaning but to setting mineral particles in motion in water so that their natural specific gravities will effect a separation as they settle or move across an inclined table. The earliest records of such processes are Egyptian 4th dynasty, about 4000 B.C., where gold washing operations are indicated in inscriptions (Hoover, 1912, p. 279); the earliest complete description of crushing and concentration is by Agatharchides, a Greek historian of the 2nd century B.C. who described an Egyptian mining operation. Rock from the mine was carried out by boys and thereafter pounded in mortars by iron pestles. The reduced fragments were then milled (probably in mills similar to those used for grinding meal) and ground fine. The fine-ground rock metal was then washed to separate the gold.

The first method of breaking rock in the mine beyond the simple application of hammer and wedge or chisel or moil was fire-setting (Hoover, 1912, p. 118). Rocks were heated by fires set in the workings and subsequently douched with cold water or 'vinegar.' The thermal shock induced cracking which was then exploited by hammer and chisel. The method was also first described in the 2nd century B.C. by Agatharchides reporting on his visit to Egyptian gold mines (Rickard, 1932, pp. 208-215). This method was used for some 2,000 years until gunpowder was introduced in central Europe at Schemnitz in 1627. It took some 75 years for explosives to cross the English Channel. The use of fire-setting persisted some 200 years longer in Norway where wood was abundant and cheap. The driving of tunnels, adits, raises and winzes, and the digging of shafts in any kind of systematic way to

FIGURE IV.1

The ancient gold mines at Fawa Khir in eastern Egypt
(after Murray, 1925, Pl. XIII, Fig. 2).

intersect projected orebodies demands at least rudimentary surveying skills and instruments such as measuring rods, levels, and devices for measuring angles. According to Hoover, the first reference made to such measurements and instruments in mining prior to Agricola in 1556 was in about the first century A.D. (Hoover, 1912, p. 129). The compass dates from the 13th century.

The minerals of prehistoric man.

The most primitive associations of human beings were concerned with fresh water and salt. Man can live without salt if he eats raw flesh and entrails but he craves salt, and with any other kind of diet he needs salt. Early man used rocks as weapons and crude tools to crack nuts and bones and as crude building blocks for hearths. Modern monkeys throw stones and crack nuts with them, and it is reasonable to suppose early humans equally able. Although some nomadic cultures evolved unusual tactics of survival in a water-scarce environment (Bushmen of the Kalihari Desert and Australian Aborigines are modern examples), the range of most nomadic or hunting cul-

FIGURE IV.2

Ancient Egyptian turquoise mines in Sinai
(after Petrie, 1906. Pls. 72 and 73).

tures was controlled by distance from water, and without receptacles for carrying water the range was short. Struggles over access to or ownership of springs, water holes, salt licks, and salt springs persisted well beyond the prehistoric era, and, in fact, are still in progress. Salt wars are no longer common in the United States as they were during frontier days, but contests over water are on the increase in the United States and over the world. Most of these are contests in the courts, but Israel's water projects on the Jordan River have brought threats of war from neighboring Arab countries. Mexico has protested vigorously that the 1.5 million acre-feet of Colorado River water it receives from the United States is too salty. Arizona and California are in conflict over the same river. The United States and Canada have negotiated for years over the Columbia (Clyde, 1965, p. 504).

Concepts of ownership of mineral recources were early introduced in primitive societies. A tribe laid claim to a spring or a salt lick, and the tribal chief representing the tribe exercised executive control and was responsible for defense of and conservation of the resource. In a sense, this was government ownership of a mineral resource. No individual within the tribe owned the water or salt or traded it to others for a consideration. More complex arrangements whereby a government monopoly obtained revenue by selling the resource, or whereby favored individuals were given concessions to exploit the resource, were yet to come.

Eolithic man used stones more than one million years ago; most ancient tools are identified simply by evidence of wear or abrasion. Shaping of stones by chipping or flaking by impact and later by pressure was the subsequent great achievement that characterized Paleolithic man, and for nearly one million years, until about 25,000 B.C., man's tools and weapons were chipped and flaked from certain kinds of stone. The importance of high-quality flint and obsidian for weapons and tools is indicated by the hundreds of miles such stone spread in the days before historical records (Forbes, 1963, pp. 122-124). Inventions and innovations came slowly in the first stages of the cultural evolution. Late in the Paleolithic, natural pigments were utilized. About 25,000 B.C., man began to fire clay to make pottery, to make implements by grinding and polishing, and to use a greater number of mineral substances. This period has been called the Neolithic. Trade in flint, obsidian, amber, salt, gold, and turquoise flourished around the Mediterranean and through Europe. By 15,000 B.C., man had discovered gold and copper. By 6000 B.C., the great written record of history was begun, and cultural evolution began to accelerate. Of

FIGURE IV. 3

Sites where bronze and iron were first exploited (3500–2000 B.C.)
(after Wertime, 1964, p. 1263).

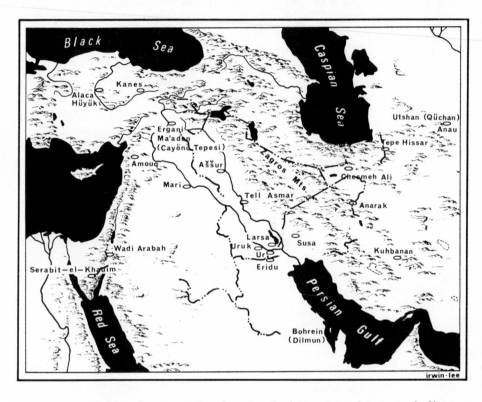

course, these dates are significant only in a general way to indicate spans of years required for change and increased utilization of environment. The cultural stages existed at different times in different parts of the world and indeed Neolithic man persists in some corners of the modern world. Neolithic salt production from Hallstadt in Austria occurred later in terms of years than Neolithic developments around the Mediterranean. Minerals and rocks used by man from about 100,000 B.C. to the beginning of the written record probably included chert, jasper, flint, chalcedony, agate, amethyst, quartz, obsidian, amber, talc and soapstone varieties, jade and serpentine, calcite, fluorspar, feldspar, iron oxides, sulfur, salt, natural asphalts, and, of course, water, and probably other ornamental stones including beryl, garnet, emerald, turquoise, malachite, lapis lazuli, gold, and copper. Ball (1931), writing on the history of gem mining, listed varieties of decorative stone used between 100,000 and 7000 B.C. and presented a series of maps showing known sources at various periods of history. Except for water and salt, man was able to get along in a simple agrarian or hunting culture without minerals and rocks. However, flint-tipped projectiles were superior to fire-hardened projectiles or even bone-tipped weapons; stone tools were better than no tools and increased the survival margin; clay pots provided a means of storing and transporting food and water and also increased survival probability; and men without such cultural aids as pigments, metal and stone ornaments, and asphalt as a preservative were willing to perform services and do work to obtain such materials. And so at the dawn of history, men took time off from farming and hunting to explore for mineral materials, produce them, and manufacture mineral products. Mining of flint and obsidian was in progress in Europe by 3000 B.C. and several thousands of years earlier in the eastern Mediterranean (Forbes, 1963, p. 120). Neolithic flint mines in chalk in France and England had a well-developed system of shafts and galleries with some shafts as much as 300 feet deep (Rickard, 1932, pp. 80-83).

Minerals in the ancient world of the Mediterranean.

About 6000 B.C., a combination of natural and human resources in the area of the eastern Mediterranean 'went critical' and resulted in a cultural explosion. Human activities expanded and diversified and created a demand for more and varied mineral materials. It is worthy of note that the earliest, settled, civilized communities were agricultural communities located in alluvial valleys, such as those of the Nile and the Tigris and Euphrates, whereas mineral materials (excepting sand and clay) needed by a growing and diversifying culture were for the most part in rocky highlands controlled through most of early history by nomadic, warlike peoples at a lower cultural level. The problems of producing mineral materials in outlying unsettled regions and transporting them to commercial trade centers are formidable even in the 20th century. The Egyptians utilized stone as a construction material and art medium at an early date because the stone was available in accessible outcrops along the Nile; the Mesopotamian cultures, on the other hand, lacked local stone and developed the ceramic arts, making bricks for construction, and utilizing ceramic materials for manufacture of household wares and as an art form. Thus, at least in its early stages, the material face of a culture is shaped by the nature of local materials. However, the lack of any substitute for metal tools and weapons forced contacts between valley and hill peoples, or between the metal-deficient, albeit food-producing, population center and mineral-rich lands. Wertime (1964, p. 1257) suggested that the first metal-oriented culture developed in the highlands east of the Mediterranean in an area including what is now western Iran and Turkey; he presented a time-scale of the development of the metallurgical arts beween 4500 and 2000 B.C. (p. 1258, Table 1). Mesopotamia and Syria imported metals from this region, from Armenia, and the Caucasus. Egypt looked for metals to the east in the Sinai Peninsula and to the south in Nubia (the Sudan). Demand for metal sparked the Neolithic metal-oriented culture which developed in the eastern Balkans. Copper was mined in Cyprus as early as 2500 B.C. Forbes (1963, pp. 131–132) listed ancient sources of minerals and metals. The rapid utilization of metals by the agricultural populations of the alluvial plains, particularly the peoples of the Nile, has prompted some to suggest that these peoples brought metal-working skills with them when they moved into the metal-deficient alluvial valleys. The use of copper, gold, and perhaps silver for ornaments is, of course, far older than the date ascribed to these agrarian civilizations. The simple metallurgical discovery that removed copper from the ornament class and increased its value enormously occurred about 4500 B.C., or at least it was exploited by the Chaldeans at about that date. It was discovered that copper can be hardened by hammering and thus constituted a raw material for a superior weaponry.

In Egypt, smaller states were consolidated into the Upper and Lower Kingdoms, and eventually united about 3400 B.C. A great theocracy developed through a series of dynasties. The creative groups that flourished around the Pharaohs and on top of the mass of workers and slaves produced artisans and engineers who developed stone industries, metal-working industries, and ceramic industries, all of which required mineral raw materials. Probably it was the Egyptian quartermasters assigned to procure quantities of mineral raw materials who first became grimly aware of the fact that gold is where you find it and that the existence of mineral deposits cannot be decreed or legislated. The political unit that was Egypt was not particularly richly endowed with minerals, and so began the first of the expansionist wars to secure control of mineral-producing real estate. Invasion of the Sinai Peninsula resulted in conquest of tur-

FIGURE IV. 4

Sites where metals were discovered in the sixth and fifth millenia, B.C.
(after Wertime, 1964, p. 1263).

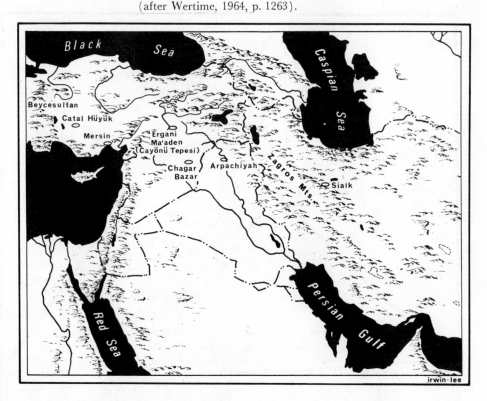

quoise and copper mines. Sir W. M. Flinders Petrie (1906) described Egyptian turquoise and copper mines in the Sinai and reconstructed the character of the mining expeditions—he dated the oldest turquoise mine as first dynasty, or about 5300 B.C. (1906, p. 41). Capture of Cyprus yielded rich copper deposits. The gold deposits of Nubia fell to Egypt. Egyptians not only took over existing inventories but actively prospected and mined in their own territory and in conquered territories. Shafts of emerald mines on the Red Sea coast are reported to have been nearly 1,000 feet deep. The Turin Papyrus of the time of Rameses II (1250 B.C.) includes a map of Egyptian gold mines.

Concepts of ownership of minerals changed drastically. The idea that resources were the property of the tribe, to be used for the

FIGURE IV.5

The Sinai Peninsula
(after Petrie, 1906, Map 1).

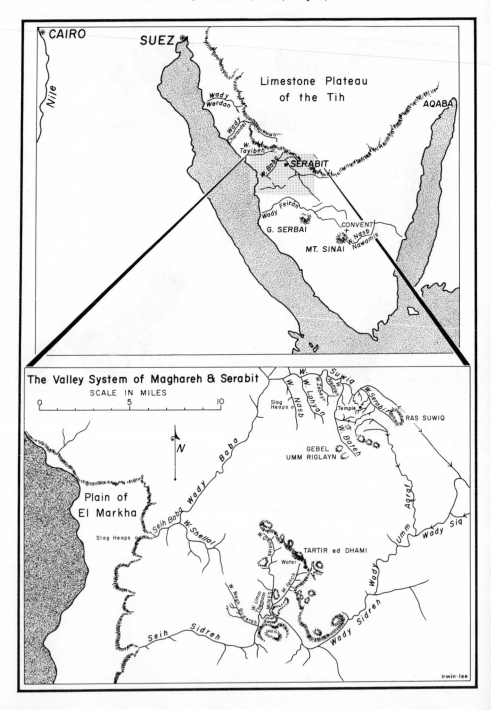

common good, gave way to the concept of absolute ownership by the god-kings—the resources of the empire were the Pharaoh's patrimony, although Forbes (1963, p. 127) stated that mines were also exploited by priests and private individuals.

It is hard to arrive at an accurate figure for the volume of metal in circulation in ancient Egypt, but Lovering (1943, pp. 41–43) has summed up evidence for estimating an order of magnitude with respect to copper and gold. Nubia's tribute to Thothmes was about 13,500 ounces. An expedition by Amenhotep III to the east of Egypt in 1400 B.C. returned with 100,000 pounds of copper and 1,000 pounds of gold. The yearly revenue of gold and silver from mines of Rameses III was stated in an inscription under a painting of him as 450,000 talents, or (using the Greek talent) nearly 5.5 million ounces per year. This would seem to be impossible inasmuch as current U.S. production is only 1.5 million ounces and world production 50 million ounces per year. Ptolemy II in the 3rd century B.C. was reported to have enjoyed an income of nearly 15,000 talents chiefly from gold mines, which suggests that the Rameses III revenue might be off by a factor of one decimal place. In the 10th century B.C., a raid on Egypt and Palestine netted a Libyan general 487,000 pounds of silver and 87,000 pounds of gold, or almost 40,000,000 dollars worth. Egypt paid Darius the Persian about 600,000 ounces in 517 B.C. as an annual tribute. It has been estimated that the yearly gold production of Egypt during the height of the empire was between 750,000 and one million ounces (Ely, 1959, p. 81). The grade of the ores worked varied from bonanzas to lean ores that probably could not be profitably worked with today's technology. Cost of mining was largely the cost of a bare subsistence diet for slave labor, although Forbes (1963, p. 130) cast doubt on the universal employment of slaves in Egyptian industry. Recovery was poor and complex ores could not be beneficiated.

The earliest iron relics in Egypt were high-priced objects, and their positioning in tombs indicates a value greater than gold. According to Rickard (1932, p. 836), iron was new and rare in Egypt about the 14th century B.C. Rickard (1932, pp. 832–841) discussed assertions that Egyptians knew how to work iron from ores before 3500 B.C. and concluded that earliest dated iron objects are of meteoric iron; as late as 1200 B.C. the large volumes of weapons were bronze. Rickard (1932, p. 836) quoted Sir W. Flinders Petrie's *Ancient Egypt* (1915, p. 20) as stating that iron manufactured from ores was not in existence prior to 1200 B.C. and evidence for industrial use of iron in Egypt points to a date of 800 B.C. Hoover (1912, p. 420), however, had reservations about the assertion by archeologists that iron metallurgy came relatively late and pointed out that iron metallurgy is simple under primitive conditions and that reduction of iron oxides to wrought-iron blooms requires a relatively low temperature without fusion. He inclined to the belief that iron and iron tools antedate the period usually assigned to their discovery. According to Smith (1965, p. 913) man-made iron first appeared in the first half of the third millenium, B.C., was not uncommon in the Hittite empire about 1500 B.C., and was an important metal by 1200 B.C. Forbes (1963, Table VII) included manufacture of wrought iron from magnetite in his Metal Age I, dated 3000–2200 B.C. A stock of 176 tons of iron bars found in Assyrian ruins in what is now Turkey and dated as 722–705 B.C. proves industrial use of iron by that time. Iron was common in Egypt at about the same date, as proved by slags in Ethiopia (700 B.C.) and iron tools (666 B.C.). Petrie (1915) discussed metals used by the Egyptians including copper, gold, silver, lead, tin, iron, and antimony.

Asphalt was probably used by the Sumerians in the pre-Babylon Euphrates Valley as early as 3000 to 2500 B.C.; the first use was as a cement, mostly in works of art. The Persians from 2800 to 2500 B.C. used asphalt in sculpture. The use of asphalt by Egyptians as a preservative in mummification began about 2500 B.C. Subsequently, the use of the material broadened, and large volumes were used in ordinary construction by the Babylonians to bind bricks and as a caulking and waterproofing agent (700 to 500 B.C.). Somewhat later the Persians used oil as well as asphalt. A well producing asphalt, "salt," and oil was described by Herodotus (Abraham, 1918, p. 9). The Sumerians and Acadians compiled lists of "stones" about 1500 B.C. which included 180 varieties, including 120 useful stones, as well as lists of bituminous substances (Forbes, 1963, pp. 78–83).

The stone industries of Egypt have amazed the world since the pyramids were constructed at the beginning of the third millenium before Christ. The quarrying, shaping, transporting, and placing of these stones attest to remarkable engineering skills. The magnitude of the projects completed is a real measure of the efficiency of this first of the highly organized governments. With a primitive agriculture, the amount of the national effort that could be diverted from food-raising over a long period of time was limited, and Egypt at the same time was forced to maintain a relatively large military establishment. Forbes (1963, p. 169, fig. 18) showed a map of the quarries of the eastern Mediterranean during ancient times and listed different kinds of stone quarried by the Egyptians including alabaster, basalt (?), diorite, gypsum, granite, syenite, limestone, marble, magnetite, obsidian, porphyry, quartzite and sandstone, steatite, serpentine, and breccia.

The fine ceramic glazes and the still-bright paints indicate an equal proficiency in the mineral arts. Egyptians were blowing glass in the XI Dynasty about 3500 B.C. (Hoover, 1912, p. 586). Wertime (1964, p. 1266) suggested that Egyptian glass-making capabilities might have resulted from developments in metallurgy in Mesopotamia. He also considered the development of high-temperature ceramics fired in reducing atmospheres in southern Mesopotamia a by-product of furnaces invented for smelting of metals. Sulfur was used as a bleach for linen textiles as early as 2000 B.C., probably the first industrial use of the mineral.

Another early invention was lime-making for plaster and mortar. In some regions, large areas were deforested to provide fuel for firing the lime kilns. In Egypt both lime and gypsum plasters were used very early (Eckel, 1928, p. 2; North, 1930, p. 385). Brickmaking was important in Egypt as in the Mesopotamian region, but brick construction in the Nile valley was overshadowed by the great stone structures.

The domestic resources of Egypt consisted of water, soil, clay, stone, and gold. The water of the Nile and the rich soil of the delta were the basic resources of the culture—and still are. They sustained the food supply. Limestone was quarried along the Nile and the famous 'black basalt'—a quartzite—came from Hammamat between Coptos and the Red Sea. The gold-mining region likewise lay in the strip between the Nile and the Red Sea, east of Coptos and Luxor. Some of the old workings include 1,500-foot drifts and 300-foot shafts. An attempt to revive the old mines was made by foreign companies between 1902 and 1921, and approximately 83,000 ounces were produced (Rickard, 1932, p. 226). Probably the largest amount of gold flowed over the southern borders of Egypt out of Nubia (the Sudan) and Abyssinia (Ethiopia). Copper also was produced in Nubia. Turquoise, malachite, chrysocolla, and copper were produced in the southwestern Sinai Peninsula, but probably the largest tonnages of copper were imported from Cyprus. Forbes (1963, p. 124) included a map of Egyptian mines in the Sinai region modified from Sir W. Flinders Petrie. Emeralds were mined along the Red Sea coast. Warring expeditions first depleted the accumulated metal and jewel stocks of a region, then an annual tribute further impoverished the conquered land. Finally, the Egyptians turned to placer mining and then lode mining to satisfy the demand for metals.

Elsewhere in the ancient world, mining of copper took place on Cyprus as early as 2500 B.C. Mining occurred in the eastern Balkans and in the Danube Valley. Bronze-age mineral industries existed in Hungary, Austria, Germany, France, Spain, Portugal, and Great Britain. The salt mines in the Tyrol (Hallstadt, Hallein, and Hull) were worked in the first millenium B.C. Adits, inclined shafts, and galleries are measured in 100s of meters.

As the ancient world grew, minerals and metals began to move long distances in regular trade. Products moved overland between India and the Mediterranean world. One route passed through Babylon and led to its prosperity. It was the hub of a network of trade routes until it was conquered by the Assyrians in 1300 B.C., and the trade routes were shifted north to pass through Nineveh. About 1200 B.C., the Phoenicians, ranging out of what is now Lebanon, took advantage of the decay of Egypt and began to open up the coasts of the Mediterranean. They encouraged prospecting by providing a market for minerals, prospected themselves, colonized, and traded. A desire to locate sources of metals was a motivating force in the Phoenician explorations. They found silver in Pontus, Siphnos, Sardinia, and Spain; tin in Drangiana (Turkestan), Asturias (Spain), and Britain; lead in Taurus, Gaul, and Spain; iron in Capadocia and Armenia; gold in Thasos, Phrygia, Thrace, and Nubia; amber in the Baltic region. Phoenicians reached Britain and started the tin trade in about 600 B.C. King Solomon, as leader of the powerful Israelite nation, organized the famous expedition to Ophir (probably in Arabia) which returned with 20 tons of gold (Rickard, 1932b, p. 242). Except for salt, there appears to have been little mining in Palestine during the bronze age; indeed, until the time of Solomon, when copper mines were opened, metals were imported. In the early 1950s King Solomon's copper mines in the southern Negev desert were reopened by the Israeli government (Eng. and Mining Jour., 1953, p. 137).

The first reference to iron mines is the discovery of iron at Mount Ida in Phrygia; according to Greek mythology, the mountains of Phrygia in Asia Minor, between the Caspian and the Black Sea, are the home of metallurgy. This is within the general area which Wertime (1964, p. 1257) concluded was the home of the first metal-oriented culture. The Jews had iron weapons prior to 1050 B.C.

because the Philistines who conquered them confiscated all iron weapons. The Bible does not mention iron tools until after the Exodus (after 1200 B.C.). Smith (1965, p. 913) alleged that "good steel was certainly being made by the smiths of Luristan (in the mountains in western Iran) at a date within two centuries (plus or minus) of 1000 B.C." India at this time was not a large producer of metals and probably imported them.

Until about 1500 B.C., tin was used sparingly in the eastern Mediterranean world and supplies were low. Possibly it moved by land from Europe (from Bohemia or Tuscany) or perhaps it came from the Caucasus region. Wertime (1964, p. 1264) discussed this problem and suggested Iran as a possible source. About 1500 B.C., large supplies of tin became available but again the source is not certain. Phoenicians arrived in Cornwall about 600 B.C., and their tin trade did not begin until after that date. Tin arrived in Phoenicia about 1300 B.C. Pure tin in the form of a ring is known from the 18th dynasty in Egypt (1580–1350 B.C.). Overland tin trade through Gaul was in progress about 300 B.C. Lead objects are rare prior to 1200 B.C., but are known from among Egyptian relics dated as old as 3800 B.C. (Hoover, 1912, p. 390); after 1200 B.C. they are common. Zinc ore was mined at least 2,000 years before the metal itself was used in Europe—it was used to make medicinal oxides by sublimation and also to make brass by direct combination with copper. Older cultures probably knew of zinc metal much earlier, but the first records of substantial production refer to shipments of zinc made to Europe in the 16th century from the Far East. Independent discovery in Europe occurred about the time of Agricola but his descriptions of zinc are not clear (Hoover, 1912, p. 410). The first adequate technical description of brass manufacture is dated as 1200 A.D. (Hoover, 1912, p. 410). A map of gem mines of circa 1000 B.C. compiled by Ball (1931, p. 696) showed sources of alabaster, amethyst, amber, beryl, emerald, lapis lazuli, jade, obsidian, olivine, rock crystal, and turquoise. Forbes (1963, pp. 234–236) published a list of precious stones of preclassical antiquity and a map of gem deposits in the eastern Mediterranean, including agate, amber, amethyst, beryl, calcite, carnelian, chalcedony, coral, garnet, hematite, jade, jasper, lapis lazuli, malachite, opal, olivine, onyx, pearl, rock crystal, sapphire, sardonyx, topaz, and turquoise.

In Greece, four mining districts were important: (1) Laurium on the Attic Peninsula southeast of Athens, (2) the islands of Thasos and Siphnos (Siphanto) farther southeast, (3) Damastium in northwestern Greece, and (4) Thrace in northeastern Greece. Laurium and the islands of Thasos and Siphnos were first opened up by the Phoenicians. The island mines were important first, but as the rich silver mines of Laurium were developed other districts paled into insignificance. Laurium provided the wealth for Athens' rise to glory, financed the Athenian war machine, and made possible the growth of a great center of trade and commerce. The Laurium mines may have been discovered as early as 1000 B.C. because they were described as ancient by writers in 355 B.C. Production of silver-rich lead ores, perhaps 2,000,000 tons of ore containing 40 to 120 ounces of silver per ton, during the classic period of three centuries came from 2,000 shafts up to nearly 400 feet deep; some of the larger stopes produced as much as 100,000 tons. The surrounding region was deforested to provide wood for mine timber and fuel. The mines were worked by slaves. On occasion, all the citizens of Athens shared in cash bonuses paid by the mines (Themistocles in Plutarch's *Lives,* pp. 234–235).

. . . and, first of all, the Athenians being accustomed to divide amongst themselves the revenue proceeding from the silver mines at Laurium, he was the only man that durst propose to the people that the distribution cease, and that with the money ships should be built to make war against the Aeginetans. . . .

By the end of the 4th century B.C., political turmoil and wars had put an end to the booming mining industry of Laurium, and the gold and silver mines of Thrace began to rise in importance (Rickard, 1932, Chapter VII).

In Greece, as in Egypt, the earliest iron was meteoric iron. Bronze was the principal metal of weaponry until the 6th century B.C. The stone industries of Greece were also advanced. Marble, sandstone, limestone, and porphyry quarries supplied stone for temples, statuary, and public buildings. Lime mortar and plaster were used in construction. Dolomite was used as a refractory (Forbes, 1963, p. 173). Likewise, the ceramic arts and glass making were well developed, and knowledge of paints and glazes was at a high level. Trade in salt, of course, continued. There are references to asphalt and bitumen—"Silician oil"— (Redwood, 1913, p. 2). About 430 B.C., Xenophon described a wall built of burned bricks laid in hot asphalt (Abraham, 1918, p. 9), and Aristotle described the asphalt deposits of Albania on the Adriatic. The famous 'Greek fire,' a super weapon of the day, was reported to have contained asphalt and other oils (Abraham, 1918, p. 10). In Greek mythology, Jason's quest for the

Golden Fleece took him to Colchis in the Caucasus on the east shore of the Black Sea where placer miners used sheep skins to line sluices and catch alluvial gold. Antimony was known to the ancient Greeks although whether it was known to Egyptians is not clear (Hoover, 1912, p. 428). It was used as a base for ointments by Greeks and Romans. The earliest mention of quicksilver was by Aristotle, and Theophrastus described its extraction from cinnabar (Hoover, 1912, p. 432). The first diamond reached Greece from India about 480 B.C. The Greeks and the ancient world in general knew about coal—the stone that burns—but because of an abundance of wood for both domestic use and primitive industries, together with a generally warm climate, it was largely ignored (Rickard, 1932, p. 783).

A variety of salts were used in Greek and Roman times and earlier but early descriptions are confusing because of use of the general term *nitrum* to include a variety of salts and mixtures of salts. Potassium and sodium salts, including naturally occurring salts and salts manufactured by leaching of ashes, and perhaps saltpeter as well (although Hoover, 1912, p. 562, doubted this), were known and are mentioned in Greek, Roman, and Biblical writings. The discovery of borax is uncertain; it was known by Agricola's time. Sal-ammoniac or ammonium chloride likewise has an uncertain history and probably was not recognized with surety before the Middle Ages. Saltpeter was in demand in the Middle Ages in the 13th or 14th century after gunpowder became a necessary war material. It was manufactured from nitrogenous accumulations by applications of lye and lime to form potassium and sodium nitrates and then leached with lye and filtered to eliminate undesirable salts. Vitriol was a term applied to both iron and copper sulfate (and later zinc sulfate). It was known to Greeks, Romans, and medieval societies. Sulfur was known to the Greeks and refined by them for various purposes. The Greeks also invented a bellows to improve the air blast in smelting operations.

The Greek mining period produced ideas as well as silver; some of the legal concepts developed endure in modern law. The silver mines were regarded as state property; however, they were not operated by the state. They were leased to an operator who made an initial payment for the lease and thereafter paid a rent (p. 150). The district was divided into tracts; leasing of the tracts was under the control of a board of magistrates. There was also a director of mines who administered the mining laws.

Not content with mere exploitation of mineral deposits, the Greeks also inquired about their genesis. The natural science philosophy of the Peripatetic school, expressed mainly by Aristotle and Theophrastus, persisted until the 17th century.

Minerals in the world of Rome.

Mineral industry flourished in the world of the Roman empire. The Romans were builders and needed materials in volume and variety; they ran a big government and military machine and needed coinage; they provided the political stability necessary to development of mining industries; they enlarged the civilized world to include new mineral territories. The stone industries flourished, and large volumes of dimension stone flowed from basalt, limestone, marble, sandstone, granite, serpentine, travertine, and other stone quarries—perhaps never before had there been such a variety of stone available to artisans. Building stones moved long distances by water. Other mineral construction materials, such as brick, cement, and lime and gypsum plaster, were produced in large volumes. It was Augustus who boasted he had transformed Rome from brick to marble. The roads, aqueducts, viaducts, stadiums, theaters, temples, and public buildings stand today as witnesses to this mineral industry. A great Roman invention in this field was pozzolanic cement made from volcanic ash occurring near Naples. Mixed with lime, this was perhaps the first manufactured hydraulic cement and permitted Roman engineers to build structures under water. Forbes (1963, pp. 174–177) discussed Roman quarries. Pliny the Elder of Rome in his treatise *Naturalis Historia* reported the use of asphalt as a protective paint for sculpture and statuary and as a medicine for boils, inflammations, coughs, epilepsy, etc. (Abraham, 1918, p. 12). The Romans, like the Greeks before them, made no attempt to utilize coal on any large scale and, instead, consumed the wood resources of their environment, at least in the Mediterranean world. In the more rigorous climate of Britain, however, the Romans, following the native custom, burned coal. Rickard (1932, p. 786) cited heaps of coal cinders in Roman ruins in England. A great Roman road, Via Salaria, was named for the salt traffic between Ostia and the Sabine country.

With regard to metals, the Romans, like other conquerors, plundered first, subsequently extracted the remainder of accumulated supplies by exacting tributes, and finally operated the mines themselves to keep the materials flowing. Thus, Greek gold and silver, Spanish gold, silver, copper, tin, and mercury, and British lead moved to the Roman capital. Although Roman invasion of Britain was

FIGURE IV.6

The Roman roads of the eastern desert of Egypt showing mines and quarries (after Murray, 1925).

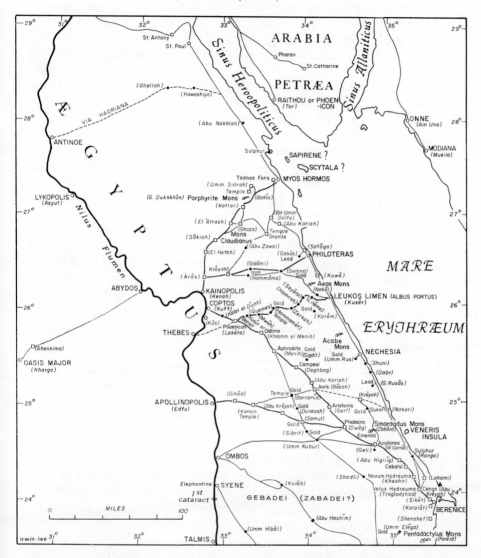

prompted by visions of gold and silver, lead turned out to be the major export metal of the island during the Roman occupation. The tin trade ended about the time of the Roman invasion (43 A.D.), perhaps due to competition from the more favorably located Spanish and Etruscan tin. Some gold, silver, tin, copper, and iron were mined by Romans in Britain for domestic use, and some iron was exported, but lead was the big trade item. Iron was mined and smelted early in the days of the Empire, and Pliny remarked on the abundance of the ores. Mines were located in Gaul, central Europe, and in Elba. Forbes (1963, p. 153) said that 10,000,000 tons of iron ore per year from Elba were treated, but this figure seems too large when compared with modern production statistics. U.S. production, for example, is about 150,000,000 tons per year. Remains of Roman iron furnaces or 'bloomeries' are widespread, particularly in Britain and northern Europe. In primitive iron furnaces the metal is produced in a spongy mass or 'bloom' and thereafter 'wrought' on an anvil. However, little is known about steel making prior to the Christian era (pp. 93, 103). Roman mines in North Africa and the Near East also furnished metals for the empire. Lead enjoyed a wider use in Roman culture than earlier—it was used for pipes, weights, and sheathing. Mercury did not become an important industrial metal until discovery of the amalgamation process for recovering precious metals in the 16th century, but quicksilver (*argentum vivum*) was known as a curiosity, a magic metal, and cinnabar was used for pigment and carving. The invention of the amalgamation process of treating gold and silver ores, whereby mercury is used as a collector and the precious metals are subsequently separated, has not been satisfactorily dated. Hoover (1912, fn. 12) said,

The recovery of gold by the use of mercury possibly dates from Roman times, but the application of the process to silver does not seem to go back prior to the 16th Century. . . . The Romans amalgamated gold with mercury, but whether they took advantage of the principle to recover gold from ores we do not know.

Becker (1888, pp. 4, 28), discussing the history of the famous Almaden quicksilver mine in Spain, noted that the mine was worked at least as early as 415 B.C. when Callias, an Athenian, invented a process for separating cinnabar from earthy matter. Cinnabar was shipped to Rome as a pigment, and Pliny II reported production of 10,000 pounds per year.

According to Hoover (1912, p. 453), the process for separating gold and silver used prior to the Middle Ages involved "cementing of the disintegrated bullion with a paste of either saltpeter and vitriol or common salt, and converting the silver to a nitrate or chloride."

Outside of resmelting the metal, it is not known how the ancients refined copper. A description by Theophilus (1150–1200 A.D.) of a process to purify copper and make it malleable is the first. Forbes (1963, p. 155) summed up the rise and fall of mining industries in the Roman provinces through the course of Empire.

According to Agricola's *De Natura Fossilum*, written in 1546, sulfur smoke was used by the "superstitious" Greeks and Romans to purify temples. No doubt sulfur was mined in the Mediterranean area, in Sicily and Italy, for a variety of medicinal purposes as well. Ball (1931, p. 698) included a map of the world's gem mines as of 1 B.C. and included sources of agate, diamond, garnet, jasper, meerschaum, opal, ruby, sapphire, and topaz in addition to the earlier used gems shown on his map of 1000 B.C. (p. 93).

Out of the Roman world there also came ideas about mineral ownership and tenure and mineral law. At one time or another, all of the resources of the then-known world except the Far East were under the legal system of the Roman empire (p. 152). The early law provided in general that ownership of the surface carried with it ownership of the minerals therein and thereunder. This idea developed early in Roman history prior to the days of empire when the Roman community was more or less restricted to the valley of the Tiber, where most mineral deposits were nonmetallics such as clay, stone, and lime materials, extraction of which involved mining of the stuff of the surface. As Rome grew, the idea was preserved so that in northern Italy in the lode-metal mining districts, ownership of the minerals went with ownership of the surface. Rome, however, according to Strabo, asserted the state's ownership of gold deposits (Rickard, 1932, p. 594). Perhaps if the land encompassed by the early republic had included significant gold deposits, the law would have evolved differently. During the days of Roman expansion, mineral deposits were acquired by conquest and lay outside of Italy proper. These deposits, acquired by conquest, became the property of the republic and later the empire. As Rome dominated the world, state ownership of mineral resources was generally accepted; state mines were leased to Roman citizens or companies of citizens. Under the famous Justinian Code of the 6th century, state mines were operated by private interests under the *usufruct,* which conveyed the right to make use of a property and profit from it so long as no damage was done to the property. A rental was paid by the holder of the usufruct to the state. The system pertained to known or existing mines, but any attempt to open a new mine on the property was a violation of the usufruct. The stultifying effect of this concept on exploration for new deposits is obvious.

The writings of Pliny the Elder indicate that there developed in Italy the idea that mining was a violation of or abuse of the land and, while permissible in conquered territory, was to be discouraged in the motherland (Rickard, 1932, p. 408). Perhaps this was due to the deforestation and accumulations of wastes around mines and silting of streams and rivers; perhaps it reflected a desire to conserve the domestic resources with which Italy was not overly abundantly endowed; or perhaps it was to avoid large slave camps near Rome. In any case, soldiering and farming were acceptable occupations, but mining was demeaning and fit only for slaves. The 'free miner' was a later concept developed in England and Germany during the medieval period. Although most writers characterize the Roman mining industry as a slave-labor industry, Forbes (1963, p. 154) stated that slaves played a minor role.

Roman know-how brought new engineering skills to mining, and for the first time, using an inefficient screw-type pump, mine waters were raised and workings were carried to shallow depths below the water level. Forbes (1963, p. 149) analyzed the work of Davies (1935) and concluded that all the mines and quarries known in 1935 in the part of Europe that was within the Roman Empire had been known and worked by the Romans.

One of the early signs of the growing instability of the Roman Empire was their balance of payments or currency drain, and perhaps there is a lesson here. The gold and silver currency of Rome began to flow backward to outlying parts of the Empire and to India and Arabia for agricultural and commercial products. The bill for imported silks, gems, and other luxury items and extravagances of the Roman capital eventually resulted in an adulteration of the currency (devaluation) (Rickard, 1932, p. 502).

The Far East.

The mineral history of the ancient civilization of the Far East, mainly India and China, is less well known. There seems to be no record of very early development of mining and metallurgical capabilities in Chinese culture, except in connection with development of the ceramic arts. Collins (1918, Chapter I) ascribed the almost exclusively agricultural character of early stages of Chinese development to a cultural origin in the alluvial plain of the Yel-

TABLE IV.3

HIGHLIGHTS OF CHINESE MINERAL HISTORY FROM THE DETAILED CHRONICLE OF COLLINS
(1918, pp. 1–38)

1. First recorded mention of mining—copper at Shuo Shan between 2700–2600 B.C., at Shansi, 2200 B.C.

2. Working of gold prohibited during reign of Emperor Shun (2255–2205 B.C.).

3. Casting of brass or bronze cauldrons by Emperor Yü (Hsia Dynasty, 2205–1766 B.C.) to collect gold and other metal from the nine provinces of China.

4. Silver 'plentiful' during the Yin Dynasty (1766–1122 B.C.).

5. Gold, silver, and lead sent to Kingdom of Yü from Chingchow; gold, silver, and copper from Yanchow; jade, iron, silver, and 'steel' from Liang-chow (2357–950 B.C.).

6. Mining official during Chow Dynasty (1122–255 B.C.) remarked that occurrence of an ore deposit is marked by the color of the surface.

7. Iron and salt made a national monopoly in 119 B.C.

8. Opposition to mining during Han Dynasty. Coal mentioned in Kiangsi Province in records of Han Dynasty (206 B.C. to 25 A.D.).

9. Gunpowder used during Wei Dynasty (220–260 A.D.).

10. Metallic currency abolished by decree in 220 A.D.

11. Gold washers working in Shansi (386–534 A.D.). Gold scarce—manufacture of gold leaf prohibited.

12. Iron coins plentiful in 525 A.D.

13. Mining and metallurgy encouraged during Tang Dynasty (618–907 A.D.).

14. Emperor Hien Tsung prohibited silver mining, encouraged copper mining A.D. 807 and then authorized silver mining.

15. Under Emperor Hsuan Tsung (847–859 A.D.) revenue from salt and iron mining was suggested as means for paying troops. Production of metals recorded as 33,333 ounces of silver, 390 tons of copper, 68+ tons of lead, 1+ ton of tin, and 317 tons of iron.

16. 914 A.D. edict permitting trade in iron and manufacture of iron tools—marked end of Government monopoly.

17. New discoveries (937–946 A.D.) of copper during Liao Dynasty. Used mainly for coinage. Beginning of general mining taxation.

18. Sung Dynasty (960–1127 A.D.) organized official mining administration and promoted the industry. Production increased. Well drilling introduced about 1013 A.D.; wells cased with bamboo in 1023–1030 A.D.

19. Suppression of mining (1078–1084 A.D.) probably due to revival of Confucian philosophy.

TABLE IV.3 (Continued)

20. Production of cement copper (copper precipitated from solution on iron) in 1102 A.D.

21. Iron monopoly reinstituted in 1083 A.D.

22. Iron smelted with coal in 1111 A.D.

23. Mineral production affected by wars during late Sung Dynasty (1100–1200 A.D.). Compulsory labor in the mines, government establishment of smelters. Mongol invasion.

24. Early Ming Dynasty discouraged mining. Famous Bawdin mine in Burma opened about 1412 under Yung Lo. In 1421, government mines relinquished to the people.

25. Mineral industry alternately encouraged and suppressed, 1435–1662. Mining again important under Emperor K'ang Hsi in 1662. Succession of imperial decrees relating to mining up to European penetration.

low River where deposits of metals were lacking, and to the pervasive teachings of Confucius whose philosophy required a simple life. As a result, mining and metallurgy were discouraged by Chinese emperors except for precious metals for currency, salt, coal, and, locally, iron; the miner occupied the lowest station in life. According to Collins (1918, p. 3), a history of mining and metals in China is largely a history of currency; he reported that analysis of early Chinese writing suggests a culture much less advanced in metallurgical arts than Western contemporary culture. However, at a later date, and without any record of a domestic primitive metallurgical culture, the Chinese developed considerable skill in mineral technology (Table IV.3). Wertime (1964, p. 1266), intrigued with the parallel developments in metallurgical arts in far-flung parts of the world, suggested that lack of evidence of the first primitive stage of metallurgical art in China indicates a ". . . sensitive technical communication out of southwestern Asia under most primitive circumstances." Wertime (p. 1266) declared himself an advocate of the theory that technical inventions were made rarely and diffused rather than independently conceived in widely separated areas. Bain (1927a, p. 71) remarked that the Chinese have mined and smelted iron for at least 2,500 years and that the Shansi iron industry is the oldest continuous mineral industry operation in the world. The earliest known iron agricultural implements in China are dated as 700 to 800 B.C. Iron chains for suspension bridges were manufactured before Christ (Merrill, 1964, p. 9). Coal was burned in China at an early date; ancient oriental engineers devised systems of piping coal gas for industrial fuel in ceramic industries (Rickard, 1932, pp. 784–785, gives sources). Probably the best known mineral structure in the East, if not the world, is the Great Wall of China built about the 3rd century B.C.; constructed of brick, stone, and earth, it extends for 1,400 miles. Chinese parmacopoeias of the 1st century B.C. list 46 varieties of stones (Forbes, 1963, p. 83). The early invention of gunpowder by the Chinese marks an early industrial use of sulfur. According to Redwood (1913, p. 2) references to petroleum and natural gas appear in Chinese and Japanese documents dating from centuries before the Christian era.

Steel was first made in India and Japan by enclosing wrought iron in sealed crucibles with charcoal and sawdust and heating over a long period. The smiths of Damascus imported Indian steel to make the famous Damascus blades prior to the birth of Christ (Rickard, 1932, p. 864). India, Ceylon, and Afghanistan were the gem centers of the ancient world. The Indian diamond industry began between 600 and 800 B.C., and sapphires were mined soon thereafter. Jade was used in China at least by 1100 B.C. In India and perhaps throughout the Far East, there was early demand for mineral substances for cosmetics and decorative pigments including iron oxides, lead oxide, red lead, antimony sulfide, cinnabar, and mercury salts.

However, despite development of a mineral technology, oriental civilizations developed basically as 'vegetable' civilizations pointed toward agriculture and animal husbandry; the mineral industry never assumed the importance it had in Western culture (Bain, 1927a, pp. 7–8). Whether this is the result of an innate cultural bias or whether it is due to lack of a varied and accessible mineral resource base is not clear. Japan, India, and China are today exploiting mineral resources, both imported and domestic, to build and sustain an industrial society but this has been brought about by competition with the West and the problems of sustaining rapidly growing populations. It is, in a sense, a western cultural stem grafted on the oriental root.

Dark or Middle Ages.

The break-up of the Roman empire and the subsequent collapse of law and order, however corrupt and bureaucratic it may have been, temporarily banked the creative fire of human culture, at

least in the part of the world where it seemed to be burning fastest. The society of the Roman empire, while not complex by modern standards, still was based on organized industry and trade,
although the larger part lived directly from agriculture, fishing, and
animal husbandry. Lifting of the protective Roman military shield
resulted in a breakdown of organized society including production,
transportation, and marketing of minerals. Construction ceased and
there was no demand for stone, plaster, or lime. Trade declined and
new coinage was not manufactured. The mines and quarries closed,
and those engaged in mining went back to subsistence agriculture or
to fighting for survival. With some exceptions, the only mineral
industry to survive was salt mining, local placer gold-washing operations, and local ceramic industries producing domestic ware.

Cultural development in the Middle and Far East did not suffer
such a drastic regression and, in fact, the violent contacts between
West and East during the Crusades probably gave some stimulus to
western recovery.

The lesson to be learned from the Dark Ages is an important one
indeed. Even in the days of near-surface high-grade ores worked without expensive machinery, political turmoil and unrest killed the
mining industry. Today, working lower grade ores in huge volumes and with tremendous capital investments in equipment and
plant, the period necessary to recover investments is commonly 20
years or longer. Such terms are only found in mature stable countries.
One might speculate on the possible results of a nuclear-war-induced
second Dark Age. The culture recovering from such a holocaust would
not be able to build, as in the past, a mineral and metal technology
by beginning with high-grade near-surface ores and gradually developing the capabilities to treat larger volumes of lower grade and less
accessible rock. Such a recovering culture would have to begin with
scrap and very lean ores. Return to a metal culture such as we enjoy
seems dubious at best. Brown and others (1958, pp. 151–152) used
the expression 'point of no return' for the point in time beyond
which a major disruption to the world-wide industrial network would
be irreversible.

However, the Roman Empire crumbled gradually and did not
collapse within a decade like a house of cards. The mineral industry
was crippled by the 3rd century when the important mining districts
of the frontiers were overrun, but it was not until the 5th century
that the nadir was reached. During the darkest period, metal demand
was satisfied from the accumulated stocks of the golden age, and

TABLE IV.4

OUTLINE OF THE EVOLUTION OF MINING AND PROCESSING OF ORES (modified from Forbes, 1963, Table VII)

Period	Mining methods	Mining tools	Stones, precious and semi-precious	Ores and natural stone	Metallurgical methods
Palaeolithic Age	Search for boulders, etc. Open workings, conical pits	Wooden or bone digging stick, horn pick. First stone tools such as hand-axe, etc.	Chalcedony, quartz, rock crystal, serpentine, obsidian, jasper, steatite, amber, jadeite, calcite	Flint and obsidian, later ochre and other natural pigments, emery	
Neolithic Age (–3500 B.C.)	Quarries, stone slabs. Open workings, sloping shafts, gradually galleries	Stone picks and hammers, chisels and celts	Amethyst, fluorspar, nephrite, jet, turquoise, lapis, lazuli, jade, agate	Granite, diorite Limestone Sandstone	
Predynastic Age (3500–3000 B.C.)	Development of square and round shafts with galleries. Ventilation and chimneys. Propping.	Stone picks and first copper tools	Hematite, alabaster, carnelian, chrysocolla, malachite, beryl, feldspar	Native metals (gold, silver, iron (meteoric), copper). Copper ores from outcrops. Alabaster, marble, rock salt	Hammering native metals. Melting and casting of metals.
Metal Age I (3000–2200 B.C.)	Systematic stripping of outcrops. Shafts with staircase (?) Filling of old galleries with gangue	General use of firesetting	Onyx, sardonyx, amazonite, azurite, callainite	Oxide, carbonate and sulfide copper ores. Galena, stibnite, cassiterite Obsidian, emery	Silver from galena Oxidation and reduction with natural blast. Wrought iron from magnetite. Copper, alloyed with lead, antimony and tin

TABLE IV.4 (Continued)

OUTLINE OF THE EVOLUTION OF MINING AND PROCESSING OF ORES (modified from Forbes, 1963, Table VII)

Period	Mining methods	Mining tools	Stones, precious and semi-precious	Ores and natural stone	Metallurgical methods
Metal Age II (2200–1200 B.C.)	Timbering of shafts (?) Drainage with pails, etc. Wider galleries	Copper tools become more general	Bloodstone, emerald, magnesite, topaz, chrysoprase	Gold-bearing quartz Oxide iron ores Copper sulfides	Short shaft-furnaces. Use of bellows Roasting of sulfide ores more general
Early Iron Age (1200–500 B.C.)	Drainage adits Large quarries	Iron tools	Sapphire, blue chalcedony, rose quartz, spinels	Limonite, hematite Copper pyrites	Wrought iron "steeled" by case-hardening, quenching and tempering
Late Iron Age (500–50 B.C.)	Mechanical drainage, transport and ventilation	gradually supersede copper and stone	Ruby, moss-agate, zircon, opal, aquamarine, meerschaum, diamond (?)	Magnetite and iron carbonate Iron pyrites (?)	Brass from copper and calamine Higher shaft-furnaces
Roman Empire (50 B.C.–300 A.D.)	Water-wheels, water-screws, etc. more common, deeper mines and large open workings	tools	Aventurine, moonstone, blue spinel, ruby spinel, pearl		"Stückofen" Mercury produced

building stone was secured by robbing existing structures. Salt continued to be mined throughout the empire, and alluvial gold-washing operations continued in Italy and Europe. The spark never went out in the ancient mining centers of Cornwall, Devonshire, and Derbyshire, England, and in Saxony and the Erzegebirge in Germany, and there the mineral arts were preserved. The Spanish mines, closed by the Visigoths, were reopened in the 8th century by the Arabs. At about the same time, industry revived in Gaul under Charlemagne, and the Church entered the mining business. By the 12th century the mineral industry was generally recovered in Europe; however, subsequently, the emancipation of serfs changed the cost structure of mining, and there was a decline in production during the 14th and 15th centuries prior to the opening of the New World.

The feudal concepts of land holding that developed in the Dark Ages, the manorial system, was a holding concept rather than an owning concept and was oriented to agriculture (p. 154). Members of the ruling classes held land in the form of large estates at the whim of the ruler at the apex of the pyramid or by force of his own war potential. The serfs raised food, and the small ruling class engaged in sports and wars. As a result of this lack of industry, the metal stocks particularly in Europe declined to the . point where iron weapons—the relics of Roman know-how—became legendary. The magic Sword of Roland and Arthur's Excalibur are examples. According to Ely (1964, p. 83), by 1500 at the onset of the Renaissance, the entire gold stock of western Europe had declined to about one million ounces or about one year's production of the fat days of the Egyptian Dynasties.

However, the mining centers of England and Germany did more than just preserve and develop ancient arts—they were also the cradles of ideas about rights of free men and the scene of struggles between miners and feudal lords to claim and enforce those rights. In the 12th century the miners of Devonshire were granted special rights and so-called stannery (tin) courts were created to settle disputes. Special courts were also established in Germany. The miner won concessions, special privileges, and then rights due to his special training and skills as he changed from serf to artisan. These special courts protected the miner from military service and other forced labor requirements associated with serfdom. Through the custom of centuries, certain 'free miners' rights were developed—the right to stake and register a claim and to hold it through work, the right of access across other lands, the right to use highways, the right to take timber for mine support and fuel. These rights were at a later time confirmed by charters. Although a tax on production or *royalty* was due to the king and/or the church from earliest times, and accounts in part for the protection the monarch gave to the miners, it was not until later (1426) that the suffering of the landowner as a result of the mining operations was compensated by a small share of the value of production. Conflicts between the miner and the worker of the surface with regard to damages, trespass, and alleged land abuse are recorded in the court records of early England (Rickard, 1932, pp. 608–611).

According to Ely (1964, p. 84), regulations for German mining districts date from the 12th century. Districts were administered by mining prefects who were responsible to a sovereign prince. Leases were acquired by individuals, and discoverers were rewarded by a larger tract—a *head meer* as opposed to a *regular meer*. The narrowness of the tracts suggests a right to follow the ore beyond the surface side lines of the tract. Ownership was vested in the sovereign who separated the mineral estate from the surface estate. Over the years free miners challenged the sovereign's ownership, and the eventual result was recognition by the sovereign of the right to prospect and the right to claim a discovery, but with reservation of a portion of the production (a royalty) to the sovereign. In England a similar evolution took place—the struggle was less bitter because of the growth of the principle of individual land ownership and the concept that the surface owner owned the mineral estate as well. However, gold and silver were recognized as the property of the crown. The base metal districts of Cornwall, Devonshire, and Derbyshire, organized during Roman days, inherited Roman customs as a father-to-son way of doing things. In Cornwall, a free tinner had the right to mark out a claim and proclaim it in the stannery courts and if it was not opposed he received a writ of possession together with the obligation to work the claim and pay a toll to the surface owner. Extralateral rights (right to follow the ore), however, were not recognized. With the full development of English common law regarding ownership of land, the right of the individual to hold land and extract minerals or metals from it became well established. The only carry-over from the latter-day Roman codes was the right of the crown to the precious metals—gold and silver.

CONCLUSIONS

In summary, a study of minerals in ancient history permits the following conclusions:

(1) Mineral materials were important to the most primitive of cultures and became increasingly important as those cultures advanced and became more complex.

(2) Through his own inventiveness and industry, man created need for a variety of mineral substances, and thus converted earth materials to resources.

(3) The prime incentive for many of man's early explorations was the need to find new sources of minerals.

(4) Peace, political and social order, and international borders open for trade have been necessary for sustained development of mineral industry from earliest times.

(5) Those western countries where mining communities fought for and established variances from the feudal order (England, Germany) gained an asset which gave impetus to their development in the later industrial Rennaissance.

REFERENCES

Abraham, Herbert (1918) Asphalt and allied substances: Van Nostrand, Princeton, 606 pp.

Adams, Brooks (1902) The new empire: Macmillan and Co., London, 243 pp.

Agricola, Georgius (1556) De re metallica, translated by Herbert Clark Hoover and Lou Henry Hoover (1950): Dover Publications, New York, 638 pp.
——— (1546) De natura fossilum, translated by M. C. and J. A. Bendy: Geol. Soc. Amer., Spec. Paper 63, 240 pp.

American Law of Mining (1964) Vol. 1, Public Domain, Rocky Mountain Mineral Law Foundation: Matthew Bender and Co., New York, 906 pp.

Bain, H. F. (1927a) Ores and industry in the Far East: Council on Foreign Relations, Inc., New York, 229 pp.
——— (1927b) Minerals in relation to possible developments in the Far East: Econ. Geol., vol. 22, pp. 213–229.

Ball, S. A. (1931) Historical notes on gem mining: Econ. Geol., vol. 26, pp. 681–738.

Bateman, A. M. (1950) Economic mineral deposits, 2nd ed.: Wiley, New York, 916 pp.

Becker, G. F. (1888) Quicksilver deposits of the Pacific Slope: U. S. Geol. Survey Monograph XIII, 486 pp.

Brown, Harrison, Bonner, James, and Weir, John (1958) The next hundred years: Viking Press, New York, 193 pp.

Clyde, E. W. (1965) Water rights problems affecting resource development, *in* Tenth Annual Rocky Mountain Mineral Law Institute: Matthew Bender and Co., New York, pp. 503–532.

Cohen, M. R., and Drabkin, I. E. (1948) A source book in Greek science: McGraw-Hill, New York, 579 pp.

Collins, W. F. (1918) Mineral enterprises in China: Wm. Heinemann, London, 308 pp.

Daniel, G. E. (1943) Three ages: an essay on archeological methods: Macmillan and Co., London, 59 pp.

Davies, Oliver (1935) Roman mines in Europe: Oxford University Press, New York, 291 pp.

DeKalb, Courtnay (1914) Mines and miners of Bible times: The Mining Mag., p. 368.

——— (1920) A visit to some of King Solomon's mines: Mining and Metallurgy, no. 1920, pp. 15–18.

East, W. G. (1962) An historical geography of Europe, 4th ed.: Methuen, London, 492 pp.

Eavenson, H. N. (1935) Coal through the ages: American Institute of Mining and Metallurgical Engineers, New York, 123 pp.

Eckel, E. C. (1928) Cements, limes and plasters: Wiley, New York, 699 pp.

Ely, Northcutt (1964) Mineral titles and concessions, *in* Economics of the mineral industries, 2nd ed.: American Institute of Mining and Metallurgical Engineers, New York, pp. 81–130.

Engineering and Mining Journal (1953) Israel to mine half million tons copper ore a year: Eng. and Mining Jour., vol. 154, no. 1, pp. 137–138.

Forbes, R. J. (1963) Studies in ancient technology, Vol. VII: E. J. Brill, Leiden and Cologne, 253 pp.

Heaton, Herbert (1948) Economic history of Europe, rev. ed.: Harper & Row, New York, 742 pp.

Heizer, R. F. (1962) The background of Thomson's three-age system: Technology and Culture, vol. 3, no. 3, pp. 259–266.

Hoover, H. C. (1950) Footnotes, *in* De re metallica (1956), translated by Herbert Clark Hoover and Lou Henry Hoover (originally published, 1912): Dover Publications, New York, 638 pp.

King Solomon's Mines (photograph): Mining Eng., vol. 5, no. 1, p. 23.

Lindley, C. H. (1914) A treatise on the American law relating to mines and mineral lands, 3d ed.: Bancroft-Whitney, Company, San Francisco, 3 vols.

Lovering, T. S. (1943) Minerals in world affairs: Prentice-Hall, New York, 394 pp.

Merrill, C. W. (1959) Significance of the mineral industries in the economy, *in* Economics of the mineral industries: American Institute of Mining and Metallurgical Engineers, New York, pp. 1–42.

Murray, G. W. (1925) The Roman roads and stations in the eastern desert of Egypt: Journal of Egyptian Archeology, vol. 11, pp. 138–150.

North, F. J. (1930) Limestones: Thomas Murby & Co., London, 467 pp.

Petrie, Sir W. M. Flinders (1906) Researches in Sinai: John Murray, London, 280 pp.

—— (1915) The metals in Egypt: in Ancient Egypt, Part I: Macmillan and Co., London and New York, pp. 12–23.

Plutarch's Lives, Vol. I, translated by John Dryden, corrected and revised by A. H. Clough: A. L. Burt, New York, pp. 213–214.

—— (1874) Themistocles, in Plutarch's Lives, Vol. I, translated by John Dryden, corrected and revised by A. H. Clough: Sampson Low, Marson, Low and Searle, London, 414 pp.

Redwood, Boverton (1913) Petroleum, 3rd ed.: Charles Griffin & Co., London, 567 pp.

Rickard, T. A. (1932a) A history of American mining: McGraw-Hill, New York, 419 pp.

—— (1932b) Man and metals: McGraw-Hill, New York, 1068 pp.

—— (1944) The romance of mining: Macmillan and Co., New York and London, 450 pp.

Sagui, C. C. (1933) Economic geology and allied sciences in ancient times: Econ. Geol., vol. 28, pp. 20–40.

Schubert, H. R. (1957) History of the British iron and steel industry from c. 450 B.C. to A.D. 1775: Routledge & Kegan Paul, London, 445 pp.

Smith, C. S. (1965), Materials and the development of civilization and science: Science, vol. 148, no. 3672; pp. 908–917.

Spurr, J. E. (1920) Political and commercial geology on the world's mineral resources: McGraw-Hill, New York, 562 pp.

Strabo (1917–1932) Strabo's Geography, translated and edited by H. L. Jones: Loeb Classical Library, Cambridge, 8 vols.

Thom, W. T., Jr. (1929) Petroleum and coal, the keys to the future: Princeton University Press, Princeton, 223 pp.

Wertime, T. A. (1964) Man's first encounters with metallurgy: Science, vol. 146, no. 3649, pp. 1257–1267.

RENAISSANCE, NEW WORLDS, NEW MINES, AND THE DAWN OF INDUSTRIALIZATION

Introduction.

The Renaissance that was brewing in the 14th and 15th centuries exploded in the 16th. It is most commonly thought of as a rebirth of the arts and sciences, of commerce, and of philosophy. It was also, however, a rebirth of engineering and industry. The demands of the creative segment of the new society could only be satisfied with new earth materials and a larger volume of earth materials. The conventional histories allege that the great voyages of discovery were motivated by demands for the spices of the East, and of course the burgeoning European population had a serious problem in extending the life of perishable foods. Spices commanded extraordinary prices in European markets. It was also known, however, that the products of the East included gold, silver, and gems, and this writer is confident that at least some of the intrepid captains and their sponsors were thinking of treasures of gold and silver as well as treasures of pepper and cloves. Rickard (1932, p. 667) stated that the lure of gold led to the discovery of the New World and documented his assertion by references to Columbus' letters. The profit motive to finding a way around the tolls levied on eastern products moving overland through Egypt, Arabia, and Turkey to Europe pushed construction of the navies and merchant marines of the developing European powers.

However, prior to the Renaissance and the discovery of the mines of the New World, beginning about 1200, an increased volume of minerals and metals from the central European deposits around the Erzgebirge in Saxony, Bohemia and Silesia (Freiberg, Joachimsthal, and Schneeberg) began to move on the rivers of central and northern Europe. These new supplies of metal relieved in part a critical European metal shortage resulting from the centuries of cultural paralysis and thereby helped to dissipate the darkness. Southeastern Germany boomed between 1480 and 1570 with silver, copper, and lead mined and exported. Antwerp became a principal metal market and smelting center.

The outstanding contributor to the central European mining Renaissance was Georgius Agricola (George Bauer), born in Saxony in 1494. Hoover (1912, pp. v-xvii) presented an excellent biography of this extraordinary man. Prior to Agricola, natural science speculations concerned with mineral deposits were restricted to Greek philosophy, mainly the contributions of Aristotle and Theophrastus, and to various theories put forth by alchemists and astrologers during the Middle Ages. Agricola's contribution was threefold: (1) He compiled in detail the knowledge of mining and metallurgy extant in the 16th century in what has become one of the most important historical documents of European civilization, *De Re Metallica,* published in 1556; this book stood for two centuries as the best technical reference on the subject. (2) He broke through the speculations, fantasies, and mysticisms of generations to classify natural phenomena on *observed* features—the form of the ore bodies. (3) On the basis of the observed features, he reasoned that the ore deposits were younger than the enclosing rocks and that they were deposited there from solutions circulating in channelways. The major contribution to the science of ore deposits between Agricola's time and the middle of the 18th century was made by Nicolaus Steno who, in 1669, concluded that ore deposits were the product of condensation of gases moving through open fractures and fissures—a view not too different from Agricola's written over 100 years earlier.

The state of mining and metallurgical arts in the 16th century is well illustrated by Agricola's summary of the things that a miner needed to know (Agricola, 1556, pp. 1–4):

For a miner must have the greatest skill in his work, that he may know first of all what mountain or hill, what valley or plain, can be prospected most profitably, or what he should leave alone; moreover, he must understand the veins, stringers and seams in the rocks. Then he must be thoroughly familiar with the many and varied species of earth, juices, gems, stones, marbles, rocks, metals, and compounds. He must also have a complete knowledge of the method of making all underground works. Lastly, there are various systems of assaying substances and of preparing them for smelting; and here again there are many altogether diverse methods. For there is one method for gold and silver, another for copper, another for quicksilver, another for iron, another for lead, and even tin and bismuth are treated differently from lead. Although the evaporation of juices is an art apparently quite distinct from metallurgy, yet they ought not to be considered separately, inasmuch as these juices are also often dug out of the ground solidified, or they are produced from certain kinds of earth and stones which the miners dig up, and some of the juices are not themselves devoid of metals. Again, their treatment is not simple, since there is one method for common salt, another for soda, another for alum, another for vitriol, another for sulphur, and another for bitumen.

Furthermore, there are many arts and sciences of which a miner should not be ignorant. First there is Philosophy, that he may discern the origin, cause, and nature of subterranean things; for then he will be able to dig out the veins easily and advantageously, and to obtain more abundant results from his mining. Secondly, there is Medicine, that he may be able to look after his diggers and other workmen, that they do not meet with those diseases to which they are more liable than workmen in other occupations, or if they do meet with them, that he himself may be able to heal them or may see that the doctors do so. Thirdly follows Astronomy, that he may know the divisions of the heavens and from them judge the direction of the veins. Fourthly, there is the science of Surveying that he may be able to estimate how deep a shaft should be sunk to reach the tunnel which is being driven to it, and to determine the lines and boundaries in these workings, especially in depth. Fifthly, his knowledge of Arithmetical Science should be such that he may calculate the cost incurred in the machinery and working of the mine. Sixthly, his learning must comprise Architecture, that he himself may construct the various machines and timber work required underground, or that he may be able to explain the method of the construction to others. Next, he must have knowledge of Drawing, that he can draw plans of his machinery. Lastly, there is the Law, especially that dealing with metals, that he may claim his own rights, that he may undertake the duty of giving others his opinion on legal matters, that he may not take another man's property and so make trouble for himself, and that he may fulfill his obligations to others according to the law.

The variety of hoisting, pumping, crushing, grinding, sizing, and washing machines employed in Agricola's day are portrayed in delightful woodcuts, as are various furnaces, crucibles, and bellows for smelting of ores.

Lopez and Raymond (1955, p. 122) published a translation of a 15th century mining lease which contained most of the elements of modern leases and showed that understanding of mining and its legal problems was not restricted to northern Europe:

[Siena, April 1st, 1445]

Before you, magnificent and powerful Lords, our most particular Lords, premising the humble recommendations, etc. . . .

It is related with due reverence by your most faithful servants, Vitale, son of Maestro Allegro of Imola, Jew, and Stefano di Giovanni of Ragusa, that they have heard through report that in some parts of your district there are certain mountains which have veins of every kind of metal; and for that reason they have come to your city and wish to mine in said mountains. They would like to ask by singular grace[1] to be allowed to mine in the territory of Montieri, that is, in the village of Bocchegianno and in the village of Roccadastra, with these pacts, conditions and procedures: that where they begin to mine no other person be allowed to mine within a mile from them for a period of twenty-five years; and if it should happen that two years pass without their mining anything, then this grace is to be understood to be null and void; and they offer forever to give your Commune out of anything they mine or find one part out of twelve. Also, in regard to everything they mine—that is, gold, silver and any other metal—they promise your Commune that they will have it melted and refined by artisans living in your town, that is, by goldsmiths; and if (the goldsmiths) themselves wish to do this they promise not to send (the metal) to others, that is, outside your city. Also, (they promise) that they will have it all struck in the mint of your Commune.

Also we wish to be allowed to use any water in the said localities and to erect there any building (needed) to work the said metal, and to be allowed to cut wood without detriment or damage to any of your communities or to private persons, (since) this grace is not to be understood to be detrimental in any part to them.

---

[1] That is, by a grant reserved exclusively to them.

And this they would like to ask by grace of your Lordships, to whom they ever recommend themselves, whom may God preserve as they wish. Praise be to God.[2]

The application of machinery to the labors of mining and milling is poorly documented until Agricola's 1556 treatise. The principles of mechanics on which such machines are based—block and pulley, windlass, water wheels, power transmission by shafts and gears, chain pumps, piston pumps and valves—were known to Greeks and Romans and were described by Ctesibius (250 B.C.), Archimedes (287–212 B.C.), and Vitruvius (1st Century B.C.) (Hoover, 1912, p. 149). Their application to mines was undoubtedly first to control water and to hoist ore and waste. The Archimedes screw was called the Egyptian screw because of its use in irrigation in Egypt. Screw pumps and water wheels were used by Romans and were found in Roman workings in the Rio Tinto mine in Spain. The Renaissance saw the first developments in ore dressing since the mortars and grindstones of the ancients. Stamp mills were invented in either the 15th or early 16th century. They are well described by Agricola who also illustrates wet stamping operations involving sizing (sieves) and washing equipment. He also published the first description of fluxes or "stones which easily melt in the fire" including fluorspar.

One of the fundamental requirements in any mining operation is knowledge of the composition of the material extracted. Of course, evaluation of the efficiency of any treatment process depends on knowledge of the composition of the material before and after treatment. Thus, as mining passed from the extraction of native metals visible to the naked eye, to extraction of mixtures of metals existing as sulfides, oxides, arsenates, etc., it became necessary to develop means of determining metal content—methods of assaying and analysis. Hoover (1912, p. 219) noted that there is little record of assaying procedures used by Greeks and Romans but inferred a system of fire-testing of metalliferous ores. A *touchstone* to determine gold and silver proportions in the mixed metal by color comparison was early described by Theophrastus. The experiments of the alchemists laid the groundwork for assay methods, though they were not concerned with quantitative analysis. The first published works on assaying are early 16th century (Hoover, 1912, p. 220); the methods are described in detail by Agricola in Book VII.

Agricola (1556, pp. 5–24) pointed up a curiously persistent idea in

---

[2] In Latin in the text: Laus Deo. The petition was approved on April 6, 1445.

human history that it is things that are 'evil' rather than the men who use them, and quoted Pliny to the point that:

Iron is used not only in hand to hand fighting, but also to form the winged missiles of war, sometimes for hurling engines, sometimes for lances, sometimes even for arrows. I look upon it as the most deadly fruit of human ingenuity. For to bring Death to men more quickly we have given wings to iron and taught it to fly.

Agricola was concerned about the contentions of those against the practice of mining who argued that inasmuch as nature concealed metals in the depths of the earth they should not be sought and extracted by men. The same sort of reasoning is heard today about space flight, population planning, and mining of minerals from the oceanic deeps.

Eighteenth-century thought on the origin of mineral deposits is well summarized by Park and MacDiarmid (1964, pp. 6–10). Ideas on the origin and composition of hot-water solutions, mineral alteration, replacement of an earlier formed mineral by a later one, concentration of elements by leaching from the country rock were advanced by European students of mines—mostly Germans working in the Erzgebirge. The major event of the century was the establishment of two opposing schools of thought which flourished in controversy for years after the passing of their founders. James Hutton, and his 'Boswell,' John Playfair, believed that the crystalline rocks such as granite which Hutton observed in his native Scotland, as well as ore deposits, were formed from molten rock generated at depth and injected as a molten fluid. His theory of ore magmas is to this day applied to certain kinds of deposits. The opposing school, founded by a German—Abraham Gottlob Werner—held that rocks and ore deposits were precipitated in a 'primeval ocean.' Although neither theory survived as broad, inclusive concepts, Hutton has undoubtedly had the best of it (p. 41). Although it has been demonstrated that a great class of ore deposits—epigenetic deposits—are precipitated from aqueous fluids moving through an earlier-formed body of rock, the igneous processes inferred by Hutton are today firmly incorporated in the body of geological science as applied to origin of igneous rock bodies. The controversy, as it persisted into the 19th century, had a beneficial effect on geological science in that it set men into the field and laboratory looking for proof to back up their theories.

The increased volumes of ores won from old mining districts resulted, as it still does, in the need for deeper workings and improved methods of breaking rocks. Renaissance engineering devised new pumps, utilized water power, and in 1627 at Schemnitz, Czechoslovakia, explosives were introduced to break rock in a mine (Rickard, 1932, p. 556). Change did not come overnight, however, and in areas of cheap and plentiful wood, such as Norway, the old method of fire-setting or heating rock with a wood fire and suddenly chilling it with water or vinegar was used to break rock until 1885, a two-century overlap of methods. The first fuel-operated power engine, the Savery steam engine of 1698, was used to pump water from British coal pits (Therring, 1958, pp. 47–48).

FIGURE V.1   Fire-setting to break the rock in a 16th century mine
(after Agricola, 1556, p. 12).

With primitive and laborious methods of breaking rock, it was, of course, necessary that only a minimum of nonpaying rock be broken to get at the ore. For this reason, the workings of many old mines where ore bodies are narrow are barely large enough to permit the passage of a wriggling or crawling man. The use of explosives made possible larger openings and improved working conditions measurably.

Enumeration of the new mining districts of the greatly expanded Renaissance world would fill several volumes without contributing a great deal to this exposition. It is enough to point out that the foundations of the first great industrial nations were laid during this period and consist of a steel industry built by the bringing together of iron, coal, and flux. These centers developed in England, Germany, France, Belgium, and Czechoslovakia, where coal and iron either occur together naturally or where iron ores could be cheaply moved to coal via water transportation. The latecomers to the industrial family, which grew to be the world giants—United States and Russia—built their industry on this same foundation of iron and coal. With the exception of Italy and Japan, who built relatively strong 19th and early 20th century industries without major coal and iron deposits, countries without such a resource base have, until the modern age, remained as agricultural countries. Countries with metalliferous ores but lacking fuels have become exporters of ores or concentrates. Political turmoil and lack of transportation facilities delayed the development of such centers from place to place so that Germany's rise took place 50 years after that of England. The industrial growth of various European nations at the beginning of the industrial era in terms of coal production, iron production, foreign trade, railroad trackage, investments in industry and population expansion was summed up by Lovering (1943, pp. 56–73).

A most important product of the Renaissance period was the codification of legal systems under which today a large part of the world's mineral resources are held (Chapter VII). In England, British common-law concepts of land tenure under which owners of land were entitled to extract from the land whatever minerals were found thereon or therein, and could, in fact, sell, lease, or otherwise dispose of the mineral estate, became firm with the only exception being the perpetuation of the Crown's traditional interest in precious metal mines. The Royal ownership of gold and silver mines presented no practical difficulty in the early days when those precious metals were won from simple ores containing native metals. However, the crown's

FIGURE V.2 Mine surveying in the 16th century
(after Agricola, 1556, p. 13).

A—UPRIGHT FORKED POSTS.   B—POLE OVER THE POSTS.   C—SHAFT.   D—FIRST CORD.
E—WEIGHT OF FIRST CORD.   F—SECOND CORD.   G—SAME FIXED GROUND.   H—HEAD
OF FIRST CORD.   I—MOUTH OF TUNNEL.   K—THIRD CORD.   L—WEIGHT OF THIRD CORD.
M—FIRST SIDE MINOR TRIANGLE.   N—SECOND SIDE MINOR TRIANGLE.   O—THIRD SIDE
MINOR TRIANGLE.   P—THE MINOR TRIANGLE.

claim of ownership caused problems when metallurgical arts advanced to the treatment of complex base metal ores containing gold and/or silver in addition to copper, lead, tin, and zinc (p. 154). The crown's rights to precious metals were in part based on the king's perogative to control coinage (American Law of Mining, 1964, vol. 1, pp. 5–6).

A similar concept of mineral tenure held in Europe, including Spain. The crown owned all precious metal mines. This concept differed from English law in that the owner of the land, although he owned the minerals other than gold and silver, was obliged to pay a royalty to the crown on production from all mines and quarries. However, in 1783, Charles III, King of Spain, decreed that *all* mines were the property of the crown. This separation of surface and mineral estate was accompanied by a complete mining code governing concessions, mine operation, and royalty payments. All of the mineral development of Spanish America, and indeed of Spanish colonies in Africa, Asia, and the Pacific, took place under this regalian or dominal theory of state ownership of mineral deposits. One important deviation from this system was French law set out in the Napoleonic Code of 1810 (pp. 159), which focused on the act of discovery, and *thereafter* provided for a royalty to the landowner while reserving to the government the control of exploitation (Ely, 1964, p. 87).

The New World.

It was not an accident that Spain built the first great Empire—Spain was already shaped as a nation when the new knowledge broke the old ways of thinking and doing things. It had been hammered into a cohesive political unit by long years of war against the Moors, so that by the beginning of the 14th century Spain had as one resource a restless cadre of men trained for fighting and nothing else.

Whereas the earliest Spanish expeditions encountered in Mexico and Peru an advanced Indian civilization with an established albeit primitive mineral industry, considerable skill in gold, silver, and copper metal working, an accumulated supply of precious metals, and known mines and quarries from which minerals had been extracted, the English, French, and Dutch landings encountered forest-hunting cultures with primitive agriculture or none at all, and no metal culture. Thus, the Spanish expeditions were able immediately to return to Spain the accumulated hoard of precious metals and to institute rapidly an exploitation of the known mines utilizing native labor. The only cash crop the English, French, and Dutch were able to reap was furs and naval stores. Nearly all elementary history texts written in the United States make much of the fact that whereas the Spanish plundered, the English colonists settled down to peaceful farming and animal husbandry. It is true that Spanish colonizing expeditions were official royal expeditions made up of teams of adventurers rather than families, whereas English expeditions included family groups departing for philosophical reasons. However, virtuous smugness about one's ancestors should be tempered by consideration that they found nothing to plunder on the Atlantic seaboard of the North American continent, at least nothing that could be exploited without hard work over the long term. A cynic might even suggest that if the first expeditions had found gold and silver, religious groups might have found it difficult to secure charters, and it might have been hard to distinguish English expeditions from Spanish ones. Subsequently, when the golden treasure of California was discovered, there was no indication of a lack of interest in gold on the part of the descendants of the colonists.

Because of the sometimes well-organized Spanish government and the continuity and stability of the always well-organized Catholic Church, records of explorations of the Spanish new world are infinitely better than anything that went before. The mineral history of Spanish America is well documented.

Both the Spanish and the Portuguese were active in early maritime explorations at the end of the 15th century. Early Portuguese expeditions along the African Coast traded in slaves, ivory, spices, and gold, while the Columbus expedition of 1492 is known to every school child. Vasco de Gama in 1503 brought home to Portugal the first East Indian cargo of silks and spices obtained by a voyage around the Cape of Good Hope—it yielded a 500 per cent return on the original investment (Adams, 1902, p. 91). In 1493 the Pope, to head off conflict, split the world between Spain and Portugal by a decree which was adjusted in 1494 by the Treaty of Tordesillas. Spain got the best of it. Portugal was restricted to explorations east of the meridian drawn through a point about 370 leagues west of the Cape Verde Islands. As extended through the Americas, Portugal received rights to Brazil while Spain got everything else. By the middle of the 16th century the flow of metal—gold and silver—from Mexico and Peru to Spain was substantial, and Spain profited hugely. After the accumulated gold supplies were located and looted (graves of Indian nobility were a prime source in both Mexico and Peru), most of the metal exported was silver. The first organized mining by Spanish, first of alluvial and then of lode deposits, was in Zacatecas, Hidalgo, and Oaxaca, Mexico, and Potosi, Peru. Portugal prospered but did not approach the gold and silver prosperity of Spain. The importance of Italy as a commercial center declined as the Atlantic Coast nations gained in prominence. The English treasury was fattened by the toll taken of homeward-bound Spanish traffic by British sea raiders. In the half-century following the conquest of Mexico, enough gold and silver was sent to Europe from the Americas to increase the existing European stocks of precious metals by 50 per cent. By 1600, after the discovery of Potosi in Peru, European gold and silver supplies increased another 400 per cent. This was the capital to finance the Renaissance or, as Rickard (1932, p. 708) said, "it broke the feudal fetters of Europe."

The Indian cultures of Mexico and Peru were in a transitional period. Copper, gold, and silver were worked by artisans as native metals, but smelting of ores was not known. The main sources of metals were placer deposits. Iron was unknown; bronze was manufactured in the high Andes but not in Mexico. Most tools were obsidian or other stone. Ceramic arts were well developed.

The preoccupation with gold and silver that accompanied explorations of the new world should not blind us to the more prosaic but also important branches of the mineral industry. Most closely tied to the precious metals was quicksilver. Prior to the discovery and development of quicksilver deposits in the Americas, silver production was a high-cost operation. The big volume of silver production from Peru and Mexico was made possible by the amalgamation or *patio* process. Before local deposits were discovered, quicksilver was shipped to the mines from the known deposits in Spain and the demand led to a mining boom in Almaden.[1] Although invention of the amalgamation

[1] Fausto de Elhuyar (1825, pp. 58–67, 94–95, 217–228) in a monograph on the influence of the mineral industry in the development of New Spain (Memoria sobre el Influjo de la Minería en Nueva España, Madrid, 1825, reprinted as Publicación 9E, Consejo de Recursos Naturales No Renovables, Mexico 1964, 228 pp.) discussed the importance of adequate supplies of quicksilver. In 1559, only two years after the discovery or re-discovery of the Patio process of beneficiating precious metal ores by amalgamation with mercury, the Spanish Crown established a strict government monopoly on export of quicksilver to the New World—a monopoly which endured nearly three centuries. The Crown set the price and controlled distribution through Royal warehouses. In Mexico, prospecting for local deposits and exploitation of them was controlled closely so as to preserve the monopoly. The small amounts of mercury produced in Mexico could not be sold at prices below those set for mercury produced in Spain (Almaden) or Peru (Guancavelica). That shortages of mercury and high prices adversely affected gold and silver mining in Mexico, is proved by the sharp increase in precious metal production which occurred after the price of quicksilver was lowered 25 percent in 1767 and another 25 percent in 1776. Over a fifteen year period increased royalties

process in the Old World is not precisely dated and probably should be credited to Roman engineering (Hoover, 1912, fn. 12), its application to the precious metal mines of the New World is well fixed, at least in time. According to Becker (188, p. 28), the process was indigenous to Mexico and was invented by a Mexican miner named Bartolome de Medina in 1557, but he gives no source. Rickard (1932, p. 706) commented:

The use of quicksilver in amalgamation was introduced (in Peru) in 1567, after Enrique Garces had disclosed the cinnabar deposits of Guancavelica. By that time the *patio* process was understood, for Bartholome de Medina had brought it to Pachuca, in Mexico, ten years previously.

Hoover (1912, footnote 12) further stated:

The question as to who was the inventor of silver amalgamation will probably never be cleared up. According to Ulloa (Relacion historica del Viagea la America Meridional, Madrid, 1748) Dom Pedro Fernandes de Velasco discovered the process in Mexico in 1566. The earliest technical account is that of Father Joseph De Acosta. . . . He states that refining silver with mercury was introduced at Potosi by Pedro Fernandes de Velasco from Mexico in 1571. . . .

Hoover (1912, fn. 12) supposed that the application of the principle of amalgamation to silver recovery was 16th century while its application to gold recovery was much older. Whether the idea for the *patio process* of amalgamation of silver ores was developed in the New World or brought to it, the process was native to the New World and certainly reached its greatest development in treatment of the silver ores of Mexico and Peru.

---

to the crown exceeded by about 6.5 million pesos revenues lost by the price cut. In 1802, there was such an acute shortage of mercury that silver royalties were reduced 50 percent so the miners could treat their ores by much more costly smelting methods.

At the outset of the Mexican Revolution in 1810 the mines were well supplied with quicksilver. In 1812, despite unsettled conditions the government distributed about 10,000 quintales. However, no more was distributed until 1819 when about 2,000 quintales, a relatively insignificant amount remaining in the Royal Warehouse in Vera Cruz, was sold.

In the early 1800s the only commercial sources of quicksilver were Almaden Idria in The Alps north of Trieste, China, and Guancavelica, Peru. The Peruvian deposits were unable to supply the demand in Peru; Chinese quicksilver was sold in small lots at high prices, as was Idria's production. To alleviate the shortages, the government in Mexico in 1811 declared local mercury deposits open for exploration and exploitation on the same basis as other metals. They found out what governments still have not learned—that it takes years to find and develop mineral deposits. In 1815, the crown terminated the 250 year old Royal monopoly on quicksilver and thereafter the Almaden production moved in commerce with other commodities. The price in the distant markets of the New World climbed.

Britain and northern Europe.

Although in some ways eclipsed by developments in the Americas, Renaissance development of British, northern and central European, and then Scandinavian mineral resources began prior to 1600. In Britain, the insatiable hunger of booming iron forges for charcoal fuel began making inroads on British forests to the point where the Admiralty became concerned about supplies of timber for building ships, and a royal edict was issued forbidding the use of certain forests for manufacturing charcoal. Schubert (1957, pp. 218–222) discussed the destruction of the British forests and the litigation about it which culminated in the Act of 1543 providing for *coppice woods* or tree lots. This must have been one of the earliest attempts at tree farming. The effect of this early effort of a government to conserve a natural resource and to determine priorities for resource use was a happy one. It helped to overcome the conservative traditions of the ironmongers developed over the centuries and forced them to use coal and ultimately coke. Although 'mineral' coal was used by iron-masters as early as 1590, it took more than 100 years for it to find general use in iron manufacture. It was not until the early 18th century that the first iron was successfully *smelted* with coke made from 'mineral' coal and the way was opened for full industrial utilization of Britain's large coal resources (Schubert, 1957, 226–229). This head start in coal technology, together with other factors, resulted in the early growth of the English iron and steel complex that marked the Industrial Revolution. At one time during the 19th century, England led the world in production of lead, copper, tin, iron, and coal. France, by accident of nature poorly endowed with mineral resources while both Germany and England were relatively abundantly endowed, felt the pinch and attempted to add to her patrimony by war. Armed conflicts over control of European mineral resources including iron, coal, and oil have persisted for centuries, although the reasons given for aggression have always emphasized more noble sentiments.

Application of the amalgamation process of treating silver ores in Europe lagged some 200 years behind developments in Peru and Mexico, being first used in 1784 by a German metallurgist. Possibly the lag was due in part to the difficulty of obtaining mercury and transporting it through Europe. In any case, the process provided a demand for mercury, which lasted several hundred years until more modern processes replaced the amalgamation process.

Other European mineral industries were also stimulated by the new explorations which required iron and steel for armaments—from cannons to cuirasses to fine Toledo blades—fittings of lead, copper, bronze and wrought iron for naval vessels, sulfur and nitrates for gunpowder, more salt for food preservation, and coinage to buy silks, jewels, ivory, and spices. Cast iron in Europe dates from about the end of the 14th century, as the first cast iron cannon date from shortly thereafter. Agricola describes iron-smelting in detail, including the forerunner of the blast furnace. The great church and public building construction consumed large volumes of construction materials, such as dressed stone, gypsum, lime and sand for mortar and plaster, brick and tile clay. And the use of coal as a replacement for charcoal in metallurgical industries must rank as one of the most important mineral events of the Renaissance.

REFERENCES

Adams, Brooks (1902) The new empire: Macmillan and Co., New York and London, 243 pp.

Agricola, Georgius (1556) De re metallica, translated by Herbert Clark Hoover and Lou Henry Hoover (1950): Dover Publications, New York, 638 pp.

American Law of Mining (1964) Vol. I, Public Domain, Rocky Mountain Mineral Law Foundation: Matthew Bender and Co., New York, 906 pp.

Becker, G. F. (1888) Quicksilver deposits of the Pacific slope: U.S. Geol. Survey Monograph XIII, 486 pp.

Ely, Northcutt (1964) Mineral titles and concessions, in Economics of the mineral industries, 2nd. ed.: American Institute of Mining and Metallurgical Engineers, New York, pp. 81–130.

Hoover, H. C. (1950) Footnotes, in De re metallica (1556), translated by Herbert Clark Hoover and Lou Henry Hoover (originally published, 1912): Dover Publications, New York, 638 pp.

Lopez, R. S., and Raymond, I. W. (1955) Medieval trade in the Mediterranean World: Columbia University Press, New York, 458 pp.

Lovering, T. S. (1943) Minerals in world affairs: Prentice-Hall, Englewood Cliffs, N.J., 394 pp.

Park, C. F. Jr., and MacDiarmid, R. A. (1964) Ore deposits: W. H. Freeman & Co., San Francisco, 475 pp.

Rickard, T. A. (1932) Man and metals: McGraw-Hill, New York, 1068 pp.

Schubert, H. R. (1957) History of the British iron and steel industry from c. 450 B.C. to A.D. 1775: Routledge and Kegan Paul, London, 445 pp.

Steno, Nicolaus (1669) De solido intra solidum naturaliter contento—dissertationis prodromus ad serenissimum Ferdinandum—The prodromus of Nicolaus Steno's dissertation concerning a solid body enclosed by process of nature with a solid, English version with introduction and explanatory notes by John Garrett Winter (1916) Macmillan and Co., New York, 283 pp.

Therring, Hans (1958) Energy for man: windmills to nuclear power: Indiana University Press, Bloomington, 409 pp.

CHAPTER VI

MODERN
MINERAL HISTORY

Introduction.

The mineral history of the 19th century was a history of world-wide discovery and development in response to steadily increasing demands of a growing industrial society. The world's most famous and romantic mining camps were born in this century, and lasting mineral trade patterns were set. The 20th century was and is both a century of discovery and a century of change with the mineral industry responding to basic changes in world society; the demand for mineral commodities such as oil and gas, uranium, phosphates, and potash, which were of limited importance prior to 1900, has provoked worldwide exploration efforts.

A chronicle of mineral discovery in the 19th century would fill a library—each new find has its own story, both romantic and practically significant in terms of politics and economics. In most parts of the world, mineral development was inextricably bound up with the winning of empires, with wars, and with political power plays. In many parts of the world the prospector was close after the hunter, and the mining camp was the first permanent settlement beyond the frontier.

Roads and railways sprouted to link the successful mining camp which produced a salable product and at the same time a market for goods to the settled lands, and so mineral exploration pulled civilization along with it just as much as civilization provided the incentive to go forth. And the people that went forth were the yeasty froth on top of the settled inert mass of humanity—the kind of people not easily intimidated, impatient with regimentation, and the kind likely to evolve new ideas. It is impossible not to wonder where these kinds of people go today. Surely the fermentation has not ceased.

During the 19th and 20th centuries, the centuries of industrialization, world mineral production has soared in a steep exponential curve. In 1962, President Kennedy, in his message to Congress, observed that in the previous 30 years the United States consumed more mineral stuffs than all the peoples of the world have consumed since the dawn of history. In 1882, the first year that the United States began reporting mineral statistics, the total value of mineral production was about 450 million dollars; in 1963 the value was 21,300 million dollars. This is a 50-fold increase in 75 years. Adjustment of the 1963 dollar value to make it equivalent to the 1882 dollar would, of course, render the increase less spectacular but it would remain at an order of magnitude that is staggering. In terms of domestic production of selected commodities, the 1882 and 1963 production compares as follows (U.S. Geological Survey Mineral Resources of the United States, 1884; U.S. Bureau of Mines Minerals Yearbook, 1963) :

	1882		1963	Increase
iron	9,000,000	tons	153,000,000[1]	x17
bituminous coal	58,000,000	tons	459,000,000	x8
petroleum	30,000,000	barrels	2,753,000,000	x90
copper	92,000,000	pounds	2,426,000,000	x26
cement	85,000	barrels	361,000,000	x4,200
phosphate	332,000	tons	20,000,000	x60
sulfur	600	tons	6,600,000	x11,000

[1] equals 74,000,000 tons of usable ore.

Consumption is, of course, higher than domestic production for commodities such as iron, petroleum, and copper which are imported in large quantities. The low 1882 figures for cement and sulfur reflect the start of those mineral industries.

Inasmuch as this chapter, or indeed this book, cannot present the complete record of 19th- and 20th-century mineral history, that history will be summarized by spotlighting the major events on the several continents, with the reservation that the treatment will not do justice to events such as the California gold rush, the great African mineral boom in gold, diamonds, and copper, the latter-day uranium boom, the demand for strange new minerals and metals resulting from the new science and industry, and the fantastic improvements in rock-breaking and earth-moving capabilities.

Throughout the latter part of this period, it is especially true that the fact of discovery cannot be separated from technology because many of the major discoveries, of iron and base metals in particular, were discoveries of value only because mining and metallurgical advances converted what was earlier only rock with an abnormal content of an element or group of elements into ore from which those elements could be won economically (Tables X.3, XI.2).

The simple enumeration of the great mineral discoveries of the 19th and 20th centuries is an invitation to controversy because a claim to greatness can be made by almost every major mine in terms of what that mine meant to national supplies in times of crisis, its sociological and industrial significance, and its economic significance. Some attach great significance to discoveries of deposits of minor metals and alloy metals such as molybdenum, vanadium, beryllium, and lithium minerals, and certainly supplies of such materials have broadened our industrial capacities.

As was pointed out earlier (p. 100), Forbes (1963, p. 149), after studying Davies' 1935 report on Roman mines in Europe, concluded that all of the mines then operating in Europe had been known to the Romans. Latter-day discovery in Europe as far as metals are concerned was limited to application of new technology in a new economy to old deposits. Truly new discoveries occurred in Scandinavia, the Balkans, and the Soviet Union beyond the old frontiers, or were discoveries of petroleum and natural gas, uranium, potash, phosphate, and sulfur not of any particular interest to the Romans. Most of the new discoveries occurred in lands new to Europeans— in the Americas, Africa, Australia, and Asia.

The beginning of the 19th century was not marked by any great new theories about mineral deposits and their origin—in fact the first half of the century was mainly a period of examination and description of operating mines. The body of data accumulated pointed clearly to one of the major tenets of economic geology—that metallic mineral deposits are commonly associated with igneous rocks. However, the 19th-century geologists proved only a spatial association and not a temporal one. This was to come later. Élie de Beaumont, a French scientist, made some outstanding contributions in general geology, principally in the field of structural geology, but at the Paris School of Mines he concerned himself with metallic mineral deposits, recognizing hydrothermal, magmatic, and contact metasomatic classes. Advances in chemistry in the 19th century had applications to geology and strongly influenced theories on the transport and deposition of elements. In France, Daubreé, Fouqué, and Michel-Lévy pioneered laboratory synthesis of minerals and proved that minerals could be deposited from solutions. Fifty-five new elements were either discovered or first isolated in the 19th century; only 27 were known prior to 1800. Clearly, without this knowledge on the fundamental building blocks of minerals, the questions about the origin, transport, and deposition of minerals could not be answered. In 1859 Von Cotta in Freiberg published a treatise on ore deposits. He recognized that all ore deposits were not the product of a single process acting at a single time. Some three decades later, Posĕpný, a Bohemian geologist, professor at The School of Mines at Przibam, launched the 'American School' of mineral deposits in a paper delivered in Chicago in 1893. This paper, taken together with contributions by Vogt (1894) and De Launay (1897), stimulated American geologists such as S. F. Emmons, Van Hise, J. F. Kemp, Waldemar Lindgren, W. H. Weed, and in 1905 the Society of Economic Geologists was launched. Bateman (1955) in the 50th Anniversary Volume of that Society's publications summed up the progress made in economic geology in the first half of the 20th century.

The United States.

The mineral industry of the United States began with the republic east of the Appalachians and, until the western expansion, remained small with local coal and metal production from Maine to Georgia. The first major event was the discovery and development of the Lake Superior copper district in the Upper Peninsula of Michigan on Keweenaw Point. (Early European explorers had knowledge of the occurrence of copper in this region since 1636, and it was used by Indians long prior to that date.) The next year, 1845, saw the first use of bituminous coal to reduce iron in Mercer County, Pennsylvania, although anthracite had been used a few years earlier in 1839. In 1848 iron mining began near Marquette, Michigan. There were several failures and regular shipments did not begin until 1856. This marks the single most important event in American mineral history—the beginning of development of the great iron ranges of the Lake Superior region. Marquette was followed by Menominee (1872), Iron River, Crystal Falls and Florence (1880), Gogebic (1884), Vermillion (1885), the famous Mesabi (1891), and subsequently Cuyuna and Baraboo (1903). The first development of the great Pittsburg coal seam in 1860 in western Pennsylvania resulted in the western shift of the United States steel industry. While the iron ranges grew, the gold and silver camps of the West were discovered. The year that iron mining began at Marquette, gold was discovered in California, and by 1849 the rush was on. The great Comstock silver camp dates from 1859 (Fig. VI.1)—the same year that Colonel Drake drilled the

FIGURE VI.1   The Comstock lode—Virginia City in the late 1870s. View toward the northwest over the long dump of the Hale and Norcross mine (Courtesy of Nevada Historical Society).

nation's first oil well in Pennsylvania. In 1864 the silver-lead ores of Eureka, Nevada, were discovered, and disseminated lead-zinc ores were discovered in southeastern Missouri. The lead-zinc ores of the Mississippi Valley had been known then for more than 100 years— the first mining in Missouri is dated as about 1742. However, the mining activity remained local and scattered until the discovery of large low-grade ores (1864) and the introduction of the diamond drill (1869). In 1871, the great copper hill at Butte, Montana, was

FIGURE VI.2   The Cane Creek (Utah) potash mine of Texas Gulf Sulfur in 1962 (Texas Gulf Sulfur Annual Report, 1962, p. 11).

nothing more than the site of a small placer mining camp. Leadville, Colorado, was opened in 1876 and the famous lead-silver camp of Coeur d'Alene, Idaho, followed in 1884.

In 1897 the great rush to Yukon and the Klondike took miners to Bonanza Creek and Dawson City. At this same time experimental work to develop a process to separate base metal sulfides by selective flotation was in process. The first patent was granted in 1905, and it was not accident that the first great porphyry copper deposit in Bingham Canyon, Utah, was opened that same year. Half a century later, 18 porphyry copper deposits in the American West had produced over 60 billion pounds of copper worth more than 10 billion dollars. The world's largest molybdenum deposit at Fremont Pass, Colorado, was developed in 1917. The last great rush, which took thousands

FIGURE VI.3   Mining with a dredge—North Carolina phosphate (Texas Gulf Sulfur Annual Report, 1963, inside back cover).

of Americans into the field to search for uranium, fanned out from the Colorado Plateau in the early 1950s and became a nation-wide effort.

Milestones in the nonmetallic field include the first manufacture of Portland cement in Allentown, Pennsylvania, in 1871, discovery of the Florida phosphate field in 1888, and the discovery of Gulf Coast salt-dome sulfur deposits in 1900. Successful exploitation by the Frasch process was delayed until 1904. The potash deposits of south-eastern New Mexico were developed in the 1930s; after World War II the booming demand for potash resulted in increased exploration and a new discovery in the paradox Basin of Utah, near Moab (Fig. VI.2). The U.S. phosphate industry was born in South Carolina in

FIGURE VI.4

Mining phosphate with a dragline in North Carolina (Texas Gulf Sulphur Company).

1867; the large Florida deposits came into production in 1888. In 1906 the deposits of the Phosphoria Formation of the Northwest were first exploited in Idaho. In the 1950s phosphate was discovered in Beaufort County, North Carolina. After exploration by several companies, extensive development was undertaken in 1961 (Figs. VI.3, VI.4). Although the beginning of the petroleum industry is dated from Colonel Drake's renowned Pennsylvania well, local developments and discoveries of such giant fields as Spindletop in 1901 and East Texas in 1930 are more significant. From 1859 to about 1900 the industry was in a lamp and lubricating oil phase; between 1900 and 1910 the demand was for fuel oil, and after 1910 the great soaring demand for motor fuel began.

Scientific inquiry into mineral deposits grew apace with discovery. The U.S. Geological Survey was born in 1879 following a series of earlier territorial surveys, and geological surveys were established in the separate states. The U.S. Bureau of Mines was established in 1910. Geological departments became a necessary part of the exploration efforts of the major mining and oil companies. Scientific societies were formed: The American Institute of Mining and Metallurgical Engineers in 1871, The Geological Society of America in 1888, the Society of Economic Geologists in 1905, and the American Association of Petroleum Geologists in 1917.

Canada.

Canada's big mineral development dates from the late 19th century and the mineral industry has steadily grown more widespread, larger, and more diversified. This is due in part, of course, to the resources of the Canadian shield and the Cordilleran region, but it is also due in no small part to the continuing strong encouragement of the mineral industry by the Canadian government in the form of liberal land-acquisition and tax policies. There was early local development of coal and metalliferous deposits in eastern Canada around the old population centers. A gold rush took place in Nova Scotia in the early 1860s. In 1878 the great asbestos deposits near Thetford and Black Lake in eastern Quebec were discovered. Gold, silver, and base metal ores were developed in British Columbia in the last decade of the 19th Century (Rossland district, 1890; Copper Mountain, 1892; the famous Sullivan lead-zinc mine in the Kootenay district, 1895). The gold rush into the Yukon Territory began in 1897.

After 1900, now famous mining districts were developed one after the other. The great silver-cobalt-nickel camp at Cobalt, Ontario, began production in 1904. Development of Sudbury, Ontario's copper-nickel ores began about 1910—the Falconbridge mine was opened in 1929. The gold and gold-copper deposits of Ontario at Porcupine (1910) and Kirkland Lake (1913) and in Quebec at Noranda (1922) are world famous. In Manitoba, copper-zinc-silver-gold ores were developed at Flin Flon (1915) and Sherritt-Gordon (1924). Gold was discovered at Yellowknife in the Northwest Territories in 1935 and subsequent discoveries in the district continued in the middle 1940s. More recently, since World War II, large base metal discoveries have been made in the Bathurst-Newcastle area of New Brunswick, near Timmins, Ontario, and in the Great Slave Lake area of Northwest Territories. Very large nickel reserves have been developed in northern Manitoba at the Thompson mine. In 1965 New Brunswick was well along with development of a huge mineral industry network to mine, concentrate, smelt, and refine a variety of metals and nonmetals including lead-zinc-copper-silver, iron (with pelletizing facilities), sulfur and sulfuric acid, and phosphoric acid. Investment of 220 million dollars is planned (Eng. and Mining Jour., 1965, pp. 70–75).

Canada was an early producer of uranium from deposits discovered in 1930 at Great Bear Lake. The extensive search for uranium ores after World War II resulted in discovery of the huge low-grade conglomerate ores of Blind River, Ontario. Oil was produced in small quantities from Eastern Canada as early as 1857 and natural gas production dates from 1889. In the mid 1920s a discovery in Montana encouraged prospecting north of the border in Alberta but production was small until the post-World War II period. Since the war, the western provinces of Canada have experienced a continuing oil boom. Large tonnages of sulfur are recovered from Canadian sour gas and some Saskatchewan gas fields contain large helium reserves. The tar sands of Alberta constitute one of the great petroleum reserves for the future and the Arctic Archipelago is a promising prospecting area. Large low-grade coal deposits occur in the same general area. Major potash deposits occur in Saskatchewan. Foreign aluminum ores have moved to hydroelectric power in western Canada.

Exploration for iron was sparked by World War II. Work on the Steep Rock Lake deposits in western Ontario, known since the 1930s, began in 1943. The great engineering project involved draining of the lake to get at the high-grade ores beneath it. By 1948 more than 2 million tons of high-grade ores had been produced. Development of the iron deposits along the Quebec-Labrador border began in the post-war period.

Mexico.

Although the flow of gold from Mexico ebbed in the post-conquest period, Mexico continued into the 20th century as one of the world's principal producers of silver from such districts as Fresnillo in the State of Zacatecas, Guanajuato and Pachuca in the State of Hidalgo, and Parral, San Francisco del Oro, and Santa Eulalía, in the State of Chihuahua. Base metal deposits are widespread in Mexico and were known in colonial days when most of them were precious metal camps. In the 19th and early 20th centuries high-grade ores and concentrates were exported, but as Mexico became industrialized in the middle 20th century more and more base metal refining facilities were built in Mexico. Lower grade ores were exploited, particularly in the copper camps of Cananea and Nacozari, Sonora.

Development of a steel industry lagged until the 20th century. The iron ores of the northern and Pacific states and the coals of the Sabinas basin in Coahuila met in the steel producing centers of Monterrey and Monclova. As industrialization progressed, interest in nonmetallic minerals grew; phosphate deposits in Baja, California, Coahuila and Zacatecas, as well as gypsum in San Luis Potosi, have been explored. The first sulfur was produced from the salt domes of the Isthmus of Tehuantepec in 1954.

Oil seeps and springs were known along the Mexican Gulf coast in the region of Tampico and Vera Cruz for many years before the turn of the century. The great Mexican oil boom began about 1900 and continued until the middle 1920s. Flush production from the Panuco-Ebano and Faja de Oro fields made Tampico the oil port of the world. Fields in the Isthmus of Tehuantepec were discovered in the 1920s and Poza Rica was brought in about 1930.

South America.

Until the 19th century, South America was from the point of view of the mineral industry a land of gold, silver, and gems. The Europeans took up where the Incas had left off, exploiting alluvial gold deposits over the continent and digging into the gold and silver lodes of the Andes, mostly in Colombia, Peru, Bolivia, and Chile. Potosi, Bolivia, has been called the richest silver hill on earth. Gold deposits were also discovered in Brazil and the Guiana highlands. Gold dredges are still working alluvial deposits in the Andean drainages. Diamonds were discovered in Brazil as early as 1720, thus ending India's long monopoly. Emeralds had been mined in Colombia in pre-conquest times; Spanish emerald production dates from 1538. Quicksilver, of course, was mined in the colonial period to permit amalgamation of precious metal ores.

Except for small local production, there was no development of base metals until the middle of the 19th century. The early 20th century saw a great boom in South American minerals which included development of the great Chilean copper deposits (Braden, 1912; Chuquicamata, 1916), exploitation of Chilean nitrate, and large scale development and production of Bolivian tin. Cerro de Pasco, Peru, an important silver producer since 1630, became a big base metal mine in 1915. Development of the vast iron deposits of Brazil and Venezuela and the smaller Chilean deposits came later. The occurrence of iron ores in Brazil, Chile, and Venezuela was known prior to World War II; the Brazilian deposits had been surveyed in the 1930s. World War II provided the impetus for development of the deposits in the State of Minas Gerais, Brazil. Immediately after the war, because of the decline in reserves of high-grade direct-shipping ores in the Lake Superior region of the United States and the 'not-proved' economic status of the great reserves of taconite ores of that region, the large American mining companies launched a worldwide search for iron deposits. In the late 1940s El Tofo and El Romeral deposits in Chile and El Pao in Venezuela were developed by Bethlehem Steel. In 1947, the exploration effort of U.S. Steel found Cerro Bolivar in Venezuela. Another fruit of this effort was discovery of large manganese deposits in Mato Grosso State, and to the north near the Guiana border in Serro do Navio, Brazil. Earlier, in 1942, the war-time search for strategic minerals resulted in development of a tungsten deposit in northeastern Brazil. Deposits of bauxite in the Guianas were discovered and developed as a result of the growth of the aluminum industry in the post-war period.

Petroleum and asphalt were known to South American Indians and were produced from springs, seeps, and shallow wells; the pitch lake on Trinidad was described by Sir Walter Raleigh as early as 1595. Information on the distribution of such occurrences in Venezuela, Colombia, Brazil, Peru, Ecuador, and Argentina accumulated during the latter part of the 19th century; exploration in Venezuela by American and European companies began about 1910. The boom in

Venezuela and Colombia occurred after 1920. Currently the major producers of petroleum in South America are Venezuela, Colombia, and Argentina, but there is also production in Bolivia, Brazil, Chile, Ecuador, and Peru. Although coal deposits occur in the Andean chain and in Brazil, a large coal-mining industry has never developed for a number of economic and political reasons.

Europe, Scandinavia, U.S.S.R., and the Balkans.

The modern mineral history of Europe and its Scandinavian, Soviet, and Balkan frontiers is a history of exploration for and discovery of mineral commodities not valued by the older culture, of application of new technology to long-known marginal deposits, of exploitation of high-cost deposits under war-time conditions, and of a great sustained mineral exploration and development program in the vast interior of the Soviet Union.

Throughout 'old' Europe the mineral industry moved into the new age by utilizing new engineering methods and new metallurgical techniques to win metals from lower-grade ores. At the great iron-copper pyrite deposit of Rio Tinto in Spain, the largest sulfide mass in the world, flotation was introduced to concentrate low-grade copper ore and more recently the plant was improved to recover sulfur. At Kokkola in northern Finland a new process (Outokumpu process) is converting 360,000 tons per year of pyrites into electricity, iron ore, sulfuric acid, and elemental sulfur. The ancient Almaden quicksilver deposit, worked for over 2,000 years, remains the world's largest quicksilver deposit. Quicksilver deposits in Italy at Monte Amiata and Idria, Yugoslavia, remain important modern sources. Lower grade base metal ores were developed in the old central European and Balkan districts. The famous minette iron ores of Lorraine were exploited first on the outcrop in Germany and then followed down dip into France. About 1920 Germany began to rely on low-grade limonitic ores and imports. Lower and lower grade copper ores became economic in the great Kupferschiefer deposits, and during World War II German technology produced liquid fuel by hydrogenation of coal. The same trends appeared in metal mining in England.

The 'new' minerals of the modern age included bauxite discovered and developed in France and the Balkans, potash deposits exploited in the famous Zechstein series of which Stassfurt is perhaps the best known deposit, manganese and chrome ores in the Balkans, the uranium ores of Joachimstahl, Czechoslovakia, the nickel ores of Petsamo,

Finland, and, of course, oil and gas. The oil fields of Rumania have produced since 1857, but only in the post-World War II period has there been serious exploration for hydrocarbons in Europe. The result has been important discoveries in France and a giant gas field in the Netherlands and under the North Sea. The Lacq sour gas field in France began recovery of sulfur from gas in 1957, and in two years captured 7 per cent of the world sulfur market.

Outside of the Soviet Union, the most significant iron discovery was the great Kiruna deposit in Sweden's Lapland which began production about the turn of the century.

The U.S.S.R., in a drive to achieve a full industrial status, has given great attention to mineral raw materials. The basis for the basic steel industry is the Krivoi Rog, Donetz Basin, and Ural iron deposits together with coals in the Kuznetsk and Donetz Basins, the Vorkuta Field north of the Arctic circle, and deposits in the Urals and Siberia. Manganese deposits are widespread; the largest and best known are Tchiaturi, Georgia and Nikopol in the Ukraine; other deposits occur in the southern Urals, middle Volga region, and in western Siberia. Copper ores have been developed in the Urals, Kazakstan, the Caucauses and Central Asia. The Soviet Union is a leading producer of precious metals including gold from the Transbaikal, Ural, and Atai areas and platinum from the Urals (discovered in 1819). Since World War II, the U.S.S.R. has become an exporter of oil and phosphate.

Africa.

In the 19th century, Africa consisted of a northern or Arab land fringing the Mediterranean and Red Seas where various cultures had exploited mineral resources for millenia, a European colony clinging to the southern tip of the continent, and a vast unknown interior referred to as 'darkest Africa.' In the Arab north, the 19th and 20th centuries brought more extensive development of long-known iron and base metal deposits in Morocco, Tunisia, and Algeria mostly by French companies, as well as exploration for and development of minerals not sought by the ancient cultures—minerals such as phosphate, petroleum, and natural gas. Except for the recent (post World War II) North African petroleum discoveries, the exciting new mineral discoveries were in the interior.

Diamonds were first. The first discovery was a 'pebble' found in 1867 on the Orange River. The rush to Kimberly followed a few years later. Gold was next. Although there were sporadic discoveries prior to 1886, that date marks the birth of the great Witwatersrand district where the thriving city of Johannesburg stands as a monument to the gold mining industry. As in ancient times, the first discoveries of both diamonds and gold were alluvial deposits; mining of the lodes came shortly after. In the first three decades of the 20th century, the great copper deposits of Rhodesia and Katanga were developed, the chromite and platinum of the Bushveldt complex and the Great Dyke in South Africa and Rhodesia began production, asbestos was found in southern Rhodesia and South Africa, the copper-lead-zinc ores of the famous Tsumeb mine in southwest Africa were exploited, and the manganese deposits of South Africa began production. The one-time largest manganese mine in the world, at N'Suta in the Gold Coast, began exporting ores in 1916. Manganese was also developed in Egypt just south of Suez. Coal fields were developed in South Africa and Rhodesia. Uranium was discovered at Shinkolobwe in the Congo, which was the world's principal source until Canadian deposits were discovered in 1930. Discovery that uranium is associated with gold in the Witwatersrand added a mid-century dividend to gold mining operations and permitted exploitation of lower grade gold ores than would have otherwise been possible. Iron deposits in Liberia were examined in the 1930s but development lagged until after World War II. First shipments to the United States from Bomi Hills took place in 1951. Bauxite was discovered in the Gold Coast.

The mineral history of Africa is inextricably tied up with exploration and settlement of the continent. The stampedes north from Capetown to the diamond and gold fields were followed by roads, railroads, and cities that opened up the 'dark' continent. Mineral exploration for petroleum, iron, and base metals continues at a high level in Africa. Modern developments include company-built transportation facilities, towns, and schools. For details on the African scene the student of mineral resources should consult a new comprehensive treatise by Nicolas de Kun (1965).

Australia.

The continent of Australia was charted and claimed for Britain in 1770 by Captain James Cook and is, therefore by virtue of its comparatively late date of settlement, a 19th and 20th century country without a long antecedent European cultural history. Its aborigines were found in a primitive society without metals; stones were in use as implements and weapons and also for decorative and magical purposes. Although gold was discovered in New South Wales east of Bathurst as early as 1838, it was not until 1851, two years after the worldwide publicity attendant on the California rush, that the Australian stampede to Bathurst and Ophir in New South Wales began. The rush quickly spread west to Victoria and gave birth to the famous gold field towns of Ballarat and Bendigo. The long delay between discovery and the rush to mine was probably due in part to a question of ownership, since in a British crown colony the crown had the right to gold and silver mines. The problem was eventually resolved *post facto* to mining by sale of licenses to the miners. The gold rush continued over the Australian continent, with ups and downs, throughout the 19th century. A rush to Darwin in the Northern Territories occurred in the '70s, and in the early '90s the great camps of Coolgardie and Kalgoolie—the golden mile—were discovered in Western Australia. Gold was also discovered in New Zealand in 1852 but it was not until 1861 that rich deposits were found and the rush took place; gold was discovered in New Guinea somewhat later.

Unlike the other newly discovered (from the European point of view) continents, however, gold was not the first metal exploited in Australia. Base metals were mined in South Australia at Glen Ozmond near Adelaide as early as 1841 (lead) and at the Burra mine by 1845 (copper). Copper was being exported from Adelaide by 1850. The lead ores of Glen Ozmond lasted about 10 years but copper continued to boom in South Australia. As the old Burra and Kapunda mines declined in the 1860s, the Walleroo and Moonta mines flourished. However, the high-grade ores were largely exhausted by the '80s. Many of the other famous base metal camps in Australia began as gold and silver mines. Mount Morgan in Queensland was a gold mine until 1886 when copper became the most important metal produced. Mount Lyell in Tasmania was likewise a gold camp from 1893 to 1902 when copper ores were developed. In 1883 the first claim was staked on the fabulous silver-lead-zinc deposit at Broken Hill in New South Wales. The copper-silver-lead-zinc ores of Mount Isa in Queensland were developed in 1923–24. An excellent account of the history of Australian mining camps is given by Blainey (1963).

Permian coals of Queensland and New South Wales were mined for local and domestic use in the 19th century, but major industrial utilization awaited construction of the first blast furnace at Newcastle in 1915. The low-grade brown coals of Victoria also became an important fuel source in the first decades of the 20th century. Iron ores for the Australian steel industry were developed about 1900 at Iron Knob in South Australia and large reserves were developed in the Middleback and Iron Monarch ranges. Exploration for iron ores beyond those needed to support the domestic steel industry was curtailed by restrictive export policies which remained in effect until 1960. When restrictions were relaxed, an iron boom resulted in the development of tremendous reserves of iron ore in the Hamersley province of western Australia about 800 miles north of Perth. Reserves of 15 billion tons are estimated and long-term export contracts with Japan have been signed.

After World War II, the worldwide search for radioactive minerals resulted in discovery of uranium ore at Rum Jungle south of Darwin in the Northern Territory. Another postwar development was the discovery and exploitation of bauxite deposits in the tropical Northern Territory. Attempts to find oil and gas in Australia met with failure until an encouraging strike in southeast Queensland in 1962 set off a wave of exploration over the continent which resulted in several natural gas discoveries in Queensland and South Australia in 1963. The oil fever continues high, encouraged by successes in 1965.

India and Burma.

The latter-day mineral history of India and Burma is the history of western culture and its material needs superposed on an ancient culture with a long mineral industry tradition. Ancient metal mines were widespread throughout India and their locations were generally known in the early 19th century; coal deposits and oil seeps were likewise a matter of record. In the late 19th century many of the old mining districts were reexamined and reexplored. It was more a time of rediscovery than discovery in a new land. Systematic, organized mining under European direction dates from the last several decades of the 19th century. The following chronology was compiled from Brown and Dey (1955).

The famous Raniganj coal field at the east end of the Upper Paleozoic Gondwana coal measures in the Indian Peninsula has been worked on a regular basis since 1814. Completion of the East India Railroad in 1855 stimulated production, and rapid expansion took place between 1880 and 1900. Iron had been mined and smelted in early times—by 326 B.C. at the time of Alexander's invasion, iron and steel weapons were used by the defenders. Early European attempts to establish a local industry based on charcoal failed. The first successful furnace was built in Raniganj coal field in 1882. Soon after the turn of the century (1904), the iron deposits in the States of Bihar and Orissa were discovered; and in succeeding years it developed that they constitute one of the great iron concentrations of the world with reserves measured in billions of tons. The Indian manganese industry of the Peninsula dates from 1891 and the chromium mining industry from about a decade later.

During the latter half of the 19th century much attention was given to the ancient gold mines of India. The most successful rediscovery was in the Kolar field in eastern Mysore where modern operations began in 1884. The ancient copper workings of the Singhbhum district were successfully reopened in 1908. The mica pegmatites of Bihar, known for centuries, began exports in 1884 and were under modern management by 1894. Other pegmatite minerals such as beryl have been produced from these pegmatites. The black beach sands of Travancore, containing ilmenite, monazite, zircon, garnet, and rutile have been mined since 1912. The bauxite ores of central India, first quarried in 1908, began to feed the first domestic aluminum plant in 1944. The first large-scale manufacture of Portland cement began in 1914.

Famous over the world are the rich silver-lead-zinc-copper ores of the great Bawdin mine in the Shan States of Burma. Worked by the Chinese as early as the 14th century, it closed in the mid-19th century because of political unrest and water problems, and reopened under European management in 1902. Burmese tin, likewise an ancient industry, expanded greatly after 1910; dredging began in the late 1920s. Tungsten mining in Burma also expanded about 1910. Oil seeps of Burma are recorded in ancient writings, and for centuries oil was bailed out of shallow wells. Commercial development by the Burmah Oil Company in Yenangyaung field dates from 1887.

Thus, the mineral industry of India and Burma, an old industry in an old land, was reborn and redirected over a period of about half a century under European impetus, the development of foreign markets for Indian and Burmese mineral products, and establishment of domestic industries.

The most romantic segment of the Indian and Burmese mineral industry is precious stones. Diamonds, rubies, and sapphires from Ceylon and southern India supplied the world for several thousands of years, and India was the only known source of diamonds until their discovery in Brazil in 1725. The rubies of the Mogok Valley in the Katha district of Upper Burma have been much prized, and stories of such gems plucked from the eyes of ancient idols have fascinated and delighted the world. In the 19th and 20th centuries there were attempts to reexplore ancient gem mines with varying degrees of success. Some mines are still in operation. Burma Ruby Mines, Limited, operated from 1889 to 1931 and produced gems valued at over 2 million pounds (Brown and Dey, 1955, p. 588).

Far East.

Information on the modern mineral history of the great Asiatic land area that is China is scant. Prior to World War II, China's principal mining industry was coal; deposits in north China and Manchuria are large. Reserves of iron, antimony, manganese, and tungsten likewise are large. The base metal picture is less clear—deposits of copper and tin in Yunnan and of lead and zinc in Hunan were the principal deposits worked prior to World War II. Information on subsequent discoveries and developments is not generally available in western countries. Deposits of bauxite, phosphate, and magnesite are probably being currently exploited. Since World War II, China has made a great effort to find and develop oil and gas deposits. It is certain that development of mineral resources is a necessary part of China's 'great leap forward' and consequently it can be deduced that China's communist state is carrying on an intense mineral exploration program. Wilson (1959, Chapter 12) visited China in 1958 and described a visit to the Institute of Geology; he reported new equipment, new geologic maps and evidence of many new mineral discoveries. In South Korea the famous Sangdong tungsten mine survived the war and is still producing.

Outside of the mainland, in Malaya and Indonesia, this century has seen large-scale tin mining, development of bauxite deposits, large-scale oil exploration and development, and development of iron deposits. In the Philippines, manganese, chromite, and gold have been produced in addition to iron. Japan has a fully developed mineral industry but resources are inadequate to satisfy the demand. It produces coal, iron, copper, sulfur, and oil in limited quantities.

Other 19th and 20th century developments.

Early in this century oil was discovered in the Middle East and by the late 1930s it was known that a large percentage of the world's crude oil reserves occur in Iran, Iraq, Arabia, and Kuwait. Large phosphate deposits have been discovered recently in Israel and Jordan. The Island of New Caledonia was for many years one of the principal suppliers of chromium and nickel ores. Chromium deposits in Turkey are mined for export to the big steel making nations. Nickel and manganese ores were exploited in Cuba and a large plant was built in the late 1950s to extract nickel from low-grade lateritic ores. The guano and underlying deposits of phosphatized rock on the Pacific islands, and to a lesser degree the Caribbean islands, have been an important source of phosphate, but by mid-20th century the smaller deposits were almost exhausted. Among the major producers in 1965 were Anguar, MaKatea, Nauru, Ocean, and Christmas Islands. For many years a rare mineral—cryolite, a sodium aluminum fluoride—has been mined in Greenland and used in the aluminum industry to make the electrolyte necessary for the electrolytic process of manufacturing aluminum. The mineral is now largely synthesized but mining of the Greenland deposit continues. In 1960 it was estimated that over a period of 50 years over 1 million tons had been mined, and reserves sufficient for 15 to 25 years operations were estimated.

REFERENCES

Bateman, A. M. (1955) Econ. Geol., 50th Anniversary Vol., Part I, pp. 1–37.

Blainey, Geoffrey (1963) The rush that never ended: Melbourne University Press, Melbourne, Australia, 367 pp.

Brown, J. C., and Dey, A. K. (1955) India's mineral wealth, 3rd ed.: Oxford University Press, New York, 761 pp.

Daubrée, Auguste (1879) Etudes synthétiques de géologie expérimentale: P. Vicq.-Dunod et Cie, Paris, 828 pp.

Davies, Oliver (1935) Roman mines in Europe: Oxford University Press, New York, 291 pp.

De Launay, Louis (1897) Contribution à l'étude de gites métallifères: P. Vicq-Dunod et Cie, Paris, 115 pp.

Élie de Beaumont, Leonce (1847) Note sur les émanations volcaniques et métalliferes: Bulletin de la Société Geologique de France, 2 série, t. iv, 85 pp.

Engineering and Mining Journal (1965) Brunswick Mining's huge complex to rely on world-wide technology: Eng. and Mining Jour., vol. 166, no. 12, pp. 70–75.

Forbes, R. J. (1963) Studies in ancient technology, Vol. VII: E. J. Brill, Leiden and Cologne, 253 pp.

Fouqué, A., and Michel-Lévy (1882) Synthése des minéraux et des roches: G. Masson, Paris, 423 pp.

Posĕpný, Ferencz (1893) The genesis of ore deposits: Trans. Amer. Inst. Mining and Met. Engrs., vol. 23, pp. 197–369.

Vogt, J. H. L. (1894) Ueber die durch pneumatolytische Processe an Granit gebundenen Mineral-Neubildungen: Zeit. prakt. Geol., v.z., pp. 458–465.

Von Cotta, Bernhard (1859) Die Lehre von den Erzlagerstatten, 2nd ed.: Freiberg, 2 vols.

Wilson, J. Tuzo (1959) One Chinese moon: Hill and Wang, New York, 247 pp.

CHAPTER VII

OWNERSHIP OF MINERAL DEPOSITS

Introduction.

History has shown repeatedly that the question of ownership of anything does not assume much importance until that thing acquires value. When the value is large, claims of ownership are tested rigorously. Many wars—in courtrooms and on battlefields—have been fought to gain control of valuable mineral resources. As population swells, distribution and adequacy of resources become more and more important, and questions of ownership or control become more vital. The so-called *tidelands* of the United States offer a good example. Whether the ownership of these submerged lands was vested in the states or the federal government was of little concern until valuable deposits of oil and gas were discovered off the shore, whereupon both parties vigorously asserted ownership. The matter was fought in the courts and finally made the subject of new legislation (p. 173). Court contests have continued. California based its claim to submerged lands beyond the three-mile limit on its historic seaward boundaries as fixed by the channel islands, but in May 1965 the Supreme Court decided against the state and in favor of federal ownership of the lands. Ownership of land and fresh-water resources is the subject of both domestic and international wrangles, and more and more the right of an owner to use his property as he sees fit is being challenged by the concept of *public good*—expressed through police powers, conservation laws, zoning laws, and expanded use of *eminent domain* by various authorities to seize land for public purposes. Thus, an owner is constrained to conform to certain practices judged as good for society in general. The owner of city real estate, for example, may be prohibited from constructing a high-rise structure on his property because of alleged detraction from the aesthetic quality of the city skyline. The competition for increased supplies of municipal, industrial, and irrigation water has spawned large-scale water transport projects which involve movement of surplus water from one region some hundreds of miles to a water-deficient region. Many residents in the region of 'surplus' protest such appropriation.

Most interesting is the serious consideration now being given to ownership of the seas and sea floors. In earlier times the sea was first a food resource and later a transportation resource. As international trade became more and more necessary for economic survival, the principle of *freedom of the seas* was thrashed out in war after war and finally established. The next question arose over rights to prime fishing grounds. Some nations have asserted exclusive rights for a distance of 200 miles off their coastlines. When these claims are not recognized by fishing boats of other nations, armed conflict and seizures are common. Now, oceanographic studies of the last two decades have demonstrated the presence of accumulations of phosphorite on parts of the continental shelves and of manganese nodules on parts of the shelf and sea floor. Do these belong to the first nation with engineering ability to harvest them? The problem was considered by two United Nations Conferences on the Law of the Sea, the First Geneva Conference of 1958 and the Second Geneva Conference of 1960; and a number of Conventions were finally ratified by the member states in 1964 (Shalowitz, 1962; Eng. and Mining Jour., 1964, p. 85; Shalowitz, 1965, p. 1412). Under the now existing convention, title to the sea floor is vested in a coastal state to a water depth of 200 meters or beyond as far as the capability to exploit the sea floor extends. The mineral industry is now waiting with interest for the resolution of ownership of valuable natural gas deposits which underlie the North Sea where England, The Netherlands, Germany, Denmark, and Norway all have interests. In December of 1965 a

White House Conference on International Cooperation heard a proposal from a special panel to the effect that ocean floor mining should be regulated by the United Nations through a special agency. The problems encountered in formulating a modern law of the sea were well stated by Chapman (1965, p. 390) :

The primary problem with which we are here engaged, it appears to me, is not a knowledge of the law of the sea, or a lack of the law of the sea, but a most frustrating inability to quickly change the law of the sea to conform either to our ideas of how it should be construed, or to keep it abreast of new demands brought about by new sorts of uses capable of being made of the sea arising from the application of advances in science and technology. The new problems arising out of the burgeoning increase in knowledge and understanding of the ocean, and of new technologies capable of utilizing this new knowledge and understanding, are thrusting themselves at us in an intemperate and uncontrollable rush; at the same time we do not have several of the old problems yet resolved.

Systems of mineral ownership.

Earliest concepts of mineral ownership were indistinguishable from land ownership and really involved land holding rather than fee ownership in the modern sense. Hunting grounds, water holes, springs, salt licks, and perhaps flint deposits were held by a tribe in a communal way. With the emergence of kings and god-kings, the interests of the tribe in real estate were vested in an absolute ruler or overlord who *owned* the property as part of his patrimony, or as a divine right, with the community subject to his overriding authority. As part of this authority he could grant or confiscate property. Such ideas of ownership culminated at an early date with the pharaohs of Egypt. The mines of Egypt belonged to the pharaoh. Although certain properties were conveyed to priests and other favored individuals in return for services, their tenure was a shaky one without any real protection under a legal system. This was the beginning of the regalian system under which mineral ownership is vested in the crown or state.

Greek creativity, the concept of the citizen, and a regard for individual rights resulted in a new system. Although minerals were considered to be state property, they were held to be resources to be developed for the benefit of people. The silver mines were regarded as state property; however, they were not operated by the state. They were leased to an operator—an individual or company—who made an initial payment for the lease and thereafter a rent of 1/24 of the production in bullion. Failure to comply was punishable by fines and ultimately by forfeiture of the lease. The lease amounted to owner-

FIGURE VII.1 Ownership of the North Sea (after Eng. and Mining Jour., 1964a, p. 85).

ship and could be sold or passed by inheritance; however, the lease terms were rather short and according to Rickard (1932, p. 371) varied from 3 to 10 years. The district was divided into tracts and leasing was under the control of a board of magistrates. A mining code administered by a director of mines spelled out the terms of the leases in detail (Ely, 1964, p. 82). The silver mines at Laurium constituted the chief asset of the city state of Athens, financing their war machine, including navies, and providing a sound, hard currency which made Athens a trade capitol. At times the income from the mines was distributed in the form of a bonus to the citizens of Athens (p. 94). The mines were of such importance to Athens that laws were passed to prevent abuse of the properties and insure proper mining methods; thus, in 339 B.C. a law was passed to prohibit removal of supporting pillars (Rickard, 1932, p. 377). Over the centuries it has been well demonstrated that a lessee system is not compatible with good mining and conservation principles. The lessee, with no vested interest in the property, tries to extract the largest possible quantity of high-grade ore during the life of his tenancy. The common result is to 'high grade' the mine, leaving the low-grade ores behind, and to destroy the support system where ore has been left as pillars. This is perhaps not true now as in the past, but the best protection for the owner is a lease which spells out operating standards and is enforced.

One of the glories that was Rome's was establishment of a single authority over the then civilized world. Roman civil law, particularly the revisions and codifications made by Emperor Justinian in the 6th century, forms the base for a substantial part of the western world's modern legal systems. The Roman concept of mineral owner-ship is called the Accession System (American Law of Mining, 1964, p. 5) and in general provided that minerals are an accessory of the surface and that the ownership of the surface carries with it the ownership of the minerals. However, throughout the long history of Rome, mining law changed and evolved as the political structure changed. Within the bounds of the early republic, the Roman citizen who owned the land also owned the mineral deposits, except for gold (p. 99). However, rich metal mines were scarce in Italy, except in the far north of the peninsula, so that mining was not a common enterprise around the Roman capital, as it was near Athens in an earlier era. In fact there developed in Italy the view that mining was an abuse of the land, was not a fit occupation for a citizen, and should be discouraged within Italy itself. Rickard (1932, pp. 406–412, 579) and Forbes (1963, pp. 153–154) speculated on the reasons for this attitude, suggesting prevention of land abuse, conservation (even to the point of giving mineral deposits time to grow back), and fear of large working slave camps near the capital as possible explanations. Perhaps this attitude would not have developed if the Romans had not been so successful in acquiring large supplies of metals as well as rich mining districts through conquest. The Romans appreciated the value and utility of metals.

Early in Rome's history, about 625 B.C., salt works were established at Ostia to supply the growing city demands (Rickard, 1932, pp. 403–404). Shallow basins were dug along the shore of the Tiber estuary and the salt was harvested following natural evaporation. The installations were public property leased to operators. After a period of profiteering, the state stepped in and took over operation in the public interest. When the properties were again returned to lease operation, the price was set by the government. A fixed rent was paid to the state.

Much the same system was followed in Rome's foreign mineral properties. Ownership was vested in the state by right of conquest. Mines were leased to Roman citizens who then were obligated to pay a royalty or rent to the state. The terms and procedures changed through history and differed in various parts of the republic and empire. At times, particularly during the latter days of the republic, private individuals made large fortunes from mines outside Italy, and by the time of the early empire many mines had been sold (Forbes, 1963, p. 154). During the later empire, the tendency was to make all mines state property and to lease them to entrepreneurs. Under one system, entrepreneurs bid on groups of mines and contracted to pay a fixed sum to the state. They then levied their own taxes up to the limit that the operation could support (Rickard, 1932, p. 415). State ownership-lease systems were even extended to Italy, overriding the old law which tied minerals to the surface ownership. Mining codes were promulgated in great detail in various districts (Rickard, 1932, pp. 582–592).

Ely (1964, p. 82) described the usufruct system which resulted from the Justinian Code in the 6th century as follows:

Usufruct was defined as the right to use another's property and to take its fruits so long as the substance was not impaired. The usufruct could be created for the life of the usufructary, the life of another, or for a term of years, but usually it was not regarded as alienable. However, the rights created by the usufructary, where mines or quarries existed on the land, were limited to the operation of those mines or quarries; the opening of new mines was prohibited as a violation of the usufruct.

As the empire declined and the need for new gold and silver supplies became urgent, the usufruct system was abandoned and mines were operated by state-appointed officials under heavy obligations to produce. As incentives, however, they had rights to own and sell land and an opportunity to profit themselves. Mines were also bestowed on individuals as rewards for service to the Emperor.

The collapse of organized government and the onset of the Dark Ages placed mines and all other land under the primitive land-holding system of feudalism whereby a nobility held lands as tenants according to the pleasure of the king. But even as the Roman legions departed, the seeds of British common law began to grow in the ancient mining districts of England. Common law is law based on principles hammered out through long custom and formalized in courts. It contrasts with civil law which is statutory and derived from government actions, either legislative or autocratic.

In England the mining communities struggled through the feudal period, contesting with kings, local lords, and the church for their long established rights to enter upon certain lands to prospect for and produce minerals, and even to cut timber and take fuel necessary for mining operations. From time to time, the king found it to his interest to take the side of the miners against their feudal lords, to curb powers of the privileged class, and to increase the revenue to the royal treasury. In the ancient lead district of Derbyshire, through long custom, claims or meers could be marked off and held by working them, even to being passed from father to son. A royalty or 'dish' was paid to surface owners. A local impartial barmaster supervised the mining activities and acted as intermediary between miner and surface owner, and a special Great Court Barmote settled disputes. In the old tin districts of Devonshire and Cornwall similar claims or bounds were marked on the ground and then proclaimed in a special stannery court; if there was no protest, a write of possession was issued. As in Derbyshire a royalty or 'toll' was paid to the surface owner. As English common law developed outside of the old mining districts, it paralleled the old Roman civil law as it was first applied in Italy. The ownership of the surface estate carried with it the ownership of everything beneath. So in England, except in the ancient mining centers ruled by custom, the freeholder owned the minerals unless they had been separated by some prior conveyance. However, the crown owned all gold and silver mines and the king had the coinage prerogative. A question was raised as to the crown's ownership of base metal mines which principally produced copper, tin, and lead but which contained minor amounts of gold and silver. During the reign of William and Mary, in the latter part of the 17th century, this problem was resolved by statutes confirming the crown's ownership of mines where gold and silver occurred in the pure state, granting to the crown ownership of all mines beneath navigable rivers and below high tide level, and giving the crown the right to purchase base metal ores containing gold and silver at the prescribed price (American Law of Mining, 1964, p. 4).

Hoover (1912, pp. 84–86) commented on the evolution of British mining law as follows:

In England the law varied with special mining communities, such as Cornwall, Devon, the Forest of Dean, the Forest of Mendip, Alston Moor, and the High Peak, and they exhibit a curious complex of individual growth, of profound interest to the student of the growth of institutions. These communities were of very ancient origin, some of them at least pre-Roman; but we are, except for the reference in Pliny, practically without any idea of their legal doings until after the Norman occupation (1066 A.D.). The genius of these conquerers for systematic government soon led them to inquire into the doings of these communities, and while gradually systematising their customs into law, they lost no occasion to assert the regalian right to the minerals. In the two centuries subsequent to their advent there are on record numerous inquisitions, with the recognition and confirmation of 'the customs and liberties which had existed from time immemorial,' always with the reservation to the Crown of some sort of royalty. Except for the High Peak in Derbyshire, the period and origin of these 'customs and liberties' are beyond finding out, as there is practically no record of English History between the Roman withdrawal and the Norman occupation. There may have been 'liberties' under the Romans, but there is not a shred of evidence on the subject, and our own belief is that the forms of self-government which sprang up were the result of the Roman evacuation. The miner had little to complain of in the Norman treatment in these matters; but between the Crown and the landlord as represented by the Barons, Lords of the Manor, etc., there were wide differences of opinion on the regalian rights, for in the extreme interpretation of the Crown it tended greatly to curtail the landlord's position in the matter, and the success of the Crown on this subject was by no means universal. In fact, a considerable portion of English legal history of mines is but the outcropping of this conflict, and one of the concessions wrung from King John at Runnymede in 1215 was his abandonment of a portion of such claims.

The mining communities of Cornwall and Devon were early in the 13th century definitely chartered into corporations—"The Stannaries"—possessing definite legislative and executive functions, judicial powers, and practical self-government; but they were required to make payment of the tithe in the shape of 'coinage' on the tin. Such recognition, while but a ratification of prior custom, was not obtained without struggle, for the Norman Kings early asserted wide rights over the mines. Tangible record of mining in these parts, from a legal point of view, practically begins with a report by William de Wrotham in 1198 upon his arrangements regarding the coinage. A charter of King John in 1201, while granting free right of entry to the miners, thus usurped the rights of the landlords—a claim which he was compelled by the Barons to moderate;

the Crown, as above mentioned, did maintain its right to a royalty, but the landlord held the minerals. It is not, however, until the time of Richard Carew's 'Survey of Cornwall' (London, 1602) that we obtain much insight into details of miners' title, and the customs there set out were maintained in broad principle down to the 19th Century. At Carew's time the miner was allowed to prospect freely upon 'Common' or wastrel lands (since mostly usurped by landlords), and upon mineral discovery marked his boundaries, within which he was entitled to the vertical contents. Even upon such lands, however, he must acknowledge the right of the lord of the manor to a participation in the mine. Upon 'enclosed' lands he had no right of entry without the consent of the landlord; in fact, the minerals belonged to the land as they do to-day except where voluntarily relinquished. In either case he was compelled to 'renew his bounds' once a year, and to operate more or less continuously to maintain the right once obtained. There thus existed a 'labour condition' of variable character, usually imposed more or less vigorously in the bargains with landlords. The regulations in Devonshire differed in the important particular that the miner had right of entry to private lands, although he was not relieved of the necessary to give a participation of some sort to the landlord. The Forests of Dean, Mendip, and other old mining communities possessed a measure of self-government, which do not display any features in their law fundamentally different from those of Cornwall and Devon. The High Peak lead mines of Derbyshire, however, exhibit one of the most profoundly interesting of these mining communities. As well as having distinctively Saxon names for some of the mines, the customs there are of undoubted Saxon origin, and as such their ratification by the Normans caused the survival of one of the few Saxon institutions in England—a fact which, we believe, has been hitherto overlooked by historians. Beginning with inquisitions by Edward I, in 1288, there is in the Record Office a wealth of information, the bare titles of which form too extensive a list to set out here. (Of published works, the most important are Edward Manlove's 'The Liberties and Customs of the Lead Mines within the Wapentake of Wirksworth,' London, 1653, generally referred to as the 'Rhymed Chronicle'; Thomas Houghton, 'Rara Avis in Terra,' London, 1687; William Hardy 'The Miner's Guide,' Sheffield, 1748; Thomas Tapping, 'High Peak Mineral Customs,' London, 1851). The miners in this district were presided over by a 'Barmaster,' 'Barghmaster,' or 'Barmar,' as he was variously spelled, all being a corruption of the German Bergmeister, with precisely the same functions as to the allotment of title, settlement of disputes, etc., as his Saxon progenitor had, and, like him, he was advised by a jury. The miners had entry to all lands except churchyards, (this regulation waived upon death), and a few similar exceptions, and was subject to royalty to the Crown and the landlord. The discoverer was entitled to a finder's 'meer' of extra size, and his title to the vein within the end lines, i.e., the 'apex' law. This title was held subject to rigorous labour conditions, amounting to forfeiture for failure to operate the mine for a period of nine weeks. Space does not permit the elaboration of the details of this subject, which we hope to pursue elsewhere in its many historical bearings. Among these we may mention that if the American 'Apex law' is of English descent, it must be laid to the door of Derbyshire, and not of Cornwall, as is generally done. Our own belief, however, is that the American 'apex' conception came straight from Germany.

The mining communities of central Europe also fought successfully to establish 'free mining' in the framework of the feudal land tenancy system. Mining districts in Germany were administered by a prefect and burgomaster (*Bergmeister*) responsible to the ruling prince. Claims or meers were marked on the ground, with a discoverer rewarded by a larger tract or head meer, and converted to lease. The mineral estate was separated from the surface but the ruling prince owned both and in him was vested the right to grant such leases. The miner had the right to follow the ore downward whether or not it passed outside of the vertical extensions of his meer boundaries. The struggle between the miners and their sovereigns was resolved when the sovereign recognized the right of the miner to free prospecting and the miner agreed to the right of the ruler to a tithe or royalty from production. Agricola (1556, Book IV) described in detail the laying out of a meer, the responsibilities of the mining prefect, *Bergmeister*, jurors, mining clerk, share clerk, mine manager, foremen, and workmen.

The Regalian Theory.

As Middle Ages passed into Renaissance, there were significant departures between English common law as applied to land ownership and mineral tenure and the various civil law systems prevailing on the European continent. In all of the prevailing systems the precious metals—gold and silver—were regarded as the patrimony of the sovereign. However, one theory separated the surface estate from the mineral estate and held that the sovereign was the absolute proprietor of the minerals; the surface owner might be compensated for damages sustained in the mining operation. Another theory regarded the two estates as one and held that the owner of the surface also owned the subsurface minerals, but that if he were unwilling or unable to exploit the minerals another might secure the right to mine. Both of these theories included the state's right to a royalty payment or tithe. The English system carried this latter theory the farthest, and save for the crown's interest in precious metals and ancient laws in certain districts, the surface landowner could mine any mineral without owing anything to anybody. The English crown's right to gold and silver mines caused repercussions in the mid-19th century during the great Australian gold rush, when the Australian government forced miners already at work to purchase a license to mine gold. The history of mining law is discussed by Rickard (1932, Ch. XI), American Law of Mining (1964, pp. 1–7), and Ely (1964, Ch. III). Various writers on the subject have alleged that all of these systems grew out of the Roman civil codes, particularly the Justinian Code. This is perhaps a reflection of how the Roman system changed from republic through empire, rather than a matter for controversy. In the early days of the Roman republic the citizen who owned the surface of the land was also the proprietor of the minerals (excepting gold which Strabo reported as property of the state). As Rome expanded by conquest, the state owned and later owned and operated mines in conquered territories. And, finally, under the autocratic Caesars all mines fell into the hands of the Roman state.

When the great voyages of discovery sallied from Spain and Portugal in the late 15th and early 16th century, the regalian theory of mineral ownership prevailed in those countries, and the crown's right to gold and silver mines was uncontested. In Spain the prevailing civil code was known as the *Siete Partidas* and dates from 1400. Francisco Xavier de Gamboa in his "Commentaries on the Mining Ordinances of Spain," published in 1761 (Heathfield Translation, 1830, Vol. I), argued that gold and silver mines should be part of the sovereign's patrimony for coinage, defense, public necessities, maintenance of good government, maintenance of his honor, and to relieve the people of taxes that would otherwise be necessary (Rickard, 1932, p. 593). Under the *Siete Partidas,* although all miners owed a royalty to the crown (standardized as 1/5 in 1504), only gold and silver mines were the property of the crown. This was changed by the royal mining ordinance of 1783 when Charles III, King of Spain, declared *all* mines as the property of the crown without regard to the kind of ores or the location of the property. This clearly and effectively separated surface and mineral ownership; at the same time, he promulgated mining regulations in detail, describing procedures for denouncements, provided for adjustment of disputes, and provided for compensation of surface owners. Royalty due to the crown was set at 1/5 of production. The right of exploitation conveyed by the concession was a temporary right; the state remained as the perpetual proprietor.

The French version of the regalian system differs from the Spanish. Under the Napoleonic Code (1810) the question of ownership of minerals did not arise until the act of discovery. Minerals were not owned by the state, as in the Spanish system, but they were under the control of the state. Following discovery, the minerals were conveyed by concession from the state to an operator. If the operator was other than the owner of the surface, then the surface owner was compensated, but the compensation was for the severed property rather than for damages. There is then an implication that the surface owner had a proprietary right, albeit subordinate to that of the state to control exploitation; the two estates, however, were separate. Ely (1964, p. 87) said:

The Mining Code of 1810, incorporated in the Napoleonic Code, made a clear distinction between surface and subterranean proprietorship, and put the estate in minerals on a basis as secure as that of real estate. The law provided that although the ownership of the surface carried with it the right to subsurface minerals, the government, through the concept of the concession, might separate the two estates, granting the estate in minerals, even in perpetuity, to one other than the owner of the estate in land, on the single condition that the latter be compensated by the payment of royalties. Mines could only be worked if actually conceded, and it was the act of concession that vested the property in the concessionaire with the power to dispose thereof in the same manner as real property, except that the area conceded could not be subdivided and sold without the consent of the government.

Napoleon is reported to have taken a personal interest in the mining code which required four years of preparation—he personally made changes in it up until one month before its promulgation on April 21, 1810. Paul A. Bailly (personal communication, 1966) on the basis of lectures by Professor Luchaire at The University of Nancy, summed up the essential features of the code as follows:

1. The government manages all the subsurface rights which are owned by the nation. This is characterized by French lawyers as owned by nobody whereas in the United States it would be labelled as publicly owned.
2. Prospecting can take place only in areas where permits have been obtained from the state. The state gives certain rights to the discoverer; but the right to develop and exploit is not conveyed automatically to the discoverer.
3. A mining concession is granted only after proof of discovery and only to a person or company which can demonstrate mining competence. The concession does not require the holder to pay to the state any royalty related to production; however, each concession stipulates certain payments or nominal rentals to the owner of the surface and a payment related to production to the dis-

coverer in case the concession holder is not the discoverer. The concession is granted in perpetuity and provides a security of tenure approaching that of a fee owner.

4. The state reserves the right to maintain public order on concession territory, the right of approval of operational plans to assure that exploitation is rational and not wasteful, and the right of approval and control of safety plans and safety measures.

State mine inspectors in France are powerful officials whose position requires a high level of academic preparation.

On the modern scene regalian principles have given rise to government monopolies—phosphate in Morocco, coal and uranium in France, petroleum in Mexico. These are commonly justified as necessary for tax revenues, the public interest, or national defense.

Mineral law in the United States.

In the early days of European settlement of the area that is now the United States, Spanish law prevailed in the southwest and in Florida and the various colonial charters obtained along the Atlantic coast. Most of these royal charters granted title to the minerals but reserved 1/5 of the gold and silver produced as a royalty to the king. The variations from the general rule included the Massachusetts Colony wherein precious stones were included in the royalty reservation, the first Virginia Charter which also reserved 1/15 of the copper, and the grant made to the Duke of York by Charles II covering the lands of New York, New Jersey, and Delaware wherein no mineral reservation was made (American Law of Mining, 1964, p. 6). According to Ely (1964, p. 89), however, the crown's reservation of gold and silver was implied whether stated or not.

Following separation from England, the State of New York asserted state ownership of gold and silver mines. Patents issued by William Penn made a similar reservation but such state ownership was never successfully asserted and was in fact abandoned about the middle of the 19th century. If either New York or Pennsylvania, or any of the other original states, had proved to be richly endowed with gold and silver deposits, the question of ownership might have been more hotly contested. The Continental Congress in 1785 passed an Ordinance regarding disposition of lands in the western territories which reserved 1/3 part of all gold, silver, copper, and lead mines, but the reservation became invalid on dissolution of the Congress, or at least was never put into effect.

Following the Revolution, the new government at first looked to the sale of the newly acquired public domain to finance its operations. Three large blocks were sold prior to organization of the government, and subsequently, in 1790, Alexander Hamilton proposed a plan to finance the government through such sales. An act passed in 1796 generally followed the earlier Continental Congress Land Ordinance of 1785 but reserved only salt springs and no other minerals. The land surveyed to be sold under this act was Ohio agricultural land. The policy of sale continued from 1796 to 1841.

Because prospective settlers were in general poor, the effect of the policy was to discourage settlement rather than promote it. By 1830 the desirability of encouraging settlement on the public domain was recognized and the result was the Pre-emption Act of 1841 which provided that a citizen who settled and improved a tract of land not to exceed 160 acres might enter the tract for a minimum price of $1.25 per acre. Prior to this act, the copper lands of Michigan were sold at auction to the highest bidder, and the lead lands of the Mississippi Valley were first leased (1807–1829) and then sold (after 1829) to the highest bidder. The Pre-emption Act of 1841 reserved to the federal government the lands containing known salt springs or saline deposits. By reserving the *lands,* the statute avoided any separation of surface and mineral estates. This policy was to cause a great deal of confusion in later years when the mineral character of certain lands had to be determined. In 1862, the Homestead Law added further inducement to settlers by removing any cash consideration on the part of the pioneer; and thus the policy of sale of public lands for revenue came to an end. Under the Homestead Law, the settler who complied with requirements relating to residence, improvement, and land use could obtain title.

The United States and its public domain grew through a series of acquisitions. The Louisiana Purchase (1803), Treaty with Spain (1819), Treaty of Guadalupe Hidalgo (1848), Gadsden Purchase (1853), Northwest Compromise (1846, 1872), and Purchase of Alaska (1867) increased the public domain by nearly one and a half billion acres. The Republic of Texas entered the Union (1845) without ceding any of its public lands to the Federal government of the United States and thus this addition to the Union did not add to the public domain; the Texas public lands were disposed of under state law much as they were disposed of under the earlier Republic of Texas (1836–1845). The General Land Office of the republic became the General Land Office of the state. Territory in Hawaii,

Puerto Rico, the Philippines, Guam, and the Virgin Islands did not become part of the public domain of the United States.

These various lands had been administered under the flags of several nations and under different legal systems of mineral ownership prior to their inclusion within the United States of America. In the former Spanish territories, for example, under the regalian system, minerals had never been conveyed to owners of the surface. To avoid injustices, treaties of cessation called for recognition of pre-existing rights, but this did not mean that the United States as the new proprietor had to adopt a foreign legal code. In 1845, the Supreme Court held that in regard to lands acquired under treaty with Spain in 1819 the United States government did not thereby succeed to the sovereign rights of the King of Spain, remarking that a nation which acquires territory by treaty or by any other means is obliged to govern that territory according to its own laws and constitution (Ely, 1964, p. 90). In an extension of this philosophy pertaining to prior Mexican grants in lands ceded to the United States by the Treaty of Guadalupe Hidalgo, the United States conveyed to the holder of the grant the full mineral estate with the confirming U.S. patent. The United States was obligated by the treaty to respect such prior grants but there were many conflicts, particularly in southern California, which arose over establishment of the validity of the Mexican grants under Mexican law.

As the United States was acquiring land in large chunks it was also disposing of lands in a variety of ways. The sale of lands for revenue began as soon as the formation of the republic, starting with the Land Act of 1796 and continuing through public auctions and the Pre-emption Act of 1841. The early land ordinance of the Continental Congress in 1785 conveyed to the individual states section 16 in each new township surveyed, as a grant-in-aid of education to maintain the public schools; subsequent legislation in 1848 added section 36, and in some of the newer states an additional two sections were granted. Mineral lands were first excluded from the school land grants and if the designated sections were mineral in character other 'indemnity' lands were granted. In such reservations there was always the critical matter of the date when the land was classified (by the Secretary of Interior) as mineral or nonmineral. This was taken as the date of survey or the date of the grant, if not surveyed. If the lands were found to be mineral after this date, the state became the proprietor of the minerals. However, the unfortunate vagueness of 'mineral character' and how and when the character was to be determined clouded titles for many years until in 1927 Congress included mineral lands in the state school selection lands provided that the states themselves would reserve the minerals, and that proceeds from them would be used to support public education. The problem of titles was not fully resolved until 1934 when Congress authorized the issuance of patents to the states to confirm state title to these mineral and nonmineral school lands irrespective of the date of classification. Further problems were resolved in 1954 in connection with lands under federal lease for oil and gas at the time they were surveyed and the school land sections designated. The Dawson Act conveyed title to the state and permitted the state to succeed the federal government as lessor.

Approximately 130 million acres of the public domain was divested between 1850 and 1871 as railroad grants or subsidies—the figure has been estimated as high as 150 million acres. The first grants went to states to encourage railroad-building and included grants for construction as well as the land for right-of-way; subsequent grants directly to railroads, mostly in the West, provided 'place' lands to aid construction to consist of ten alternate odd-numbered sections per mile within a strip ten miles wide on both sides of the right-of-way. Mineral lands (except for coal and iron deposits) were excluded so the railroad was given the right to select 'indemnity' lands composed of odd-numbered sections in a second ten-mile-wide strip. Much the same problems with respect to minerals arose as with the school land grants. Because of the long term which customarily elapsed between vesting of title in the railroad (when the line was constructed in the case of place lands and when the selection was made in the case of indemnity lands), the railroads argued that the mineral character of the land should be determined when title was vested and that any subsequent discovery of minerals prior to the issuance of the patent should not withdraw the lands from the grant. However, in 1893, the court held that the Secretary of Interior could determine the mineral character up until the U.S. patent was issued and withdraw the land from the grant if it was found to be mineral in character. The question of whether or not the railroad right-of-way itself was conveyed in fee without a reservation of the minerals was not decided until 1957 (American Law of Mining, 1964, p. 14) when the Supreme Court held in divided opinion that the minerals did not pass. This verdict has been attacked on the grounds that it was a hindsight judgment involving a policy of separation of surface and minerals that did not exist at the time the grant was made—when the policy was to exclude mineral lands rather than to separate the two estates. In Texas between 1852 and 1882, the state granted some 32 million acres to railroads with the proviso that the railroad company undertake the surveying job. Sixteen sections per mile were granted to the company providing they would locate a like amount for the state. As elsewhere in the West, the railroads took odd-numbered sections and the state took even-numbered sections. In the case of the M.E.P. and P.R.R. line, later the Texas and Pacific, the company for a period of time was given exclusive option to locate its certificates in a belt 40 miles wide along its route. Through later trading, some of the railroads consolidated their alternate sections into blocks which could be operated or leased as grazing units on an economically sounder basis. In Texas no mineral or mineral lands were reserved so that the railroads acquired an endowment which, now that the early financial strains of construction and maintenance have been replaced by financial strains due to competition and changing social and economic patterns, serves them in good stead. However, because much of the Trans-Pecos country of Texas was poorly surveyed, there was much uncertainty about section corners, and therefore much uncertainty about mineral ownership of particular tracts of land. This uncertainty resulted in much hardship for prospectors and, in fact, made Texas an unfavorable region for prospecting. In an address in 1903, William B. Phillips (1903, p. 26), Director of The University of Texas Mineral Survey, said:

It has also been held that the difficulty of knowing just where the boundary lines between the public school sections and the railroad and private lands were to be found has kept prospectors and miners from opening mining property.

Questions about mineral ownership also arose over the swamp-land grants (1849–50) which granted to the states various swamps and lands subject to flood to promote reclamation projects; the minerals, in light of the U.S. government's failure to reserve minerals or mineral lands, passed to the states (Ely, 1964, pp. 92–93). The various agricultural acts (Pre-emption, Homestead, Desert Land Entry, and Enlarged Entry Acts) excepted mineral *lands* from entry. Likewise, the scrip issued by the government to be exchanged for lands did not entitle the holder to select mineral lands. It was not until 1916, with the passage of the Stock Raising Homestead Act, that the United States severed mineral estate from surface estate and reserved minerals instead of mineral *lands*.

Mining law in the United States was forged in the gold camps of

California and is in many ways a tool of strange design. During the period 1848–1866, in the absence of any state or federal law, the miners organized into districts, formulated their own laws, and enforced them. By 1866 there were perhaps a thousand such organized districts in California and other western territories. In 1851 the California legislature recognized mining district customs so long as they did not conflict with state law. There was thus established the grounds for a common law of mining which in general recognized that a valid mining claim rested on discovery, appropriation, and development and that in any conflict a priority in time constituted a priority in right. These principles were subsequently validated by mining legislation. There was also introduced in some districts the 'extralateral'

FIGURE VII.2

A lode claim under United States mining law.

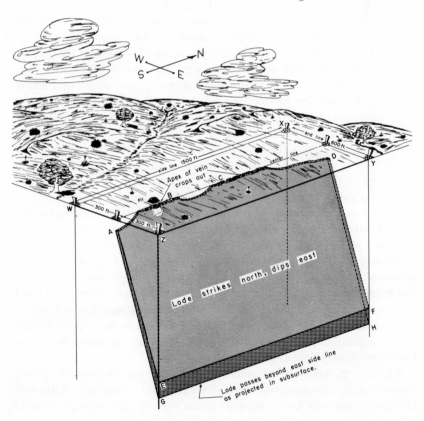

right, that is, the right of a miner working a lode to follow the deposit downward even though the natural dip or inclination of the body caused it to pass beyond the downward vertical extension of the side line of the claim as marked on the surface (Fig. VII.2). This "right" to follow the lode downward had its antecedents in the ancient practices developed in Derbyshire, England, or in Germany (p. 157), and some historians have credited 'Cornish' miners with importing these ideas into the western mining districts of the United States after the California gold rush. Because water was necessary for mining as well as agricultural operations, water law developed with mining law as miners and farmers and ranchers contested for water. Here again the first appropriator was vested with the prior right, notwithstanding the use of the water for mining or agricultural purposes.

Out of the need for order on the public lands of the states and territories grew the federal mining legislation of 1866, 1870, and 1872. The first law of 1866 legalized the existing state of affairs. A distant Congress thereby showed considerable wisdom and probably prevented years of anarchy and violence on the public lands of the West. The act provided that (1) all mineral lands in the public domain were free and open to exploration and development; (2) rights previously acquired under local rules through acquiescence and implied sanction on the part of the government were recognized and confirmed; and (3) through compliance with regulations of the statute, title might be obtained to mineral deposits. The 1866 act was subsequently modified by the acts of 1870 and 1872 which provided for the patenting of lode and placer claims; this law, although criticized in this time as archaic and unworkable, remains as the law governing mineral location on the public domain.

The act of 1866 was not passed without opposition. An eastern faction favored sale or lease of federal mineral lands to raise money to defray the costs of the Civil War. A Senate amendment, defeated, proposed to declare all the gold extracted from the mines of California as U.S. property and to pay the miners for the service performed in extracting it. Another, the Homestead Law for Gold and Silver, proposed to auction mineral lands in 40-acre tracts, requiring that a tract be mined out before the owner would be permitted to buy another tract (O'Callaghan, 1962, p. 36). But finally ideas of extracting a royalty from the miners was abandoned.

The Placer Act of 1870 amended the 1866 act by defining placer deposits and providing for their location and patenting. Although the earlier act was broad enough to include placers, certain sections were applicable only to lodes. Subsequently, both the act of 1866 and the act of 1870 were combined into the Mineral Location Law of 1872.

Very briefly summarized, the act of 1872 provided that a citizen of the United States (including corporations) or an individual who had expressed the intention of becoming a citizen might enter upon the public domain and, upon making a discovery of minerals, might mark his claim, or any number of claims containing a discovery, on the ground and hold his claim by performing a minimum amount of assessment work on it each year (work valued at 100 dollars) or by working it to produce minerals therefrom. Most state laws required that notice of the claim be filed in the county courthouse where records of such claims are maintained. However, this is not a federal requirement, and prior to application for a patent, there is no federal record of the claim. State laws commonly impose location requirements over and above the federal requirements. These mostly concern details of discovery and corner posts and the nature of the discovery shaft or pit. The locator may seek title from the United States by applying for a patent. Notice of intent must be posted on the claim, in the Land Office (Bureau of Land Management), and in the local newspapers. The applicant must offer proof of citizenship, proof of the mineral character of the land, proof that at least 500 dollars worth of improvements have been made, and an official survey of the property. Conflicting claims are resolved in the courts. The price is 5 dollars per acre for lode claims and 2.5 dollars per acre for placer claims. After the patent is issued the full title including title to the surface passes to the locator and thereafter he may make any use of the land that he sees fit. Prior to receiving a patent, the locators' rights to a claim are protected under a doctrine known as *Pedis Possessio;* it means 'actual possession' and has been variously construed to refer to the area immediately surrounding the working area or, more liberally, to the entire surface of the claim (Ladendorff, 1961, pp. 80–81). The history of legal contests over unpatented mining claims indicates clearly, however, that the best title insurance is diligent and persistent work on the claim.

The distinction between lode claims and placer claims is an important one. Placer deposits are deposits of valuable minerals occurring as loose grains in sand and gravel, commonly along stream courses or beaches. Lode deposits are commonly more or less tabular bodies enclosed within hard rock and dipping at an angle so as to have a hanging wall and a foot wall (Fig. VII.2). Because of the complexity of nature the distinction is not always easy to make, particularly in flat-lying stratiform bodies. In 1881 in Nevada a court held that the law was drawn for the protection of miners and not by or for geologists and a lode was liberally interpreted as ". . . a continuous body of mineralized rock lying within any other well-defined boundaries on the earth's surface and under it. . . ." (Ely, 1964, p. 100). A placer location, under the law, may consist of no more than 20 acres (or 160 acres for associations) located so as to conform with the legal surveyed subdivisions of the public lands. The holder of a placer claim has no right to go beyond the vertical extensions of his side lines—he has no extralateral rights. A lode claim is prescribed as no more than 1,500 feet along the vein and 300 feet on each side for a total of slightly in excess of 20 acres. The end lines and side lines should be parallel. The most confusing aspect of the lode claim law is the provision that if the claim includes the apex of the vein, the locator has the right to follow the vein downward beyond the vertical downward extension of the side lines of his claim, but within the projected end lines. The difficulty lies in correctly determining the apex—and many a law suit has been fought to determine who has the apex and who has the faulted segment of the vein in structurally complex areas (Fig. VII.3). This 'right' has been relinquished by miners in certain districts. For example, title to parts of the large low-grade porphyry copper ore bodies in the Southwest was in many places clouded by extralateral rights of lode claim holders. It was not until claim holders within a district agreed to vertical downward extensions of claim boundaries that development proceeded.

The act also allowed acquisition of up to 5 acres of nonmineral land for mill sites and encouraged deep drainage and haulage tunnels by granting to the owners of a tunnel driven 3,000 feet into a hill the right to previously unknown lodes intersected by the tunnel.

Subsequent to the 1872 legislation there arose contests as to what constituted a valid discovery since the test is the rather vague test as set forth in a court opinion in 1894—". . . where minerals have been found and the evidence is of such a character that a person of ordinary prudence should be justified in the further expenditure of labor and means, with a reasonable prospect of success. . . ." (p. 178). Contests over prior locations, contests over the validity of the discovery shafts required by state laws, contests over the validity of assessment work done to hold claims in the year prescribed, and contests over what was a mineral (p. 5) and what kinds of minerals were included under the Mineral Location Act of 1872 are a common

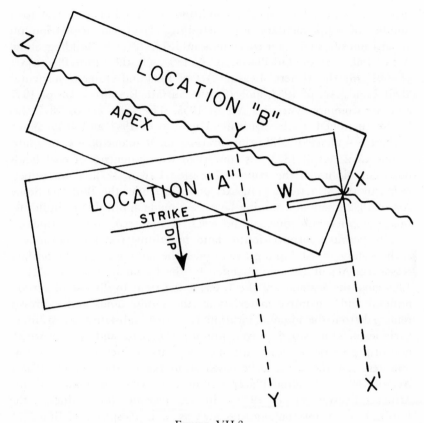

FIGURE VII.3

Lindley's exposition of the apex law
(1914, p. 364, Fig. 34).

. . . The figure represents two locations—A and B. The outcropping vein is exposed in a steep hillside, so that the course of the outcropping apex is widely divergent from that of the true course of the vein on a level,—i.e., the *strike*-line. This is not an uncommon occurrence. It is plain that the course of the apex, *x-y-z*, is the 'true course of the vein upon the surface.' Let *x* represent the point of discovery, and let the strike be determined by means of a short discovery tunnel, *x-w*. The question suggested is, Should the discoverer on making his location follow the line of strike as in location A, ignoring the segment of the apex, *y-z*, or should he follow the apex as in location B?

If he selected A, he would lose all rights on the vein after it departed out of the side-line at *y*. This has been conclusively determined by the courts.

matter of court record. Special circumstances relating to certain rock and mineral substances which do not fit the definitions of lodes or placers or which have special conditions of location gave rise to a number of supplementary acts including (1) special legislation on acquisition of patents on coal lands in 1873, (2) the Building Stone Act of 1892, (3) the Oil Placer Act of 1897, (4) the Saline Placer Act of 1901, (5) the Mineral Leasing Act of 1920 and Outer Continental Shelf Lands Act of 1953, and (6) the Surface Resources Act of 1947 and the Common Varieties Act of 1955. The basic act of 1872 was further modified by the Multiple Use Acts of 1954 and 1955. None of these acts affected valid prior locations made under pre-existing law.

The Coal Act of 1873 was concerned with patenting of coal lands not locatable under the Mineral Location Law of 1872; it was superceded by the Mineral Leasing Act of 1920. Under the Building Stone Act of 1892, the placer-mining laws were made applicable to building-stone deposits. Subsequently, however, it was recognized as undesirable to permit appropriation of land containing common substances, such as stone or sand and gravel, under the mining laws. The Surface Resources Act of 1947 as amended by the Common Varieties Act of 1955 gave the Secretary of the Interior the right to dispose of certain mineral and vegetative materials on the public lands and expressly removed from the mineral location laws such substances as ordinary varieties of sand, stone, gravel, pumice, pumicite, and cinders which do not possess properties giving such deposits distinct or special value. The test of value seems to be based on marketability. The Oil Placer Act of 1897 and Saline Placer Act of 1901 were superseded by the Mineral Leasing Act of 1920. This act provides for leasing of the Public Domain for commodities such as coal, phosphate, sodium, potassium, oil, oil shale, or gas. It has been amended to change regulations governing prospecting and to permit multiple use. Provisions include wildcat or noncompetitive leases issued on a first-come, first-served basis and competitive leases for lands within a known mineral area. Acreages are limited and rentals and royalties are set. The Multiple Use Act of 1954 and the Common Varieties Act of 1955 provide for mineral locations under the mining law and mineral leases under the leasing act to exist simultaneously on the same tract. They, of course, are concerned with different kinds of mineral substances. Conflicts have occurred as in the case of oil wells drilled through potash orebodies in New Mexico, but these have been resolved through special requirements for development or compensation to the damaged party.

The would-be prospector on the public domain of the United States, therefore, must first determine which land is open to prospect-

TABLE VII.1

CHRONOLOGY OF MAJOR UNITED STATES MINERAL LEGISLATION[6]
(from American Law of Mining, Vol. 1, Chapters II, III, V)

(1) Mining Laws of 1866 and 1870
(2) Mineral Location Law of 1872[7]
(3) Coal Act of 1873
(4) Building Stone Act of 1892
(5) Oil Placer Act of 1897
(6) Saline Placer Act of 1901
(7) Mineral Leasing Act of 1920[8]
(8) The Atomic Energy Act of 1946
(9) Mineral Leasing Act for Acquired Lands, 1947
(10) Surface Resources Act of 1947[9]
(11) Public Law 250, 1953[10]
(12) Submerged Lands Act and Outer Continental Shelf Lands Act of 1953
(13) Atomic Energy Act of 1954
(14) Multiple Mineral Development Act of 1954[11]
(15) Common Varieties Act of 1955[12]

[6] Does not include the various public land acts authorizing reservations or withdrawals.
[7] Replaced (1).
[8] Superceded (3), (5) and (6).
[9] In part superceded (4).
[10] Stop-gap legislation to resolve conflicts between (2) and (7) and permit multiple use.
[11] Also known as Public Law 585. Superceded but did not abrogate (11).
[12] Amended (10). The Amended Act, known as the Multiple Surface Use Act, superceded (4).

ing, which mineral substances can legally be located under the mineral location laws, which are subject to prospecting permit and lease, and which are sold by competitive bid. All federally owned land is not public domain; a land status map that shows the general land ownership situation can be secured from the Bureau of Land Management but detailed information on ownership must be obtained from the Bureau office or from courthouse records. The following other federal lands are subject to mineral development under special procedures or not at all:

(1) Indian lands including reservations and individual allotments are subject to leasing for mineral development with approval of the tribal council and Secretary of Interior or in the case of individually owned tracts, with consent of the allottee and the appropriate federal agent.

(2) Military reservations are generally excluded from mineral entry except that prior rights are recognized.

(3) National parks and monuments are in general not open to mineral entry but the wording of the specific act of withdrawal governs the land use and there are some exceptions to the general rule

(Mount McKinley National Park, Glacier Bay National Monument, Organ Pipe Cactus National Monument). Prior rights are recognized.

(4) National forests generally are open to mineral location and leasing except that the forest regulations must be observed. The Forest Service in general does not encourage mineral development within its preserves and carefully scrutinizes mineral locations to confirm the fact of a valuable discovery.

(5) Reclamation withdrawals under the act of 1902 include lands required for irrigation works and lands that might be irrigated therefrom. The former are not open to entry, although prior locations are recognized; the latter are open for mineral entry and development.

(6) Power Act Reservations under the Federal Water Power Act of 1920 leave mineral entry and development to the discretion of the Federal Power Commission or to Congress.

(7) Patented townsites are not open to mineral entry under the mineral location law. Minerals discovered are the property of the owner of the patent; however, prior to issuance of a patent the lands are open for entry. Incorporated towns, villages, and cities are not open under the mineral-leasing act of 1920 as amended in 1946.

(8) The Pickett Act of 1910 authorized executive withdrawal of public lands for development of water power, irrigation, classification, or other public purposes. Withdrawals under this authority included petroleum reserves and oil shale deposits, but these lands remained open for location of metalliferous deposits (and uranium) under the mineral location law.

(9) The Taylor Grazing Act of 1934 together with the previously cited Pickett Act of 1910 was used in 1934 and 1935 to effectively put a stop to what had become a rather uncoordinated disposal of the public domain. By a series of executive orders, the President withdrew all vacant and unappropriated public lands in the major public land states of the West, prohibiting sale, settlement, location, or entry until the land could be classified to determine the most desirable land use. Of great importance to the mining industry, however, was the provision of the act which, while preventing disposal for agricultural purposes, permitted location and development of mineral deposits under the mining law.

(10) After World War II oil companies began extensive prospecting and development of oil and gas on the continental shelves of the United States, mostly off California and the Gulf of Mexico states. The resulting ownership contest between the federal government and

the several states resulted in the Submerged Lands Act of 1953 which gave to the states submerged lands up to 3 miles from the coast in the Atlantic and Pacific oceans and up to 3 marine leagues (10.35 miles) in the Gulf of Mexico. On the basis of their historic boundaries, the seaward limits of Texas and Florida are set at three marine leagues, but the boundaries of Louisiana, Mississippi, and Alabama are restricted to three miles. Beyond these boundaries the lands are subject to special leasing by the Secretary of Interior under the provisions of the Outer Continental Shelf Lands Act of 1953. A study by Shalowitz (1962) entitled "Shore and sea boundaries" explores the problems of submarine lands in detail.

(11) While disposing of the federal domain during the last 50 years, the federal government has also acquired or reacquired tracts totaling nearly 60 million acres. These acquired lands are not open to mineral location but are subject to prospecting permit and lease by the Secretary of Interior under the Acquired Lands Act of 1947.

(12) In 1964 after vigorous contest Congress passed the Wilderness Act, Public Law 88-577, setting aside 9.1 million acres of public lands as a permanent National Wilderness Preservation System. These lands are open for mineral location until December 31, 1983. That is to say, lands not proved mineral in character and claimed for minerals under the appropriate location and leasing laws before that date are thereafter removed from entry. Mining interests are expected to use only a minimum of land for equipment and transportation facilities and to restore land as nearly as possible to its original state on cessation of mining. Prior rights are recognized under the act:

(2) Nothing in this Act shall prevent within national forest wilderness areas any activity, including prospecting, for the purpose of gathering information about mineral or other resources, if such activity is carried on in a manner compatible with the preservation of the wilderness environment. Furthermore— such areas shall be surveyed on a planned, recurring basis consistent with the concept of wilderness preservation by the Geological Survey and the Bureau of Mines to determine the mineral values, if any, that may be present; and the results of such surveys shall be made available to the public and submitted to the President and Congress.

(3) Notwithstanding any other provisions of this Act, until midnight December 31, 1983, the United States mining laws and all laws pertaining to mineral leasing shall, to the same extent as applicable prior to the effective date of this Act, extend to those national forest lands designated by this Act as 'wilderness areas.' . . . (Section 4(d)).

The need for modernization of United States mineral law.

It is to be expected that legislation passed to regulate mining in 1872, based on the economics of that time and the state of knowledge about the occurrence of mineral substances that prevailed, might not meet the problems of 100 years later. It is, in fact, quite a tribute to the legislators of 1872 that the basic provisions of the mineral location law still endure. If the law had been drawn by the scientists of the day it would perhaps be now less satisfactory than the act that was passed. However, in the last 20 years changes in methods of prospecting and exploration and changes in economics of mining have made the old mining laws much less than satisfactory. The deficiencies of the law on the modern scene were recognized by the Hoover Commission in 1949 and a number of recommendations were made but not put into effect. As a result of growing pressure for modernization, Congress in 1964 set up the Public Land Law Review Commission to make a 4-year study of public land laws and make recommendations by the end of 1968.

The basic faults of the mining law of 1872 are as follows. The law is inapplicable to concealed deposits because it requires that valuable minerals be exposed to prove a discovery. This is a serious fault because most of the mineral deposits that remain to be found are concealed or blind deposits which do not crop out. Discoveries will be made through drilling of geological, geophysical, and geochemical targets. The exploration involved in delimiting such targets is expensive and time-consuming, and there is nothing in the current law which protects the right of a prospector to acquire a property discovered as a result of his exploration. The investment in conducting geological, geophysical, and geochemical investigations to define targets and then test the targets by drilling is very large and without some security of right to acquire the fruits of this investment in exploration, the exploration will not be prosecuted. In dealing with a blind or concealed orebody a valid discovery can be confirmed only by drilling or underground workings. The rather rigid requirements set up by some states to define a discovery shaft should be liberalized to permit acceptance of the kind of exploratory work which is recommended by geologists or engineers as the most economical way to confirm a discovery. Only in recent years has drilling been recognized as a valid method of confirming a discovery on a surface claim. Nevada (1960) and Arizona (1964) have recognized drilling as a means of satisfying location laws. The presence of a geophysical anomaly or geochemical anomaly detected through considerable effort and expense by the prospector should be sufficient to confirm a discovery; at least it should be sufficient to hold the claim for a reasonable length of time until the anomaly can be tested. Likewise, a target defined by geological work through detailed mapping and projection should be sufficient to protect the prospector's interest in the property for a reasonable time until the projection can be tested. The provision whereby a claim can be held in perpetuity by performance of 100 dollars worth of assessment work per year is no longer in the public interest. Some locators hold large numbers of claims by annually blowing a hole in a hillside or 'making a pass' with a bulldozer blade. A hundred dollars worth of work is quite different in 1965 than it was in 1872. The claim holder should assume the burden of proving he has done the required assessment by filing an affidavit; this is required in some states. Claims would be explored and either abandoned or developed more expeditiously if the assessment requirements were increased from year to year. In any case, claims should be cancelled after a reasonable length of time for development has expired without action on the part of the owner. Considering the change in prospecting methods, it would also make good sense to increase the size of claims during the exploration period. Ladendorff (1961, appendix) presented a bill drafted by the Hard Minerals Committee of the Section of Mineral and Natural Resources Law of the American Bar Association designed to provide for the location of 'exploration claims' not necessarily based on a discovery. Under this proposed legislation, geological, geochemical, or geophysical indications of mineralization would be sufficient grounds for holding the prospect until it could be explored. Such exploration claims would encourage mining companies to employ a regional approach to finding new deposits. The hope for the future lies in the kind of regional analysis used by oil companies who are able to lease exploration ground in large tracts rather than in the more limited property approach forced upon mining companies by the necessity of acquiring exploration ground in 20-acre rectangular claims.

At the time the 1872 law was passed, the West was sparsely populated and no one could foresee the pressure for land for living and recreational purposes or the value of timber resources. The provision of the 1872 act which provided for acquisition of the surface rights to a mining claim through a patenting process has been much abused by persons exploiting the mining laws so as to acquire at a low price ownership of building sites on mountain streams or in timbered regions. The use of the surface is, of course, necessary for some mining operations, for construction of milling and transportation facilities, for example, and timber cut from mining claims has been used in mine construction and for support. The law should be corrected to permit use of surface and timber only for purposes necessary to the mining operation. The Multiple Surface Use Act of 1954 as amended in 1955 prevents nonmining use of claims prior to patenting.

Anyone who has tried to construct a map of claims as described in county courthouse records in a region being actively prospected can testify to the need for a federal register of mining claims properly surveyed and properly described. Claims staked over claims staked over claims with side and end lines trending in all directions make it impossible to ascertain ownership. In fact, some claims are fraudulently staked with the purpose of confusing the ownership situation so that legitimate prior owners are forced to pay for quit claim instruments. In some courthouses indifferent clerks have not properly recorded even the vague descriptions filed.

The law should also be free of regulations tied to the supposed geometry, form, or origin of the deposit. Distinctions between lodes and placers are not really necessary, particularly if extralateral rights are abandoned. The question of the apex of a lode or vein, then, is of little practical interest. If extralateral rights are abandoned and the locator ·receives only the ownership of the minerals within the vertically projected lines of his claim, then he should have the option of staking adjacent claims to cover the dipping or plunging extensions of the orebody as projected from geological and geophysical evidence, as suggested earlier. Uncertainties of the present law are illustrated by uranium deposits where uranium minerals are disseminated in a body of sedimentary rocks. Should such deposits be located as lode or placer claims? They are technically neither lodes nor placers even under the most liberal interpretations. The orebodies are not continuous, nor are they enclosed between recognizable datums such as hanging walls and footwalls; on the other hand, neither are they loose minerals in dirt or gravel. A distinguished jurist once suggested that both kinds of claims should be filed on the same deposit. Clearly, the law breaks down here.

Any new mineral act should clarify the status of various mineral substances now treated in a variety of acts (p. 171). Nonmetallic minerals, commonly called industrial minerals and rocks, are commonly used in bulk with a minimum of processing or refining; they are of value because of certain chemical or physical properties they possess, in contrast to ores which are mineral aggregates from which one or more minerals are extracted. The status of these materials is not clear because they are subject to appropriation under the mining laws when they have an unusual value (American Law of Mining, 1964, pp. 166–178). The value is usually the result of their location. This means that a deposit of sand and gravel near a growing city where there is a large demand for aggregates is a mineral deposit, whereas the same material in a terrace on a distant mountain stream is not a mineral deposit and therefore not available for mineral location because there is no market for it. Subsequently, if a dam is located on the stream, the same deposit might, through a new economic situation—a demand—become available for entry under the mineral location laws. Likewise, land underlain by ordinary stone cannot be appropriated under the mineral laws unless it can be demonstrated that the stone in some way has a value that similar stone in other areas does not have. The Internal Revenue Code likewise has been confused in its treatment of mineral substances (p. 207).

The mineral-leasing laws have been less subject to criticism, but recently the government, through the Bureau of the Budget, has requested that all noncompetitive bidding be eliminated. The government argues that noncompetitive wildcat leases cost the government large sums in potential revenue and permit middlemen and speculators to make large profits. Such leases are now permitted on lands where mineral deposits are not known to exist. It might be argued that the middleman performs a service in searching out such lands, determining their potential, and then selling the leases to potential developers, but for the most part the contribution is indeed slight. Large tracts are tied up and the middleman does nothing except wait for a wave of mineral exploration to sweep toward his holdings.

It is also in the public interest that lands not now open for prospecting and leasing, particularly the large tracts of lands held as military reservations, be opened for mineral development where such development would not interfere with the primary purposes of the reservation. This is, after all, no more than an extension of the multiple-use concept already adopted by Congress.

The multiple-use concept is curiously enough being locally subverted by agents of federal agencies such as the Forest Service and Bureau of Land Management where these agencies are responsible for management of tracts of land legally open for mineral locations. In their zeal to prevent abuse of forest and range, individuals in authority have harassed the bonafide prospector to discourage location of mineral claims (Knoerr and Pitman, 1964, p. 98). The 'prudent man' test (p. 169) of a mineral location which governed mineral discovery provisions for many years has, through administrative ruling of the Department of Interior, been replaced by the test of whether or not the discovery is a valuable deposit under today's economic conditions. This so-called 'marketability test' is no less vague than the 'prudent man test' and, from the point of view of the prospector and miner, it is less workable. Moreover it is easy to misapply it as a 'profitability test.' Profitability and marketability are not the same thing. Profits are controlled by vagaries of the market and efficiency of operation, as well as the overall cost structure. Profitability can hardly be used as a test for location and development of a mineral claim. According to W. Howard Gray as quoted in Engineering and Mining Journal (1964, p. 108), the Department of Interior is contesting mineral patent applications on the basis of marketability. Revisions of the public-land laws to set forth clearly the rights of the prospector under the concept of multiple use are very much needed.

Canadian mineral law.

This section was summarized from an article by Harry Macdonell (1965) entitled "Comparative Analysis of American and Canadian Hard Mineral Laws" and from Northcutt Ely's "Summary of Mining and Petroleum Laws of the World" (1961).

In Canada the original provinces retained titles to public lands, and exercise jurisdiction over them; the Canadian Dominion government has jurisdiction over the public lands of the Northwest Territory, Yukon Territory, and the Far North. Except for Quebec, provincial laws are rooted in English law and the freeholder in general received all rights except to the royal minerals—gold and silver. In most provinces the minerals pass with the land unless specifically reserved; in Quebec the minerals do not pass unless specifically conveyed. Mining laws within the several provinces differ substantially. The concept of the apex which provides for extralateral rights was generally rejected in Canada. Some Canadian provinces grant mineral patents, others employ the mineral lease system.

Unlike the United States where the basic mining law has remained unchanged since 1872, Canadian mining law has been several times modernized. It is summarized as follows:

(1) As in the U.S., aliens may locate claims on dominion lands; upon converting to an exploitation lease, the title must be placed in a company which is either 50 per cent Canadian-owned or which lists its shares on a Canadian exchange.

(2) Canada has dropped the discovery provision and mining claims are not located with reference to the geometry of a vein. This is a recognition of the validity of geochemical and geophysical prospecting and of drilling in finding concealed deposits. Claims are rectangular and marked by a regulation metal tag in provinces where staking is a requirement. Details of location and staking differ in various provinces. In some provinces claim lines must be run North-South and East-West. In Nova Scotia prospecting and developing rights are conveyed by licenses which rely on national topographic maps for reference. The various provinces and the Dominion government have various forms of exploration and production licenses and leases for oil, gas, and coal.

(3) Since discovery is no longer the basis for location in Canada and the claim is not drawn with relation to the supposed geometry of the lode, then extralateral rights cannot logically exist and do not exist in Canada.

(4) In Canada there is no overlap in jurisdiction between provincial and Dominion government, and both have established locating and recording systems for their respective lands.

(5) After location and recording, under most Canadian law, the locator has the right to investigate and explore his claim, but he does not automatically have the right to mine. Assessment work must be done as in the United States, while the claim is being evaluated. Before mining, the locator must obtain an exploitation lease or a patent, depending on the jurisdiction. Where lands are patentable, it is more difficult to secure patent than in the United States.

(6) Canada has numerous special tax provisions relating to mining and the tax structure is completely different from that of the United States. There is a percentage depletion allowance of $33\frac{1}{3}$ percent for all operators of metalliferous mines, oil and gas wells, and certain industrial mineral mines. New mines may be granted income tax exemption for 36 months.

(7) The Atomic Energy Control Act of 1946 affects all mining of radioactive substances.

Mineral Law in the U.S.S.R.

Ely (1961, pp. 97–98) summarized Soviet mineral law as follows: All land and subsurface resources were nationalized by the first Land Law of 1917, and state ownership of minerals was emphasized in the constitution of 1923. Despite provisions in the mining law which permit operations by foreigners, all mining is conducted by Soviet government organizations and to a small extent by industrial cooperatives. Under the law of 1927, prospecting by individuals is encouraged; exploitation rights are conveyed by license.

REFERENCES

Agricola, Georgius (1556) De re metallica, trans.: Herbert Clark Hoover, and Lou Henry Hoover (1950) New York, Dover Publications, 638 pp.

American Law of Mining (1964) Vol. 1, Public Domain, Rocky Mountain Mineral Law Foundation: Matthew Bender and Co., New York, 906 pp.

Chapman, W. M. (1965) Statement before Sub-committee on Oceanography, of the House Committee on Merchant Marines and Fisheries, respecting H.R. 5175, the law of the sea, and public policy: National Oceanographic Program Legislation, Serial No. 89–13, pp. 388–447.

Ely, Northcutt (1961) Summary of mining and petroleum laws of the world: U.S. Bureau Mines Inf. Circ. 8-17, 215 pp.

——— (1964) Mineral titles and concessions, in Economics of the mineral industries, 2nd ed.: American Institute of Mining and Metallurgical Engineers, New York, pp. 81–130.

Engineering and Mining Journal (1964a) Who owns the continental shelf?: Eng. and Mining Jour., vol. 165, no. 10, p. 85.

——— (1964b) AMC speakers stress trends affecting the business of mining: Eng. and Mining Jour., vol. 165, no. 10, pp. 107–108.

Forbes, R. J. (1963) Studies in ancient technology, Vol. VII: E. J. Brill, Leiden and Cologne, 253 pp.

Hoover, H. C. (1950) Footnotes, in De re metallica (1556), translated by Herbert Clark Hoover and Lou Henry Hoover (original edition, 1912): New York, Dover Publications, 638 pp.

Knoerr, A. W., and Pitman, Frank (1964) Colorado mining convention reflects industry rebound: Eng. and Mining Jour., vol. 165, no. 3, pp. 98–102.

Ladendorff, G. H. (1961) Proposed legislation to enlarge prediscovery rights of mineral locators: Natural Resources Jour., vol. 1, no. 1, pp. 76–94.

Lindley, C. H. (1914) A treatise on the American law relating to mines and mineral lands, 3rd ed.: Bancroft-Whitney Company, San Francisco, 3 vols.

Macdonell, Harry (1965) Comparative analysis of American and Canadian hard mineral laws, in Tenth Annual Rocky Mountain Mineral Law Institute: Matthew Bender and Co., New York, pp. 423–466.

O'Callaghan, J. A. (1962) Historical pattern of mineral exploitation in the United States: Colo. Sch. Mines Quarterly, vol. 57, no. 4, pp. 31–42.

Phillips, W. B. (1903) The mining laws of Texas: The Univ. of Texas Mineral Survey Bull. No. 6, 37 pp.

Rickard, T. A. (1932) A history of American mining: McGraw-Hill, New York, 419 pp.

Shalowitz, Aaron L. (1962) Shore and sea boundaries, Vol. I: U.S. Coast and Geodetic Survey Publ. 10-1, 420 pp.

Shalowitz, Aaron L. (1965) The continental shelf (Letter to the editor): Science, vol. 148, no. 3676, p. 1412.

CHAPTER VIII

MINERALS
AND GOVERNMENT

Introduction.

The preceding chapters on history and mineral ownership have already introduced the subject of this chapter—the relationship between mineral resources and government. That there should be a relationship is immediately apparent. Government has the responsibility for defense of the nation and therefore must be concerned about supplies and availability of mineral raw materials which in the modern age constitute the power to make war. These are metals to build the machines of war, fuels to operate them, and a host of nonmetallic industrial minerals to construct operational and training facilities and to feed the chemical and metallurgical requirements of an industry straining to support the war and the domestic economy. Government has the responsibility for the economic well-being of the country in peace or war. In the modern era this can be translated into a concern for the health of an industrial economy which consumes vast quantities of mineral raw materials to produce goods for domestic use and for export. The government has the responsibility for agricultural policies which insure that the population is fed. Today the mineral crop nutrients are part of the problem. Thus, both domestic and international government policy is concerned broadly and in myriad detail with minerals, mineral deposits, and mineral resources —with minerals moving in international trade, with mineral deposits in the process of being exploited, and with future supplies of minerals.

The legitimate interest of government in mineral resources is not in question. There is, however, considerable difference of opinion on how the government should express its interest, that is to say in the posture and policy of government in regard to minerals. On one side is the philosophy that mineral resources are the patrimony of the people and the government should closely control the mineral industry as a 'public utility.' On the other side is the philosophy that minerals are the private property of the land owner and government should limit itself to promoting policies designed to maintain the health of a free market economy. In the United States there now prevails a mixture of the two philosophies. In the interests of national security, the government has from time to time been forced to make allocations of mineral commodities and currently maintains a large stockpile of mineral commodities. It is both a major buyer and a major seller of minerals. From time to time the federal government has provided direct assistance to segments of the mineral industry in the form of grants, bonuses, subsidies, premiums, loans, advances against production, purchase contracts, protective tariffs, import quotas and tax concessions. As part of its responsibility to maintain a sound currency, government is concerned with silver and gold. As part of its general responsibility to plan for the future, the government has resorted to conservation laws which control certain mining activities.

GEOLOGY AND MINERALS IN THE NEW CONSERVATION MOVEMENT[1]

Stewart Udall (1963) in his book "The Quiet Crisis" chronicled the history of conservation in the United States in a series of chapters whose titles themselves summarize development of the movement: Chapter IV, The Stir of Conscience—Thoreau and the Naturalists;

---

[1] The material in this section was presented in an address to the American Institute of Professional Geologists, Denver, Colorado, October 8, 1965, and to the Interstate Oil Compact, Corpus Christi, Texas, December 6, 1965, and subsequently published in *Science*, vol. 151, pp. 409–412, January 28, 1966.

Chapter V, The Raid on Resources; Chapter VI, The Beginning of Widsom—George Perkins Marsh; Chapter VII, The Beginning of Action—Carl Schurz and John Wesley Powell; Chapter VIII, The Woodlands—Pinchot and the Foresters; Chapter IX, Wild and Park Lands—John Muir; and Chapter X, Men Must Act—the Roosevelts and Politics. The Conference of Governors and the North American Conservation Conference called by President Theodore Roosevelt in 1908 and 1909, respectively, marked the beginning of a nationwide awareness of natural resource problems and were the culmination of a series of reports, recommendations, and laws written over the preceding half century (Allen, 1959, p. 8). Between 1910 and World War II, the conservation movement was concerned mainly with preventing the destruction and waste of natural resources—with soil erosion, deforestation, and the waste of mineral resources. Since World War II a new dimension has been added to the conservation effort—cleanliness and beauty—and, for the first time, air and water have been a major focus of attention. In previous years conservationists became alarmed and exercised about local pollution but only in the present decade has pollution of the atmosphere and of ground and surface waters and the destruction of natural beauty been nationwide problems. Through sudsy streams, salty wells, and smog, pollution has touched a large body of citizenry.

Conservation today means different things to different people. Some of the most vocal conservationists are really preservationists—opposed to change. They resent the march of row houses into the rural scene, they fight subdivisions which rout wildlife from its woodland homes, and they bitterly oppose the extractive industries which consume natural resources and convert them to material and energy products. Within cities, they attempt to prevent destruction of fine old buildings no longer economically useful to make way for new modern structures. They are strongly motivated to preserve the past as part of the heritage of the future. Perhaps they really are reacting against the disappearance of the world of their youth, a world which most of us remember as a better world than the present-day one, probably because young people usually feel better than middle-aged or old people. Organized into heritage societies, historical societies, sportsmen's clubs, garden clubs, and conservation federations, these groups have locally been effective in forcing a careful review of projects which propose to make major changes in the natural scene or raze structures of historical interest. But, however worthwhile the preservationist movement might be in some instances (and this writer confesses to preservationist sympathies), in others it is unrealistic in asking present society to pay too high a price for the past. The preservationist lives in our modern industrial society and enjoys its benefits. These are not without their price. The preservation of an old building simply as an architectural and historical monument in the midst of a growing city where there is great demand for space can rarely be justified unless the building can be converted to serve a useful purpose as well as be a monument. This is the concept of multiple use. Likewise, preservation of a potential rock quarry site as a woodland glade constitutes elimination of a valuable mineral resource and costs society a substantial amount in lost tax revenues and lost payroll. If crushed rock must be hauled a long distance because the more conveniently located resource is denied to society, then construction costs in the area rise accordingly. In line with the multiple-use concept, the rock could be quarried over the economic life of the deposit and thereafter the area could be landscaped and restored for other uses. The question is—what is the price of *preservation* and can we afford to pay it? In some cases, we can and should pay the price; in others, the price is too high. *Conservation,* on the other hand, is long-term economy and we must pay the short-term price for it.

The concept of multiple use is a difficult one to criticize because it embodies the give-everyone-a-chance spirit of America, and makes good economic sense. But although the concept is appealing, it is not easy to apply because some uses preclude others. For example, grazing, forest industries, recreation, wildlife management, and mineral exploration can go on concurrently with only a reasonable amount of accommodation between the diverse users. However, farming, urban development, industrial development, highway development, and military installations require exclusive use for the period of their life. Where present uses are exclusive in nature, the multiple use doctrine can be applied only sequentially—that is, (*b*) can use the land only after (*a*) has finished. The problem then is to determine the sequence of use. In a democratic system the test of the 'highest and best use' is commonly applied by land appraisers. The highest and best use is not necessarily the most productive use on a dollar-per-acre basis, but rather the use that is most in the public interest. The mineral industries are probably the most productive in terms of contributing the highest value from the smallest acreage. Surface mining is an exclusive use, but underground mining, where subsidence is eliminated, can exist concurrently with other use of the surface. White (1961) considered the multiple use problem in an article titled "The Choice of Use in Resource Management." He listed the elements in decision making as: (1) Quantity and quality of the resource, (2) Present value of gains and losses accruing from future use of the resource, (3) The technological changes which might effect future demand, and (4) The relation of any given use to other resource use. These are more or less the same elements which must be considered in the valuation of mineral property as discussed in Chapter I.

Although conservation is frequently defined as effecting a harmony or balance between man and his environment, such a goal can never be achieved in an industrial society, because an industrial society by its very nature consumes and changes its environment. It devours huge quantities of minerals—nonrenewable natural resources—and spews great quantities of toxic products into the environment. Only an agricultural or pastoral culture with a more or less stable population can achieve true harmony with the environment. The best an industrial society can do is, through knowledge of ecology and through planning, to minimize disruptive changes, to dispose of toxic waste products in safe systems, and to use nonrenewable resources conservatively in the most advantageous way possible. Conservation in this sense is applied ecology and goes beyond the former emphasis on wise use and elimination of waste. The 1964 Conservation Yearbook of the Department of Interior stated (p. 9):

The program of more and prophetic stewardship being forged today is both careful and daring. Conceived on a truly national scale, it is deeper than soil conservation, broader than wildlife preservation, more penetrating than forest husbandry, more encompassing than control of air and water pollution.

It should be obvious that the success of the new conservation movement, or any conservation movement, depends on control of population. Projection of rates of growth of the world population today, ranging from slightly less than 1 per cent in the developed countries to over 4 per cent in some of the developing areas, makes it clear that the matter is one of very grave concern (National Academy of Sciences, 1963). These projections indicate a world population of 6 to 7 billion at the turn of the century, and continuing the same rate, of 25 billion by the year 2070. These rates are higher than any foreseeable economic growth rate so, at best, we are faced with a declining living standard and increasing competition for the earth's food and material resources. There are bacterial cultures that multiply to the point where their population exceeds the food resources of their environment and they starve to death; there are bacterial cultures that multiply to the point where the toxic products they produce so befoul their environment that they poison themselves. Commonly, the self-destruction results from both factors operating simultaneously. To draw an analogy with the human culture is not pleasant but is clearly indicated. Only the time scale is different.

It is difficult for students concerned with the preservation and re-generation of renewable natural resources to fit minerals, a non-renewable resource, into a working conservation definition. Indeed, it is impossible to do so under any limited definition of conservation—how can you conserve something which is being irreplaceably consumed? In order that nonrenewable natural resources could be brought within the conservation ethic in a positive way, the concept was broadened to include *wise use* and *efficient management*. Thus the 1952 official statement of the President's Materials Policy Commission with regard to conservation read:

A sound concept of conservation is one which equates it with efficient management—efficient use of resources, and of manpower and materials: a positive concept compatible with growth and high consumption in place of abstinence and retrenchment (Vol. I, p. 21).

This stretching of the term *conservation* is forced by the realities of an industrial society which cannot build a fence around its mineral resources. Allsman (1962, p. 87) stated:

Because of the responsibilities assigned to us by the Congress, we in the Bureau of Mines consider that conservation in metal mining (as it is with other minerals), is specifically concerned with (1) preventing loss of life and protecting health of labor, (2) maximum efficient use of manpower, materials, energy, and equipment, and (3) full extraction and full utilization of mineral resources with minimum waste, all consistent with the welfare of the community.

McKelvey (1962, p. 143) interpreted the federal philosophy as follows:

. . . the essence of the federal philosophy on mineral resources is not that they must be hoarded for future generations or reserved for wise use but rather that they are to be efficiently developed and fully used to sustain the national security and our growing economy.

This definition urges full and efficient use. McKelvey proceeded to document his assertion that current federal actions are in support of the full-use concept.

One of the most thoughtful definitions of conservation was formulated in 1935 by a geologist, C. K. Leith (1935, pp. 109–110). It presented a clear preview of the conservation movement of the 1960s.

Conservation is the effort to insure to society the maximum present and future benefit from the use of natural resources. It involves the inventory and evaluation of natural resources, calls for the maintenance of the renewable resources at a level commensurate with the needs of society, and requires the substitution, where the conservation of human energy permits, of renewable or inexhaustible resources for those which are non-renewable, and of the more abundant non-renewable resources for the less abundant ones. It not only seeks to eliminate waste of resources if use be economically feasible, but also looks forward to improvements in techniques of production and use, and requires that there be prompt and proper adjustments to advances in technology. It thus appears that conservation involves the balancing of natural resources against human resources and the rights of the present generation against the rights of future generations. It necessitates, moreover, the harmonizing of the procedures and objectives of conservation with the conditions of the present or future economic order, and calls for a careful allocation of duties and powers among private and public agencies.

This definition requires careful study and raises many questions because it includes many elements. It calls for inventory and evaluation of resources. With regard to minerals, this is an extremely expensive program if carried out in any detail. Who should do it and on what scale (p. 21)? It calls for maintenance of renewable resources at an optimum level. This involves economic studies and projections to determine the proper level and some kind of action to insure that production will be adequate. Is it really necessary to program production of renewable resources, or is a free-market economy the best way of matching production and demand? The answer to this question is intimately bound up with political science and philosophy of government. Leith's definition calls for substitutions. Are these to be effected through government controls and allocations or through operation of a free market system? During World War II the government found it necessary to allocate certain commodities for certain purposes and to require substitutes for less critical purposes. The war was in a sense a prelude of the future because demand exceeded supply and priorities had to be established and enforced. Most definitions of conservation call for elimination of waste. How? Through inspection of extractive industries by government engineers and the closing of wasteful operations? Drastic legislation would be required to legalize such supervision, although some such legislation already exists in special cases—for example, to prevent flaring (burning) of natural gas where no market exists. The definition calls for balancing the rights of the living against the rights of those unborn. Those to come have no representation except those living who have a strong sense of human destiny and they are all too few.

This brief analysis attempts to point out that the mechanisms required to implement the worthy objectives of conservation present very knotty problems in themselves and are inextricably tied to philosophy of government. If on the one hand government's responsibility is to protect the rights of the individual and guarantee maximum individual liberty, and on the other hand the government is to enforce conservation of natural resources, some difficult compromises must be made. One of the basic individual rights in the United States is the right to own property. This is certainly in conflict with government management of the land. But what good is planning if the plans cannot be implemented? Perhaps relinquishment of private property rights is too high a price to pay for conservation? These questions are raised to present some idea of the gravity of the conservation decisions which must be made.

Planning and implementation of those plans on a nationwide scale can be most efficiently accomplished where the government has complete authority and the individual has none. Under such a system, for example, an oil field can be exploited solely on the basis of engineering considerations uncomplicated by the rights of property owners. Resources can be allocated to their highest use; silver, for example, might be reserved exclusively for the photographic and electronic industries with use for tableware and jewelry prohibited by decree. To a degree, private property rights are already subordinate to conservation laws and, for this reason, conservation has been called by some the road to socialism. Our system of government has attempted to achieve a balance between individual rights and the public interest. Clearly, a property-owner should not be allowed to dump poisonous wastes in a stream and thus damage a large number of other individuals. Clean water is an essential to survival. In other cases, however, definition of the public interest is not so easy. Should a property-owner be prohibited from building a structure on his property simply because his neighbors do not like the looks of it? Aesthetic considerations are, after all, a matter of personal preference and are not subject to measurement by ordinary standards. What good is the right to private property if it cannot be exercised? Or should the owner of a valuable mineral resource be prevented from mining it and required to put it in the bank for the future because foreign suplies of the commodity are currently plentiful?

An interesting conservation decision was made recently in the State of New Mexico by the New Mexico Oil Conservation Commission. An oil company with a lease on state land proposed to drill a deep exploratory well to test a promising structure. However, as located, the well bore would pass through the unmined part of a potash ore-body at a much shallower depth and cause revisions in the mining program of a potash mining company. The potash mining company moved to deny a drilling permit to the oil company. There was considerable testimony offered concerning the damages that would be suffered by the mining company and how much potash ore would have to be left around the well bore in the interest of safety to prevent subsidence. At the conclusion of the hearing, the New Mexico Commission denied the permit to the oil company on conservation grounds, reasoning that it would prevent waste if drilling of the well were delayed until after all the potash ore had been mined, following which time the potential oil structure could be tested without requiring that any extra potash ore be left in the workings.

Another conflict between resource users is currently being fought along the Texas Gulf Coast where miners of oyster shell have come into conflict with commercial fishermen and sportsmen. Shell from dead reefs is mined by dredge and sold as a high-calcium raw material for the chemical industry, including lime and cement manufacture; because of a shortage of hard rock along the Texas Gulf Coast it is also valuable for its physical properties and used as a concrete aggregate and road base material. Supplies of shell have been depleted in some parts of the coast, and the operators are desirous of moving into new ground previously denied to them because of proximity to live oyster reefs. The dredging operation muddies the water and is harmful to the living oyster colonies. Oyster fishermen have moved to deny the request and they have been supported by other commercial fishermen and sportsmen's groups who regard live reefs as an asset to their business and pleasure. A compromise by the Texas Parks and Wildlife Commission, the state regulatory agency, was unacceptable to the fishermen and is being challenged in the courts. Oyster shell is a high-quality chemical grade raw material. Its use as an aggregate and as a road base material is a lower use in the sense that material which meets the higher specifications for chemical grade raw material is also consumed in uses which require only that it be hard and abrasion resistant. In the absence of competing gravel and crushed stone deposits, it is also the cheapest aggregate and road-base material available. The question might be raised, Is it in the best long-range interest of Gulf Coast industry for oyster shell to be used up in construction or should it be conserved for higher industrial uses? One reason that the question cannot be answered is that there is no inventory of shell reserves. The amount of shell that remains to be recovered is not known. As a practical matter, the shell industry produces about 11 million cubic yards of shell per year valued at more than 15 million dollars; more than half is used in road building and constructional industries. Many other industries are related to or based on the shell industry. Royalty paid to the State of Texas is more than 1.5 million dollars. Thus any conservation decision made in this case must weigh many factors and the interests of many groups, some of which do not even know they might be affected by the decision.

Conservation decisions, like other decisions, can be rapidly made obsolete by technology or changes in economics. In a world guaranteed completely open to free trade and perpetually at peace, conservation policies governing domestic mineral industries probably would be very different than in the present world where foreign supplies might be suddenly interrupted and national security is of overriding importance. In such an ideal world mineral stuffs would flow from regions of abundance to regions of scarcity, from raw material producer to consumer, solely along economic gradients. But even in such an ideal world, the need to industrialize to support burgeoning populations and raise living standards would gradually alter trade patterns so that more and more minerals would be consumed by the producing country and eventually, as presently dictated by reasons of security, a big industrial consumer like the United States would have to look to its low-grade ores and its lean oil fields. It would be unwise if conservation decisions based on the current availability of cheap foreign minerals should strip us of our capabilities to move down the domestic resource ladder, exploiting lower and lower grade earth materials. It is true that we wrong future generations by wastefully consuming the high-grade resources of the earth; it is equally true that we commit a wrong if we leave them no capability to utilize the low-grade materials they inherit.

There is a disturbing aspect of the new conservation movement in that that extractive industries and the mineral industries in particular are regarded as rapacious despoilers and looters of the nation's resources. To what extent this attitude is based on past history and to what extent it is due to the ugliness of a scar on the land left by a mine or a quarry is not clear. It is true that a noisy, dusty quarry with its snorting diesels and endless parade of heavy trucks is not pleasant to the eye as is a green meadow. However, it is certainly unrealistic for the lover of beauty who lives in the 20th century to expect that all such quarries should be located in someone else's area. If conservation teaching is honest and objective it must evaluate what the mineral industry contributes to modern society—what we get in return for the local ugly scars (which nowadays do not have to remain ugly after the minerals have been harvested). For example, the oil industry in Texas produces unpleasant smells, unsightly well fields, and salt water which is difficult of disposal. It also produces a product valued at about 4 billion dollars per year, which is indispensable to modern society, pays half a billion dollars in royalties to land owners, nearly 250 million dollars in state taxes, and 150 million dollars to counties, cities, and school districts. It also produces jobs for some 216,000 people—one out of every 17 Texans—and pays them salaries of nearly 1.5 billion dollars per year. Needless to say, the employees pay taxes and support local businesses. The myriad satellite industries are not included (Faggioli, 1965, p. 17). Much of the blame for pollution placed on the oil industry has been misplaced. Recent studies indicate that concentration of salts from heavy irrigation and from natural salt and brine bearing formations is the major cause of salt pollution in many parts of Texas (Langdon, 1965, p. 6; Faggioli, 1965, p. 12).

Many modern writers and commentators judge the modern mineral industry guilty because of the past deeds of the industry. In a sense this is analogous to the Ministry of Truth in Orwell's superstate which was engaged in rewriting history to make it conform to the present, or to the Communist practice of rewriting textbooks to eliminate a past hero in current disfavor. The Appalachian coal fields, for example, were developed in a different society in a different time by an industry which cannot be held guilty for violation of laws passed fifty years thereafter. It was a time of wasteful exploitation of resources, when some individuals abused the land and appropriated the cream of the nation's resources for their own gain. It was also a time of human exploitation—of child labor and sweat shops in manufacturing industries such as the garment industry. We condemn all these practices today but do not find today's garment industry guilty because their 19th century predecessors followed the practices of the 18th century. On the contrary, the manufacturing industry is praised for its contribution to America's way of life. What about the mineral industry that built the great steel complex at Pittsburgh and along the Great Lakes? Perhaps it is not more guilty than the garment industry, and its contributions to society should be balanced against the excesses of the early exploiters.

What then is the place of minerals in this new conservation movement which attempts to exercise stewardship over the land through science and engineering? As long as America remains an industrial power, the mineral industry must expand to supply minerals for materials, minerals for energy, and water and crop nutrients to sustain life. Thus conservation cannot hope to decrease the volume of earth minerals being extracted. On the contrary, government policies must encourage the industry on a broad front. It will, however, in the opinion of this writer, exercise a good deal more control over the industry in the future so that in many aspects of the mineral industry there will be overt or covert government—business partnerships or perhaps economic relationships. There are many ways that this can be effected without the government assuming a proprietary interest in the enterprise. The economics of the mineral industry will change to meet new conservation laws—costs of land restoration will have to be recovered from income; costs of eliminating and disposing of pollutants, both air and water, will likewise have to be borne by the industry. Sulfurous gases will no longer be discharged into the air. Large volumes of wastes will be disposed of by injection into secure subsurface hosts.

In order to plan effectively, the government will have to know a great deal more about the mineral resources of the United States and will need to make a modern inventory of the various kinds and categories of mineral resources left for future use. This will include detailed studies of the cost boundaries of various grades of resources. It will also require a great deal of data from environmental science and engineering studies which have not yet been made. Most important, the government, through administrative agencies or the courts, will have to act as arbiter between various conservation groups whose interests conflict. For example, it may be advisable in terms of wise use of mineral resources to mine sand and gravel from terraces along a river and even to dredge the river channel. Such activity might very likely be opposed by fish and wildlife groups. The conflicts must be resolved on the basis of full information about the place of these various resources in an overall resource plan. The success of the conservation movement in the future will depend on how effectively the various segments of the movement can be pulled together into a comprehensive natural resource ethic. Although some of the most famous of early conservationists were geologists—men like John Wesley Powell, John Muir, C. R. Van Hise, and C. K. Leith—they are conspicuous by their absence from today's natural resource planning groups, local, state and federal, which seem to be controlled largely by representatives of forest and range, recreation, water, and wildlife interests. Probably the geologists' greatest contributions to modern conservation have been their efforts, with petroleum engineers, to make state oil and gas conservation laws work and to more efficiently produce oil and gas reservoirs through unitization. Perhaps geologists are regarded in government circles as champions of the mineral industry, rather than as conservationists. They are both. The counsel of geologists is essential in the development of a comprehensive natural resource ethic.

This need for a comprehensive ethic was expressed in a White House release dated May 1965 calling for a conference on natural beauty. A panel of land reclamation experts recommended:

An all-out joint Federal-State-local effort is urgently needed to restore the landscape, with the Federal Government providing the incentive and leadership. The Federal and State governments should participate by acquisition of certain despoiled lands for public use, and by grants, loans, and cost sharing with the private sector and local subdivisions of government where the public interest will be served.

A Federal Commission is needed to establish standards and criteria, including economic values, for the enhancement and protection of the beauty and attractiveness of the United States and to implement national policy as needed in effecting both rehabilitation and preservation of the landscape, including rivers. This Commission should promote coordination of planning and action among all levels of government.

The national study of surface-mine rehabilitation presently under way under the Appalachian Regional Development Act of 1965, Public Law 89-4, should be carried forward at greater speed, with sufficient detailed on-site studies of conditions and with studies in depth by professional people to develop a meaningful program of action.

The Federal Government must take the initiative on Government-owned lands to establish standards of land maintenance and rehabilitation before it leads others into taking similar action. The planning for this rehabilitation must involve the competence and skills of all appropriate disciplines so that the total environment and ecology of the region is recognized.

Public investment in restoration efforts should be protected by appropriate statutes.

State or regional compacts pertaining to surface mining, water pollution, terrain damage, and land rehabilitation should be encouraged.

For an excellent collection of readings in resource management and conservation, the student should see Burton and Kates (1965).

STOCKPILES AND OTHER ASPECTS OF A NATIONAL MINERAL POLICY

It is a matter of fact that the world in which mineral policy must be formulated is not an ideal world. Past wars have proved that mineral production and national security are closely related. During World War II the diversion of manpower and shipping to procure strategic mineral materials was of such magnitude that, following the war, stockpiles were established to insure supplies of essential minerals in the event of a future war. In 1946, Congress passed the Strategic and Critical Materials Stockpiling Act and created what has since come to be known as the Strategic or National Stockpile. This act enlarged a prewar Strategic Materials Act which provided for purchase of only a very few mineral commodities. The intensification of the cold war and the Korean war resulted in the Defense Production Act of 1950 which in effect created a second stockpile—the DPA Inventory or Stockpile. A third stockpile—the Supplemental Stockpile—was established in 1954 to receive foreign mineral commodities bartered for U.S. agricultural products. The bartered goods were received by the Commodity Credit Corporation and then transferred to the Supplemental Stockpile. Thus, in effect, materials held by the Commodity Credit Corporation constituted a fourth stockpile called the CCC or 'pipeline' stockpile (Table VIII.1). Materials in the Defense Production Act Inventory as well as those held by the Commodity Credit Corporation can be disposed of under presidential authority as long as they are not sold below current market price. Congressional action is required to release materials in the National or Strategic Stockpile and the supplemented stockpile, unless the President invokes the issues of national defense or obsolescence. In 1965, some 95 items were in the stockpiles—the National Stockpile was the biggest with 5.9 billion dollars worth of goods, the DPA Inventory contained about 0.9 billion dollars worth, and the Supplemental Stockpile about 1.3 billion dollars worth. Other government agencies have from time to time accumulated inventories of minerals but these are not formally called stockpiles; for example, the Atomic Energy Commission acquired substantial amounts of mercury in the 1950s, a large part of which was declared surplus in 1964 (52,000 flasks). The General Services Administration manages the National Strategic Stockpile, the Defense Pro-

TABLE VIII.I

Inventories of Mineral Commodities in U.S. Stockpiles

(Bureau of Mines, Mineral Facts and Problems, 1965 ed., and Chemical Week, August 21, 1965, p. 76) [1]

Commodity	Strategic Stockpile	DPA[2] Stockpile	CCC[3] Stockpile	Supplemental Stockpile	Total 6/30/64	Sold prior to May 1965	Declared excess as of May 1965
Aluminum (thousand short tons)	1,127	819	—	—	1,946	50	1,450
Asbestos (thousand short tons) All grades	19,496	2,348	10,352	70,074	101,270	14,000	61
Bauxite (thousands of long dry tons)							
Metal grade	5,843	1,370	806	8,707	16,726	—	6,400
Refractory grade	299	—	—	—	299	—	—
Beryllium (short tons beryl, ~11% BeO)							
All grades	23,230	2,543	6,576	17,778	50,127	?	?
Beryllium metal and alloys	1,075	—		6,465	7,540	?	?
Chromium (short tons of ore and concentrate) Chromite—							
Chemical grade	559,452	—	—	699,584	1,259,036	25,000	4,000,000
Metallurgical grade	3,795,102	532	172,028	1,543,110	5,510,772		
Refractory grade	1,047,159	—	—	179,775	1,226,934		
Cobalt (thousands of pounds contained cobalt) All grades	76,067	25,067	—	1,065	102,199	—	60,000

(Continued on following page)

Copper (thousands of short tons)	1,008	96	—	11	1,115	53	290
Diamond, Industrial (millions of carats)	39.4	—	—	20.9	64.3	?	?
Fluorspar (thousands of short tons)							
Acid grade	458	17	—	669	1,144	350	266
Metallurgical grade	369	—	—	43	412	—	.243
Lead (thousands of short tons)							
Refined lead	1,050	—	—	328	1,378	50	1,300
Magnesium (short tons)							
Primary	173,484	—	—	—	173,484	4,000	25,000
Manganese (thousands short ton Mn ore)							
Battery grade	165	4	—	138	307	100	53,000
Chemical grade	31	—	—	217	248		
Metallurgical, all grades	5,852	3,057	112	3,683	12,704		
Mercury (76-# flasks)	184,501	—	—	16,000	200,501	500	365[4]
Mica (thousands of short tons)							
Strategic, all grades	25.78	3.28	.16	4.30	33.52	.10	20.2
Molybdenum (thousands of pounds contained Mo)	80,086	—	—	—	80,086	10,000	1,000
Nickel (short tons)							
Stockpile grade	166,914	52,364	—	—	219,278	7,000	162,000

TABLE VIII.1 (Continued)

INVENTORIES OF MINERAL COMMODITIES IN U.S. STOCKPILES

(Bureau of Mines, Mineral Facts and Problems, 1965 ed., and Chemical Week, August 21, 1965, p. 76).

Commodity	Strategic Stockpile	DPA² Stockpile	CCC³ Stockpile	Supplemental Stockpile	Total 6/30/64	Sold prior to May 1965	Declared excess as of May 1965
Platinum group (thousands troy ounces)	820	—	—	698.1	1518.1	—	316
Rutile (thousands short tons of concentrate)	19	17	—	12	48	?	?
Tin (long tons pig tin)	314,129	—	—	7,505	321,634	30,000	94,000
Titanium (short tons sponge metal)	—	22,356	—	9,021	31,377	—	—
Tungsten (thousands pounds contained metal) Ore and concentrate	120,071	77,864	—	5,775	203,710	800	158,900
Vanadium (thousands of pounds contained vanadium)	15,730	—	—	—	15,730	—	12,000
Zinc (thousands of short tons)	1,257	—	—	324	1,581	100	1,500

[1] Includes only those commodities discussed in Chapter X. Also included in the various stockpiles are: antimony, bismuth, cadmium, columbium-tantalum, corundum, graphite, iodine, kyanite, quartz crystal, rare-earths, selenium, strontium, talc and soapstone, and thorium.

[2] DPA = Defense Production Act.

[3] CCC = Commodity Credit Corporation.

[4] There have been more recent sales through 1965 of about 35,000 flasks.

duction Act stockpile, and the Supplemental Stockpile; the Commodity Credit Corporation manages its own pipeline stockpile. However, a large number of different boards and agencies have been and are involved in stockpile matters. Prior to the Korean war, the Munitions Board (Defense Department) and the National Security Board (Executive Office of the President) had the most responsibility. During the Korean war, the Defense Production Administration became the central authority. Subsequently, in 1953, the Office of Defense Mobilization took over the then existing Strategic and DPA stockpiles. The Commodity Credit Corporation came on the scene in 1954 when the Supplemental Stockpile was created. Administration of the stockpiles, procurement policies, disposal, and objectives have come under a great deal of criticism in recent years. In 1965 a so-called Omnibus Stockpile bill was considered by Congress. Formally titled the Materials Reserve Stockpile Act of 1965, the Act proposed to consolidate the existing accumulations of materials into the National Stockpile and the Materials Reserve Inventory and provide for rotation of materials for sale and disposal. It would also eliminate the present requirement that Congress approve each sale and give the President the authority to make sales and determine prices. Congress, however, was reluctant to turn its prerogatives with regard to stockpiles over to the executive branch and the bill was postponed indefinitely after extensive hearings. Recently a number of mineral commodities have been sold as excess or surplus from the stockpiles including cadmium, copper, lead, magnesium, mercury, nickel, tin, tungsten, zinc, zircon, and others (Table VIII.1). In general, the consumers of mineral raw materials have favored such sales while mineral producers have opposed them. Critics of the stockpile program protest that the government, as a major buyer and seller, can control supplies and prices. They are concerned that elimination of congressional approval will result in producers having no voice in stockpile sales. That there is some substance to this concern was well illustrated in November of 1965 when the government, in a determined attempt to prevent aluminum and copper price increases, threatened immediate and massive stockpile sales of these metals. Congress was by-passed because the President considered the Vietnam fighting as sufficient reason to invoke emergency powers in the interests of national defense. The position of those opposed to the action was well illustrated by a cartoon in E&MJ Metal & Mineral Markets for November 15, 1965 (Pendergast, 1965, p. 5) reproduced here as figure VIII.1.

However, from the consumer's point of view, stockpile sales have

FIGURE VIII.1

The government stockpile and the aluminum price crisis of November, 1965 (after Pendergast, 1965, p. 5).

'Let us reason together'

eased many painful temporary shortages and smoothed out irregularities in mineral supply. It was proposed in the case of copper that the government make loans from the stockpile to be repaid at times of more abundant supply, but this plan was not approved. In any case, the stockpile is a reality and despite problems of management is important to national security.

Apart from strategic necessity, the stockpile has been of value as an economic stabilizer. It has been used for this purpose—to maintain productive capacity at a desirable level, to alleviate distress in domestic mineral industries, to ease shortages and guarantee an orderly flow of needed raw materials to industry for a number of years (Netschert, 1962, p. 183). But although there has been *de facto* commodity stabilization through purchase and sale of stockpile items, even the producers and consumers who were most benefitted have avoided endorsement of the procedure as a proper and continuing function of government. Each transaction is an extraordinary event carefully considered by the cumbersome machinery of Congress. A sale sets no precedents. If a materials reserve apart from the strategic stockpile were to be established to operate as an efficient economic stabilizer it would require continuing purchases to make up for disposition by sales with an acquisition-disposal system that does not require congressional authority for each transaction. Such a stockpile or materials reserve puts the government in the market place as a regular buyer and seller of minerals, permits the government to set and control prices, and in short is a further step toward a managed economy. In this writer's opinion, however, future burgeoning demands for minerals and the likelihood of sporadic political interruptions in supplies from foreign sources will require some sort of in-and-out domestic materials reserve to prevent segments of U.S. industry from facing serious shortages. Excesses in existing stockpiles will not last forever and will have to be replaced for cold-war industrial protection even if not required in a strategic sense for a hot war. Lovering (1953, p. 123) called for a National Materials Reserve apart from the military or strategic stockpiles:

I propose a large government-owned reserve of industrial raw materials as suitable to the economy of a great industrial power. Such reserves would constitute reservoirs of mineral wealth of far greater value and economic power than any gold treasure in Fort Knox or the Denver mint and would represent a perennial addition to national wealth.

Stockpile inventories of major mineral items as of June 30, 1964, with modification through May 1965 are shown in Table VIII.1. There are a total of 95 materials (including nonmineral materials) inventoried but 18 of them now carry objectives of zero, so there are quotas for some 77 items. How much copper and lead should we stockpile? How are the objectives determined? This question is, of course, the central issue in the stockpile program. To answer it requires evaluation of United States needs during war, conventional or nuclear. Thus, as planners attempt to peer into the future, stockpiles change. New materials are added, old materials are increased, reduced, or eliminated. Specifications are changed. Some materials declared excess are sold in times of domestic shortages, others remain as 'excess.' Presently (1965) the Office of Emergency Planning is studying the needs of the United States in the event of a nuclear war. With widespread devastation, return of order would depend on how fast transportation and communications systems could be restored. Copper and aluminum wire would be needed in large quantities. Petroleum would undoubtedly be vital. Lead and zinc, on the other hand, would not be so critical during a recovery period when manufacture of items such as automobiles and appliances would be at a standstill. If fabricated or manufactured products are stockpiled there is a loss of flexibility and a high risk that the manufactured article will become obsolete while in the stockpile. Thus the general policy has been to stockpile only raw materials.

As national security is threatened by shortages of minerals in time of war so, in a sense, is it threatened by abundant low-cost foreign supplies in time of peace. There are parts of the world where rich high-grade deposits can be produced at costs substantially below prevailing costs in the United States. If such commodities are freely imported in large volumes, higher-cost domestic industries can be crippled or killed. The government must consider, then, the effect on national security if such supplies are cut off and there is no domestic industry to supply the necessary mineral commodity or commodities. The question of national security is perhaps more closely tied to oil than to any other mineral commodity because of the essential nature of this mineral fuel. Foreign oil producers, most of them U.S.-based companies, want a share of the United States market for their abundant cheaply-produced foreign oil; domestic producers want to limit oil imports. Walter J. Levy, an international oil expert, was recently quoted by the *Oil and Gas Journal* as follows (Oil and Gas Journal, 1965, p. 46):

Let me add that the importance of ample U.S. oil reserves and excess capacity is immense—not just for the direct national defense in the narrow sense but in terms of our worldwide power position. If we were ever to become decisively dependent on imports of foreign oil, we would soon become subject to unacceptable economic and political pressures by a few major oil producing countries— as would western Europe.

In the present aligned world there is another side to this coin which is of concern to foreign policy makers. If friendly nations are shut off from profitable U.S. markets, their own economies are threatened—particularly in the case of one-crop countries which depend on a single mineral commodity such as oil, copper, or lead-zinc for a large part of their foreign exchange. Good will toward the U.S. is likewise damaged and a potential source of the mineral commodity during times of need becomes less secure. If such action on the part of the United States results in economic depression—albeit short term—in the exporting country, political stability may be destroyed.

An editorial in the Oil and Gas Journal (1965, p. 47) commented on the U.S. oil import policy and stated:

Imports will not be held down to the point of outright protectionism, as desired by independents. To do so might cause repercussions from domestic consumers and certainly from foreign producing countries. National Security is envisioned not as economic self-sufficiency but as access to diverse global supplies and fostering the goodwill and economic progress of many foreign nations.

Some years ago the domestic lead and zinc mining industry in the United States was in a state of severe depression. Import quotas were put on lead and zinc with specific quotas allotted to various producing countries. Countries selling large quantities of lead-zinc to the United States, including Australia, Canada, Mexico, and Peru, protested these quotas vigorously. Inasmuch as trade is a two-way street and we also are a major exporter, such action did not help the United States position in general tariff negotiations. Recently it has been argued that lead-zinc import quotas are no longer necessary because of the economic recovery of the domestic industry. The quota system was ended by presidential proclamation October 22, 1965. This particular industry is also assisted by a small-producer's subsidy geared to a base price. Another example is the domestic fluorspar industry. It has been unable to compete with cheap imported fluorspar, mostly from Mexico, and has urged a higher protective tariff. A high tariff might result in severe depression in the Mexican states of Coahuila and Chihuahua where fluorspar mining is a major industry.

The goal of all these mechanisms, quotas, tariffs, subsidies, tax policies, and even stockpile purchases and releases, is to strike a balance between domestic industry and foreign trade which will be in the best interests of national security, overall foreign relations, and the United States mineral economy. To what extent the various contesting forces are brought into balance is really a test of United States mineral policy. There is perhaps no official U.S. document which presents *the* mineral policy of the United States. Such policy is the sum total of laws and administrative regulations extant. Ridge (1962, p. 291) has expressed the opinion that this vague and formless collection of statutes and orders is not adequate:

I would contend, however, that these laws and regulations as they now stand, do not constitute a truly adequate program on which to base our industrial economy. A sound national mineral policy should have as its clearly expressed and legally possible goal the supply of mineral raw materials this country needs at the times and places and in the quantities required. This our present laws and regulations do not guarantee.

It might be well to point out here that under the broad economic theory which built the United States, the *lack* of laws and regulations is just as much policy as their existence. Ideally, in a market system, laws and regulations are at a minimum and are designed chiefly to impart enough stability for long-term planning. Any mineral policy must concern itself with the health of the domestic industry and its capabilities, foreign mineral trade, and national security. Domestically, the concern must be equally divided between the manufacturing consumer of mineral raw materials who must be guaranteed his supplies and the producer who must be guaranteed an economic climate in which he can operate. The importance of the exploration phase of the producers' effort is commonly overlooked or deemphasized but is really the long-term key to a healthy domestic industry. Any national policy which does not recognize the domestic industry's need to enter upon and explore the public lands of the United States will result in a United States more dependent on foreign sources. Perhaps the most valid criticism of U.S. mineral policy is not the lack of statutes and regulations but the patchwork structure that has been built. A full review with the goal of coordinating domestic and foreign policy is in order.

TAXATION

The mineral industry, like other industry, pays income taxes, federal and state, and *ad valorem* property taxes. In addition, they have been and are subject to a variety of special state taxes variously called mining taxes, occupation taxes, production taxes and severance taxes. There are also sales and excise taxes on mineral products. There is a wide variation from state to state. Taxation of mineral property has been reviewed by Roberts (1944) and Borden (1964).

In some states, mining property has been taxed at a higher rate than nonmining property. In Michigan, for example, until recently, iron mining properties were taxed at full market value whereas nonmining property was taxed at some fraction of market value. This discriminatory approach was changed in 1963 so that mining and nonmining properties are now assessed on the same basis (Act No.

66, Public Acts of 1963). In Minnesota, prior to 1964, the iron mining industry was in decline. Although excluded from the state's corporate income tax, it was burdened with occupation and royalty taxes that resulted in iron mining corporations paying about three times the state's corporate income tax rate. In order to attract industry to invest in the state's huge reserves of low-grade siliceous iron ore (taconite), Minnesota voters in 1964 passed the Taconite Amendment which guaranteed that for a period of 25 years taxes on taconite production will not be increased above the general corporate level.

The federal government has used tax policy to encourage development of mineral properties by permitting accelerated 'write-off' of capital investment (recovery of capital through accelerated depreciation or amortization schedules), rewarding new investment by allowing investment tax credits, and providing options for recovery of exploration and development expenditures. Boericke and Bailey (1964, pp. 258–259) described government aid in financing the White Pine project of the Copper Range Company in the early 1950s through (1) a long-term loan of capital funds, (2) certification of a part of the cost for accelerated depreciation, and (3) a procurement contract at a base price. Certain foreign countries have gone further. Canada provides a 3–3½-year income-tax-free period for new mines, with liberal depreciation schedules and depletion allowances (p. 179). Puerto Rico allows a 10-year tax-exemption period for new industries, including mining; in Jamaica the tax-free period is 7 years; Ireland provides for half-rate tax for the first four years; in Greece a special initial tax rate is negotiated (Koenig, 1964).

The most important aspect of U.S. tax policy as far as the mineral industry is concerned is the depletion allowance provision of the Internal Revenue Code. The understanding of the application of depletion allowances to nonrenewable mineral resources is fundamental to understanding of the economics of the domestic mineral industry.

Percentage depletion provisions of the U.S. Internal Revenue Code.

Probably no aspect of government-mineral industry relations has been debated as long or as hotly as the percentage depletion provisions of the Internal Revenue Code. These are the provisions which entitle the mineral producer to deduct from the gross income from property a percentage allowance as specified under the code so long as the deduction does not exceed 50 per cent of taxable income computed without the depletion allowance. Gross income from property means the gross income from the mining or extractive process; rents or royalties on the property can be excluded from calculation of gross income. The percentage allowance varies from 5 per cent for commodities such as sand and gravel, to 10 per cent for coal and asbestos, to 15 per cent for most metals, to 23 per cent for sulfur and uranium, to $27\frac{1}{2}$ per cent for oil and gas.

The reason for the percentage depletion allowance is part of overall U.S. income tax philosophy which holds than an individual or corporation should be taxed on income after legitimate costs of doing business are deducted. Thus, if a manufacturer must purchase a building and machines to produce a marketable product he is entitled to recover the cost of the building and machines from gross income prior to computation of the net income on which the tax is based. He does this by capitalizing the building and machines and deducting a percentage of their cost each year over the life of the building and working life of the machines. This is called depreciation.

The mineral producer may not have to buy a factory, but he does have to buy or find a concentration of minerals which can be economically produced. Thus his capital cost, or a large part of it, is in the mineral deposit. Like the manufacturer's factory and machines, the mineral deposit has a 'working life' in that when the deposit is mined out it is exhausted. Because mineral deposits are nonrenewable resources, they are termed wasting assets. The percentage depletion allowance, then, permits the producer to recover his capital investment in the deposit, whether through purchase or the cost of exploration. This principle as stated by the U.S. Supreme Court in *Anderson* v. *Helvering* (310 U.S. 408) reads:

The granting of an arbitrary deduction in the interests of convenience of a percentage of the gross income derived from the severance of oil and gas merely emphasizes the underlying theory of the allowance as a tax-free return of the capital consumed in the production of gross income through severance.

Percentage depletion is a method adopted by Congress in 1926 to simplify various earlier conceived depletion systems based on cost (1913), value as of March 1, 1913, or value as established 30 days after discovery (1918). The so-called cost depletion and discovery-value depletion methods of recovering the capital invested in a wasting asset in general proved so complex and cumbersome that the government, after study of a large body of industry data, established percentage depletion as a more workable system for certain industries. The operator, however, still has the option to calculate a depletion schedule based on his original cost instead of using percentage depletion.

There is no question that in permitting recovery of some exploration costs from gross income prior to tax computation, this procedure encourages exploration and draws capital into the mineral extraction industries. If exploration expenditures had to be recovered from net income, exploration programs would be more conservatively budgeted and the domestic mineral resource base would be adversely affected.

Some of the critics of percentage depletion object to the percentages, stating that they are too high; others object to the principle, arguing that it is a tax loophole or a special favored treatment for one industry. The percentages are admittedly arbitrary. They are supposed to reflect the different cost ratios of various industries, the extraction rates or duration of operation, and an average of acquisition costs. As the mineral industry changes, revisions (up or down) in the percentage allowance might well be in order. The well-known $27\frac{1}{2}$ per cent depletion for oil and gas, for example, is the result of a compromise between the U.S. Senate which recommended 30 per cent and the U.S. House of Representatives which recommended 25 per cent. If it can be shown that such an allowance permits recovery of more than the costs of finding and acquiring deposits of oil and gas, then that extra amount is nothing more than an incentive to stimulate exploration. In such a case, there is some basis for referring to percentage depletion as a subsidy. However, petroleum industry figures reported by Hiestand (1960, pp. 419–420) show that a $33\frac{1}{3}$ per cent allowance is necessary to return the cost of acquiring reserves to replace those produced and that the existing $27\frac{1}{2}$ per cent shortchanges the industry. Without percentage depletion (or cost depletion), it would be more attractive economically to sell mineral properties under the long-term capital gains provisions of the tax laws than to operate mines or oil fields (if anyone wanted to buy them under those conditions).

The Internal Revenue Code of 1939 as amended in 1951 provided for depletion at different rates for (1) stone and marble, 5 per cent; (2) calcium carbonates, magnesium carbonates, and dolomites, 10 per cent; and (3) chemical and metallurgical grade limestone, 15 per cent. By allowing three different rates for what is generally limestone, the stage was set for prolonged and expensive litigation to do nothing more than define for tax purposes terms in common use in industry and to determine whether or not the allowance should be based on the physical and chemical specifications of the product or the use to which it is put (Cooper, 1965). The 1954 code corrected some of the mistakes of 1951 but relied on the dubious guide of product-use rather than physical and chemical specifications to determine which allowance shall be permitted. Depletion allowances under the 1954 code are as follows (American Law of Mining, 1964, pp. 70–72):

(1) 27-½%—oil and gas wells.

(2) 23%—sulfur and uranium. Also included is a lengthy list of metallic and non-metallic minerals to which the 23% rate applies if the minerals are produced from deposits in the United States. If such minerals are produced from deposits outside the United States, the applicable rate is determined under group (3), (4), or (6), whichever is appropriate.

(3) 15%—ball clay, bentonite, china clay, sagger clay, metal mines (if the 23% rate for domestic minerals is not applicable), rock asphalt and vermiculite.

(4) 10%—asbestos (if the 23% rate for domestic minerals is not applicable), brucite, coal, lignite, perlite, sodium chloride and wollastonite.

(5) 5%—brick and tile clay, gravel, mollusk shells (including clam and oyster shells), peat, pumice, sand, scoria, shale and stone (except stone described in group (6). Also included in the 5% group are bromine, calcium chloride and magnesium chloride if they are produced from brine wells.

(6) 15%—all minerals not included in groups (1) through (5). A number of minerals are specifically named in this residual or "catchall" group but with no limiting intent. Stone, if used or sold for use as dimension stone or ornamental stone, is included in this group; otherwise, it is in the 5% group. Certain minerals specifically named in this group are eligible for the 23% rate if produced from deposits in the United States; otherwise, the 15% rate applies. Any mineral in this 15% group, whether specifically named or not, is depletable at the 5% rate if used or sold for use as rip rap, ballast, road material, rub-

ble, concrete aggregates, or for similar purposes unless sold on bid in direct competition with a bona fide bid to sell a mineral listed in group (3). For example, limestone is depletable at 15% if used or sold for use other than as rip rap, ballast, road material etc. However, if it is used or sold for use in any of these applications, it is depletable at 5% unless sold under the specified competitive conditions with, for example, rock asphalt, which is entitled to the 15% rate under group (3). Specifically excluded from group (6) and therefore not eligible for percentage depletion are soil, sod, dirt, turf, water, mosses, and minerals from sea water, the air, or similar inexhaustible sources.

A practical difficulty in applying the allowable percentage depletion has arisen in some mineral industries where the mined product is not sold but manufactured into a mineral product. The difficulty lies in determining gross value from mining under those circumstances. For example, there is rarely a market for clay used to manufacture common brick or for some kinds of cement rock used to make Portland cement. However, it is the raw material that is being depleted, not bricks or cement. In such cases, the U.S. Internal Revenue Department has moved to establish area values for the mined raw material at some point in its flow from mine through mill. Industry costs are considered in establishing value. Many of the problems of codifying depletion allowances could be avoided by better communication between the authors of government tax law on the one hand and geologists and engineers on the other.

The United States is not the only country with depletion provisions under the tax laws. For example, Canada allows a $33\frac{1}{3}$ per cent for metal mines, oil and gas wells, and some industrial mineral mines; France allows $27\frac{1}{2}$ per cent for oil providing that a like amount is invested in oil activities in France or the French Union within 5 years. Of course, in the many parts of the world where minerals are owned by a national government, the operator does not own the mineral deposit but acquires rights to produce it through concession and lease. He does not have a cost of acquisition beyond exploration and operating costs which commonly are recovered under the terms of the concession-lease prior to full profit-sharing with the national owner.

Those who object to the basic theory of depletion are really objecting to a long-established United States tradition that capital should not be taxed. Furthermore, they seem to be unable to appreciate special factors in the mineral industry which have to do with the origin and distribution of mineral deposits (pp. 22–30). Particularly, they seem not to appreciate the risks in exploration where large sums must be spent without any guarantee of recovery of any part of the investment. If the failures cannot be paid for by the successes, then exploration will not be privately financed. The proposition that acquisition costs, including exploration costs, can be recovered out of net income by increasing the price of the product would result in erosion of capital by taxation because the amount recovered by sale and allocated to purchase or discovery of a new deposit to replace an exhausted one would be subject to income tax at the prevailing corporate or individual rate.

Thus, existing depletion provisions are a recognition of the nature of a wasting asset. Modification or alteration of them would change the economics of the mineral industry and have far-reaching effects on the U.S. economy. Clearly, any such changes should be made only after exhaustive study of the entire industry; piecemeal or patchwork alterations are to be avoided. The depletion provisions are a part of the nation's mineral policy and must be considered together with other foreign and domestic mineral problems.

MINERALS AND MONEY

Introduction.

Are gold and/or silver necessary for sound currency systems?

This question is debated more heatedly—and sometimes more acrimoniously—than any other economic question now before our society, and the correct answer to it is perhaps more important to the well-being and security of the United States—or any nation—than any other. There can be no long-term military strength without economic strength. Although the battle lines are not sharply drawn, there is a tendency for bankers to answer the question with an emphatic Yes!, whereas theoretical economists and political scientists respond with a resounding No!

Those who answer in the negative argue that the amount of gold or silver hoarded by a country is no real measure of its economic strength or ability to pay debts. A thriving, productive society with full employment is able to maintain favorable trade balances through productiveness, whether or not there is an ounce of gold in the treasury; money should be managed so as to bring about full employment. Those who believe in the importance of gold and/or silver, the bankers who conduct the world's financial transactions on a day-to-day basis, reply to this argument by calling history as a witness. The economic health of a nation, they say, is like that of an individual, variable and can change suddenly; prosperity is temporary and a matter of degree. A reserve of gold, a commodity with a recognized value the world over, lends stability.[2] The currency of a country without a reserve of precious metal is an unsecured promissory note and its value is difficult to measure, or rather, difficult to relate to the values of other currencies secured all or in part by gold. In the world market place, the value of the currency of a nation without gold reserves may be subject to fluctuations depending on short-term analysis of its economic well-being.

This introduces the concept of value or worth. According to the dictionary, *value* is the desirability or worth of a thing as compared with the desirability of something else, and *worth* is the qualities and circumstances on which, taken together, such desirability depends. Economists have attempted to define the value of something in several different ways—on the degree of demand for it, on the amount of labor embodied in the item, or on the cost of reproducing it. Practically, however, the value of something is measured by what it can be exchanged for in terms of goods or services, at a given time in a given place.

Since prehistoric times, gold and to a lesser extent silver, have had value in this practical sense in nearly all cultures—that is, they could be exchanged for some quantity of goods or services. Paper currencies, on the other hand, have many times in the course of history been reduced to little or no value through the collapse of the issuing institution. Some analysts on the modern scene are impatient with introduction of the historical record as a witness for the importance of gold or silver in backing up paper currencies. Perhaps it is natural for an individual to regard his own time as somehow different or even unique, and to believe that progress or changes have made it impossible for past events to repeat themselves. To this writer, however, the lessons of 8,000 years of history are impressive indeed. It is very difficult for the most articulate of economic and political theorists to persuade individuals who have experienced the ephemeral and

---

[2] Although historically important as a monetary standard, silver is not now held as international reserves.

unstable character of political systems in the past, and seen so-called hard currencies turn soft, that gold and silver have no real value outside of an industrial value for jewelry, electronics, and photography. A glance at the world free gold market shows that the highest price for gold—with a premium for easily transportable coins—prevails where there is the least political security. In the final analysis, a commodity has value because someone else wants it.

The nature of money.

Money performs several different functions in world society. It is, of course, a convenient medium of exchange, replacing the cumbersome barter systems which prevailed in pre-money or money-short societies. By reducing grains, hogs, soap, and the worth of a day's labor to a common unit of value, the business of the market place was rendered infinitely simpler and more convenient. Monetary units provide a uniform common denominator for keeping accounts and records of such business. Money also performs an important purpose in providing a way of accumulating or storing up wealth. A surplus of labor, perishable goods, and durable goods can be converted to money and accumulated. Money is of two kinds—money with *intrinsic* value and money with *token* value.

Money with intrinsic value is, of course, money wherein the circulating medium is itself recognized by society as valuable. Gold and silver coins are historically the substance of intrinsically valuable money, but other durable and easily transportable substances such as gems could serve the same purpose. However, a money system using gems would be awkward because of their relative scarcity, the difficulty of judging their value, and the problem of reducing them to standard units of weight or value. It is important that the value of money be easily measurable without complicated testing and analysis, but the basic premise is that the substance be generally recognized as having value in itself. Of course, when a society is under extreme pressures, even long and well-accepted standards of value fall. Thus a starving man will exchange his goods and labor for something to eat rather than for gold. It is not difficult to imagine situations where such items as fishhooks, nails, and blankets would take on extraordinary value as compared to gold. But these situations are or have been isolated and temporary whereas gold, silver, and gems have been recognized as having value over millenia. Other metals such as copper, iron, and lead, as well as alloys, have been used for coins at various times in various parts of the world, but these were more tokens than intrinsically valuable.

Token money, commonly paper but also including coins with a monetary value in excess of metal value, is merely a record of a promise of payment by a responsible institution. Historically, this token money became acceptable in society only when the holder had the option of converting it to money with intrinsic value. As society became accustomed to token money, however, the option of conversion was denied or restricted; confidence was maintained by public belief that the issuing institution held a reserve of gold, silver, and other assets to back up the token currency. In the United States, over a period of many years, the legal requirements for the gold reserve which must be maintained by institutions issuing currency, namely Federal Reserve Banks, has been twice reduced. In 1963 in the United States, money with intrinsic value—silver coins—constituted about 8 per cent of U.S. currency and about 92 per cent was token money. The token currency consisted of about 85 per cent Federal Reserve notes, 5 per cent silver certificates (which could be exchanged for silver), and 2 per cent other paper. In 1965, however, the silver certificates, the only remaining convertible token currency, were being retired and were rapidly disappearing from circulation. In July of 1964 there were about 2.1 billion dollars of silver certificates in circulation; by March of 1965 the total had declined to 1.1 billion dollars. Under the law, Federal Reserve notes must be backed up by gold certificates held by issuing banks in the amount of not less than 25 per cent of the value of the circulating currency. In mid-1965, the back up gold reserve ratio stood at about 39 per cent and was falling. The requirement that Federal Reserve Banks must also secure the deposits of member banks by gold certificates up to 25 per cent of their value was quietly dropped in early 1965. These progressive decreases in gold back up requirements reflect, of course, decreases in the United States gold reserves and increases in Federal Reserve notes.

Gold, silver, and the gold standard.

Gold through history has been a mobile metal flowing with the currents of conquest and political power. As an undisputed symbol of wealth, it flowed as loot from conquered lands to the victorious nations. It has also been an index of economic health, moving away from societies which consumed more than they produced. Rickard

(1932, p. 501) remarked on the outward flow of gold and silver currency which marked the decline of the Roman Empire—profligate spending for luxuries (silks, ivories, spices) without balancing exports resulted in heavy flows of Roman gold and silver to India and the Far East.

As of 1963, the world monetary gold reserve outside of the Communist Bloc was about 42 billion dollars. Annual world production is about 53 million ounces. The price of gold is held within narrow limits by United States' maintenance of a fixed price of 35 dollars per ounce. Foreign central banks can exchange dollars for gold at this price—that is to say, the United States will sell gold for 35 dollars an ounce and thereby holds a ceiling on the price. The United States will purchase gold at 35 dollars per ounce and therefore has established a floor under the price. In 1958, the United States held a gold reserve of 20.6 billion dollars—about half the world supply exclusive of the Communist Bloc whose reserves are not public information. In mid-1965, the U.S. gold reserve had declined to 13.9 billion dollars or about one-third of the world supply exclusive of the Communist Bloc. According to Triffin (1964, p. 82) Soviet stocks have been estimated as low as 2 billion dollars, but probably the more reliable estimate is 7.5 to 9.5 billion dollars (as of 1963). If correct, this would raise the known world supply of government-held gold about 10 per cent. Private hoards and jewelry are not included in the total.

World production of silver is about 256 million ounces per year. This production, plus accumulated supplies, is not adequate to meet current and projected demands for both industrial purposes and coinage. Policies of the U.S. Treasury control or strongly influence the world silver market. U.S. Treasury stocks, accumulated by buying over a period of many years, have been sharply depleted in recent years and, if the depletion rate is continued, face exhaustion in a very few years. Buying by the Treasury ceased in May 1963. Between 1958 and 1964 the Treasury stocks declined from about 2.1 billion ounces to 1.2 billion ounces. The Treasury sold silver at about 0.91 dollars per ounce until November of 1961 when sales were halted; thereafter the price rose rapidly until June 1963 when it reached 1.293 dollars per ounce, a price equal to the monetary value of the silver dollar. This price will hold as a ceiling as long as silver certificates can be exchanged for silver metal. When these are largely converted, the price may rise so that it would be profitable to melt silver coins. Legislation passed in mid-1965 reduced sharply the silver content of U.S. 50-cent pieces and eliminated silver from smaller coins. Reduction of coinage requirements will tend to relieve demand, extend the life of existing Treasury stocks, and stabilize the price.

The gold standard came upon the scene as a result of the British Parliament's Gold Standard Act of 1816. It was the product of several centuries of money problems and attempts to work out a money philosophy. The single metallic currency standard thereby initiated endured for 93 years and transformed the British sterling currency into a world-wide hard currency. The gold standard is a monetary standard under which the basic unit of currency is defined by a stated quantity of gold; it is usually characterized by coinage and circulation of gold, unrestricted convertibility of other money into gold, and the free import and export of gold for settlement of international obligations. Under the classic gold-standard system, both domestic and international currencies are tied firmly to gold. An international trade deficit thus reduces the amount of domestic money and initiates a corrective action by lessening domestic demand, lowering prices, and increasing competitive exports.

The United States embarked on its monetary philosophy with the Mint Act of 1792 which provided for a bimetallic standard, gold and silver, until 1873 when the gold-standard system was adopted. The Gold Standard Act of 1920 strengthened the system. In 1933, however, a presidential order closing the banks effectively suspended the gold standard and successive laws (Banking Act of 1933 and Gold Reserve Act of 1934) conveyed to the Executive broad powers to manage the money of the United States. The United States now operates on what is called the limited-gold-bullion standard under which the coinage and circulation of gold is prohibited, but a gold-bullion reserve is maintained to support the currency and the shipment of gold in international transactions is permitted. It is limited because only foreign central banks can convert dollars into gold.

Since World War II, the economies of many countries have experienced large-scale changes; currencies once stable in world markets became soft. Periods of profligate public spending brought some countries near disaster. Inflation was followed by austerity and by more inflation as governments came and went. Some countries under the economic philosophies of Karl Marx or Lord Keynes instituted a 'managed currency system' wherein purchasing power of the currency was adjusted by a monetary authority to influence business activity and prices; such a managed currency has no fixed relationship to a metal standard. Under Lord Keynes' theory, management of money is the mechanism by which full employment is achieved.

Currently· prevailing in most of the free world is a gold exchange standard. Under this system, domestic currency is maintained at parity with the standard money of a foreign gold standard or gold bullion standard country. Gold is not used to back up domestic currency but only as an international reserve to settle net import-export differences. The international reserve includes reserves of so-called hard currencies—dollars and sterling—as well as gold. In most countries, the central bank charged with responsibility for maintaining international reserves limits the amounts of foreign hard currencies held, and thus when dollars or sterling accumulate above a certain level they are exchanged for gold. The practice of using some national currencies as international reserves has been attacked by some economists (Triffin, 1960; Boarman, 1965). The drain on U.S. gold reserves, which has been continuous since 1957, shows that since that time the U.S. has been spending, lending, and giving away overseas more dollars than it takes in through trade. Military spending and foreign aid are large items in this overdraft; another substantial item is foreign investment by U.S. corporations. It is these dollars which accumulate in foreign banks and are exchanged for gold. Under the gold standard, these balances would be settled on a regular basis.

One result of post-war economic confusion and the need for order and stability in world trade was the creation of the International Monetary Fund.

International Monetary Fund, international currency reserves, and international liquidity.

The International Monetary Fund (IMF) is a special agency of the United Nations, officially authorized as early as 1944 and formed in 1946. In the late 1950s, the fund's membership had grown to 67 members; by 1965 there were 102 members. The mission of IMF is to stabilize international money exchange rates through assistance to member nations in the form of technical advice and by loans of gold or hard currencies to meet temporary difficulties in settlement of international balances. Each member nation subscribes to the fund in terms of a quota. Of this quota, 25 per cent, or 10 per cent of the nation's gold and dollar reserves (whichever is smaller) must be subscribed in gold. The remainder is in the national currency. In 1958 the fund contained over 9 billion dollars of which about 2.5 billion was in gold and convertible currency. Member nations cannot substantially alter exchange values or devalue without prior approval of the IMF. Quotas were increased in 1965 by 25 per cent. As a result, the IMF now holds a substantial part of the world's gold supply.

Liquidity is a measure of money available in a monetary system and international liquidity refers to the amount of money available to finance world trade—namely, gold, dollars, sterling, and access to credit. Practically, it is the total of international reserves. These total about 70 billion dollars, 40 billion of which is gold, 25 billion is in dollars and sterling, and the remainder is in IMF drawing accounts (Triffin, 1964, Table 8). That part of world reserves made up of gold rose from 85 per cent in 1913 to 95 per cent in 1933–34, and then declined steadily to about 60 per cent in 1962 (Triffin, 1964, p. 27). Because of a great post-war expansion in world trade and a diminishing world monetary reserve as compared to world imports, some economists hold that more international liquidity is needed. Other economists have challenged this view, stating that continued inflation proves there is *too much* liquidity and pointing out that reserves are used to settle differences, not to consummate transactions. According to this conservative view, monetary discipline to cure inflation will solve the problem of liquidity. In any case, a number of plans to increase international liquidity have been offered such as (1) expansion and reorganization of the International Monetary Fund to a money-creating world central bank, or (2) simultaneous world-wide currency devaluation. The latter plan involves increasing the price of gold, or, looking at it another way, increasing international reserves and international liquidity by making the gold security worth more. At the present price, the world supply of gold is not sufficient to serve as security for an expanded world currency. Wonnacott (1963) suggested that a gradual upward revaluation at a rate of 2 per cent per year, or at a rate less than that prevailing for government bills, would eliminate the economic shock of a sudden major change not previously announced, and at the same time make speculation unprofitable. An increase in the price of gold, by whatever means, is of great interest to the student of mineral resources; it will change the economics of gold mining the world over and make exploitable low-grade deposits that cannot now be profitably worked.

Proposals to meet the alleged shortage of reserves through the IMF are exemplified by the so-called Roosa Plan put forward by former Under Secretary of the U.S. Treasury Robert V. Roosa. His recommendations include creation by IMF of a new asset which would be held with gold, dollars and sterling as national reserves. These new units would circulate among governments only; they would be initially contributed by industrial countries with currencies generally accepted in world trade (Wall Street Jour., September 8, 1965). Reserves would be thus expanded because although a country cannot hold its own currency as a reserve, it could hold the new IMF units received in exchange for currency contributions.

TABLE VIII.2

COMPOSITION AND DISTRIBUTION OF
GROSS INTERNATIONAL MONETARY RESERVES, 1913–1962
(after Triffin, 1964, Table 8)
(In millions of U.S. dollars)

End of	1913	1928	1933[1]	1933[2]	1937	1949	1957	1962
I. GOLD	4,110	9,850	11,380	19,265	25,285	33,500	37,305	39,230
A. World	4,110	9,850	11,380	19,265	25,290	35,005	38,765	41,430
B. International Institutions (—)	——	——	——	——	—5	—1,505	—1,460	—2,200
II. IMF GOLD TRANCHES*	——	——	——	——	——	1,660	2,315	3,795
III. RESERVE CURRENCIES	700	3,160	1,115[3]	1,115[3]	2,370	11,710	12.925	22,545
A. U.S. Dollars[4]	——	600	60	60	430	3,200	8,705	17,745
B. Pounds Sterling[5]						6,420	6,420	6,420
C. Other and Discrepancies	700	2,560	1,055	1,055	1,940	2,090	2,620	3,400
TOTAL	4,810	13,010	12,495	20,385	27,655	46,870	57,365	65,570

[1] Gold valued at $20.67 per ounce.
[2] Gold valued at $35 per ounce.
[3] Rough estimate calculated from League of Nations publications, on basis of old pound parity ($4.8665), around which the pound was fluctuating again in the latter part of 1933.
[4] Estimated at about nil in 1913; and from 1957 on basis of April 1963 Federal Reserve Bulletin (p. 423) and Survey of Current Business (for breakdown of "notes and bonds" between "official" and "private"), but including in 1962 $251 million of non-marketable securities.
[5] Residual estimates until 1949; rough estimates for 1949 and 1957, including downward adjustment of previously published estimates (of Bank of England Bulletin) to improve comparability with new 1962 gross estimates.
* The gold tranche position of a member country equals the member's quota minus the Fund's holdings of the member's currency. In other words, it equals the

MINERALS IN THE DEVELOPING NATIONS

Introduction.

A number of yardsticks are used to measure the degree of 'development' of a nation or a region of the world and these include: (1) the extent to which the nation or region is industrialized, (2) per capita income of the population, (3) the Gross National Product per unit of area or per capita, and (4) the literacy of the populace or average level of education. There are other, less tangible criteria—the political and cultural maturity of the people as indicated by the stability of their political system, their birth rate, and contributions made to the arts, humanities, and science. These do not all indicate the same kind of development, but most students would agree that if all the above indexes are high the nation is a developed nation by today's standards. Most commonly, the degree of development is related to the degree of industrialization. It can be argued in an intellectual sense that purely pastoral or agricultural cultures could be fully

---

member's gold subscription, minus its net drawings, plus its repurchases of currency subscription, plus the Fund's net sales of its currency, and plus or minus the Fund's administrative and operational expenditures or receipts in its currency. The importance of the gold tranche lies in the fact that it measures the amount that an individual member may draw from the Fund on an essentially automatic basis. Under the Fund's gold tranche policy members are given the overwhelming benefit of the doubt in relation to requests for transactions that do not increase the Fund's holdings of the member's currency beyond an amount equal to the member's quota.

Sources: These can only be regarded as rough estimates (particularly for earlier years) calculated from a variety of sources, such as:

   (1) *International Financial Statistics* (November 1963 and Supplement to 1963–64 issues), starting in 1937, with personal estimates of missing data, and excluding throughout claims of EPU (to avoid misleading impression of sudden contraction of foreign-exchange reserves at the end of 1958).

   (2) For earlier years International Reserves and Liquidity (IMF, 1958) Federal Reserve Board and League of Nations publications, supplemented for most of 1913 foreign-exchange reserves by A. I. Bloomfield's estimates in *Short-Term Capital Movements Under the Pre-1914 Gold Standard* (Princeton University, International Finance Section, 1963).

These estimates exclude *throughout* Communist countries' reserves, unreported in recent years (approximately $1,145 million in 1913, $525 million in 1928, $695 million in 1933 in old dollars, and $1,130 million in the same year in new dollars).

Minor discrepancies in the totals arise from the rounding of estimates to the closest $5 million. Even this conveys an unjustified impression of precision in these estimates, most of which are certainly subject to much larger errors.

developed in nonindustrial countries and that pastoral and agricultural cultures might be more successful over the millenia than industrial cultures as far as adaptation to environment is concerned, particularly if they have evolved stable populations and do not pollute earth or atmosphere. But the fact is that in the world today the industrialized nations are the ones with successful agricultural systems and the nonindustrialized nations are for the most part laboring with bare subsistence agriculture. There are some nations such as Austria, Finland, Iceland, and New Zealand which are not generally considered as industrial nations but which have very successful agricultural, forest and fishing economies; it is interesting to note that they also have low to moderate population growth rates.

Although it is interesting to argue whether industrialization (e.g., development in the current sense) is good or bad, the fact is that as long as populations are growing at rates substantially higher than replacement rates, and as long as higher per capita incomes are considered a good thing to have, the argument remains purely academic. Nations must industrialize; the world must industrialize, because industrial areas can support larger populations at a higher standard of living than nonindustrialized areas. If population growth can be brought under control and world-wide political maturity attained, the relative merits of agricultural and pastoral cultures as opposed to industrial cultures can be profitably debated.

It is also interesting to consider why some parts of the world remain undeveloped while other parts have developed to a high level. Because of national pride and the sensitivity of questions of racial capacity, it is difficult to discuss dispassionately the cause of differentials in degree of development. It is obvious that resources, environment, and cultural factors are all involved. It is perhaps more profitable to inquire into what is required for development today. Six ingredients are necessary to turn an undeveloped nation into a developed nation capable of sustaining its population at a high standard of living: (1) an educated people, (2) investment capital, (3) a national drive or purpose, (4) a low or controlled population growth rate so as to maintain a proper balance between population and resources, (5) resources or access to them, and (6) a political system which encourages initiative and rewards both individual and collective accomplishment. Equal opportunity for all citizens to achieve the limit of their own abilities is a first step, but the society must be realistic and admit that advances are made largely through the efforts of a relatively small number of extraordinarily well-endowed individuals. Their creative efforts provide the opportunities for others. Such individuals must be encouraged to be productive and be rewarded for it.

McCracken (1963), addressing the question, Why does economic growth occur?, assigned natural resources to a secondary role and concluded that investment capital, education, and research backed up by the will to innovate and compete are the principal causes of growth. These factors are clearly the prime requisite for growth and development, but, in this writer's opinion, natural resources or access to them are the fundamental materials with which human culture, however creative and energetic, must work and their importance should not be underemphasized.

If we look at one undeveloped nation in the world which has developed with extraordinary rapidity in the short span of a quarter century—Israel—we find all of the above ingredients in abundance, except perhaps a stable population. Large amounts of capital were poured into Israel from the Jewry of the world and from United States' aid. That this alone was not sufficient is indicated by the simple fact that the large investments of the United States in so-called foreign aid in other parts of the world have not produced any such desirable results. Israel also offered a home to the educated and capable Jews of Europe who emigrated in large numbers to offer their new country their considerable skills and abilities. Thus, Israel had the human resources. National purpose was engendered by a fierce desire to build something secure for themselves and was hardened by hostile neighbors to the point of a religious fervor. The political system encouraged and rewarded individual initiative. It is difficult to assess Israel's population growth rate because of the policy of unlimited immigration. This is perhaps a larger threat to Israel's success than hostile neighbors. Immigration of 60,000 per year plus the native birth rate has resulted in an uncomfortable growth rate of 4 per cent.

If other nations which have made substantial progress in development are examined, for example, U.S.S.R., Japan, and Spain, most or all of the six factors listed previously are found to be involved in their success. Great stress on education and available capital for investment are present in all cases. The Soviet Union drew on a vast resource base and was not troubled by overpopulation; a system of incentives was established to reward individual and collective accomplishments; recently the Soviet economic system took on suspiciously capitalistic aspects in recognizing consumer demand. Japan, with national drive to rebuild, negotiated access to resources in Australia, western U.S. and Canada, and embarked on a population control program to keep a balance between resources and population. Spain's progress can perhaps be best ascribed to a people awakened through increased contact with the surrounding rapidly developing world. Because of a European labor shortage, large numbers of Spaniards left home and returned with new skills and capital; the mineral resources of Spain were needed by a fast-growing European community and foreign capital sought admittance.

In all developing countries the consumption of minerals and mineral fuels increases exponentially. Indeed, the role of minerals in development is fundamental. No nation without mineral resources or access to them has ever industrialized. Exploitation of mineral resources can, in an early phase of development, provide income that, if invested in education, agriculture, and arts and crafts industries, will measurably shorten the time required for a boot-strap development program. Later in the development program, the same mineral industry, if properly managed, can provide raw materials for domestic heavy industry, including chemical and metallurgical industry. The country with high-value mineral resources is a country with a built-in bankroll. The problem is to assure the maximum benefit from the fortuitously located asset. If income from it circulates to numbered accounts in Swiss banks, it does not assist in solving the capital requirements of the country.

The previous discussion considered the benefits to be derived from a discovered and developed mineral deposit. Of course, substantial capital investment is required in a still earlier phase of development —exploration for mineral deposits. Modern mineral exploration is expensive. It requires regional aerial photography and mapping, geological and geophysical surveys, and testing of targets by drilling and underground workings. The country wishing to explore and evaluate its mineral potential must find a source of (1) capital and (2) technically competent people to conduct the exploration. It can look to domestic sources of capital or to foreign sources. One domestic source is the national treasury or the national credit. In most underdeveloped countries both are low. The cost of supplying minimum social services so strains the financial resources that there is no surplus to divert to an expensive mineral exploration program. Likewise, without visible sources of income with which to repay loans or bonds, a country has difficulty in securing financing unless there are overriding political considerations which persuade a foreign government to write off or discount the risk. Private capital in underdeveloped countries is usually not available for several reasons. Because of political instability, the nation's wealthy keep their funds invested outside the country. Also, in countries where there is a shortage of capital, investors receive high interest rates for low-risk capital—invested, for example, in city real estate—and there is no incentive to put money into high-risk mineral ventures except at extraordinary rates of interest. Even if the underdeveloped nation can raise enough domestic capital to undertake mineral exploration, it commonly lacks the trained people needed to carry out and evaluate the surveys. The work must be contracted to foreign groups, either private or government.

Foreign sources of capital include foreign companies, foreign governments, or supranational organizations such as United Nations, various economic unions, and international banks. The private corporation operating in the field of minerals is not organized as a charitable or altruistic organization. It is in the business of finding, producing, processing, and selling minerals and mineral products to make a profit. Its first responsibility is to its shareholders, although most major companies today conduct themselves as good citizens and do not ignore the humanitarian aspects of their normal activities. However, if such companies do not operate at a profit they are not able to contribute much to humanitarian projects such as construction of schools and hospitals. Moreover, companies that undertake to explore and develop concessions in foreign countries do so as a business enterprise. They take risks with their own capital; and in return for taking the risk they expect an opportunity to get their capital back, to be paid for their labor, and to make a profit if they are successful. In the modern world, particularly in the case of metal mines where the trend is to development of large low-grade deposits, the period of operation necessary to recover initial investments may be a matter of 20 years or more, instead of the relatively few years required to pay out high-grade deposits in the past. A company, then, must have reasonable assurance of long-term political stability, assurance that changing governments will honor the original agreements which governed the operation. Political opportunists who cry Nationalize! before a country has adequate capital and knowledgeable people to operate mineral industries do their country a disservice, whether or not the seized industry is paid for. Political opportunists who seize property and pay for it with worthless bonds, or not at all, destroy their country's credit before the world and thereby adversely affect possibilities for future development. The son who inherits a

FIGURE VIII.2
A modern mining community in an undeveloped land: Oranjemund, built by
Consolidated Diamond Mines of South-West Africa (Courtesy Anglo American
Corporation of South Africa, Limited, Johannesburg).

profitable business built by his father and then, impatient for money,
ruins it by trying to take too much money out of it, is foolishly
killing a goose that might have provided eggs or income for a multitude of investments. One benefit which accrues to a country that
succeeds in developing a mineral industry is the training of a body
of domestic engineering talent which can provide leadership in a
variety of other projects and in government. The industry as it grows
and develops provides a nucleus for the middle class, which is the
backbone of developed countries.

The distribution of income from a successful mining operation
rarely supports the frequently heard complaint that mineral indus-

tries are 'bleeding' the host country. To be judged successful by
ordinary business standards, an extractive mineral industry must
have annual gross earnings of at least 20 per cent of the invested
capital. After payment of operating expenses and taxes (70 per cent
to 80 per cent of gross income) and making appropriate reserves for
re-investments and working capital (10 per cent to 15 per cent of
gross income), only 5 per cent to 10 per cent of gross income is
available for distribution as dividends. Thus a very large percentage
of gross income remains in the host country. In a favorable investment
climate it is not uncommon for some of the dividends to come back
in the form of new investments.

In many countries, underdeveloped and developed, the extractive
mineral industries have been hampered by misguided conservation
groups who want to keep the commodity in the ground as a heritage
for future generations. That is, on the face of it, a worthy objective
and it raises an interesting philosophical point of the debt of the
living to the living as against those who will come. Minerals are not
converted to wealth until they are extracted and used, and in industrial societies, demand for mineral commodities has a way of changing.
For example, those nations who mistakenly hoard iron ores for the
future may find that in the great market places of the world where
steel is made, the future demand will be for ores specially tailored
for certain processes and kinds of furnaces. As the demand in the
world market changes to require pelletized self-fluxing and self-
reducing raw materials, those who have restricted development of
local ores may find themselves stuck with a noncompetitive commodity marketable only after a substantial investment in a beneficiation plant. Those who protected coal reserves are today dismayed to
find coal losing out to oil and nuclear fuels in the energy markets
of the world. Economical processes to extract aluminum from common clays will cut off markets for distant bauxite ores, so that the
politician who through ignorance or greed prevented development of
bauxite ores has cut off a source of income that could have been invested to better the lot of his people. When the truth is known, he
will be historically viewed as a betrayer of his trust. Technology and
engineering progress do not stand still; mineral resources should be
developed now for the benefit of the living, but they should be developed to permit maximum recovery and eliminate waste. Waste, not
full development, is the crime against tomorrow. This is not to say
that volumes of rock which through natural processes of concentration
contain abnormally high amounts of certain minerals or metals will

lose their value as potential commercial sources of those minerals or metals. Eventually, the undeveloped ores or minerals in the ground will be developed and exploited, but cost and market conditions may defer their development as a source of wealth for many years to come, and the progress of the hoarding country may lag accordingly.

In the early phase of mineral discovery and development, valuable commodities may be dug or pumped out of the ground and shipped out of the country of their origin in the crude form with little or no processing. Minerals with a low unit-value, such as gypsum, cement raw materials, or glass sands, will be passed over because they cannot be developed without local markets, unless by chance they are located on tidewater. In this early phase the valuable minerals are not processed where they are produced because of (1) lack of market for the product, (2) lack of processing facilities which cost money, (3) lack of a trained labor force to man such facilities, or (4) a political climate which discourages investments. However, as the country develops, it commonly exercises its rights to control its own raw materials and may insist that beneficiation and refining be carried on within its own borders. In a mature stage of development with large local markets, an educated labor force, and local capital to participate in the construction of domestic chemical and metallurgical industries, such growth comes naturally. It can be politically encouraged but only at the right time economically; such development cannot be forced successfully. Portland cement plants, for example, should have a capacity of at least 50,000 tons per year to be economic and thus the local market must be able to absorb that much portland cement. In the United States the average plant has a capacity of about 500,000 tons per year. A cement plant constructed for political reasons before the market is ready for it will be a losing proposition and will either close or require subsidy from the government.

Ideally speaking, there is no reason why national or government companies cannot operate successfully according to normal business standards. Practically, there is a very good reason. Industry decisions must be made on the business elements of a problem if the decisions are to be sound and the enterprise is to function efficiently. The location and construction of facilities cannot be influenced by political considerations without raising the costs of the operations. Likewise, expensive high-risk mineral exploration projects must be decided on scientific, engineering, and business criteria without regard for political considerations. Only a courageous political executive, for example, would be likely to undertake a risky high-cost offshore oil exploration venture because if he failed he and his party would be subject to political attack. It would be safer for him to drill off-sets to existing production. Mineral exploration and development cannot be concentrated in the regions of a country that are politically allied to the in-power establishment; they must go where the prospects for discovery are best. Nor does the support of marginal mineral operations for political purposes result in a strong healthy mineral industry. If a government company is directed toward social and political goals as well as the normal business function, there is a price to be paid.

The Alliance for Progress.

In March 1961 the United States proposed a plan for overcoming the capital deficiencies of one of the large underdeveloped areas of the world—Latin America. The plan, *La Alianza para el Progreso,* or Alliance for Progress, was formalized and organized in two subsequent meetings, at Punta del Este, Uruguay (the Declaration of Punta del Este) and at Montevideo, Uruguay (Accord of Montevideo). The expressed goal was to raise per capita income in Latin America by 2.5 per cent per year. The three elements for implementing the Alliance were set forth as (1) planning, (2) self-help, and (3) external assistance. The 10-year program was built around a minimum of 20 billion dollars of outside assistance from (1) the United States, (2) international agencies including International Bank for Reconstruction and Development (World Bank), International Finance Corporation, Inter-American Development Bank, and International Development Association, (3) private U.S. capital invested directly at a projected rate of 300 million dollars per year, and (4) public and private capital from other developed countries.

The element of *self-help* as proposed in the Alliance carries a strong mandate for social reform—land and tax reform, commodity stabilization, economic integration, and labor legislation—which really points toward overhaul of political systems toward government management rather than toward free-market development. Simultaneous encouragement of both private capital investment and government-managed economics requires acceptance of business partnerships between private industry and government. The difficulty with such partnerships lies not so much in the profit-sharing arrangements as in the management. Private corporations want to retain management so that decisions will be based on business and economic factors; governments want to assume management so that social and political factors can be considered. Those governments which acquire a working interest—that is, those who put up part of the capital are, under normal business attitudes, entitled to more voice in management than those countries which have a royalty interest only, that is, those which invest no capital but share in the profits. Recognizing the problems of private industry, the U.S. government has instituted a program to insure private companies against nationalization or confiscation of their investments.

In stressing the capital requirements for development, it seems that the Alliance for Progress underemphasizes the other factors which history has shown are necessary for development and which have been discussed here, namely, an educated people, a national purpose or drive, a reasonable population growth rate, and a political system which encourages people to work. It is true that education is part of the self-help element of the plan and that the social reforms are designed to give opportunity to those who have lacked it heretofore, but perhaps these are really the key to the plan and deserve more attention. To ignore the population problem in Latin countries which have growth rates in excess of 3 per cent is an ostrich approach. Education for a continent is a magnificent idea but hardly something that can be made part of a ten-year program. Perhaps the Alliance would have more chance of success if instead of a continental approach, the area were selectively analyzed to determine where the necessary elements for development can now be found so that the support can be focused or concentrated in those areas. These nuclei would grow and expand by themselves if the human energy required for development was in fact present. If the environment is right, an initial cultivation and some fertilizer once applied will result in healthy growth, if not, the growth will always be sickly and will require continuing care (investment). Perhaps political considerations can justify continuing investment but this is not a sound approach to economic development. Investment in the raw materials or mineral industry sector of the Latin American economy by private firms in the light of the world-wide demand for raw materials of all kinds would be immediate and large if reasonable partnerships with Latin American governments were offered and guaranteed as part of the Alliance. Income from such enterprises could underwrite a substantial part of the self-help phase of the program.

Zambia (Northern Rhodesia), a case history.

F. Taylor Ostrander (1963, pp. 4–11) has discussed the development of the Northern Rhodesian copper belt. His remarks are reproduced here (with minor changes made by letter of December 21, 1965) as a case history of an area in the earliest stages of development:

Consider the case of the Northern Rhodesian Copperbelt. Many tributes have been paid to those who pioneered the copper industry in this heart of darkest Africa. Where there was only the African bush thirty years ago, there is today an urbanized population of 250,000 people, including over 200,000 Africans. It constitutes one of the largest industrial complexes that exists anywhere south of the Equator. There are modern roads and towns and just about the best African housing on the continent. Over 625,000 tons of copper are produced each year with an annual sales value of around $350 million. One-fifth of the gross value of those sales, over $70 million a year, is paid to the various levels of Rhodesian government as tax revenues accruing from the production of copper. Great modern hydroelectric projects located far from the Copperbelt supply the needed power. A railroad network takes the copper 1200 miles to various seaports. To reproduce this whole industrial complex and its essential supporting services today might cost as much as $1 billion.

The Northern Rhodesian copper industry is large-scale, efficient, benevolently paternalistic, a source of abundant tax revenues for the state, a center of attraction for great numbers of indigenous peoples who flock in to work in the copper mines. It has had a profound influence on their lives as they have become in the short space of a quarter century, in a single generation, a stable urban people, largely detribalized, dependent on and enjoying the fruits of modern industry.

During the past thirty years the copper industry has also had many wider repercussions on economic development in Northern Rhodesia. For example, the turnover of workers in the mines has always been high—something the mines have been working successfully to reduce—but this high turnover during an entire generation has meant that a constant flow of knowledge of modern tools and modern industrial organization has been carried back to the rural villages. Men who have learned how to use wrenches and motors and how to work under industrial discipline, their wives who have visited clinics and domestic science classes, can never be quite the same again when they return to their villages.

Today, under the mines' pension system, several thousands of pensioned long-service employees who have had the longest exposure to modern, urban, industrial life have retired to live in the rural areas, and they have capital—their substantial savings and their monthly cash pensions. This is creating new small-scale entrepreneurship in many cases.

Nevertheless, the principal tasks of economic development have still to be accomplished in most of Northern Rhodesia—an area larger than Texas with a population of about three million. That population is still primarily dependent upon subsistence farming in primitive rural areas. Perhaps half of that population is not yet in any meaningful way in touch with a money economy. Millions still live in crude huts of saplings and reeds, they sleep on the ground, they use primitive instruments of agriculture and work, they are subject to floods and famine and have little reserves even of the seeds of the products they grow, the women are the toilers in the field, and one-third or more of all the children born do not reach the age of five. Let me quote the findings of an English team from the Royal Commonwealth Society for the Blind which last month visited the Luapula Valley, about 200 miles from the rich Copperbelt of Northern Rhodesia. They reported:

> Most of the villagers live at a bare subsistence level and the majority are too poor to buy soap and what we call the necessities of life.

The endemic diseases they found included bilharzia, hookworm, malaria, smallpox, measles, night blindness and tuberculosis.

It is obvious that too small a proportion of the African population has benefited from minerals development and economic development in Northern Rhodesia.

No one can deny that Northern Rhodesia is better off than other African states. Indeed, because of its great mineral reserves and flourishing copper industry, Northern Rhodesia is probably the richest of all African states. But, after thirty years of mineral development, the real task of economic development, of bringing the modern world to the populace of the country as a whole, has scarcely begun. Thirty years of copper mining has not created the needed agricultural revolution (see pp. 3–4 of full text).

We must first recognize that large-scale tax revenues from copper production did not begin to accrue to Rhodesia until after World War II. During the world depression of the 'Thirties, copper prices and consequent profits were low and the Copperbelt mines used what cash they could generate to recoup their initial capital, which under local law had a prior claim over tax payments. During the war years, copper prices were fixed. Although production rose and taxes on profits went to rates of over 60%, most of the increased taxes went to the British Government in London, where the companies were registered. Finally, in 1953, when the companies transferred their domicile to Northern Rhodesia, the Federation of Rhodesia and Nyasaland had just been created and the new Federal Government was assigned responsibility for collecting all corporate taxes—and for spending the bulk of the proceeds. As a result of all these factors, the Northern Rhodesian Government enjoyed only about five years of its own rising affluence from copper revenues, from about 1949 until 1953. Then the new Federal Government took over. Each year after 1953, some $20 to $30 millions of the annual tax revenues the Federal Government received from copper were in effect transferred to Southern Rhodesia and Nyasaland. If, instead of these transfers over the past nine years of Federation, a sum totaling, say, a further $250 million had been available to the Northern Rhodesian Government to spend, rural and urban economic development in that Territory might have come much further along.

Not until Rhodesian Selection Trust, Limited, one of the two groups that comprise Northern Rhodesia's copper industry, as a voluntary act of good citizenship, made a five-year interest-free loan of $5.5 million to the Northern Rhodesian Government in 1956, did that Government initiate the first comprehensive rural development program, the Northern Provinces Development Program—and then it was arbitrarily limited to about one-quarter of the Territory. To this day, no such comprehensive program has been introduced in the rest of the Territory.

We have to bear in mind, moreover, that until recently—certainly until after World War II and perhaps not before the late 'Fifties—economic development was not conceived as a function of colonial administration. The objective of government was to maintain law and order and to balance the budget on the basis of local resources, without burden to the mother country. Colonial administrators brought up in this tradition do not change easily, nor do they have the necessary knowledge.

Also, it must be recognized that the technical know-how of economic development just did not exist. Neither those who developed the minerals nor the colonial governments were at fault for this. Until recently, the state of the art of economic development had not yet reached a point where government expenditures could be directed with sure aim at the achievement of an agricultural revolution. Even today, we do not know with certainty how to achieve it. At least, however, we know that agriculture must be broadly revolutionized or more years will be wasted. And, a good deal more than that is known today about how to proceed with this task.

In the light of modern knowledge, we can perhaps define one area in which the copper companies might have made it possible for minerals development to spill over on a broader scale into general economic development. They could have adopted a program of deliberately developing indigenous enterprise around the copper industry. Industrial and foreign investor statesmanship can see to it that any central enterprise deliberately stimulates the maximum amount of satellite local entrepreneurship by subcontracting wherever possible, by hiving off parts of the central enterprise for transfer to local enterprise, by giving capital subsidies and management training to help get such satellite activities under way, etc. Such a policy would superimpose a new objective of a longer run nature on normal management decisions based on efficiency alone. The objective would be the creation of a healthy economic environment within which the central enterprise would live. The aim, by the way, would be the development of *native* entrepreneurship, not satellite enterprises under expatriate control. This is one way modern management might see its development task today. It is a new concept. It would result in some greater tendency for mineral development to contribute to broader economic development. It could be done by mining companies alone, without encouragement or direction from the state, although any such sponsorship of activities designed to promote wider economic development must remain a secondary objective of minerals management.

Even this policy, of course, would not come close to creating the necessary agricultural revolution in primitive subsistence native agriculture.

It cannot be overemphasized that the principal responsibility of those who developed minerals is to mine at low cost and high safety, to pay their taxes and insure that the relations with their labor force are in accord with the principles of modern industrial management.

The primary responsibility for economic development must belong to government. It is *not* a function of private industry.

For a long time ahead, those governments which want to develop their mineral resources must seek to attract the necessary technical skills and the capital from the Old World.

None of the skills and techniques needed in minerals development are available today to any important degree among the populations of the undeveloped countries. They must be attracted, they must be persuaded, to go out to the undeveloped world.

World Bank.

Considering the giant capital requirements for finding, developing, extracting, and processing the mineral resources needed for the future, it is worthwhile examining one of the best known international sources of capital, the World Bank or, more properly, the International Bank for Reconstruction and Development. The following summary is from McDivitt (1963, pp. 59–67). The bank was organized at the end of World War II as a mechanism of funding reconstruction efforts, primarily in western Europe. As reconstruction proceeded, more and more emphasis was shifted over the years to development loans to assist the emerging nations in other continents.

As of 1962, the bank had made some 300 loans totaling about 6.5 billion dollars to finance 600 projects in 60 different countries or areas. The money has been allocated about equally between electric power, transportation, and industry (including agriculture, minerals, and basic industries, such as steel).

The bank operates as a special agency of the United Nations. The capital is subscribed by member nations and raised through sale of the bank's bonds in financial world markets. Only about 25 per cent of the 6.5 billion dollars loaned was put up by member nations— the rest was raised by bond sales, resale of loans to commercial banks and other investors, interest, and repayments. The fact that the bank has operated successfully largely through its own efforts and that there is a ready market for its bonds is evidence that it is an economically sound enterprise rather than a politically motivated dispenser of free money. Applications are screened to insure that the borrower can repay the loan, the project is economically sound, and the project will aid in the country's development. For the most part, the bank meets a part of the costs and expects the borrower to make a substantial investment. The interest rate is at the bank's rate of borrowing money with 1 per cent annual commission added—the range has been from $4\frac{1}{4}$–$6\frac{1}{4}$ per cent. Although the bank makes loans for projects considered too risky by ordinary commercial money sources, it requires that the loan be guaranteed by the government of the borrowing country. Two other organizations, although autonomous, are affiliated with the bank and have less stringent requirements for making loans; the International Finance Corporation can make loans to private corporations without government guarantee, and the International Development Association has a liberal policy of very low interest or no interest loans to undeveloped countries. The bank's participation in the mineral industry has been in four areas: (1) loans for mineral development, (2) loans to improve power and transportation facilities in areas where mineral resources are known to occur, (3) loans for construction of mineral-processing facilities to permit development and treatment of ores in the borrowing country, and (4) technical advisory services. Examples of loans for mineral development include loans to Chile for modernization and expansion of the coal industry, loans to India for improvement of the coal industry, a loan to Gabon to finance development of a manganese property including transportation facilities, and a loan to Mauritania to develop iron ore properties.

A first step.

A first step for any undeveloped country is to answer the question —are there mineral resources that can be developed and, if so, where are they? The answer can only come through a geological survey. A country with an established geological organization needs to check the capabilities of its staff to do the job and then provide the financing. Countries without geological surveys must build them or contract the work to outsiders. The work cannot be done overnight nor can it be done for nothing. The country or region must be mapped. Aerial photographs and topographic base maps on scales large enough for detailed geological work come first. When an adequate base is available, the modern approach utilizes geophysical and geological surveys. As the work proceeds the focus narrows to areas of potential mineral accumulation and as a final phase the targets are tested by core-drilling and underground workings. Costs of exploration and development are substantial—the general magnitude of a combined electromagnetic, induction, magnetic, and radiation survey is 20,000 to 25,000 dollars per thousand square kilometers. Bailly (Table I.3; Fig. I.1) has tabulated costs on a square-mile basis and illustrated the relationship between acreage and investment at various stages. Estimates on geologic mapping have recently been presented by Noakes (1965, p. 400):

New techniques in regional mapping have had a profound effect on the search for mineral resources be they metals, non-metals, rock materials, oil or water; but despite new techniques, the regional mapping of large areas, even where outcrop is plentiful and vegetation light, is a major task. The experience of the Bureau of Mineral Resources [Australia] indicates that, on a general average, mapping on 1:50,000 scale with final publication at 1:250,000 costs 1 field geologist/year per 1,000 square miles, with the essential support on one unit/year of sub-professional and clerical assistance, 0.5 unit/year of specialist support (petrology, paleontology, etc.) 0.3 units/year of all grades of supervision and 0.3 unit/year of drafting. On this basis the regional mapping of a province or a basin of 50,000 square miles involves approximately 50 geologist/years, 50 sub-professional and clerical/years, 25 specialist/years, 15 supervision/years and 15 draftsman/years.

The U.S. Geological Survey estimates the cost of a 7½′ geologic quadrangle map (scale 1:24,000) as between 10,000 and 20,000 dollars, depending on the complexity of the geology.

Of course, mapping of the country is basic to many other kinds of engineering projects, including construction of transportation networks, dams, harbors, and general land-use studies involving agricultural potential, so general mapping should not be budgeted solely against mineral development. Systematic large-scale geologic quadrangle mapping comes later—maps of this kind are most helpful in development of water supplies and large-volume low-unit-value nonmetallic industrial minerals during later stages of the country's development.

The student of resources can find more on minerals in developing nations by consulting Buck (1963), Clawson (1964), Bonini and others (1964), and various publications of the United Nations (1951, 1963).

MINERALS AND CITIES[3]

The latter half of the 20th century has seen the rise of the giant city or megalopolis and this social phenomenon will undoubtedly characterize whatever period of time remains to modern industrial civilization. No one has proposed that cities might have a critical size limit—indeed, demographic projections indicate cities of 35 to 40 million inhabitants by the turn of the century. The accelerating construction of these human hives has already wrought profound environmental changes in and around the urban areas. Tremendous volumes of food, water, and materials flow into the urban area to sustain the human activity; these raw materials are consumed, altered or modified in form, and ejected in the form of both beneficial and waste products. The beneficial products—for the most part manufactured goods in the broad sense—are distributed through a multitude of surface, air, and water transportation systems. The waste products, however, are spewed into the atmosphere, dumped into natural surface distribution systems such as rivers, streams and oceans, or pumped underground, the care taken in disposal being dependent on the toxicity of the waste. Thus the urban area is a nucleus of atmospheric, hydrospheric, and lithospheric contamination. In addition to liquid, solid, and gaseous waste materials, urban activities produce large quantities of heat which is also discharged into the environment with marked ecological effects.

Cities and minerals come together in several different ways. Cities are centers of consumption of raw mineral products, and in the manu-

---

[3] Part of this text has been previously published in slightly different form in an article entitled "Geology and Urban Development" in *Texas Town and City*, Vol. LII, No. 7, pp. 9–10, 20.

facturing processes become centers of secondary minerals recovered from wastes and scrap. Satellite mineral industries sustain the urban area by providing water and construction materials. In a sense, the iron mines in Minnesota which provide steel beams and the refined crude oil from Texas which operates city equipment are also sustaining mineral industries. This chapter, however, is concerned mainly with the low-unit-value minerals which are produced in or close to the urban area—commodities such as water whose value is measured in cents per thousand gallons, and sand, gravel, crushed stone, clay, and earth fill whose value is measured in cents per yard or per ton.

Water is, of course, the prime municipal resource, and with few exceptions the availability of water controlled the original site of settlement. In the early history of community growth, water supply

FIGURE VIII.3   A quarry in the path of urban expansion (after Bauer, 1965, Fig. 45, p. 38).

was usually the first municipal service provided after provision for maintenance of law and order. From a community spring or well, water supply was improved by distribution systems, and its quality was controlled to meet public health standards. In nearly all cases the early city water systems tapped local sources—streams, rivers, lakes, shallow aquifers. As demand grew, cities were faced with the problem of expanding the water supply for residential, commercial, and industrial users, and it soon became clear that an abundant supply of cheap water was an attraction to industry and a mechanism to achieve community prosperity. Expansion of supplies through construction of new reservoirs, deeper well fields, aqueducts to more distant surface sources, and treatment plants required large capital investment and cities turned to bond issues for financing. Some communities in dry regions with no surface water and limited prospects for ground-water development had such a serious water problem that growth stopped. As population and demand grew, conflicts between cities and prior water users and between one city and another became more common and more heated. In the mid-1960s for the first time large-scale desalination of sea water or saline ground water appeared to offer hope of water at costs of 20 to 30 cents per thousand gallons (p. 373). This new source could solve many of the problems of coastal cities and some inland cities in sedimentary basins containing large volumes of saline ground water. The most ambitious water project on the current scene is the California Water Plan which is designed to meet the immense water needs of urban southern California. The first stage known as the State Water Project and financed by a 1.75 billion dollar bond issue will construct the dams, aqueducts, power plants, and pumping stations necessary to move large volumes of water from north to south. The aqueduct will be 444 miles long. Engineering is complicated by earthquake hazards. Even more imaginative plans have been suggested; one, costing perhaps 100 billion dollars, would transport water from the Pacific Northwest, including Canada, eastward into the Great Lakes region and southward into the dry southwest of the United States, and is known as the North American Water and Power Alliance. This plan is justified by projecting the population growth and needs of the large cities in the continental interior and the southwest. Very large concentrations of people have political power and can use it to achieve their objectives. There is, however, an alternative to this concept which regards regional population growth as an independent variable and requires huge investment and environment modifications to bring water to the area. Populations are mobile; perhaps if the water is not supplied in the quantities demanded, the regional population growth would be slowed as people moved to the area of abundant water supply and the overall needs could then be revised downward.

There are few cities that have not grown over and around peripheral sand and gravel pits, stone quarries, clay pits, or cuts from which sanitary fill has been taken. The relationship between the city and the urban mineral industry is embodied in the concept of place value. The construction materials resources which are of concern to a city are used in large volumes but have a low value per unit of production. Of paramount importance, then, is their location with respect to a city's growing parts. If a commodity has a value of 1.00 dollar per ton at the quarry, and if it costs 5 cents per ton-mile to transport it, one can easily see that at the end of a 20-mile haul, one-half the cost of the commodity is haulage cost; at 40 miles, the cost of transport is twice the value of the commodity at the source. When multiplied by a factor of thousands of tons, the cost increment is substantial indeed. This is another way of saying that a large de-

FIGURE VIII.4

Haulage costs of selected rock materials
(after Fisher, 1965, Fig. 2).

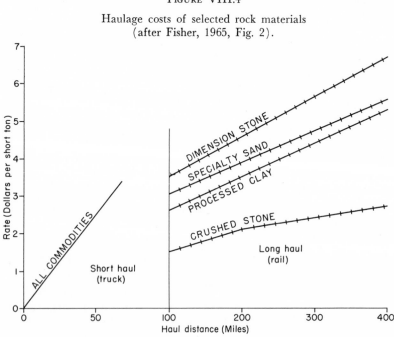

posit of sand and gravel within the city limits is a valuable asset, whereas a simlar deposit 100 miles away may be worthless (Figures VIII.4, VIII.5). The operator producing minerals for the urban

FIGURE VIII.5

Delivered costs (per cubic yard) of common aggregate materials in Central and Coastal Texas (after Fisher, 1965, Fig. 3).

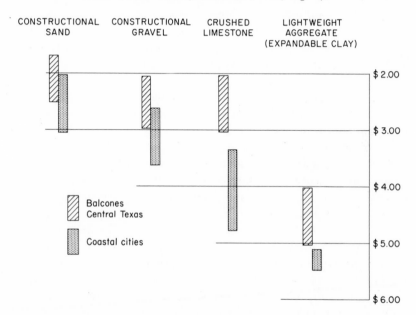

market, therefore, is constrained by transportation economics to locate the closest deposit to the urban area that is satisfactory from the mineral product standpoint. The occurrence of mineral deposits, however, is determined by geologic factors and not by the shape and symmetry of the growing city. Deposits of sand and gravel and of stone suitable for aggregate and base material are not ubiquitous and around many large cities either never existed in adequate quantities, have been depleted through use, or have been rendered unavailable through unplanned urban growth. The planning group of a city that becomes concerned about depletion of sand and gravel or crushed stone sources cannot simply find the least desirable land in the city—the old dump—and zone it for quarry sites. Mineral resources cannot be created by administrative decision or legislation. Intelligent planning for and management of urban mineral resources must be based on sound information about the occurrence of the resources. Detailed knowledge of the geology of a city is basic to any resource or environmental planning and of first priority is an accurate and detailed geologic map or model. The same kind of advance planning used by city departments concerned with power, traffic, sewage, and parks should be applied to mineral resources. Such is already the case in regard to water; no city can be managed efficiently without long-range water planning. The concept needs to be extended to the construction materials. If sand and gravel must be hauled in from distant points, the price of concrete will go up, construction costs will go up, and the city's bill for municipal projects will be higher.

Demographers predict that a large number of fast-growing urban areas in the United States and elsewhere will merge into giant cities or megalopoli in the near future. In the United States about 1 million acres of land per year are being converted to residential home sites, and most of this land is in and around existing population centers. Every mile of federal highway consumes 40 acres. Planning, zoning, exercise of eminent domain and condemnation of private land in the public interest are natural results of population growth, increased competition in the human hive, increasing conflicts between potential land users, and the overall pressure for land. The dismal alternative to planned urban complexes are urban jungles such as exist around the old nuclei of New York and Chicago, and which cost society so much in so many ways. It is cheaper to plan now, and the mineral producer must have a place in the planning. He competes for land in the urban area and is restricted in his area of use by the natural occurrence of the mineral deposit. He is not regarded as a desirable neighbor—he scars the land, detonates explosives, makes noise with heavy equipment, spews dust over the landscape, and is a terminus for fleets of trucks. Many of these nuisances can be modified or controlled —but at extra cost. According to Ahearn (1965), "zoning ordinances have treated sand and gravel operations with the junk yard, rendering plant, trash incinerator, stockyard, and sewage treatment facility." In the first half of the century when deposits were more abundant and the city's perimeter expanded at a relatively slow and predictable rate, the quarry or pit operator was more easily able to locate in an area where he bothered few neighbors and where he could count on an adequate term to work the deposit. In the second half of the century, with many deposits already depleted, his chances of being engulfed by a much more rapidly expanding perimeter and closed down by high taxes, restrictive zoning regulations, or even injunctions are greatly increased. He now needs the protection of a city authority. Citizens who do not understand the importance of an abundant supply of cheap construction materials, and commonly led by conservation groups who regard the pit and quarry operator as a despoiler or plunderer, need to be better informed. The operator needs to look at his public relations and to make plans to reclaim and restore the land after the minerals have been harvested. In Lincoln, Illinois, a wet pit operated for years by Lincoln Sand and Gravel Company has

FIGURE VIII.6   A sound-proofed drilling rig on a one-acre site in the Los Angeles area (after Spaulding, 1965, p. 203).

been reclaimed and developed as Lincoln Lakes—a recreation-oriented community. Such reclamation more than recovers its cost. The obvious answer to urban land shortage is multiple use. Los Angeles has included mineral deposits in its planning. The city surveyed a number of sand and gravel deposits in San Fernando Valley, evaluated them by drilling, and zoned a number of gravel pit sites. After the deposits are quarried, the pits will be first used for waste disposal, and then restored for normal urban development.

Cities which have grown up in areas where high-value mineral deposits have subsequently been discovered or which have grown around high-value deposits are presented with a different kind of problem. Exploitation of the deposit can cause the city major difficulties but at the same time yield much needed additional revenue to the city and private property owners alike in the form of increased taxes, rentals, royalties, and bonuses. An example is the oil and gas which lies under parts of the general Los Angeles urban area. Because of the high value of the deposits, operators have been willing and able to work with the city to minimize the nuisance. Drilling rigs are enclosed, soundproofed, operated electrically insofar as possible, and removed after completion of the hole. Well-heads are sunk below the surface. Successful exploration for and production of oil and gas from within this urban area is an excellent example of multiple land use and conservation through prevention of waste. Hartsook (1965) examined the history of Huntington Beach, California, which had a population of 5,000 in 1959, 75,000 in 1964, and a predicted 150,000 to 200,000 for 1975. The program of the Huntington Beach Company (first a land company, then an oil company) for developing its urban mineral properties while preserving a good community image included extensive studies of geologic, geographic, engineering, economic, social, and political factors affecting successful adaption of the company to the fast-changing scene. Cities which have expanded over old mine workings are in some areas faced with serious foundation problems as a result of collapse of supports in the workings. In some places, these old workings can be turned into an asset by backfilling them with wastes to solve the collapse problem or reconditioning them for a higher level of underground storage or even for use as shelters. Some abandoned underground mines contain large volumes of water and are capable of maintaining a steady, sustained flow of fresh water. In the Joplin, Missouri, area, industry draws more than 1 billion gallons per year from old lead-zinc mines.

THE ROLE OF THE MINERAL INDUSTRY IN THE ECONOMY OF THE UNITED STATES

Minerals and the mineral industry contribute to the national economy in a variety of ways—as a basic source of income or wealth, as cargo for a host of carriers, as a source of jobs, as a payer of local, state and federal taxes, and as a 'mother industry' for myriad satellite industries. It is difficult to measure anything but the first contribution made to the economy by the extractive and mineral processing segments of the industry. Thereafter, mineral products flow into the manufacturing, chemical, agricultural, and energy industries, and their contributions are not credited to the mineral industry. Some idea of the importance to the economy of mineral materials and mineral fuels can be developed in the minds' eye by an imaginative consideration of the U.S.-manufactured automobile: Iron from the Lake Superior ranges, moved through the Great Lakes by an ore carrier, and manufactured into steel in Cleveland or Pittsburgh; limestone, coke, manganese, and fluorspar used in the blast furnace; mining, processing and beneficiation of these minerals; the manufacturing of the machinery to do the mining and hauling; the other metals—copper and aluminum and ferroalloys required for electrical systems, radiator, trim, and for fatigue-resistant steels such as piston rods, lead for the storage battery; the manufacture of the battery; mineral pigments in the paint; gasoline for the tank; glass for the windshield and windows . . . . With a little imagination you can see people all over America mining, processing, smelting, refining, carrying, fabricating, and finally assembling the component parts to make an automobile in, say, Detroit. Then the finished product, largely mineral, leaves Detroit. It is carried by truck or rail. It is housed temporarily and then sold. Through the years of its useful life it is serviced and maintained. In a last phase it is junked. But then the scrap recovery operation begins and the process, in a more limited way, starts all over again.

Mineral statistics—for the first phase only, the mining and mineral processing or manufacturing industries—are reported yearly in the U.S. Bureau of Mines Minerals Yearbook. Most recent statistics available generally lag about two years, a remarkably short time considering the monumental task of collecting, collating, and publishing the data. Data for 1963 are summarized in Table VIII.3. These data, however, present a minimal picture. As Merrill pointed out (1964a, p.

TABLE VIII.3

ROLE OF MINERALS IN THE ECONOMY OF THE UNITED STATES
SALIENT STATISTICS 1963
(except as otherwise stated)
(U.S. Bureau of Mines Minerals Yearbook)

	Dollars
(1) Value of production—	
Metals, non-metals, fuels	19,620,000,000
(2) National income, generated by the mineral	
industry (except manufacturing) —	
Mining (including fuels)	5,414,000,000
Primary metals industries	10,497,000,000
Stone, clay, glass	4,530,000,000
Total	20,441,000,000
(3) Investments in new plants and equipment—	
Mining and fuels	1,040,000,000
Mineral oriented manufacturing industries	
(primary iron and steel, nonferrous metals,	
stone, glass, clay, chemicals, petroleum, and coal)	6,790,000,000
Total	7,830,000,000
(4) Salaries and wages—	
All mining industries, including fuels	3,798,000,000
Primary metal industries	7,930,000,000
Stone, clay, glass	3,310,000,000
Total	15,038,000,000
	Short tons
(5) Freight generated by mineral industries—	
Rail and motor (1962)	1,365,396,000
Truck (only includes sand and gravel, stone, cement, slag)	1,456,810,000
	People
(6) Employment—	
Mining (nonfuel)	202,100
Mineral fuels	432,100
Mineral oriented manufacturing (fertilizers,	
cement, steel, primary nonferrous metals)	666,300
Total	1,300,500
Scientists and Engineers (1960)	104,600

18), statistics commonly conceal a substantial amount of mineral industry activity under the general heading of 'Manufacturing.' In item (2), Table VIII.3, for example, the total contribution of all mineral industries to national income in 1963 was 20,441 million dollars. This is only 4+ per cent of the total industrial contribution of 478,793 million. Merrill (1964a, p. 18) estimated the real contribution as much as 10 per cent of the total. The same observation applies to item (4), Salaries and wages, and to item (6), Employment. The statistics show that the mineral industry work force makes up only 2 to 3 per cent of the total nonagricultural work force of the United States. If the full complement of mineral industry employees in manufacturing were included the total would be higher. Consider, then, the result of including all of the satellite industries concerned with minerals and the people directly employed with them—for example, Trucking: Item (5) indicates that nearly 1.5 billion tons of sand and gravel, stone, cement, and slag were moved by truck in 1963. If the average load was 10 tons, there were 150 million trips involved. Mineral freight accounted for about 59 per cent of all rail traffic and 83 per cent of all water traffic in the United States in 1962.

Taxes paid by the mineral industry in the form of corporation income taxes, individual and partnership income taxes, franchise taxes, state and local property taxes, and severance taxes make up a significant part of U. S. tax revenues. Corporate income taxes alone amount to more than 3 billion dollars and constitute some four per cent of national tax income (Merrill, 1964b, p. 19). In Texas in 1963, the oil industry paid 223 million in states taxes, and 150 million to counties, cities, school districts (Faggioli, 1965, p. 17). Add to this the personal income taxes paid by mineral industry employees and taxes on income of shareholders and it becomes clear that a large part of the mineral-created wealth of the United States, notwithstanding the fact that minerals in the United States are not owned by the government, goes to pay the cost of government.

Economists have recently given much prominence to an economic index called GNP—Gross National Product—which is defined as the total value of goods and services measured at market prices. It is supposed to be a measure of national economic growth and commonly other growth curves, for mineral commodities for example, are compared to the GNP curve and rated, then, as more or less than GNP growth. Merrill (1964, p. 20) observed that value of all mineral products (measured as raw materials) amounted to about 4 per cent of the Gross National Product. Purchases of goods and services (by

TABLE VIII.4

TRENDS IN CONSUMPTION OF MINERALS AND OTHER NATURAL RESOURCES

(after Romney, 1965, pp. 10, 13)

A. CONSUMPTION—MILLIONS OF DOLLARS—ON 1954 DOLLAR Base—1870–1915–1957

Year	Non-Metallic Minerals	Metals	Mineral Fuels	All Minerals	Agricultural Products	Timber Products	Population 000's Omitted
1870	60	57	269	386	5,000	2,300	36,905
1915	504	1,009	3,410	4,923	15,700	3,620	100,549
1957	2,079	2,344	11,375	15,798	26,100	3,615	171,196
Factor of Increase of Total Consumption and of Population—1870 = 1							
1870	1	1	1	1	1	1	1
1915	8.4	17.70	12.68	12.75	3.14	1.57	2.51
1957	34.65	41.12	42.29	41.00	5.22	1.57	4.30
Factor of Increase in Per Capita Consumption—1870 = 1							
1870	1	1	1	1	1	1	
1915	3.38	7.05	5.05	5.08	1.25	0.62	
1957	8.06	9.56	9.84	9.52	1.22	0.36	

B. CONSUMPTION OF NATURAL RESOURCES, YEARS 1870–1957–2000   In 1954 $ Value (Millions of Dollars)

Year	All Natural Resources	Mineral Resources	% of Total	Agricultural Products	% of Total	Forest Products	% of Total	Population
1870	$ 7,686	$ 386	5%	$ 5,000	65%	$ 2,300	30%	39,905
1957	45,513	15,798	34.5%	26,100	57.3%	3,615	8.0%	171,196
2000	108,979	46,154	42.4%	52,567	48.2%	10,249	9.4%	330,000
Factor of Increase of Total Consumption and of Population—1870 = 1								
1870	1	1		1		1		1
1957	5.92	41.0		5.22		1.57		4.3
2000	14.20	119.6		10.51		4.45		8.28

individuals, corporations, and *the government*), investment, and net exports all go into making up the index. There seems to be a widespread misconception that the GNP index is a measure of economic health; it is a measure of economic *activity* and the two are not necessarily synonymous. For example, the index is positively affected by government spending programs even if the programs are financed by deficit spending. The index would also be affected by a frenzy of economic activity such as might preceed an economic crisis to the extent that such activity affected prices of commodities; a rise in prices due to inflation raises the GNP. Inasmuch as mineral raw materials make up only 4 per cent of GNP, and the other 96 per cent of the index is derived from other goods and services, GNP is perhaps not the best economic index with which to compare growth in demand for mineral commodities, even though the mineral commodity turns up in different form again and again in a procession of manufactured products. For these reasons, comparisons of mineral growth and demand with GNP for various commodities as given in Chapter X should be made with full knowledge of what GNP is.

Romney (1965), using statistics published by Resources for the Future, Inc. (1962, 1963), summarized trends in mineral consumption in the United States (Table VIII.4) and concluded that:

(1) Between 1870 and 1957 the minerals demand explosion exceeded the population explosion in the ratio of 9.5 to 1.

(2) Mineral consumption in 1957 was 41 times that of 1870, while manufacturing output increased 36.25 times, agricultural products increased 5.22 times, forest products increased 1.57 times, and GNP increased 19.41 times.

(3) By the year 2,000, it is predicted that mineral consumption will increase by a factor of 2.92, agricultural products by a factor 2.01, timber products by a factor of 2.83, GNP by a factor of 4.80, and population by a factor of 1.92 (Romney, 1965, p. 12).

REFERENCES

Ahearn, V. P. (1965) Urbanization, land use controls, and the mineral aggregates industry: Paper presented at Annual Meeting of American Institute of Mining, Metallurgical and Petroleum Engineers, Chicago, February 17, 1965.

——— (1958) The zoning problem and its significance to the sand and gravel producer: National Sand and Gravel Association, 38 pp.

Allen, S. W. (1959) Conserving natural resources, 2nd ed.: McGraw-Hill, New York, 370 pp.

Allsman, P. T. (1962) Conservation in metal mining, *in* Minerals and energy, Part I: Colo. Sch. Mines Quarterly, vol. 57, no. 4, pp. 87–95.

American Law of Mining (1964) Vol. 5, Rocky Mountain Mineral Law Foundation: Matthew Bender and Co., New York, 282 pp.

Bauer, A. M. (1965) Simultaneous excavation and ore rehabilitation of sand and gravel sites: National Sand and Gravel Association, 60 pp.

Boarman, P. M. (1965) The world's money: Wall Street Jour., May 10, 1965.

Boericke, W. F., and Bailey, C. C. (1964) Mine financing, *in* Economics of the mineral industries, 2nd ed.: American Institute of Mining and Metallurgical Engineers, New York, pp. 245–279.

Bonini, W. E., Hedberg, H. D., and Kalliokoski, Jorma (1964) The role of national governments in exploration for mineral resources: Littoral Press, Ocean City, New Jersey, 220 pp.

Borden, G. S. (1964) Taxation of mineral property, *in* Economics of the mineral industry, 2nd ed.: American Institute of Mining and Metallurgical Engineers, New York, pp. 463–509.

Buck, W. K. (1963) Mineral development policy: Canada Department of Mines and Technical Surveys, Mineral Resources Division., Min. Inf. Bull. MR64, 14 pp.

Burton, Ian, and Kates, R. W. (1965) Readings in resource management and conservation: University of Chicago Press, Chicago, 609 pp.

Clawson, Marion (1964) Natural resources and international development: Fifth Annual Forum, Resources for the Future, Inc., Johns Hopkins Press, Baltimore, 462 pp.

Cooper, Byron N. (1965) Limestone and dolomite: geologists and percentage depletion allowances: Paper presented to the First Midwest Forum on Geology of Industrial Minerals, The Ohio State University, February, 1965.

Faggioli, R. E. (1965) Oil and gas versus water in the Southwest: conflict or compromise? *in* Oil and water—related resource problems of the Southwest, a symposium, edited by P. T. Flawn: Bureau of Economic Geology, The University of Texas, Austin, 64 pp.

Fisher, W. L. (1965) The search for nonfuel minerals: Bull. South Texas Geol. Soc., vol. 5, no. 2, pp. 6–12.

Goldman, H. B. (1959) Urbanization and the mineral industry: Calif. Div. of Mines, Min. Inf. Service, vol. 12, no. 12, 5 pp.

Hartsook, E. A. (1965) Population pressure and mineral industries: Paper presented at Annual Meeting of American Institute of Mining, Metallurgical and Petroleum Engineers, Chicago, February 17, 1965.

Hawtrey, R. G. (1947) The gold standard in theory and practice, 5th ed.: Longmans, Green, London, 280 pp.

Hiestand, T. C. (1960) Application of geology in computing depletion of producing properties: Bull. Amer. Assoc. Petrol. Geologists, vol. 44, no. 4, pp. 409–422.

Johnson, H. G. (1962) Money, trade and economic growth: Harvard University Press, Cambridge, 199 pp.

Kemmerer, E. W. (1944) Gold and the gold standard: McGraw-Hill, New York, 238 pp.

Keynes. J. M. (1930) A treatise on money: Macmillan and Co., London, 2 vols.
——— (1931) Essays in persuasion: Hart-Davis, London, 376 pp,
———(1936) The general theory of employment, interest and money: Macmillan and Co., London, 403 pp.

Koenig, R. P. (1964) National attitudes—vital key to effective mineral development: Mining Eng., vol. 16, no. 7, pp. 95–97, 100, 102.

Landsberg, H. H., Fischman, L. L., and Fisher, J. L. (1963) Resources in America's future: Resources for the Future, Inc., Johns Hopkins Press, Baltimore, 1017 pp.

Langdon, J. C. (1965) Resources and the state government, in Oil and water —related resource problems of the Southwest, a symposium, edited by P. T. Flawn: Bureau of Economic Geology, The University of Texas, Austin, 64 pp.

Leith, C. K. (1935) Conservation of minerals: Science, vol. 82, no. 2119, pp. 109–117.

Lovering, T. S. (1953) Safeguarding our mineral-dependent economy: Bull. Geol. Soc. Amer., vol. 64, pp. 101–126.

McCracken, P. W. (1963) Basic sources of economic progress, in Symposium on economic growth: Proc. of American Bankers Assoc., Washington, D.C., pp. 21–37.

McDivitt, J. F. (1963) The world bank: Mining Eng., vol. 15, no. 5, pp. 59–67.

McKelvey, V. E. (1962) National goal for mineral resources: efficient development and full use in Minerals and energy, Part I: Colo. Sch. Mines Quarterly, vol. 57, no. 4, pp. 143–152.

Merrill, C. W. (1964a) The significance of the mineral industries in the econimy, in Economics of the mineral industries, 2nd ed.: American Institute of Mining and Metallurgical Engineers, New York, pp. 1–41.
——— (1964b) Gold and silver—money and credit, in Economics of the mineral industries, 2nd ed.: American Institute of Mining and Metallurgical Engineers, New York, pp. 709–728.

National Academy of Sciences (1963) The growth of world population: NAS-NRC Pub. 1091, 38 pp.

Netschert, B. C. (1962) The strategic stockpile—hindsight and foresight, in Minerals and energy, Part II: Colo. Sch. Mines Quarterly, vol. 58, no. 1, pp. 175–187.

Noakes, L. C. (1965) Economic geology in Australia (Australia newsletter): Econ. Geology, vol. 60, p. 400 (pp. 399–403).

Oil and Gas Journal (1954) What's ahead for oil abroad (Interview with Walter J. Levy): Oil and Gas Jour., vol. 63, no. 26, pp. 43–46.

——— (1965) Editorial—How the oil-import policy looks now: Oil and Gas Jour., vol. 63, no. 28, p. 47.

Ostrander, F. T. (1963) The place of minerals in economic development: Amer. Inst. Mining, Met. and Petrol. Engrs., Preprint No. 63177, 25 pp.

Pendergast, R. A. (1965) M&MM analysis: The aluminum price debacle, *in* E&MJ Metal & Mineral Markets, vol. 36, no. 46, pp. 4–5.

Potter, Neal, and Christy, F. T., Jr. (1962) Trends in natural resource commodities: Resources for the Future, Inc., Johns Hopkins Press, Baltimore, 568 pp.

President's Materials Policy Commission (1952) Resources for freedom, Vol. I, *in* Foundation for growth and security: U.S. government Printing Office, Washington, 184 pp.

Ridge, J. D. (1962) A national mineral policy, *in* Minerals and energy, Part II: Colo. Sch. Mines Quarterly, vol. 58, no. 1, pp. 291–321.

Roberts, W. A. (1944) State taxation of metallic deposits: Harvard Economic Studies, vol. 77, 400 pp.

Rommey, M. P. (1965) Minerals in the life of man: Utah Mining Association, Salt Lake City, 16 pp.

Shannon, Ian (1963) The economic function of gold: Cheshire, Melbourne, 139 pp.

Smutz, H. E. (1954) Zone regulation of oil drilling and related administrative problems, Planning Advisory Service Special Report: American Society of Planning Officials, Chicago, 9 pp.

Spaulding, A. O. (1965) Drilling in city brings on no civic hostility: Oil and Gas Jour., vol. 63, no. 10, pp. 190–202.

Triffin, Robert (1960) Gold and the dollar crisis: Yale University Press, New Haven, 195 pp.

——— (1964) The evolution of the international monetary system: Princeton Studies in International Finance No. 12, Princeton University, Princeton, 87 pp.

Udall, S. L. (1963) The quiet crisis: Holt, Rinehart and Winston, New York, 209 pp.

United Nations (1951) Proceedings of the United Nations Scientific Conference on the conservation and utilization of resources, 1949, Vol. 2, Mineral Resources: Geneva, 303 pp.

——— (1963) Report on the United Nations Conference on the Application of Science and Technology for the Benefit of the Less Developed Areas, Geneva, 1963, Vol. 2, Natural Resources: Geneva, 243 pp.

U.S. Department of the Interior (1965) Quest for quality, *in* U.S. Interior Conservation Yearbook: 96 pp.

White, G. F. (1961) The choice of use in resource management: Natural Resources Jour., vol. 1, pp. 23–40.

Wonnacott, Paul (1963) A suggestion for the revaluation of gold: Jour. Finance, vol. 18, no. 3, pp. 49–55.

CHAPTER IX

MINERALS, MINING, AND ECOLOGY

Introduction.

In 1922, R. L. Sherlock in a delightful book entitled *Man as a Geological Agent* called attention to the extent of man's modification of the earth, and attempted to quantify insofar as possible the results of human activities over the centuries that man had inhabited Great Britain. His chapters treated excavation, attrition, subsidence, accumulation, alterations of the sea coast, the circulation of waters, climate and scenery, and the total of the alterations effected by man in the London urban area. The London chapter, although dealing with a city then just emerging from the horse and buggy era, is instructive to anyone concerned with modern urban geology studies. Sherlock concluded in 1922 that man is many times more powerful as an erosive agent than all of the natural denuding forces combined. He compared man to a glacier which tends to make the land surface uneven, forming terraces, holes, and mounds in a sporadic manner and wreaking big changes in a short period of time.

Consider now, if you will, the acceleration in number, kind, and magnitude of changes wrought by human activity since 1922. From the air the face of any industrialized nation can be seen to be scarred by innumerable pits, cuts, and scrapes. The contour of the land is modified on a large scale. Most major and minor drainages are characterized by engineering works. Natural resources are moved long distances in large volume by trucks, rail, ship, pipeline, or aqueduct. The composition and temperature of the soil, water, and air are changed by a vast array of chemical and industrial processes. This discussion will not consider biological changes resulting from human activity or the changes brought about by civil engineering projects in general. However, inquiry into the effect on the environment of extraction and processing of minerals is pertinent to a general study of mineral resources, particularly in view of the definition of conservation recently expressed in the U. S. Department of Interior Conservation Yearbook for 1964, *Quest for Quality*; conservation is defined as "applied ecology." Ecology is the science which is concerned with the mutual relationships between organisms and their environments.

The following section, then, considers the ecological effects of the mineral industry segment of modern industrial society, including (1) effects of mining, (2) effects of water resource projects, (3) effects of concentrating, beneficiating, and refining of mineral products, and (4) effects of redistributing the mineral 'stuff' of the crust. It is common to consider any ecological changes wrought by man as somehow 'bad' and any undisturbed natural scene as 'good.' However, if good and bad are defined in terms of adapting the environment to support large numbers of human beings at a high standard of living, then some changes are good and some are bad. For example, pollution of water, where it occurs, is clearly a bad effect of human activity. On the other hand, impoundment of water behind a dam may be a good change. Storage of water to prevent wasteful floods; provide adequate water supplies to sustain the population; generate power; create a recreation resource; and provide a habitat for fish, waterfoul, and other wildlife, must be evaluated as good by anyone with the well-being of human society as his principal interest. However, the fact that water impoundment affects the overall regimen of the river, prevents large surges of fresh water from cleaning out the channel and reaching the sea, and thereby perhaps changes the salinity of the estuary or bay, is considered as bad by those whose first concern is minimizing the ecological changes resulting from human activity.

Mining.

The ecological effects of mining can be conveniently considered under the headings underground mining, open pit mining, and dredging. Any underground mine is marked by a number of supporting surface installations—headframe, hoist-house, mill, laboratory, administration building, and living quarters, all served by a network of roads. Around a large mine there may be also a school, hospital, commissary, and recreational facilities—in short, everything to be found in a small city, including water supply and sewage disposal systems. When plans for development of the great San Manuel copper mine in Arizona were laid, two contracts were signed—the first in 1952 called for construction of a town including 12 miles of paved streets, 1,000 dwellings, 3 school buildings, a hospital, a park and shopping center, together with water supply, sewage, gas and electricity; the second contract for the mining installation, signed in 1953, involved expenditure of some 65 million dollars. At the end of 1955, capital investment was over 110 million (Parsons, 1957, p. 250). Thus, there takes place around a mine the same modification of terrain which characterizes any sizable colony of people, together with the special changes which accompany the digging out of the ground of several thousand or more tons of rock per day, crushing it, separating the desired elements, and disposing of the waste. In forested areas timber is cut for use in supporting the underground workings. The principal undesirable ecological changes resulting from underground mining have been, and still are in some areas, those caused by uncontrolled deforestation and resulting soil erosion, dumping of the crushed and ground rock waste—the mill tailings— in the local drainage system, the discharge of highly mineralized or acid mine waters into the local drainage system, and subsidence of the surface due to collapse of the underground workings after the mine has been abandoned. None of these abuses *has* to occur, and in the future legislation will prevent it, albeit at some cost to the mineral producer and thus to the consumer. Timber for support can be taken according to modern forest management procedures, or concrete supports can be substituted for timber. Collapse of the surface can be prevented by backfilling or maintenance of a support system. This high-cost procedure, however, is practical only where valuable improvements have been built over the mine workings, such as in urban areas. Filling of anthracite mine workings to prevent subsidence of part of northwest Scranton, Pennsylvania is expected to cost in excess of 1 million dollars. Value of improvements in the area is more than 13 million dollars. In the area of Cleveland, Ohio, pillars in underground salt mines are equipped with strain gauges to measure build-up of stress. Only about 50 per cent of the salt is recovered. One company engaged in extracting salt brines monitors a network of surface benchmarks to detect any changes of surface level due to withdrawal of the brine. For future planning in as yet undeveloped areas, it should be sufficient to maintain maps showing areas of potential surface subsidence. Disposal of waste rock or tailings and mine waters, however, is a major problem. Waste rock dumps and finely ground tailings accumulate in huge piles. The coarser broken and crushed rock of the dumps is relatively stable and is rarely moved in large volume by natural processes. It can be used to backfill workings and, if it meets specifications for aggregate and road base material, it can be put to good use in a local market. Tailings, however, behave as fine sand or silt and in many ways they present the same engineering problems as sand dunes. Natural erosion agents attempt to reduce the unstable piles and carry away the comminuted rock as sediment in the streams of the area. Such a sudden load of fine sediment chokes the streams and destroys the equilibrium previously achieved. An effective disposal system must protect natural drainage from the tailings. Tailings can be used to fill abandoned workings; where they are available close to an expanding urban area tailings might be marketed for low-grade constructional purposes such as sanitary fill. Commonly, however, a high content of iron sulfides in dumps and tailing piles result in a chemically unstable material unsuitable for constructional uses. In many cases, the only practical approach is to stabilize the tailing piles, perhaps with vegetation or perhaps by spraying with an asphaltic compound, so that they remain as fixed manmade mounds after the mining operation has terminated.

Mine or oil field waters can be treated to alter their objectionable chemical character or disposed of by injection into a secure subsurface formation. This is an expensive procedure. In the early days of the petroleum industry, salt water was pumped into local surface pits. Leakage contaminated surface and ground water supplies. Subsequent practice reduced contamination by lining the disposal pits, casing off fresh-water-bearing strata, and drilling salt-water disposal wells. Commonly the water is returned to the reservior as part of secondary recovery operations. Fresh-water pollution by the mineral industry has occurred and still occurs, but to a lesser degree than is commonly realized. The pollution charges against the mineral industry, based on past abuses, are in many cases no longer just (Faggioli, 1965, pp. 10–16). The coming years will see conservation laws in most states set pollution control standards which the mineral industry and other industries will have to meet one way or another. In Texas, the oil and gas regulatory body, the Texas Railroad Commission, is attempting to eliminate all surface disposal pits.

In open pit mining, modification of the surface is on a much larger scale than underground mining, and in the modern mining industry far more waste and ore is moved in open pit operations than in underground mines. Wolfe (1964) reported that today open-pit mining, dredging, and solution-evaporation methods account for 95 per cent of the total value of metals and nonmetals extracted while underground mining methods account for only 5 per cent. In the United States about 80 per cent of the metallic ores and 95 per cent of the nonmetallic minerals and rocks are mined by surface methods. Modern shovels, draglines, and trucks have capacities measured in tens of cubic yards; recently-manufactured giant trucks for use off-the-highway have capacities of up to 135 tons. In the coal mining industry, the largest single unit yet designed is a 200-cubic-yard shovel as tall as a 21-story building and capable of dumping 150 yards from the excavation; a new coal hauler has a 240-ton capacity. Draglines with buckets up to 85 cubic yards and booms up to 275 feet long are in operation in strip coal mines. In the largest operations, millions of yards of overburden are removed to depths of several hundred feet until the orebody is reached and mining commences. Pit dimensions are measured in thousands of feet. The very biggest operations produce on the order of 100,000 tons of ore per *day*. In the Twin Buttes area south of Pima, Arizona, the Anaconda Company in 1965 began a stripping operation designed to remove 165 million tons of alluvial overburden to a depth of 460 feet over a 4-year period. They will use 80-ton capacity scrapers and 100-ton capacity bottom dump trucks (Beall, 1965, p. 80). Recently it was proposed to strip overburden to a depth of 1,000 feet (1.3 billion cubic yards at a cost of 25 cents per yard) to open up for open-pit mining about 3.1 billion cubic yards of oil shale (Engineering and Mining Journal, September, 1965, p. 101). The great open pit of the Utah Copper Division of Kennecott Copper Corporation at Bingham Canyon, Utah, has been called the biggest man-made excavation in the crust of the earth (Parsons, 1957, p. 27). At the end of 1965, about one billion cubic yards (2.5 billion tons) of ore and overburden had been moved, and the pit was about 2,200 feet deep (Figure IX.I). The record was set on July 29, 1965, when 132,801 tons of ore and 267,077 tons of waste were moved (Paul A. Bailly, personal communication, 1966). Such great excavations must be drained. The huge volumes of overburden must be disposed of in addition to the large volumes of mill tailings from the day-to-day crushing, grinding, and concentrating operation. In areas where the water table is intersected by the pit, care must be taken not to contaminate the fresh water. Of course, subsidence is not a problem, but slumping of pit walls and slopes can be serious if there is nearby

FIGURE IX.1   Utah Copper's great pit in Bingham Canyon in 1964 (Courtesy of Kennecott Copper Corporation).

surface construction. Proper engineering for slope stability is necessary. The major problem is waste disposal. In most populous areas, the pit itself can be reclaimed for some beneficial use after the minerals have been harvested—if wet, for a pond or lake, if dry, for waste disposal or some facility where a sunken, below-surface location is desirable. In less thickly populated areas, the pit, although unsightly, causes no damage if it is properly fenced against livestock. Backfilling coal strip mines is already common practice in many areas—costs are reckoned at from 10 to 40 cents per recovered ton of coal depending on whether the pit is simply filled or whether the original contour of the land is restored and reforestation is undertaken. On an acre basis, costs range from about 50 to 400 dollars (Brooks, 1966, pp. 26–28). In any case, unless the original soil is saved and stockpiled for reclamation purposes, the spoil is new land without an established soil profile; this may be good or bad, depending on the character of the original soil.

Dredging is open-pit mining with a floating mineral factory. The principal ecological effects are the result of disposal of the spoil. In dredges operating in small drainages (as opposed to large rivers or oceans), the impounding of water to float the dredge also results in environmental changes. Any change in sediment distribution in an aqueous system which has reached equilibrium, particularly one in which there are strong currents, will set into operation natural processes working to restore equilibrium. Erosion, sediment transport, and deposition will occur. Thus, dredging of sand and gravel from a bay or estuary may cause rapid erosion of beaches; dredging of sand and gravel from rivers may cause deposition of the sediment load from upstream and an increase in erosive capacity below the dredged area. The same kind of changes are caused by construction of dams and jetties. The spoil from dredges, consisting of mud, silt, and sand rather than ground or crushed rock, if distributed on the land surface may, depending on its composition, greatly increase fertility in the same way that the mud and silt spread over the land by floods restores its agricultural potential. Such spoil cannot be heaped in one place but must be spread and contoured. Thus, one by-product of dredging might be improvement of pasture and agricultural land. During operation of a dredge the water is roiled and fine sediment is thrown in suspension. Such conditions kill certain kinds of flora and fauna. Live oyster reefs, for example, can be injured by dredging in such close proximity that the live organisms are smothered by fine sediment churned up by the cutting-head. In Texas where dredging

of shell from dead reefs is big business, the shell dredges are prohibited from operating so close to live reefs as to result in damage
to the living organisms, but there is debate over the radius of protection to be afforded the live reefs. For many years the distance was
1,500 feet. Now, due to a shortage of shell reserves, dredges may
operate to within 300 feet of a live reef. The long-term effects may be
inimical to live oyster growth along the Texas coast (p. 190).

Water resource projects.

In attempting to capture water, store it for use, and distribute
it through irrigation systems, man has probably caused more ecological
changes than in any other mineral enterprise. Throughout the
United States, there are stock tanks and ponds behind simple earth
dams on sags and swales, there are small lakes behind more elab-
orate dams on tributary drainages, and there are major reservoirs
behind the great dams on major rivers. These store water for use in
times of need, provide convenient watering places for stock, and render more orderly and less catastrophic the progress of heavy precipitation to the oceans. Ecologic effects are many. According to some
engineers, the proliferation of small ponds and lakes on the upper
reaches of drainage basins increases the evaporation rate to the
point where contributions to big reservoirs on major rivers are reduced and the ultimate result is a net loss of water. Changes in
stream regimen affecting water flow, sediment transport, erosion,
estuary and bay environment, and coastal processes accompany the
construction of dams. Increase in area of water surface behind impounding structures increases evaporation, and by increasing marginal
vegetation, also increases transpiration. Resulting additions of water
vapor to the atmosphere result in slight weather and climate modifications. The transport of water through irrigation systems into
previously dry regions results in great changes through conversion
of land from desert or semi-desert to productive agricultural land.
However, prolonged irrigation with evaporation of part of the water
applied to crops result in progressive enrichment of salts in the soil
and eventually renders the soil unproductive.

Withdrawal of ground water in large volumes commonly results in
subsidence of the surface, particularly in areas of unconsolidated or
weakly consolidated formations, and presents many engineering problems as long as withdrawal continues without natural or artificial
recharge. Desalination of large volumes of sea water or saline ground

water will produce effluent brines and present a disposal problem (p. 373). Return of these highly saline waters to the ocean will result in local ecological changes that will be largely biological. Finally, the huge engineering projects designed to transport very large volumes of water for hundreds of miles, from wet areas to dry areas, will cause profound ecological changes in both the intake and discharge ends of the systems. It is alleged that tapping of the headwaters of the Snake and Columbia Rivers, for example, would so change the regimen of the river as to limit salmon migration and spawning.

Concentration, beneficiation, and refining.

The variety of processes required to separate a desired mineral substance from the host earth material and refine it to meet industrial specifications produces waste—solid, liquid, and gaseous wastes. The amount of waste which accrues from any particular operation is, of course, a function of the original concentration of the desired substance. Thus, a mining operation which mines and concentrates ores containing a fraction of an ounce of gold per ton produces large volumes of waste in relation to the mineral substance recovered, while an operation which mines gypsum for manufacture of wallboard uses nearly all of the rock mined and has a relatively small volume of waste in relation to the mineral substance recovered. The kind of waste produced depends on the nature of the process used to convert the mineral material into a useful product. Washing operations produce sediment and slime-charged water (which can be clarified in settling tanks); leaching operations produce spent acids; concentration by flotation produces sediment in the form of tailings and liquid in the form of water contaminated by various reagents; chemical processes involving liquid and ion exchanges produce spent reagents and contaminated water solutions; and smelting processes result in slags and gases, commonly high in sulfur compounds. Today, solid wastes accumulate in heaps on the surface; liquid wastes are discharged into surface drainages if they contain a low level of pollutants, or are chemically treated to reduce toxicity and then discharged, or are retained in surface pits or pumped into an underground disposal formation; and gaseous wastes are discharged into the atmosphere or if especially poisonous are treated to eliminate toxic constituents. The trend is toward legislation requiring that (1) solid wastes be put back into the excavation or otherwise landscaped and planted,

(2) liquid wastes be injected into a secure subsurface formation or chemically treated to produce clean water and a concentrated liquid or solid waste which in a reduced volume can be disposed of efficiently, and (3) gaseous wastes either be eliminated by prohibiting the process (e. g., burning of high-sulfur fossil fuels); beneficiating the fuel before burning (e. g., removal of pyrite); or by chemically removing the pollutant before discharge of the gas. Recently a process has been developed for converting coal burning wastes into marketable products. Fly ash is sold as a pozzolanic material. Prices range from 2 to 7 dollars per ton. Consolidated Edison of New York now converts fly ash into an aggregate which is marketed under the name Edicrete for about 4.5 dollars per yard. American Electric Power sells boiler slag as a superior road base material for 3 dollars per ton.

The biggest disposal problem is that of radioactive wastes produced by atomic fission. At present, highly radioactive wastes are retained in specially designed tanks and no one seems to know what to do with them. These wastes are highly dangerous and cannot be permitted to escape into the lithosphere, hydrosphere, or atmosphere. They also are highly mobile because they produce heat through the normal process of radioactive decay. One promising method is to stabilize them by absorption into a clay body and to dispose of them by deep burial in restricted areas. Less potent wastes can be injected into deep geologically secure subsurface hosts or disposed of in deep sea 'sinks.'

Another problem is CO_2—the universal product of combustion. The mineral industry is only one of many contributors to the rising carbon dioxide content of the atmosphere. The mineral industry supplies the fossil fuels—coal, lignite, oil, and gas—but they are burned by the home-heating plant, the automobile engine, and the electric utility producing power as well as the smelter and blast-furnace. Carbon dioxide is not toxic in the way of sulfurous gases. The potential danger lies in changing the heat balance of the earth by increasing the absorption of solar radiation and thereby raising the temperature of the earth's surface. If the CO_2 content of the atmosphere were to double, the average surface temperature would increase 3° to 4° C. A possible consequence is melting of the polar caps, flooding of coastal cities, and drastic effects on fish population (Conservation Foundation, 1963).

The seriousness of pollution by metallic elements produced and distributed by combustion is now under study. Of principal concern is lead, a well-known poisoner, which is widely distributed by combustion of leaded motor fuel.

Redistribution.

All natural processes of erosion result in redistribution of crustal material. Such processes include weathering which effects chemical and physical changes resulting in a disaggregation and size reduction of the earth material and subsequent transportation by mass movement, water, wind, and moving ice. The ultimate result of these processes is to move material from higher elevations to lower, and to reduce the mountains and fill up the basins. Through time, materials are in this way moved for great distances—thousands of miles. Man, in his worldwide digging up and carrying off, is at the same time much more selective and much less systematic. Centuries of digging up the metals of the world and carrying them to the industrialized countries of Europe and North America has certainly resulted in a major redistribution of the metallic elements in the upper thousand feet of the earth's crust. To some degree these metals are returned to the source area in the form of manufactured products, but the net result is a concentration of the metals in the industrial areas. Moreover, within the industrial areas, there is a concentration in the urban regions. In a larger view, however, man is a dispersing or homogenizing agent because he destroys the great natural concentrations of minerals—such as iron, copper, phosphate, and potash deposits—and distributes them around the world. Unless there is an exceptional case, such as Mexico City where part of the city is foundering as water is removed from its unconsolidated sedimentary foundation, urban communities build up the crust and form mounds of accumulated debris. Archeologists are well acquainted with the stratified accumulations of long-occupied city sites. Thus man, like an earthworm, burrows into the earth and turns over its surface; like a bird, he brings materials from elsewhere to build his nest; and like the pack rat, he accumulates quantities of trash. Sherlock (1922, p. 189) estimated that debris has been added to the site of London at the rate of one foot per century—a rate similar to that estimated from a study of ancient cities. The debris included bricks, masonry and concrete fragments, ashes, clinker, cinders, glass, household rubbish, wood, asphalt, organic material, and sewage sludge.

The effect on the environment of man's redistribution of earth materials is difficult to measure except in cases where changes are drastic and obvious. Changes in chemistry of the urban soil are rarely noticed because they come slowly—the land is no longer used for agriculture so its productivity change is not measured. Only where poisonous accumulations of oils or chemicals or salts produce bare spots is the change obvious. Changes in texture of the soil are toward greater mechanical stability. Clay and mud are stabilized by addition of lime, or by mixing of gravel or crushed stone, or by covering with a pavement. Moisture content is changed. Pavement increases run-off and decreases soak-in, but also decreases evaporation. The most pronounced biologic effects are on the aquatic flora and fauna in response to dumping of solid and liquid mineral material into drainages. Redistribution of water, of course, brings about the most profound changes in flora, fauna, and atmosphere (p. 258). The oasis around an artificial lake in a desert region is perhaps the most striking example of change through redistribution of minerals.

Conclusion.

In the overall view of man's development the use of minerals has been of such immense benefit as to render inconsequential the local injurious environment effects—one has but to contemplate human culture without mineral materials, mineral fuels, or mineral crop nutrients. To deny these facts is to distort appreciation for pristine wilderness into an irrational obsession. In this generation, however, the human population and its effects on environment have reached a point where injurious effects of the mineral industry must be dealt with in a constructive fashion. The answer is not to deny society the use of minerals but to minimize the injury. It does not make much sense to kill the industrial culture to preserve the environment. For whom would it be preserved?

REFERENCES

Beall, J. V. (1965) Southwest copper—a position survey: Mining Eng., vol. 17, no. 10, pp. 77–92.

Brooks, D. B. (1966) Strip mine reclamation and economic analysis: Natural Resources Jour., vol. 6, no. 1, pp. 13–44.

Doerr, A. H. (1962) Coal mining, landscape changes, and reclamation recommendations for Oklahoma, in Minerals and energy, Part 1: Colo. Sch. Mines Quart., vol. 57, no. 4, pp. 97–111.

Engineering and Mining Journal (1965) Open pit mining in 1965: Eng. and Mining Jour., vol. 166, no. 9, pp. 100–121.

Faggioli, R. E. (1965) Oil and gas versus water in the Southwest: conflict or compromise? *in* Oil and water—related resource problems of the Southwest, a symposium, edited by P. T. Flawn: Bureau of Economic Geology, The University of Texas Austin, pp. 7–20.

Mining Engineering (1965) Pennsylvania's Land Reclamation Act: Mining Eng., vol. 17, no. 7, pp. 145–146.

Parsons, A. B. (1957) The porphyry coppers in 1956: American Institute of Mining and Metallurgical Engineers, New York, 270 pp.

Sherlock, R. L. (1922) Man as a geological agent: H. F. & G. Wetherby, London, 372 pp.

Sullivan, G. D. (1965) A new science—mined land reclamation: Mining Eng., vol. 17, no. 7, pp. 142–144.

The Conservation Foundation (1963) Implications of rising carbon dioxide content of the atmosphere: The Conservation Foundation, New York, 15 pp.

Wolfe, J. A. (1964) Impact of technology on mineral economics: Paper presented to the Southwest Metals and Minerals Conference, American Institute of Mining, Metallurgical and Petroleum Engineers, Los Angeles, California, May, 1964.

CHAPTER X

OCCURRENCE, DISTRIBUTION, AND OUTLOOK

Introduction.

It is difficult to treat the occurence and distribution of mineral resources briefly and at the same time meaningfully. One common approach is to list the occurrence the world over of each commodity; another is to sum up the mineral wealth of each region or political subdivision. Both require presentation of mineral statistics. These statistics are essential to the support of the discussion and to the inquiry of any serious student of mineral resources, but they are also a formidable mass of detail which if not properly presented tends to impound the smooth flow of general principles. The author of comprehensive works on mineral resources is in a perplexing damned-if-he-does-and-damned-if-he-doesn't situation with regard to presentation of mineral statistics. The difficulty lies in the several significant data that are required for a summation that means anything. Production, reserves, and demand are interrelated and must be examined together for an understanding of the resource problem. For example, from the resource viewpoint, figures on current and past production of a particular mineral commodity in the various countries of the world are significant only when considered with the various classes of reserves remaining in the mineral deposits and the economic conditions under which they can be produced. These figures are difficult to obtain and, in fact, in many countries do not exist. Likewise of importance is an analysis of factors which will affect future demand for the commodity; in planning for the future, data on available reserves are meaningful in terms of forecasts of demand for the commodity. Increases in demand for minerals can be examined in terms of two growth elements: (1) an increase due to a higher level of consumption—an increase in per capita consumption, and (2) an increase due to an increase in population. For example, if the per capita annual increase in consumption of mineral X is 2.5 per cent and population increases at the rate of 1.5 per cent per year, the combined annual increase is slightly more than 4 per cent (4.03%).[1] A reminder about rates of increase is in order here. The geometric progression, as expressed by the compound interest formula, produces formidable in-increases over relatively short term periods:

X increasing at 2% per year=2X *in*	35 years
3%	23½ years
4%	18 years
5%	14 years
6%	12 years
7%	10 years
8%	9 years
9%	8 years
10%	7½ years

Also of significance to any student of mineral resources is the likelihood of new discoveries of major importance. Some parts of the

---

[1] If 100,000 people use 5 pounds of X per year, the consumption in that year is 500,000 pounds of X. If the population is increasing at 1.5%, there will be an additional 1500 consumers at year end, or 101,500 people. If this population uses 2.5% more of X than in the previous year, it will consume 5.125 pounds of X per person or a total of 520,187.5 pounds of X. The additional 20,187.5 pounds represents an increase of 4.03%. This simplification assumes that a consumer born into the population at any point in the year is a full consumer. If an additional consumer who comes into the population is weighted on the basis of the part of the year he is present (for example, a consumer born at mid-year would be considered half a consumer), the compound growth rate is very slightly less.

earth's crust are richer in a particular element than other parts; in these provinces chances for discovery are greater than outside of them. It is also important to know whether the world production of a particular mineral commodity is made up of contributions from a large number of deposits or whether it is coming from one or two very large deposits which also contain the bulk of the known reserves. The problem is compounded because of lack of data from that vast area of the earth's surface controlled by the Soviet Union and China. A great mineral exploration effort has been carried on in the Sino-Soviet area over the past two decades but the results are not available to western students.

What was known about the distribution of mineral resources at mid-century is ably presented in a mineral atlas by Van Royen and Bowles (1952). This chapter will review the most important mineral commodities and attempt to present the significant geologic, geographic, economic, and political factors as of this date. The interests of the United States are emphasized. Statistics are included in a series of three tables: Table X.1 gives a summary of current world mineral production as distributed (in percentages) among the various nations; Table X.2 presents current production figures and reserve estimates for important mineral commodities—the reserve data indicate in general the quantity of material available in known deposits that can be extracted with current technology under existing economic conditions; Table X.3 shows the minimum degree of concentration of the various elements necessary for exploration under today's economic system and with existing technology. The meaning of these figures is discussed in the separate sections dealing with each commodity.

The single most important fact about mineral resources is that they are not distributed equally over the world; some nations are richly endowed, others are poor in minerals. Some nations have very large reserves of one particular commodity and as a major exporter of that commodity have a large voice in world mineral trade. Their own economy is tied to the world market for the commodity. Very large countries, because their area generally takes in several geologic provinces, have a broader mineral resource base than countries whose borders include only part of one geologic province such as a coastal plain or an interior plateau. But no country today, however large, is completely self-sufficient in mineral resources. This is because modern industrial society consumes a tremendous volume as well as a wide variety of minerals. As a result, then, of the fact that political boundaries are not drawn on geologic criteria, and as a result of

TABLE X.1

APPROXIMATE PERCENTAGE DISTRIBUTION OF WORLD MINERAL PRODUCTION IN 1963[1]

(U.S. Bureau of Mines Minerals Yearbook, Vol. IV, Table 6, pp. 10–11)

| | WESTERN HEMISPHERE | | | EASTERN HEMISPHERE | | | | | | WORLD | | |
	North and Central America	South America	Total	Europe Free[2]	Europe Eastern[2]	Africa	Middle East and Asia Free[3]	Mainland China, Mongolia, North Korea, and North Viet-Nam	Oceania	Total	Free	Cuba, Eastern Europe, Mainland China, Mongolia, North Korea, North Viet-Nam
Metals:												
Aluminum:												
Bauxite	31.9	19.3	51.2	16.2	18.8	5.8	5.5	1.3	1.2	48.8	79.9	20.1
Ingot	49.7	.5	50.2	19.6	21.4	1.0	5.2	1.8	.8	49.8	76.8	23.2
Antimony	11.0	14.8	25.8[5]	6.4[5]	14.5	21.4	5.0	26.8	.1	74.2[5]	58.7	41.3[6]
Arsenic, white[4]	[5]	1.3	[5]	[7]		1.1	2.1	[6]	—		100.0	[6]
Beryl	10.2	39.2	49.4	7.4	15.0	33.5		—	2.1	50.6	85.0	15.0
Bismuth	[5]	[5]	62.8	[5]	3.7	.3	15.6	10.2	—	37.2	86.1	13.9
Cadmium	47.3	1.5	48.8	16.9	21.9	1.0	8.3	—	3.1	51.2	78.1	21.9
Chromite	1.3	.4	1.7	2.7	38.0	29.4	27.0	.8	.4	98.3	59.9	40.1
Cobalt[4]	[5]	—	[5]	[5]	[6]	81.4	[5]	[6]	.2	[5]	100.0	[6]
Columbium-tantalum[4]	25.3	18.5	43.8	4.0	[6]	50.1	1.8	[6]	.3	56.2	100.0	[6]
Copper:												
Mine	33.5	16.6	50.1	3.3	16.2	20.7	5.1	2.1	2.5	49.9	81.6	18.4
Smelter	31.6	14.4	46.0	9.5	15.7	19.0	5.8	2.2	1.8	54.0	82.1	17.9

(Continued on following page)

Gold	11.5	1.8	13.3	.4	25.0	56.8	1.8	.4	2.3	86.7	74.6	25.4
Iron and steel:												
Iron ore	20.2	6.8	27.0	25.4	28.5	4.1	6.3	7.5	1.2	73.0	64.0	36.0
Pig iron (including ferroalloys)	26.1	1.2	27.3	27.5	26.7	1.0	9.8	6.4	1.3	72.7	66.9	33.1
Steel ingots and castings	28.1	1.2	29.3	28.1	27.2	.8	10.0	3.4	1.2	70.7	69.4	30.6
Lead:												
Mine	24.0	8.2	32.2	13.7	20.4	7.4	4.0	5.9	16.4	67.8	73.7	26.3
Smelter	28.6	4.9	33.5	22.8	19.8	2.0	4.6	5.1	12.2	66.5	75.1	24.9
Magnesium	54.5	—	54.5	20.5	22.7	—	1.6	.7	—	45.5	76.6	23.4
Manganese ore	1.8	9.6	11.4	.7	48.4	22.1	10.1	6.9	.4	88.6	44.2	55.8
Mercury	15.7	1.4	17.1	52.4	15.2	—	4.3	11.0	—	82.9	73.8	26.2
Molybdenum	72.1	8.7	80.8	.6	13.7	[r]	1.3	3.6	—	19.2	82.7	17.3
Nickel	65.5	[r]	65.5	.8	24.4	.8	.1	—	8.4	34.5	70.7	29.3
Platinum-group metals	25.7	1.9	27.6	—	52.2	20.0	.2	—	[r]	72.4	47.8	52.2
Selenium[4]	67.2	.9	68.1	13.8	[6]	3.0	14.9	[6]	.2	31.9	100.0	[6]
Silver	45.4	18.4	63.8	6.6	13.8	2.6	5.0	.6	7.6	36.2	85.6	14.4
Tellurium[4]	87.4	8.4	95.8	—	[6]	—	4.2	[6]	—	4.2	100.0	[6]
Tin:												
Mine	[5]	[5]	13.7	1.1	11.0	10.2	47.7	14.7	1.6	86.3	74.3	25.7
Smelter	1.5	2.3	3.8	17.5	10.7	6.3	45.7	14.6	1.4	96.2	74.7	25.3
Titanium:												
Ilmenite[4]	57.1	[r]	57.1	20.9	[6]	2.2	9.7	[6]	10.1	42.9	100.0	[6]
Rutile[4]	5.4	.1	5.5	—	[6]	1.0	.9	[6]	92.6	94.5	100.0	[6]
Tungsten	8.8	6.5	15.3	3.8	18.7	1.0	13.2	45.3	2.7	84.7	36.0	64.0
Uranium oxide (U_3O_8)[4]	74.1	[r]	74.1	6.9	[6]	15.0	[r]	[6]	4.0	25.9	100.0	[6]
Vanadium[4]	55.1	[r]	55.1	8.8	[6]	36.1	—	[6]	—	44.9	100.0	[6]
Zinc:												
Mine	32.7	5.9	38.6	14.8	17.6	6.9	6.3	5.9	9.9	61.4	76.5	23.5
Smelter	32.3	2.2	34.5	24.5	20.7	2.9	7.6	4.5	5.3	65.5	74.8	25.2
Nonmetals:												
Asbestos	41.6	[r]	41.6	3.4	37.7	11.9	1.5	3.4	.5	58.4	58.9	41.1

TABLE X.1 (Continued)

APPROXIMATE PERCENTAGE DISTRIBUTION OF WORLD MINERAL PRODUCTION IN 1963[1]

(U.S. Bureau of Mines Minerals Yearbook, Vol. IV, Table 6, pp. 10–11)

| | WESTERN HEMISPHERE | | | EASTERN HEMISPHERE | | | | | | | WORLD | |
	North and Central America	South America	Total	Europe Free[2]	Europe Eastern[2]	Africa	Middle East and Asia Free[3]	Middle East and Asia: Mainland China, Mongolia, North Korea, and North Viet-Nam	Oceania	Total	Free	Cuba, Eastern Europe, Mainland China, Mongolia, North Korea, North Viet-Nam
Barite	39.4	7.0	46.4	30.9	9.7	3.9	3.4	5.5	.2	53.6	84.8	15.2
Cement, hydraulic	19.7	3.7	23.4	31.9	23.6	2.5	14.4	3.2	1.0	76.6	73.1	26.9
Corundum	—	—	—	—	42.5	54.5	3.0	—	—	100.0	57.5	42.5
Diamonds:												
Gem	—	4.2	4.2	—	3.7	92.1	ᵇ	—	—	95.8	96.3	3.7
Industrial	—	.8	.8	—	9.2	90.0	—	—	—	99.2	90.8	9.2
Diatomite	30.1	.4	30.5	32.7	21.7	.8	13.9	—	.4	69.5	78.3	21.7
Feldspar[3]	35.0	3.8	38.8	39.6	13.6	2.7	4.8	—	.5	61.2	86.4	13.6
Fluorspar	34.1	.4	34.5	31.2	13.9	2.8	4.3	13.3	—	65.5	72.8	27.2
Graphite	ᵇ	ᵇ	ᵇ	ᵇ	10.1	2.5	47.7	16.5	—	ᵇ	73.4	26.6
Gypsum	33.9	1.3	35.2	34.2	19.2	1.9	7.1	1.0	1.4	64.8	79.8	20.2
Magnesite	9.2	1.1	10.3	25.0	38.7	1.3	3.1	20.8	.8	89.7	40.5	59.5
Mica, including scrap	55.4	.7	56.1	ᵇ	16.9	2.2	18.9	5.6	.3	43.9	77.5	22.5
Phosphate rock	39.6	1.6	41.2	.2	21.8	26.2	2.7	3.3	4.6	58.8	74.9	25.1

(Continued on following page)

Potash, K$_2$O equivalent (marketable)	29.0	.2	29.2	37.6	32.2	—	1.0	—	—	70.8	67.8	32.2
Pumice[4]	17.8	.1	17.9	81.1	[6]	.1	.8	[6]	.1	82.1	100.0	[6]
Pyrites, including cupreous	6.6	[7]	6.6	34.2	21.9	2.7	25.5	8.0	1.1	93.4	69.9	30.1
Salt	34.6	2.5	37.1	24.7	15.4	1.6	8.9	11.7	.6	62.9	72.8	27.2
Strontium minerals[4]	38.5	1.5	40.0	60.0	[6]	—	—	[6]	—	60.0	100.0	[6]
Sulfur:												
Native	78.4	1.2	79.6	.5	15.2	.2	3.0	1.5	—	20.4	83.3	16.7
Byproduct, elemental	47.0	—	47.0	37.7	11.7	.1	.8	2.7	—	53.0	85.6	14.4
Talc and soapstone	27.4	2.2	29.6	21.4	12.3	.5	29.7	6.0	.5	70.4	81.7	18.3
Vermiculite	68.8	.9	69.7	—	[6]	30.1	.2	[6]	—	30.3	100.0	[6]
Mineral fuels:												
Coal, all grades including lignite	16.8	.3	17.1	22.3	40.8	1.7	5.4	10.9	1.8	82.9	48.3	51.7
Coke:												
Metallurgical	19.0	.7	19.7	32.7	31.8	.8	8.3	5.7	1.0	80.3	62.5	37.5
Other types	.5	1.0	1.5	41.8	39.6	.5	13.9	.9	1.8	98.5	59.5	40.5
Fuel briquets	.5	—	.5	31.0	59.2	[7]	7.7	—	1.6	99.5	40.8	59.2
Petroleum, crude	33.3	14.7	48.0	1.4	17.1	4.6	28.3	.6	[7]	52.0	82.3	17.7

[1] Based on production data (including estimates) as presented in world production tables in commodity chapters of Volumes I and II. In some cases, revised figures have been incorporated in individual country chapters of Volume IV, thus percentages given here do not necessarily agree with totals of production based on data in individual country chapters. Regional divisions of total conform to those used in the Table of Contents of Volume IV, except as noted.

[2] As used here, Free Europe includes all countries listed under Europe except: Albania, Bulgaria, Czechoslovakia, East Germany, Hungary, Poland, Rumania, and the U.S.S.R.

[3] As used here, includes all Middle East and Asian countries except China (Mainland), Mongolia, North Korea, and North Viet-Nam.

[4] Distribution of free world output only; no estimate of production made for Communist countries except Yugoslavia.

[5] Production data not available but recorded distribution for other areas based on a world total which includes an estimate for this area.

[6] Does not apply; see footnote 4.

[7] Less than 0.1 percent.

[8] Production by China (mainland), Mongolia, North Korea, and North Viet-Nam unknown; no estimate included in world total on which percentage figures are based.

world industrialization, access to mineral raw materials is of primary importance to any national economy based on industry; therefore a degree of freedom of world trade must be assured. An industrial nation shut off by war from mineral raw materials can survive for a short time by ingenious use of substitutes and by accumulated stock-piles, the length of survival depending on its own domestic resource base. Eventually, however, its industry will suffer drastic shortages and perhaps its social and economic system will collapse. From time to time, nations have attempted to overcome strategic mineral defi-ciencies by armed aggression—by bringing the mineral-rich area under their political control, either as conterminous territory or as a foreign colony. Some such expansions have been resisted and have not proved to have long-term stability, others have persisted for generations. German attempts to seize Balkan oil supplies failed; Soviet seizure of the important nickel deposit at Petsamo in what was Finland has been successful and the security of possession does not appear to be threatened. Attempts by Egypt to bring all Middle East oil under control of a United Arab Republic are currently in progress.

Reserve index.

$$\text{The ratio of } \frac{\text{reserves}}{\text{annual production}} \text{ or } \frac{\text{reserves}}{\text{annual consumption}}$$

is useful if considered with appropriate reservations about possible changes in demand, economics and technology. It means something different for each commodity, depending on how the reserves are esti-mated or calculated (pp. 9–13 and Table X.2 explanatory footnotes). Herein these ratios are called the reserve-production index and the reserve-consumption index and are expressed in years:

$$(1) \quad \frac{\text{reserves}}{\text{annual production}} = \text{reserve-production index}$$

$$(2) \quad \frac{\text{reserves}}{\text{annual consumption}} = \text{reserve-consumption index}$$

Clearly, a new discovery will increase the index, while an increase in production or consumption due to increased demand will decrease it. A decrease in demand due to use of substitutes will increase the index. Consideration of the indexes for the various commodities (pp. 273–350) shows immediately large differences in indicated long-term availability as of 1964, ranging from 14 years for mercury to more than 5,000 years for potash.

The reserve index can be calculated on a worldwide, continental, or national basis. On a worldwide basis, ignoring stockpiles and other inventories, and considering that world consumption cannot exceed world production and that what is produced is consumed somewhere in the world, the reserve-production index is sufficient to give a measure of world ability to meet current demand from known reserves. However, it is profitable in calculation of a national reserve index, and we are concerned primarily with indexes for the United States, to consider both production and consumption. The national reserve-consumption index supposes that all domestic requirements will be met from domestic resources and is therefore a self-sufficiency index. The national reserve-production index is a measure of the length of time the domestic mining industry can continue to produce at prevailing rates; it is not affected by the percentage of domestic consumption satisfied by domestic production, the amount of exports, or the amount of imports. If the U. S. reserve-production index is less than the reserve-consumption index it obviously indicates that the United States is exporting or stockpiling part of its production; if the reserve-production index is more than the reserve-consumption index, then domestic production is not adequate to supply demand and the commodity is being imported. In the case of petroleum, for example, *proved* domestic crude oil reserves are 31 billion barrels, domestic reserves are being consumed at a rate of 2.8 billion barrels per year, but total consumption is at a rate of 3.3 billion barrels per year. The deficit is made up from 0.5 billion barrels of imports. Domestic reserve-production index as of 1964 is, thus, 11 years but the domestic reserve-consumption index is only 9.3 years (see p. 15 for discussion of classes of crude oil reserves).

The reserve-consumption index, as used herein, is based on the assumption that all of the domestic consumption is supplied from newly mined domestic minerals—it is a measure of a nation's ability to supply domestic demand from domestic resources. In the case of metals for which there has accumulated a substantial scrap pool of recycling metal—for example, iron, copper, lead—the amount of metal in the scrap pool (old scrap) must be subtracted from the total consumption to determine the number of years that domestic reserves can satisfy the demand for new metal at current rates. The amount of minerals in the various stockpiles also constitute a reserve and should be added to reserves-in-the-ground in evaluating self-sufficiency in an absolute sense. However, the stockpiles are a fluid reserve, increasing and decreasing with purchases, sales, and revisions of objectives. Table VIII.1 gives the amounts of various mineral commodities in the several stockpiles as of June 30, 1964. These totals have *not* been considered in calculating U. S. domestic reserve-consumption indexes presented in this chapter. Due to reevaluation of objectives, most commodities are held in amount in excess of present objectives and many commodities are held in quantities which exceed present objectives by several hundred percent. Unless objectives are changed again, the coming years will see substantial sales from the various stockpiles.

The reserve index is a changing index, increasing or decreasing with time. To be useful it must be dated. The reserve index which obtained for a particular commodity in 1950 might be substantially different from that in 1960 or 1970. It is interesting to note, however, how little these indexes have varied in the past for some commodities. Despite the large yearly production and consumption of crude oil, for example, the reserve-production index for petroleum has varied little over past decades. New discoveries have more or less kept pace with withdrawals from the reserve bank account and maintained a steady production/proved reserves ratio. This is true also for other mineral commodities. Operating companies do not believe it good practice to invest large sums of money in development before it is necessary. For the most part, reserves are developed one or two decades prior to the time they are scheduled for extraction.

MINERAL FUELS

Coal.

Bituminous coal and lignite are widely distributed in large quantities. Coal is an essential part of the formula for industrialization. Modern substitutes are oil, natural gas, hydropower, and nuclear energy; but technology has not yet developed a satisfactory process for substituting these fuels for coke in the blast furnace, and thus coking coal remains as an indispensable raw material for steel production— the common yardstick for measuring industrial potential. However, direct reduction processes and use of natural gas have been successful in pilot operations and widespread industrial application seems near. Oil and natural gas, as cleaner, more easily transportable commodities, have replaced coal in many of its former fuel markets outside of steel manufacture.

In the United States about 3 per cent of the mines produce 53 per

TABLE X.2

WORLD DISTRIBUTION OF MINERALS IN TERMS OF 1963–64 PRODUCTION, RESERVES, AND RESOURCES

(from U.S. Bureau of Mines, Commodity Data Summaries, January, 1965, Mineral Facts and Problems, 1965 edition, and other sources as cited).

est.   = estimated.
NA   = not available.
confidential = company confidential, data not released because of limited number of producers.

A. MINERAL FUELS

1. *Coal, bituminous, and Lignite*

	PRODUCTION				RESERVES[1]	
	1963		*1964 (est.)*		*(est. recoverable)*	
	Coal[2]	*Lignite*[3]	*Coal*[2]	*Lignite*[3]	*Coal*[2]	*Lignite*[3]
	(thousand short tons)				*(million short tons)*	
United States	474,490	2,705	493,360	3,040	604,118	223,760
Australia	27,664	21,000	30,150	20,500	19,800	22,560
Belgium	23,609	––	23,550	––	3,260	––
Canada	8,702	1,874	9,315	1,950	20,935	13,390
France	52,640	2,728	57,100	2,600	6,675	160
Germany, West	158,685	117,569	158,600	123,800	64,100	34,000
India	72,672	1,093[4]	70,800	1,500	34,700	280
Japan	57,377	1,008	56,100	840	5,350	140
Netherlands	12,686	––	12,500	––	1,350	5
South Africa, Republic of	46,798	––	48,700	––	37,050	––
United Kingdom	219,291	––	215,000	––	22,200	––
Other Free World	61,107	50,667[4]	61,500	52,100	23,825	21,700
Sino-Soviet Bloc	914,265	597,402[4]	959,850	605,500	1,170,000	146,300
World Total	2,129,986	796,046[4]	2,196,525	811,830	2,013,363	462,295

2. *Crude petroleum* (millions of barrels, 42 gal.)

	PRODUCTION		PROVED RESERVES[5]
	1963	*1964 (est.)*	
United States	2,753	2,805	31,000
Iran	538	664	38,000
Iraq	423	449	25,000
Kuwait	705	776	63,000
Saudi Arabia	595	621	60,500
Venezuela	1,186	1,238	17,000
Other Free World	1,662	1,991	72,500
Soviet-Sino Bloc	1,673	1,706	30,800
World Total	9,535	10,250	337,800

[1] Recoverable reserves represent 50% of the conservatively estimated total reserve.
[2] Includes bituminous and anthracite.
[3] Includes brown coal and lignite.
[4] Includes some lignite.
[5] Proved reserves only; does not include potential reserves in unexplored basins, continental shelves, oil shales, or tar sands.

TABLE X.2 (Continued)

A. MINERAL FUELS (Continued)

3. *Natural gas* (billions of cubic feet)

	MARKETED PRODUCTION		RESERVES
	1963	*1964 (est.)*	
United States	14,747	15,464	276,000
Canada	1,005	NA	37,000
Italy	271	NA	5,000
Mexico	424	NA	10,000
Middle East	NA	NA	178,000
Other Free World	NA	NA	NA
Sino-Soviet Bloc	NA	NA	83,000
World Total	NA	NA	NA

4. *Uranium* (tons of uranium oxide, U_3O_8)

	MINE PRODUCTION		RESERVES	
	1963	*1964 (est.)*	*Tons U_3O_8*	*Grade (% U_3O_8)*
United States	14,723	13,960	160,000	0.24
Australia	1,200	800	10,000	0.26
Canada	8,141	5,000	210,000	0.12
France	2,021	2,000	36,000	0.14
South Africa, Republic of	4,532	4,000	150,000	0.02
Other Free World	70	100	55,000	0.06–0.18
Sino-Soviet Bloc		Not	available	
Free World Total	30,700	26,000	621,000	——

B. IRON AND FERRO-ALLOY METALS

1. *Iron ore* (thousands of long tons)

	MINE PRODUCTION		RESOURCES[6]	
	1963	*1964 (est.)*	*Quantity*	*Approximate Grade*
United States	73,599	82,000	15,000,000	25–60% Fe
Australia	5,685	6,000	16,000,000	55–68% Fe
Brazil	8,137	10,000	28,000,000	40–66% Fe
Canada	26,906	28,000	28,000,000	22–60% Fe
France	56,971	50,000	8,000,000	35% Fe
Germany, West	12,694	10,000	1,600,000	30% Fe
India	14,690	16,000	21,600,000	55–60% Fe
Sweden	23,258	25,000	3,500,000	58–70% Fe
United Kingdom	14,912	15,000	4,600,000	25–30% Fe
Venezuela	11,676	13,000	3,800,000	40–58% Fe
Other Free World	77,085	88,000	13,000,000	NA
Sino-Soviet Bloc	184,295	170,000	50,000,000	40–46% Fe
World Total	509,908	513,000	195,000,000	NA

[6] Does not include large low-grade deposits containing less than 20 per cent iron.

TABLE X.2 (Continued)

B. Iron and Ferro-alloy Metals (Continued)

2. *Manganese* (thousands of short tons)

	MINE PRODUCTION		RESERVES[7]		
	1963	1964 (est.)			
United States	11	confidential	small	=	1,000
Brazil	1,320	1,300	large		
Gabon	702	1,000	large	=	800,000
India (including Goa)	1,300	1,300	large		
South Africa, Republic of	1,442	1,400	large		
Other Free World	2,351	2,300	moderate	=	10,000
Sino-Soviet Bloc	8,964	9,200	large	=	1,600,000
World Total	16,090	16,500	large	=	2,411,000

3. *Chromium* (thousands of short tons)

	MINE PRODUCTION		RESERVES	
	1963	1964 (est.)	Quantity	Grade %
United States	——	——	8,000	35–40
Philippines	503	500	6,000	+30
Southern Rhodesia	412	550	600,000	35–50
South Africa, Republic of	873	1,000	2,000,000	+44
Turkey	445	550	10,000	40–48
Other Free World[8]	486	500	22,000	18–50
Sino-Soviet Bloc	1,756	1,900	15,000	35–55
World Total	4,475	5,000	2,661,000	

4. *Nickel* (short tons of metal)

	MINE PRODUCTION		RESERVES	
	1963	1964 (est.)	Quantity	Grade %
United States	13,394	15,000	500,000	0.7
Canada	219,941	220,000	4,500,000	0.9–1.6
Cuba (est.)	18,400	24,000	17,000,000	0.5–1.0
New Caledonia (est.)	32,200	40,000	16,000,000	1.1
Other Free World	5,255	6,500	12,000,000	0.8–1.2
Sino-Soviet Bloc	94,810	96,500	NA	NA
World Total	384,000	402,000	NA	NA

[7] Mineral Facts and Problems, 1965 ed., Manganese, pp. 10–11. Does not include potential reserves in sea-floor manganese oxide nodule accumulations.
[8] Judging by volume of exports, reserves may be much larger.
[9] Do not include potential nickel reserves in sea-floor manganese nodule accumulations.

TABLE X.2 (Continued)

B. IRON AND FERRO-ALLOY METALS (Continued)

5. *Molybdenum* (thousands of pounds of contained molybdenum)

	MINE PRODUCTION		RESERVES	
	1963	1964 (est.)	Quantity	Grade
United States[10]	65,011	65,000	Over 3,000,000	About ⅔ in ores containing less than 0.4% MoS_2 and about ⅓ in copper ores containing less than 0.2% MoS_2
Canada	1,000	2,000	NA	NA
Chile	6,704	7,000	Over 1,000,000	In copper ores containing less than 0.2% MoS_2
Japan	732	800	NA	NA
Other Free World	2,353	3,000	NA	NA
Sino-Soviet Bloc	15,800	16,000	NA	NA
World Total	91,600	93,800	NA	NA

6. *Tungsten* (short tons, 60% WO_3 basis)

	MINE PRODUCTION		RESERVES		
	1963	1964 (est.)	Predominant type	Quantity	Grade %
United States	confidential		Scheelite[11]	143,000	0.3–1.0 WO_3
Australia	1,771	1,800	Scheelite	40,000	0.5 WO_3
Bolivia	2,513	2,600	Wolframite	87,000	2.0 WO_3
Canada	—	10	Scheelite	1,200	1.5–5.0 WO_3
Korea, Republic of	6,724	7,000	Scheelite	111,000	1.7 WO_3
Portugal	1,635	1,750	Wolframite	31,000	0.4–1.2 WO_3
Other Free World	10,000	10,000	NA	175,000	NA
Sino-Soviet Bloc (est.)	41,400	41,000	NA	1,962,000	NA
World Total	64,700	66,000		2,550,200	

[10] Recent information (U.S. Bureau of Mines, Mineral Facts and Problems, 1965 ed., Molybdenum, p. 8) indicates U.S. reserves may be as high as 10 billion pounds of contained "moly."

[11] Mostly below currently commercial grade. Total reserves estimated by the U.S. Bureau of Mines in 1957 were 9 million short ton units WO_3 containing 142.5 million pounds of tungsten (Mineral Facts and Problems, 1965 edition, Tungsten, p. 10).

TABLE X.2 (Continued)

B. IRON AND FERRO-ALLOY METALS (Continued)

7. *Cobalt* (short tons of contained cobalt)

	MINE PRODUCTION		RESERVES	
	1963	*1964 (est.)*	*Quantity*	*Grade %*
United States	confidential		140,000	0.06–0.7
Canada	1,408	1,500	200,000	0.06
Congo, Republic of the	8,050	8,000	800,000	0.02–8.0
Morocco	1,511	1,500	15,000	1.6
New Caledonia	—	—	450,000	0.2
Northern Rhodesia, Southern				
Rhodesia and Nyasaland	778	600	390,000	0.02–0.2
Other Free World	18	20	NA	NA
Cuba	192	250	large	0.02–0.2
Sino-Soviet Bloc	NA	NA	large	0.5 –6.5
World Total	14,000	14,500	large	0.5

8. *Vanadium* (thousands of pounds of contained vanadium)

	MINE PRODUCTION		RESERVES
	1963	*1964 (est.)*	
United States	7,724	8,500	moderate
Other Free World	6,612	6,300	large
Sino-Soviet Bloc	NA	NA	large
World Total (excludes Sino-Soviet Bloc)	14,336	14,800	large

C. NON-FERROUS INDUSTRIAL METALS

1. *Copper* (thousands of short tons)

	MINE PRODUCTION		RESERVES	
	1963	*1964 (est.)*	*Quantity*	*Grade %*
United States	1,213	1,251	32,500	0.80
Canada	458	480	8,000	1.70
Chile	663	670	46,000	1.97
Congo (Leopoldville)	298	321	20,000	4.00
Northern Rhodesia	648	684	25,000	3.71
Peru	196	200	12,500	0.91
Other Free World	791	880	30,000	2.00
Sino-Soviet Bloc	953	1,000	38,000	2.20
World Total	5,220	5,486	212,000	2.03

TABLE X.2 (Continued)

C. NON-FERROUS INDUSTRIAL METALS (Continued)

2. *Lead* (thousands of short tons)

	MINE PRODUCTION		RESERVES—MEASURED AND INDICATED—LEAD CONTENT
	1963	1964 (est.)	
United States	253	280	6,000[12]
Australia	459	430	6,000
Canada	199	220	9,000
Mexico	209	190	3,500
Peru	163	170	2,500
Other Latin America	82	70	500
Other Free World	733	720	12,400
Sino-Soviet Bloc	702	750	NA
World Total	2,800	2,830	50,000[13]

3. *Zinc* (thousands of short tons)

	MINE PRODUCTION		RESERVES[14]	
	1963	1964 (est.)	Quantity	Grade % zinc
United States	529	570	12,000[15]	NA
Australia	394	395	6,000	NA
Canada	497	725	19,000	NA
Mexico	266	265	4,000	NA
Other Free World	1,370	1,410	30,000	NA
Sino-Soviet Bloc	914	915	20,000	NA
World Total	3,970	4,280	91,000	NA

4. *Tin* (long tons)

	MINE PRODUCTION		RESERVES	
	1963	1964 (est.)	Quantity	Grade
United States	confidential		Negligible	NA
Bolivia	22,752	24,000	750,000	NA
Congo (Leopoldville)	6,488	5,000	500,000	NA
Indonesia	12,947	16,400	1,000,000	NA
Malaya, Federation of	59,947	60,500	1,200,000	NA
Nigeria	8,723	8,500	250,000	NA
Thailand	15,587	16,000	300,000	NA
Other Free World	15,000	15,500	200,000	NA
Sino-Soviet Bloc	49,000	49,000	NA[16]	NA
World Total	190,300	195,000	4,700,000	NA

[12] Weigel (1965, p. 77) estimated new discoveries in Southeast Missouri as containing *potential* reserves on the order of 30 million tons of contained lead.

[13] Mineral Facts and Problems, 1965 ed., Lead, p. 9.

[14] Probably will be increased by new discoveries in Southeast Missouri (Weigel, 1965, p. 77).

[15] Includes zinc in slags.

[16] Soviet reserves are estimated at 500,000 long tons (Mineral Facts and Problems, 1965 ed., Tin, p. 6).

TABLE X.2 (Continued)

C. NON-FERROUS INDUSTRIAL METALS (Continued)

5. *Aluminum* (thousands of short tons) and *Bauxite* (thousands of long tons)

	ALUMINUM PRIMARY METAL		
	PRODUCTION		CAPACITY (EST.)
	1963	*1964 (est.)*	
United States	2,313	2,540	2,540
Canada	719	791	905
France	329	340	344
Germany, West	230	232	232
Japan	247	267	297
Norway	242	270	309
Other Free World	603	665	640
Sino-Soviet Bloc	1,412	1,510	1,500
World Total	6,095	6,615	6,775

	BAUXITE			
	MINE PRODUCTION		RESERVES	
	1963	*1964 (est.)*	*Quantity*	*Grade % Al_2O_3*
United States	1,525	1,600	50,000	50
Australia	350	600	2,000,000	50
British Guiana	2,210	3,500	150,000	58
France	1,971	2,000	70,000	58
Jamaica	6,903	7,500	600,000	50
Surinam	3,427	3,500	250,000	58
Other Free World	7,379	7,600	2,090,000	55
Sino-Soviet Bloc	6,070	6,700	550,000	50
World Total	29,835	33,000	5,760,000	

D. PRECIOUS METALS

1. *Gold* (millions of troy ounces)

	MINE PRODUCTION		ORE RESERVES— MEASURED & INDICATED	
	1963	*1964 (est.)*	*Content*[17]	*Grade oz./ton*
United States	1.47	1.47	20	0.01
Australia	1.02	0.96	moderate	NA
Canada	4.01	3.78	moderate	NA
South Africa, Republic of	27.43	28.84	500	0.30
Other Free World	5.05	5.00	NA	NA
Sino-Soviet Bloc	12.72	12.70	large	NA
World Total	51.70	52.75	large[18]	NA

[17] Includes gold recoverable as a by-product of base metal ores.
[18] May approximate 1 billion ounces (Mineral Facts and Problems, 1965, ed., Gold, p. 5).

TABLE X.2 (Continued)

D. PRECIOUS METALS (Continued)

2. *Silver* (millions of troy ounces)

	MINE PRODUCTION		ORE RESERVES—MEASURED & INDICATED	
	1963	*1964 (est.)*	*Content*[19]	*Grade oz./ton*
United States	35.0	36.4	590	0.3
Canada	30.7	30.0	640	NA
Mexico	42.8	44.0	730	NA
Peru	36.4	38.0	530[20]	NA
Australia	18.9	20.0	260	NA
Other Free World	68.8	71.5	NA	NA
Sino-Soviet Bloc	35.7	35.7	NA[21]	NA
World Total	249.4	255.7	5,000	NA

3. *Platinum-group* (thousands of troy ounces)

	MINE PRODUCTION		RESERVES (EST.)
	1963	*1964 (est.)*	
United States	confidential		small
Canada	345	400	12,000
Columbia	29	30	5,000
South Africa, Republic of	306	600	12,000
Other Free World	—	—	—
Sino-Soviet Bloc	800	1,000	10,000
World Total	1,530	2,000	40,000

E. MINOR METALS

1. *Beryllium* (short tons of beryl containing 10–12% BeO)

	MINE PRODUCTION[22]		
	1963	*1964 (est.)*	BERYLLIUM RESOURCES
United States	1	17	The United States has very little beryl that can be hand-sorted economically from pegmatites. The resource of disseminated beryllium minerals is promising. A belt of pegmatites extending through King Mountain, N. C., is reported to contain 823,000 pounds of beryl per ton of rock. Certain nonpegmatite deposits in Utah, Nevada, and Colorado contain beryllium as phenacite and bertrandite; the Spor Mountain area, Utah, contains considerable bertrandite in submarginal deposits.
Argentina	718	500	
Brazil	2,169	2,200	
Mozambique	600	750	
South Africa, Republic of	425	500	
Other Free World	1,637	1,433	
Sino-Soviet Bloc	1,100	1,100	
World Total	6,650	6,500	

[19] Includes silver recoverable as a by-product of base metal ores.
[20] From Merrill et al. (1965, p. 17) and Hardy (1964).
[21] Estimated as 5 billion ounces in 1960 (Mineral Facts and Problems, 1960 ed., Silver, p. 4).
[22] Excluding small tonnages of low-grade Colorado ores containing about 3% BeO.

282   MINERAL RESOURCES

TABLE X.2 (Continued)

E. Minor Metals (Continued)

2. *Magnesium* (short tons) [23]

Primary Metal

	Production		Capacity
	1963	1964 (est.)	
United States	75,845	79,000	103,000
Canada	8,695	8,700	11,000
Italy	6,300	6,300	7,000
Japan	2,500	2,800	3,000
Norway	18,700	22,000	27,000
United Kingdom	4,200	4,200	6,000
Other Free World	2,560	2,000	5,000
Sino-Soviet Bloc	36,000	36,000	50,000
World Total	154,800	161,000	212,000

3. *Mercury* (flasks of 76 pounds)

	Mine Production		Reserves
	1963	1964 (est.)	Quantity thousand flasks
United States	19,100	15,000	75
Italy	54,564	55,000	700
Mexico	17,800	18,000	125
Spain	53,000	60,000	1,000
Yugoslavia	15,838	17,000	400
Other Free World	15,000	15,000	200
Sino-Soviet Bloc	61,000	62,000	700
World Total	236,000	240,000	3,200

4. *Titanium* (short tons of sponge metal) , *Ilmenite* (thousands of short tons of concentrates) , and *Rutile* (short tons of concentrates)

Titanium Sponge Metal

	Production		Capacity (est.)
	1963	1964 (est.)	
United States	7,879	confidential	11,500
Japan	1,939	2,700	4,900
Other Free World	30	500	1,700
Sino-Soviet Bloc	NA	NA	NA
World Total	9,848	NA	18,100

[23] Sources include sea water and large domestic magnesite and dolomite reserves.

TABLE X.2 (Continued)

E. MINOR METALS (Continued)

4. *Titanium, Ilmenite,* and *Rutile* (Continued)

	ILMENITE			
	MINE PRODUCTION		RESERVES	
	1963	1964 (est.)	Quantity	Grade % TiO_2
United States	888	930	41,000	0.14–20.0
Australia	224	250	Medium	NA
Canada	379	380	150,000	35.0
Norway	276	300	200,000	17.0
Other Free World	455	500	41,000	NA
Sino-Soviet Bloc	NA	NA	NA	NA
World Total	2,222	2,360	NA	NA

	RUTILE			
	MINE PRODUCTION		RESERVES	
	1963	1964 (est.)	Quantity	Grade % TiO_2
United States	11.9	12.0	1,000	0.5–3.0
Australia	203.8	250.0	3,000	0.5–3.0
Other Free World	4.4	10.0	3,000	NA
Sino-Soviet Bloc	NA	NA	NA	NA
World Total	220.1	272.0	NA	NA

F. SELECTED NONMETALS

1. *Asbestos* (thousands of short tons)

	MINE PRODUCTION		RESERVES	
	1963	1964 (est.)	Fiber content	Average Grade, %
United States	67	100	4,000	NA
Africa	384	400	13,000	NA
Canada	1,272	1,300	60,000	NA
Other Free World	167	160	3,000	NA
Sino-Soviet Bloc	1,320	1,400	30,000	NA
World Total	3,200	3,360	110,000	NA

2. *Fluorspar* (thousands of short tons)

	MINE PRODUCTION		RESERVES	
	1963	1964 (est.)	Quantity	Average grade
United States (shipments)	200	209	18,400	At least 40% CaF_2
Canada	67	70	5,000	70–75% CaF_2
Germany, West	96	95	4,400	25–78% CaF_2
Italy	137	135	3,300	At least 35% CaF_2
Mexico (exports)	531	534	19,600	At least 65% CaF_2
Other Free World	683	676	24,100	NA
Sino-Soviet Bloc	626	633	13,200	NA
World Total	2,340	2,352	88,000	

TABLE X.2 (Continued)

F. SELECTED NONMETALS (Continued)

3. *Industrial Diamond* (millions of carats)

	MINE PRODUCTION		RESERVES	
	1963	1964 (est.)	Quantity	Average grade
United States	—	—	—	—
Congo[24]	19.8	20.0	500	NA
Ghana	2.1	2.1	25	NA
South Africa, Republic of	2.6	2.6	45	NA
Other Free World	2.8	3.1	15	NA
Sino-Soviet Bloc	2.8	2.7	NA	NA
World Total	30.1	30.5	600+	

4. *Mica, strategic and nonstrategic* (thousands of short tons)

	STRATEGIC			
	MINE PRODUCTION		RESERVES	
	1963	1964 (est.)	Quantity	Average grade
United States	0.05	0.04	Small	NA
Brazil	0.1	0.10	Large	NA
India (exports)	9.8	9.5	Very large	NA
Other Free World	0.3	0.3	Moderate	NA
Sino-Soviet Bloc	1.4	1.4	Large	NA
World Total	11.7	11.3	Large	

	NONSTRATEGIC			
	MINE PRODUCTION		RESERVES	
	1963	1964 (est.)	Quantity	Average grade
United States	109.0	107.0	Moderate	NA
Brazil	1.4	1.5	Large	NA
India (exports)	27.8	23.0	Very large	NA
Other Free World	7.5	7.0	Moderate	NA
Sino-Soviet Bloc	33.0	30.0	Large	NA
World Total	175.7	168.5	Large	NA

5. *Phosphate Rock* (millions of long tons)

	PRODUCTION		INDICATED RESERVES
	1963	1964 (est.)	Quantity
United States	19.8	20.5	14,500
Algeria	0.2	0.2	1,000
Morocco	8.4	9.6	21,000
Togo	0.6	0.7	120
Tunisia	2.3	2.2	2,000
Other Free World	6.5	6.8	1,930[25]
Sino-Soviet Bloc	12.6	13.0	7,800
World Total	50.4	53.0	48,350[26]

[24] Brazzaville and Leopoldville.
[25] Mostly Brazil, Peru, Egypt, Spanish Sahara, Pacific and Indian Ocean islands, and Senegal.
[26] Do not include large potential reserves on the continental shelves.

TABLE X.2 (Continued)

F. SELECTED NONMETALS (Continued)

6. *Potash* (millions of short tons, K_2O equivalent)

	PRODUCTION		INDICATED RESERVES
	1963	*1964 (est.)*	*Quantity*
United States	2.87	3.00	450
Canada	0.60	0.65	17,500
France	1.90	1.95	350
Germany, West	2.15	2.30	9,500
Israel and Jordan	NA	NA	2,000
Italy	0.21	0.25	NA
Spain	0.28	0.30	300
Other Free World	0.13	0.15	7,000
Sino-Soviet Bloc (Russia and East Germany)	3.86	4.00	34,000
World Total	12.00	12.60	71,100

7. *Sulfur* (thousands of long tons)

	NATIVE SULFUR				RECOVERED SULFUR	
	MINE PRODUCTION		RESERVES		PRODUCTION	
	1963	*1964 (est.)*	*Quantity*	*Grade*	*1963*	*1964 (est.)*
United States	4,882	5,900	NA	NA	947	991
Italy	41	43	NA	NA	—	—
Canada	—	—	—	—	1,037	1,525
Japan	218	222	NA	NA	—	—
France	—	—	—	—	1,396	1,500
Mexico	1,486	2,000	NA	NA	43	45
Germany, West	—	—	—	—	85	86
Other Free World	140	170	NA	NA	263	272
Sino-Soviet Bloc	1,373	1,400	NA	NA	644	645
World Total	8,140	9,735	NA	NA	4,415	5,064

cent of the total production. Fifty-two per cent is consumed by electric utilities for power generation, 20 per cent by coking plants, and the balance by other manufacturing and mining industries. A significant development in the U. S. coal industry in recent years has been the opening of new mines in the west in Arizona, New Mexico, Utah, and other Mountain States. The big market is for steam coal to fire boilers of western utilities. Extra-high-voltage electric power transmission permits cheap long distance power transmission which coal men refer to as 'coal-by-wire.'

World reserves are shown in Table X.2. South America seems to be the most deficient continent, with some deposits in the Andean chain and in southern Brazil. Because of their low quality and unfavorable distribution, coal deposits in South America have not been extensively developed and consequently coal-based heavy industry has been retarded. Reserves are also small in Canada and Africa. Geologically, most coal and lignite occur in late Paleozoic, Mesozoic, and Tertiary age strata as beds and seams of wide areal extent. Areas where ancient rocks of the continental shields crop out do not contain coal deposits. Largest reserves are in the United States (one-third of the world's resources), China, and the Soviet Union. European reserves, after more than a century of industrial age production, are still substantial. In general, in traditional world trade patterns, iron ore moves to coal, but more recently both coal and iron have moved to tidewater metallurgical complexes. Bauxite also moves to sources of power, mainly hydroelectric but also including large coal and lignite fields. The 1964 world reserve index for coal and lignite is more than 800 years. For bituminous coal only, the index is more than 900 years. The United States reserve-production index as of 1964 for bituminous coal is in excess of 1,200 years, and the reserve-consumption index is more than 1,400 years.

There are opposing trends recognizable on the modern scene which at the same time tend to increase and decrease future demand for coal. Coal is the major fuel for industrial energy, for generation of electric power, and the demand for industrial energy is increasing. According to calculations made by the Energy Policy Staff of the Department of the Interior (1963, Table 1) 83 per cent of known recoverable fossil fuel energy reserves in the United States are in the form of coal; if all classes of reserves are considered (marginal and undiscovered as well as known recoverable), the figure is reduced to 68 per cent. Hubbert (1962, Fig. 53) calculated that 78 per cent of the total recoverable energy reserves available to the United States (already used and remaining) are in the form of coal. As the steel industry expands, the demand for coking coal will increase. There is also increasing demand for coal as a chemical raw material. In the more distant future, as supplies of petroleum and natural gas are depleted, more coal will be converted to gas and liquid fuels. However, working in opposition to this projected increase in demand is a current shift away from coal to oil, gas, and nuclear energy, and of great potential significance, concern about atmospheric pollution as a result of coal-burning will result in more legislation to prevent combustion of high-sulfur fuels. Concern about the rising CO_2 content of the atmosphere may eventually result in curbs on combustion of coal and other fossil fuels (pp. 260). The cost of beneficiating coal to remove pollutants prior to burning and the cost of reclaiming strip-mined land will increase the price of coal in the market place and make it less competitive. Clearly it is in the best interests of the coal industry to devise cheap and efficient methods to combat pollution and to minimize post-mining clean-up and land reclamation. Notwithstanding the adverse factors, the U. S. Bureau of Mines "Mineral Facts and Problems," (1965 ed., p. 26) forecast an increase in production in the United States of about 75 per cent within the next 15 years to an estimated 775 to 800 million tons per year in 1980. However, even in the unlikely event that an increase of such magnitude was worldwide and there was no offsetting increase in reserves, the world reserve index would remain at more than 400 years in 1980. In the case that a high *rate of increase* were maintained, a rate that would double demand every 20 years, for example, the reserve index would decrease rapidly. In such a case, deeper and thinner coal seams would be added to the reserve inventory until for one reason or another, coal became too high priced to burn for energy. Another technological development which may well affect the long-term demand for coal is in the field of nutrition. The U. S. Bureau of Mines announced in September of 1965 that certain microbes which feed on coal chemicals produce protein at a very high rate and that a coal-derived high protein food supplement can be manufactured.

Crude oil.

Although petroleum and related substances were used by the ancients (p. 90) and the beginnings of the United States oil industry dates from the mid-19th century, oil is a 20th-century, mineral resource by any standards of exploration, production, and consumption. It is the prime fuel of the transportation industry, has taken many other markets from coal, particularly residential and commercial heating, and increasingly is used for petrochemical feedstock. Geological knowledge has advanced to where it can be proved that hydrocarbons are a normal constituent of sedimentary basins the world over, and that where thick accumulations of Paleozoic, Mesozoic, and Tertiary sediments occur, the probability is that deposits of oil also occur. Further, it is known that the stable or shelf sides of basins are more likely to be productive than the mobile sides, and that foreland facies sedimentary rocks are more likely hosts than orogenic facies rocks. The elements required for accumulation of petroleum are (1) a source rock, (2) a reservoir, and (3) a trap—structural or stratigraphic. Oil in some quantities has now been discovered in all continents, the most recent addition to the ranks of producers being Australia. However, the great bulk of the world's known reserves are concentrated in the Middle East (Iran, Iraq, Kuwait, Saudi Arabia), Venezuela, and the United States (Table X.2). Other areas outside the Sino-Soviet Bloc with substantial reserves include South America (Colombia, Peru, Argentina, Trinidad), Mexico, Canada, North Africa (Libya and Algeria), and the East Indies (Borneo and Indonesia). Soviet and Chinese reserves are probably very large. Except for recently discovered giant gas fields in France and the Netherlands, Europe's known reserves of hydrocarbons are small. New ground remaining for exploration has been considerably broadened by technology which permits deeper drilling and exploration of the continental shelves. Off-shore lands, together with Alaska, the Arctic islands, and Australia, are current busy exploration frontiers. Weeks (1965, p. 132) estimated a potential 700 billion-barrel reserve in the continental shelves.

In the United States production comes from nearly 600,000 wells in 31 states, with Texas, Louisiana, and California as leading producers. Although the major producer of petroleum, the United States is also a major importer, bringing in nearly half a billion barrels (1964) mainly from Venezuela, Canada, Kuwait, Saudi Arabia, and Colombia. Nearly all nonproducing areas must import some oil and a great deal of the foreign exchange of nonproducing countries is spent for petroleum; India and Brazil import nearly all of their requirements. Industrial Europe is a major importer. Any threatened interference with the flow of oil causes international crises.

The 1964 world reserve index is 33 years based on *proved* reserves (see p. 15). U.S. reserve-production index is 11 years; U.S. reserve-consumption index is 9+ years. At present, consumption of crude oil in the United States is increasing at a rate of about 3 per cent per year, whereas outside of the U.S. the increase is a staggering 10 per cent per year. The combined increase is 6 to 7 per cent per year over the world. This extraordinary rate of increase of demand for petroleum reflects the industrialization of large parts of the world where there previously was no substantial petroleum market and the general population increase. In the more mature economy of the United States, part of the growth is due to increase in use of petroleum for manufacture of petrochemicals. Also, petroleum is consumed in great quantities by modern war machines so that any increase in military activity increases demand for petroleum.

It is clear that worldwide increase in the demand for petroleum at rates which double the consumption every decade means that without a high rate of new discoveries and without augmentation of supplies through improved recovery techniques, the reserve index will decline rapidly from its present 33 years (based on proved reserves). The domestic industry is, in fact, hard-pressed to maintain a comfortable ratio between production and proved reserves. The future is brightened considerably, however, by improved technologic capability to extract oil from oil shale and bituminous sands, and to produce oil by hydrogenation of coal. Please refer to the discussion of petroleum reserves in Chapter I (p. 15). On the domestic scene, and considering only liquid crude oil reserves, it can be calculated that if reserves of all classes aggregate 600 billion barrels, a 3 per cent per year increase in consumption starting from 3 billion barrels per year production will exhaust 340 billion barrels, over half, of the total reserve by the end of a 50-year period.

Natural gas.

Of fast-growing importance as an energy source and as petrochemical feed stocks is natural gas. It is a widespread constituent of sedimentary basins and commonly, but not everywhere, is found in association with petroleum. It is a highly mobile substance that, like petroleum, is found in traps where a reservoir is sealed by a relatively impermeable material. Gas is produced from wells, the natural gas liquids or distillates that it contains are separated, and the gas is transported by pipelines to market areas. Recently, natural gas has been liquified and transported by tanker to gas-deficient regions. Natural gas is a blanket term including a variety of gaseous hydrocarbons, mostly methane and ethane, mixed with water, carbon dioxide, nitrogen, and hydrogen sulfide. It is commonly sold by the MCF (thousand cubic feet) but there is a trend to sale on a BTU basis, and to pricing on an area rather than a cost basis. So-called 'sour gas' containing quantities of hydrogen sulfide is an important source of recovered sulfur (p. 348).

The great bulk of known gas reserves are in the United States and the Middle East with substantial reserves also in the Sino-Soviet bloc, Canada, and Mexico. Major discoveries have been made in Europe (France, Netherlands) in recent years and the North Sea basin is a promising area for new fields.

In the United States production is from more than 100,000 gas wells together with oil wells in 31 states. Texas and Louisiana account for 42 per cent and 27 per cent respectively. Relatively small amounts of gas (about 3 per cent of total consumption) are imported from Canada and Mexico; a negligible amount is exported. About 67 per cent of production is used by industry with the balance distributed between residential and commercial consumers.

For the past 10 years demand for natural gas has grown at a yearly rate of between 5 and 6 per cent and predictions for the balance of the century suggest a 3 to 4 per cent growth (Zaffarano and Lankford, 1965, p. 34). Domestic reserve indexes, 1965, for production and consumption are about 20 years. Were it not for the conservative method used to report petroleum and natural gas reserves (p. 15), these indexes, in view of the high growth rate, would be a matter for concern. With the present demand, a 6 per cent growth rate, and no new discoveries, domestic proved reserves would be exhausted in a little more than 12 years. However, the outlook for discoveries of new and deeper gas fields in the United States is good. Like petroleum, a larger portion of natural gas production will in the future be used in petrochemical manufacture. Gas will probably remain competitive in the energy market for many decades because it is clean, easily transportable fuel, and its production and use is accompanied by less of a pollution problem than occurs with fossil fuels.

Uranium.

Uranium is commonly listed as a minor metal rather than a mineral fuel; but, except for weaponry, the major markets of the future will probably develop in the areas of fuel for power-generating and desalinating nuclear reactors and for propulsion of naval, air, and space craft. Uranium is rather widely distributed over the world in fissure vein deposits, in irregular disseminated deposits in sandstone and limestone, and in very large low-grade stratiform deposits in Precambrian conglomerates. Low concentrations of uranium have been recovered from phosphate rock in manufacture of phosphoric acid and very low concentrations in black shale and sea water may one day be a source, but these are not included in reserve figures used herein. The bulk of the world's reserves, so far as is known at present, occur in Precambrian conglomerates in Canada at Blind River, Ontario, and in South Africa associated with gold in the Witwatersrand deposits. The large reserves of the United States are mainly in disseminated deposits in sandstone. Other significant deposits occur in

Australia (Rum Jungle), Canada (Great Bear Lake), the Congo (Shinkolobwe), Czechoslovakia (Joachimstahl), France (including the Malagasy Republic and Gabon), India, Portugal, and Spain. The Sino-Soviet position is not known but deposits are known to occur in East Germany, central Europe, the Balkans, Soviet Union, and China. The Congo, Great Bear Lake, and Joachimstahl deposits were known sources before the great demand following World War II; the Shinkolobwe deposit ceased production in 1960 and is reported to be largely depleted.

United States production in 1963 came from about 600 mines with about 80 per cent from 75 principal mines. Imports of concentrates came from Canada, Republic of South Africa, Australia, and Portugal.

Because of military applications and the huge future energy potential, uranium and other fissionable minerals are under strict government control in nearly all countries of the world. There is no free trade. Because of government restrictions, even in countries without the technological capacity to exploit uranium deposits and because of the short history of demand, the true reserve picture is probably not known and major deposits remain to be discovered. O'Brien (1964, p. 13) compared the energy content of the known world reserves of energy raw materials in terms of BTU content and reported that the energy in known reserves of nuclear raw materials is about 21 times the total energy in coal, oil and gas, oil shale, and tar sands as follows:

Coal	21.0×10^{18} BTU
Oil and gas	5.0×10^{18} BTU
Oil shale	1.0×10^{18} BTU
Tar sands	0.2×10^{18} BTU
Nuclear fuels	575.0×10^{18} BTU

The 1964 world reserve index is 24 years (excluding Sino-Soviet Bloc). U. S. reserve-production index is only 12 years but this is in a way misleading because much of the production is being absorbed and stockpiled for military requirements; some is exported. On the basis of *industrial consumption* only, the reserve-consumption index would be much larger. Demand over the next decade will be largely military and will depend on exigencies of the international situation

and the success of the present nuclear powers in limiting the proliferation of nuclear weapons. Demand will be high in nations newly
capable of manufacturing nuclear weapons as they attempt to build
a stockpile; demand will be less in the established nuclear powers
depending on their own estimate of 'overkill' capabilities. According
to Atomic Energy Commission forecasts, domestic civilian demand
will be 1,600 to 4,000 tons per year of U_3O_8 in 1970, 8,900 to 14,000
tons per year in 1975, and 19,000 to 27,000 tons in 1980 (Baroch,
1965b, p. 28). This predicted increase is based on a probable boom
in nuclear power and desalination facilities. New reactors require a
large initial charge. In view of the current low level of uranium exploration, surges in demand could rapidly lower the reserve index.
Roscoe (1965, pp. 14-15) examined growth in demand for nuclear
fuels and concluded that after 1976 it will not be possible to supply
the need from deposits now known, and that production increases in
the late 1970s will have to come from deposits not yet discovered in
1965. The rate of growth of nonmilitary applications is very sensitive
to engineering advances in design of breeder reactors using thorium
and in successful utilization of nuclear fusion; success in either could
adversely affect the long-term nuclear-power market for uranium.
Although the uranium market does not appear to be threatened by
developments in these areas in the near future, the problem of disposing of radioactive wastes from nuclear fission acts as a spur to
research in nuclear fusion. Although contaminants are produced in
the fusion, they are less abundant.

Because of the complex military, industrial, and research factors
which must be evaluated, and the possible alternatives leading to
boom or slow-down, the resource future of uranium is perhaps more
difficult to predict than for any other mineral.

The successful development of a breeder reactor in which surplus
neutrons from uranium or plutonium fission are used to convert
thorium into uranium 233 would immediately make thorium a prime
energy source, change its traditional market patterns, and put it into
competition with other energy minerals. Thorium minerals occur in
placer deposits (monazite sands), vein deposits, and in concentrations
in both igneous and sedimentary rocks. Major known deposits are in
India, Canada, the United States, Soviet Union, eastern Europe, and
Brazil. Known deposits probably contain on the order of a million
tons of thorium oxide (Baroch, 1965, p. 7), and 1964 production was
on the order of one or two thousand tons. Domestic consumption over
the last five years has averaged about 200 tons of thorium oxide.

IRON AND FERRO-ALLOY METALS

Iron.

Iron, the workhorse metal of the industrial age, is a common substance all over the world with giant high-grade deposits occurring in all continents and usable smaller or low-grade deposits in many nations. The large deposits containing reserves measured in billions of tons of high-grade ore occur in Australia, Brazil, Canada, India, Soviet Union, and the United States (Table X.2). In the United States 179 mines produced iron in 1963; 140 mines accounted for 97 per cent of total domestic production. Minnesota and Michigan produced 76 per cent of the total, Alabama produced 4 per cent, and the remainder was divided between 19 other states. In addition to a very large domestic production (Table X.2), the United States imports about 40 million long tons of ore (1964), mainly from Canada, Venezuela, Chile, and Peru.

FIGURE X.1

Sources of United States Iron Ore Supply 1940–63 and Predicted Sources 1964–80 (Reno, 1965, Fig. 3, p. 23).

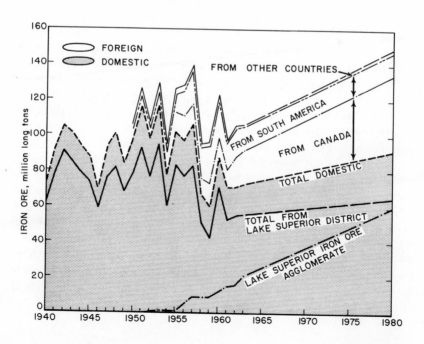

Geologically, the giant deposits all over the world occur in Precambrian iron formations in the continental shields where iron-rich sedimentary rocks, commonly siliceous, have been enriched by weathering. Important iron deposits also occur around igneous intrusions where emanations from the hot molten body invaded the country rock and reacted to form bodies of hematite and magnetite. Such deposits are widespread. Although smaller and more irregular than the Precambrian iron formations, they are commonly very high grade. In some areas, beds of hematite and limonite occur in a marine sedimentary sequence. The extensive minette ores of Europe and the Clinton ores of the Appalachain region are of this type. In some areas sedimentary rocks containing iron silicate and carbonate minerals have been converted to limonite ore by weathering. The Tertiary brown iron ores of East Texas are an example. Generally, such ores are of low grade and of local interest. So-called lateritic iron ores occur in tropical and semi-tropical areas where weathering has leached away silica and left a concentration of iron oxides. These are generally low-grade deposits; in some areas they are nickeliferous.

Technological changes have had a great effect on iron reserves since World War II. In order to utilize the low-grade siliceous ores of the Lake Superior iron ranges, a technique of concentrating and pelletizing the ore was developed. This uniform, easily-handled, high-grade feed so improved blast furnace performance that pellets are now preferred over high-grade direct shipping ore in many plants.

The 1964 world reserve index is 380 years, *not* including the enormous low-grade deposits containing less than 20 per cent iron. Consumption of iron will continue to increase as the world industrializes and population expands. As steel, it has little to fear from substitutes except where metals with special properties are needed. Large deposits are widespread and availability is assured. However, the large known reserves and large 1964 world reserve index should not lead to complacency. The United States, consuming 120 million tons of iron ore per year, producing 80 million tons and importing 40 million tons, has a 1964 reserve-production index of 190 years based on the present domestic production/imports ratio, and a 120 year reserve-consumption index if the total demand is satisfied from domestic ores. With an annual increase of only 2 per cent, the demand will be 240 million tons per year by 2000. The U. S. Bureau of Mines (Reno, 1965, Fig. 3, p. 23) presented predictions of sources and growth to 1980. These predictions are much more conservative than those made by Fuller (1959, p. 17) who, to illustrate the potential magnitude of growth in resource use, based a prediction for iron ore on a 1950 consumption of 130 million tons, a per capita increase in steel production at the rate of 2.5 per cent, and a population growth rate of 1.5 per cent. He pointed out that with such growth rates demand for iron ore in the year 2000 would be 800 million tons per year. At such a rate, domestic reserves of 15 billion tons would last less than 20 years. Fuller made his point; his illustration also clearly indicates the magnitude of the differences in long-range predictions that result from slight differences in the growth rates used in the forecast. If Fuller's growth rate is applied to the 1950 consumption of 130 million tons for the period 1950 to 1963, the United States in 1963 would have consumed 210 to 220 million tons of iron ore. It is difficult to compare this with actual consumption because of uncertainties about what kind of ore was included in Fuller's 130 million tons. According to the U. S. Bureau of Mines, Minerals Yearbook for 1963, total crude ore mined was about 153 million tons which was equal to about 74 million tons of usable ore and agglomerates (made at the mine). This was supplemented by about 33 million tons of imports and decreased by some 7 million tons of exports. The total industrial consumption of iron ore and agglomerates was reported at 112 million tons. The reason that consumption does not balance production plus imports minus exports in any one year is that large stocks are maintained at mines, consuming plants, and ports. In 1950, domestic crude ore mined was 126 million tons equal to 98 million tons of usable ore, imports were about 8 million tons, and exports about 2.5 million tons; consumption, according to the U. S. Bureau of Mines Minerals Yearbook for 1950, was 106.6 million tons. If a 4 per cent growth rate is applied to this figure for a period of 13 years (to 1963) it would increase to about 178 million tons per year or about 66 million tons more than actually consumed. The actual growth rate since 1950 has been closer to 1 per cent than 4 per cent (U.S. Bureau of Mines, Minerals Yearbook 1964, Table 8, p. 13).

Manganese.

Although manganese oxides are common in nature and small concentrations of manganese minerals are geologically ubiquitous, large high-grade deposits are relatively rare. The United States has none. Domestic production is negligible and close to 2 million tons per year of ore is imported mainly from Brazil, Africa, India, and Mexico. The largest known deposit is in the Soviet Union; most of the reserves elsewhere are in Brazil, Gabon, India and Republic of South Africa. The large manganese oxide deposit at N'Suta on the old Gold Coast (Ghana) is now depleted but a substantial manganese carbonate deposit has reportedly been discovered. Manganese is currently produced from deposits in many countries in Central America, South America, Europe, Asia, Africa, and Oceania (Dehuff, 1965a, Table 1, p. 13). Accumulations of manganese oxide in nodules on the sea floor have been estimated on the order of billions or trillions of tons. The future industry might change drastically, depending on what part of this enormous reserve is economically and technologically recoverable.

There are no economic substitutes for manganese in the metallurgical and chemical industry. About 93 per cent of the manganese consumed in the United States was for metallurgical purposes (steel production), 5 per cent was for chemical and other miscellaneous purposes, and 2 per cent was for manufacture of dry-cell batteries. In the case of a crisis, the United States could develop production from numerous small and low-grade deposits and recover manganese from open-hearth slags.

Geologically, manganese occurs in large sedimentary deposits where earthy masses and nodules of manganese oxide are included in beds of sandy clay and marl (the Soviet type) or limestone and in residual deposits where weathering of manganese silicate and carbonate minerals has resulted in accumulations of manganese oxides (India, Brazil). Some of the residual concentrations have been subsequently metamorphosed and now occur as tabular bodies and lenses in deformed and altered rocks. Manganese carbonate and silicate deposits in fissure veins are worked in some areas but generally such occurrences are small.

The 1964 world reserve index is 146 years. This does not take into account sea-floor manganese oxide nodules. Inasmuch as about 35 pounds of manganese are used to make a ton of steel, and more than 90 per cent of all manganese produced is consumed for such metallurgical purposes, it seems clear that manganese is tied firmly to steel. According to the U. S. Bureau of Mines (Harris, 1960, p. 21), domestic steel growth rates in the recent past have been at the rate of 2 per cent per capita. With a 1 to 1.5 per cent population increase, yearly growth rate would be about 3 per cent. For the future the U.S. Bureau of Mines predicts a 2 per cent growth through 1975 (U.S. Bureau of Mines, Minerals Yearbook 1964, Table 8, p. 13). Thus, growth of the steel industry will result in a steady increase in demand for manganese at a rate which will double demand in 20 or 30 years. Barring disruptions in world trade, conventional deposits can supply this estimated demand until well into the next century. Low-grade deposits and sea-floor nodule deposits are adequate insurance against any shortage in an absolute sense. Scattered deposits in the United States which can be treated by in-use methods to produce a 35 per cent Mn concentrate aggregate perhaps 1 million tons. Inasmuch as the United States currently consumes about 2 million tons of ore per year, the domestic reserve-consumption index is only six months. If there are disruptions in world trade, therefore, the United States would have to rely on its stockpile (p. 197) until domestic low-grade ores and slags could be brought into production and utilized.

Evaluation of the long-term outlook for manganese is really (1) an evaluation of the likelihood of a major change in the steelmaking process, and (2) an evaluation of prospects for new uses. Batteries, the one significant nonmetallurgical market, can be made without manganese. The only steelmaking process now in industrial use which promises to reduce manganese consumption is the basic oxygen process, but there is no firm quantitative information on the reductions which might occur over the long term. Rapid growth of the process might reduce the rate of increase in demand for manganese but probably will not cut back manganese consumption. One result of the basic oxygen process is a decrease in manganese content of slags so that slags from the new process will not be a low-grade resource for the future.

Chromium.

Chromite deposits are relatively rare and the Western Hemisphere is notably deficient in chromium. The United States has a low-grade high-cost deposit in Montana which has been shut down since 1961 when a stockpile contract was filled. The United States imports about 1 million tons per year, mostly from the Republic of South Africa, Rhodesia, Soviet Union, and the Philippines. The United States metallurgical industry consumes about 58 per cent of imported ores, 30 per cent goes to the refractory industry, and 12 per cent is distributed among the chemical industries. By far the largest known reserves are in the Republic of South Africa, with additional large reserves in neighboring Rhodesia (Table X.2). Substantial deposits also occur in Turkey, the Philippines, Soviet Union, Finland, and the Balkans (Yugoslavia, Greece, Albania). Smaller reserves are distributed over a large number of African, Asiatic, and Oceanic nations with small amounts also credited to Cuba and Canada (Holliday, 1965a p. 9, Table 5). The fact that nearly 98 per cent of the world's known reserves of high-grade chromium ore is concentrated in a relatively small area in the southern part of the African continent has great political significance and cannot but affect economic relationships between the Republic of South Africa and Rhodesia and the rest of the world.

Geologically, chromite occurs in basic and ultrabasic igneous rocks, generally in stratiform bodies such as the Bushveldt complex of South Africa. Chromite also occurs in residual deposits formed by weathering of ultrabasic rocks such as peridotite and serpentine, but such deposits are of minor economic significance.

The 1964 world reserve index is 532 years; the U. S. reserve-consumption index based on 1964 consumption of 1 million tons of ore (and concentrates) and reserves of only 8 million tons, is slightly more than 6 years. This index is not now being reduced by production. Considering that the large reserves of the world are distant from the United States, the difference between the world reserve index and the domestic index is a matter for concern.

Projections for 1980 consumption by the U. S. Bureau of Mines (Holliday, 1965a, pp. 14–15) are in terms of metallurgical uses (1.4 million tons), refractory uses (0.5 million tons), and chemical uses (0.25 million tons). Based on 1963 consumption, growth rates are as follows:

	Millions of tons of chromite		
	1963	Annual growth rate	1980
Metallurgical	.63	4+%	1.40
Refractory	.37	2-%	.50
Chemical	.19	2+%	.25
Total	1.19		2.15

These projections are based on an estimated 1980 steel production of 147 million tons of which 2.3 millions tons is estimated to be stainless steel requiring 1 million tons of chromite. Other alloys will consume 0.4 million tons of chromite. The demand for refractories will increase at a much lower rate because of changes in steelmaking processes. The refractory growth predicted by the U. S. Bureau of Mines is based on use of 3.5 tons of chromite per 1,000 tons of steel. The estimated chromium chemicals growth rate is about 2 per cent.

If the 1980 prognostication of the U. S. Bureau of Mines is correct, and the ratio between U. S. and world consumption is more or less maintained, world demand in 1980 will be 6 to 8 million tons. Without any increase in reserves, the 1980 world reserve index will be a comfortable 340 years, the 'comfort' depending on unobstructed world trade. U. S. reserves are not likely to increase materially. The most promising area for substitutions is in the refractory industry where the abundant magnesium refractories can replace chromite in part. There does not appear to be a wholly satisfactory substitute for the largest consumer of chromium—stainless steel. Titanium probably will replace stainless steel in some applications if a shortage of chromium occurs due to interference with imports.

Nickel.

Like chromium, large concentrations of nickel are not distributed equally throughout the world. The United States is nickel-poor with only one small operating mine in Oregon. Imports of about 125,000 tons per year of nickel metal come mainly from Canada and Norway but since Norwegian raw material comes from Canada, nearly 99 per cent of United States nickel has a Canadian origin. It is used to make various ferrous and nonferrous alloys and electroplating anodes. There are three principal types of deposits— (1) nickeliferous copper sulfide deposits, (2) nickeliferous silicate deposits, and (3) nickeliferous laterites and serpentines. The great nickeliferous sulfide deposits are in Canada in Ontario and Manitoba; a similar deposit occurs at Petsamo. Formerly Finnish, this deposit is now in Soviet territory. The major nickeliferous silicate deposit is in New Caledonia, with smaller occurrences in South America, Indonesia, and the United States (Oregon). The bulk of the terrestrial reserves are nickeliferous laterites formed by deep weathering of serpentine and other ultrabasic rocks. The largest known deposits are in Cuba, the Philippines, the Celebes, and Borneo. Smaller deposits are in Japan, Madagascar, Soviet Union, Greece, and Puerto Rico; chances for discovery of additional deposits in the equatorial region are good. Another potential source is the sea-floor manganese nodules which commonly contain up to 1 per cent nickel.

World reserve index (excluding the Sino-Soviet Bloc reserves but including Sino-Soviet production) is >124 years. Sino-Soviet reserves, judging from current production, are probably large Geologically, it might be expected that the bulk of Sino-Soviet reserves are in sulfide or silicate deposits, inasmuch as laterite deposits occur in tropical and semi-tropical countries.

The U. S. 1964 reserve-consumption index is perhaps 4 years, but since neighboring Canada is the major nickel producer the source is much more secure than in the case of chromium. Disruptions in supply due to political factors are unlikely. Growth rates in nickel consumption are expected to reflect general industrial growth. Demand will be decreased by economically attractive substitutions and increased by new uses. A major marketer of gasoline is currently advertising the virtues of nickel as a gasoline additive. This is a dissipative use. With increase in demand of 2% per year and modest success in expanding reserves through new discoveries, North American supplies (exclusive of Cuba) would be çapable of sustaining U.S. industry for at least 35 years or until the turn of the century. There is, moreover, a reassuring cushion in other Free World ores and of lower-grade ores in the laterites of the tropics. A new facility recently announced for Guatemala will add 12,500 tons of nickel per year to existing capacity (Wall Street Jour., August 27, 1965). Plans to develop a large nickeliferous laterite deposit in the Dominican Republic were cancelled by Falconbridge in 1965 because of the political and social unrest in that nation Barring drastic increases in demand, U. S. nickel supplies are more secure than for any other ferro-alloy metal for which domestic supplies are negligible.

The removal of Cuba from the United States political and trade sphere was most significant in regard to nickel. The loss of the huge low-grade reserves developed by Freeport Sulfur at Moa Bay, together with the investment in U. S.-based facilities for processing the ore to a nickel-rich liquor for subsequent nickel extraction and refining represent a major mineral resource consequence of a political realignment.

Molybdenum.

Molybdenum is the only one of the ferro-alloy metals with which the United States is abundantly endowed. In 1964, nine U. S. producers produced nearly 65 millions pounds of molybdenum (in concentrates). About 70 per cent of the total production was from one producer in Colorado, where the Climax mine is the world's largest deposit. Other producers in the western states produced molybdenum as a by-product from copper ores. Molybdenum is exported from the United States in quantities of about 25 million pounds a year. In the United States, about 80 per cent of production was used by the iron and steel industry; the remainder went to the chemical industry. Outside of the United States, the major known deposits are in Canada, Chile, and Peru. According to Engineering and Mining Journal Metal and Mineral Markets for March 29, 1965, 48,900,000 pounds per year of additional production will be available by 1968 from new ore or increased production facilities in Colorado, New Mexico, Arizona, Utah, Chile, British Columbia, Ontario, and Quebec. Smaller deposits occur in Australia, the Balkans, Greenland, Japan, Mexico, Norway, Turkey, and Yugoslavia. Judging from Sino-Soviet production of some 16 million pounds per year and known deposits in the Soviet Union and Manchuria, reserves of some magnitude must exist in Asia but no detailed information is available. China has claimed the largest reserves in the world and more than 100 deposits are known in the U.S.S.R. (Holliday, 1965b, p. 8).

Geologically, molybdenum is associated with granitic igneous rocks. Molybdenum occurs (1) as the principal sulfide mineral in fissure veins and replacement deposits—the ore in the Climax mine is a stockwork of molybdenum-quartz veinlets, (2) with copper in porphyry copper deposits, and (3) with tungsten in contact metasomatic deposits.

Recently available data indicate U. S. reserves of more than 5 million *tons* of molybdenum (about 2 million tons of which are in deposits now being mined or investigated), a Canada-Chile-Peru reserve of about 1,000,000 *tons* and a Sino-Soviet reserve of 2 million *tons* or more (Holliday, 1965b, p. 8). Canada's Endako mine in British Columbia is reported to be the second largest in the world with reserves of over 66 million tons of ore containing 0.20 per cent MoS_2 (Engineering and Mining Journal, 1965, p. 81). This would suggest a minimum world reserve index of more than 100 years. Lacking additional reserve figures, it is not possible to calculate a more accurate 1964 world reserve index; the United States reserve-consumption index based on consumption of 25,000 tons per year and reserves of 5 million tons, is 200 years.

Despite a relatively large reserve index due to large reserves in relation to present demand, the rate of growth in demand for molybdenum indicates the probability of a rapid decline in the index

FIGURE X.2

Projected Production and Consumption of Molybdenum in the United States
(Holliday, 1965b, Fig. 2, p. 10).

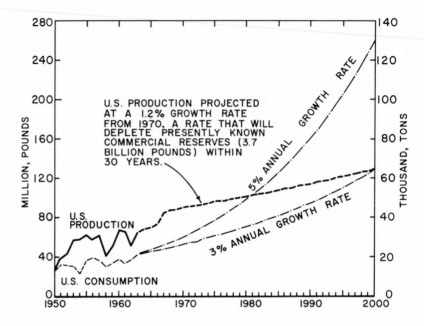

(Figure X.2). The relatively attractive price of molybdenum, its ability to substitute for other higher-priced ferro-alloy metals in shorter supply, and the security of a large domestic supply have resulted in a steadily increasing consumption of 'moly' per ton of steel and a growth rate higher than that of domestic steel production. These considerations led the U. S. Bureau of Mines to project a whopping 5 per cent growth rate as long as the metal is available at or near 1964 prices. Such a growth rate (doubling consumption every 14 years), if supplied wholly from domestic deposits, would exhaust the 5 million ton reserve in 50 years.

Tungsten.

Tungsten is an Asiatic element; although there are deposits in the Americas, Africa, Europe, and Australia, by far the greatest reserves are in China (Table X.2). Other significant deposits occur in Korea, Cambodia, Burma, Malaysia, Japan, and Thailand. Production figures for the United States were classed as "Company Confidential" in 1963 and 1964, which generally reflects a very limited number of producers. In 1962 production amounted to about 8 million pounds, mainly from Bolivia, Republic of Korea, Portugal, and Argentina. About 40 per cent of the tungsten used in this country is for manufacture of carbides, 20 per cent is used as pure metal, 17 per cent goes to the high-speed tool steel industry, and the remainder is distributed over a large number of industrial applications.

Most tungsten deposits are quartz vein and contact metamorphic deposits associated with granitic rocks. Erosion of such deposits has resulted in placer accumulations of commercial importance in some areas. In some deposits tungsten minerals predominate, in others tungsten occurs with other metals such as molybdenum, antimony, tin, copper, silver, and gold.

World reserve index as of 1964 is 40 years. The fact that about 77 per cent of the world's known reserves are in China is of strategic significance. A great deal of metallurgical research has gone into investigation of titanium, tantalum, zirconium, and molybdenum substitutions for tungsten, but substitutions have not been completely successful. U. S. 1964 reserve-consumption index is only about 12 years based on reserves of 140 million pounds and annual consumption of about 11 to 11.5 million pounds. U. S Bureau of Mines predictions that consumption will increase from 11 million pounds in 1963 to 25 million pounds by 1980 requires a growth rate of slightly less than 5 per cent (Stevens, 1965, p. 15). This is based on increase in use of tungsten in aircraft, nuclear, and space industries.

From the U. S. point of view the tungsten outlook is bleak. The world's principal reserves are distant from the U. S. and in a part of the world which cannot be considered a secure source. Only increased use of substitutes, increased secondary recovery, new discoveries, and utilization of unconventional sources can improve the resource outlook. One unconventional source which promises to increase domestic reserves is the Searles Lake, California, brine deposit which contains an estimated 135 million pounds of tungsten. If this low-grade concentration of tungsten can be efficiently recovered, domestic reserves will be almost doubled.

Cobalt.

Cobalt occurs in associations with copper, nickel, iron, silver, manganese, lead, zinc, and is rarely found in concentrations by itself.

The largest·known deposits are (1) with nickel in laterite deposits such as those of Cuba and (2) with copper in the great Katanga-Rhodesia copper belt in Africa. In the famous old district of Cobalt, Ontario, cobalt was associated with silver and nickel in fissure vein deposits. The largest currently recoverable cobalt reserve is in Katanga Province of the Republic of the Congo. Large reserves also exist in neighboring Zambia. Erratic cobalt mineralization occurs with the nickel ores in New Caledonia and reserves are reported to be large. Morocco also has significant reserves of cobalt ores. The lateritic nickel ores of Cuba contain the largest reserves in the Western Hemisphere. Substantial quantities of cobalt are found in the copper-nickel ores of Ontario and Manitoba, Canada. There is only one producer in the United States, at Cornwall, Pennsylvania, and the quantity of production is confidential. Substantial reserves, however, exist in Pennsylvania, Idaho, and Missouri (Table X.2). Some 12.5 million pounds of cobalt were imported in 1964, mainly from the Republic of the Congo, Belgium-Luxembourg, West Germany, and Norway. The European sources are from metallurgical plants treating foreign ores, not from European mines. Cobalt is used mainly in the manufacture of alloys, although a substantial percentage is used in nonmetallic compounds, salts, and driers.

Lacking reserve figures for much of the world, a 1964 world reserve index cannot be calculated. The Free World index is about 150 years. U. S. reserve-consumption index is about 25 years. Because cobalt is produced throughout the world as a by-product of mining other metals, principally copper, nickel, and iron, production of it is a dependent variable with available supplies pegged to other metals rather than demand for cobalt. Current demand for the principal associated metals is strong so there is a surplus of cobalt. Its high price has made it difficult to develop new markets. Prospects for growth appear to be in special-property materials for new technology —such as both ferrous and nonferrous alloys, high-temperature and high-strength materials, and in permanent magnets.

Domestic resources are largely in the form of low-grade ores where cobalt occurs with lead or with iron. Only the cobalt-bearing iron deposits are now being worked so that the U. S. reserve index is not declining very rapidly. Removal of Cuba to the Communist sphere politically removed a very large reserve of cobalt-nickel ore just being brought into production, and favorably located geographically with respect to United States markets (p. 300). However, as long as the cobalt ores of Africa reach the market place, present trade patterns will continue and the United States will have ample sources. Canadian reserves and the domestic reserves provide a cushion against times of politically induced shortages. New Caledonian reserves are very large but also distant and subject to political interdiction.

Vanadium.

Vanadium is a widely distributed element over the earth, but high-grade deposits in which vanadium is the principal ore element are rare. Probably the richest concentrates were the vanadium-rich asphaltite veins in the Peruvian Andes (Mina Ragra). In Africa, lead and copper vanadates occur in the oxidized parts of base metal deposits in Rhodesia and Southwest Africa. Titaniferous magnetite deposits in Finland and South Africa contain appreciable content of vanadium and are important sources; similar deposits exist in the United States and the Soviet Union. Some clays and shales are vanadium-rich—phosphatic shales in Idaho and Wyoming are a potential domestic source. In some areas coals contain vanadium, and coal ash is a potential source. Crude oil in Venezuela and Mexico is high in vanadium which can be recovered from residues. Bauxite and laterite carry high vanadium values in some areas; the vanadium can be recovered during the processing of bauxite for alumina. Major known reserves and resources are in the United States, Republic of South Africa, U.S.S.R., Finland, and China (Dehuff, 1965, p. 5). For the last 20 years vanadium has been recovered from Colorado Plateau uranium ores in the United States, and the U. S. has been the world's largest producer. However, the reserves are not very large and will not be a major source after about 1970 (Dehuff, 1965, p. 5). As Colorado Plateau reserves are diminished, the United States will turn to the large potential reserves in phosphatic shales and titaniferous magnetites.

The United States production in 1963 came from six firms, producing mainly from uranium-vanadium ores in the Colorado Plateau but also including some from impure ferrophosphorous sources. Over 90 per cent was consumed by the metallurgical industry for ferrous (83 per cent) and nonferrous (10 per cent) alloys; the remainder went to the chemical industry and was used largely for catalysts. The United States exports substantial quantities of vanadium.

Inasmuch as vanadium is produced mainly as a coproduct or by-product, the economics of its recovery from abundant low-grade sources is tied to the demand for associated products such as phosphate rock, titaniferous iron ore, and uranium ore. From reserve and resource data presented by Dehuff (1965b, p. 5), the 1964 world reserve index is very large, probably more than 1,500 years. Based in 1964 consumption and only the Colorado Plateau reserves, the U. S. reserve-consumption index is only about 10 years. However, the enormous low-grade reserves in phosphate and magnetite ores constitute a secure back-up for the currently exploitable Colorado Plateau ores. Production of vanadium from such low-grade sources would be tied to or complexly interrelated with the economics of phosphate and iron, but if they are included the 1964 U. S. reserve-consumption index is increased by at least several hundred years. Some of the shales in the Phosphoria Formation which are highest in vanadium content are low in phosphate; if these potential sources of vanadium are utilized, vanadium will be the principal product rather than a by-product of phosphate production.

Conventional metallurgical and chemical demand for vanadium will grow apace with the steel industry and with production of vanadium catalysts. There are, however, prospects for extraordinary growth in demand for vanadium catalysts in controlling atmospheric pollution, specifically in cleaning up internal combustion engine exhausts. In the event of widespread use of such catalysts, demand for vanadium could perhaps grow at a rate in excess of 5 per cent per year. In this event the low-grade ores where vanadium is a co-product or by-product will be exploited sooner rather than later, conceivably within the next several decades and certainly before the turn of the century, depending on availability of foreign ores to make up the difference between U. S. demand and production.

NONFERROUS INDUSTRIAL METALS

Copper.

Copper, one of the first, if not the first, metal used by man and certainly the first metal used for tools and weapons, is still one of the most important industrial metals. The United States, the world's largest producer (Table X.2), also imports about half a million tons, mainly from Chile, Canada, Peru, and Republic of South Africa. Because of the low grade of currently worked domestic ores and the very large tonnages mined and milled, production in the United States is concentrated in a relatively few large companies; as of 1963, four companies accounted for 72 per cent of mine output and 85 per cent of refined metal production, ten other companies supplied 26 per cent of mine output; four companies accounted for the other 14 per cent of refined metal production. Arizona (55 per cent) and Utah (16 per cent) are the principal producing states. Half of the copper is used as pure metal, the other half in manufacture of alloys.

The bulk of the world's reserves are in large deposits in copper-rich parts of the crust. About 85 per cent of known reserves are in the six principal producing areas; in order of magnitude of reserves, these are (1) the Andean western slope—Chile and Peru, (2) central African copper belt—Northern Rhodesia and Congo, (3) western United States, (4) U.S.S.R.—Ural Mountains and Kazakstan region, (5) central Canada, and (6) the Lake Superior region of the United States and Canada (Table X.2). Other significant deposits occur in Bolivia, Cuba, Cyprus, Finland, India, Mexico, Norway, Sweden, and Turkey (Wideman, 1965, p. 21).

Copper is concentrated in many different kinds of geological environments. Large tonnages occur in so-called porphyry copper deposits where mineralization is associated with intrusive igneous rocks of acid to intermediate composition. The diagnostic characteristic is more or less even dissemination of copper through large volumes of rock, so that although the grade of the ore is relatively low, tonnages are enormous. Some deposits were formed through enrichment of original lean mineralization by secondary processes. Where sources of natural solvents (such as pyrite) were present, weathering processes removed copper from the oxidized zone and precipitated it at or just below the water table, making a rich blanket of copper ore. Some of the highest-grade ores come from vein and contact metamorphic deposits where copper minerals fill fractures, pores, and vugs and replace parts of the host rock; tonnages are not very large except in a few places such as Butte, Montana. Large tonnages of copper ores also occur in extensive stratiform bodies in sedimentary rocks such as sandstone, shale, and conglomerate. The occurrence of ore seems to have been controlled by sedimentary features and also by later structures. Deposits in central Africa are of this type. In the old Precambrian shield areas such as central Canada, copper is associated with nickel in ultrabasic rocks. In the Lake Superior region copper is in lava flows and associated conglomerates, sandstones, and shales.

World reserve index as of 1964 is 40 years, based on material minable under existing economic conditions with existing technology. History has shown that the copper mining industry, through improved technology, has been able to utilize lower and lower grade ores at little or no increase in cost. U.S. 1964 reserve-consumption index is 18 years in terms of new copper, 27 years if the 0.4 million ton scrap pool is subtracted from the total consumption. Reserve-production index is 26 years. Despite large production, the United States imports copper. About half the imports are from Chile and Peru where national governments are exercising sovereignty over resources to an increasing degree and where nationalization of resource industries is possible (Peru) and likely (Chile). Only the Canadian source (19 per cent of imports) can be regarded as secure. Although the greater part of African copper goes to European industry rather than to the U.S., interruptions in flow of African copper would seriously curtail overall Free World supplies and thus adversely affect the United States resource position. Copper is a basic industrial metal. Demand will increase with overall growth of the economy and population but because copper faces stiff competition from aluminum and other metals and materials (plastics), and because of a nearly half-million-ton copper scrap pool, the growth rate was predicted to be 1.5 per cent per year, less than that projected for general economic growth (Wideman, 1965, p. 33). But the current fighting in Vietnam illustrates how quickly increased military demands can change market patterns and forecasts. Copper, a traditional munitions metal, has new military uses in the proliferation of military electronics equipment. The surge in military demand for copper in late 1965 caused a shortage and the price began to rise. To meet the shortage and hold the price the U. S. Government (1) released 200,000 tons of copper from stockpiles, (2) limited exports of copper scrap, (3) requested Congress to suspend the 1.7 cents per pound import tax, (4) urged the Commodity Exchange, Inc., to discourage speculation in copper futures by raising margin requirements, and (5) asked defense contractors to request priorities. Whether or not the increase in military demand will become drastic enough and be sustained long enough to require allocations and destroy the free market remains to be seen.

A vigorous exploration program throughout North America promises to augment reserves substantially and will increase the reserve index. Barring drastic and sustained military increases in demand, the United States position appears to be satisfactory through this century. Demand outside of the United States, due to industrialization of previously undeveloped areas, electrification, and construction, will probably increase at a rate in excess of the U. S. rate of 1.5 per cent per year, and possibly will be as high as 3 per cent (Wideman, 1965, p. 33), This demand will result in more competitive buying in world markets. Union Carbide Corporation recently announced development of a new cable composed of a sodium metal core and a plastic sheath. If testing is successful, such an invention could make possible a saving in copper for power transmission.

Lead.

Lead is a widely distributed element. There are significant deposits on all continents and in some 50 countries of the world. The largest reserves are in Australia, Canada, China, Mexico, Morocco, Peru, Southwest Africa, United States, U.S.S.R., and Yugoslavia. World reserves are estimated at 50 million tons (Moulds, 1965, p. 9) with 18.7 million in North America, 3 million in South America, 4 million in Africa, 6 million in Australia, 10.1 million in eastern Europe, mainly in the Soviet Union, 5.6 million in western Europe, and 2.6 million in Asia (Table X.2).

Although a major producer (Table X.2), the United States imports large quantities of lead (about 400,000 tons per year) mostly from Australia, Canada, Mexico, and Peru. In the United States, 25 mines produced 92 per cent of the output, 10 yielded 77 per cent, and the four top producers were responsible for 53 per cent. Production was centered in the southeast Missouri district, Coeur d'Alene district of Idaho, West Mountain district of Utah, Butte, Montana, district, Metaline, Washington, district, and Upper San Miguel, Colorado, district. About 96 per cent of domestic production is from west of the Mississippi River. Recent large investments in lead mines and smelters in southeast Missouri are designed to raise U. S. lead production from the present 280,000 tons to about 600,000 tons by 1968. In the United States lead was used for batteries (38 per cent), gasoline additives (17 per cent), red lead and litharge (6 per cent), caulking lead (7 per cent), and the remainder in various industrial uses including alloys, sheathings and coverings (such as cable covers), ammunition, and the building industry.

Most of the world's lead deposits occur as cavity-filling and replacement deposits. The high-grade deposits are in contact metamorphic zones, in fissure veins, mantos, pipes, and breccias; the large low-grade deposits are disseminated through large volumes of rock but are also cavity-filling and replacement deposits. Although some large deposits have no clear association with intrusive igneous rocks, it is believed that lead-bearing solutions were derived from subjacent igneous bodies. Lead is relatively insoluble and tends to remain in the oxidized zone during weathering; in some areas enrichment of lead ores has occurred through removal of soluble constituents.

World reserve index as of 1964 is 18 years. Prospects for substantial increase of reserves through current worldwide exploration programs are excellent. The 1964 domestic reserve-consumption index is 4 years if the total consumption is considered in terms of (1) new lead and (2) measured and indicated reserves. If the 0.5 million ton scrap pool is subtracted from the total consumption the domestic reserve-consumption index is increased to 8 years. The 1964 reserve-production index is 22 years. New discoveries in southeast Missouri will substantially improve the U.S. position; *potential* reserves in that area are estimated at 30 million tons of contained lead (Weigel, 1965, p. 77). Of the total domestic consumption, about one-third is newly mined domestic lead, one-third is imports, and one-third is secondary lead. Principal import sources—Australia, Canada, Mexico, and Peru —are politically stable but the more distant sources could be rendered insecure by regional wars. The annual growth rate in demand predicted by the U. S. Bureau of Mines (Moulds, 1965, p. 19) is 2 per cent, based on projected increases in demand for storage batteries and gasoline additives and declines in other traditional uses. If studies initiated in 1966 to evaluate the effects on the environment of widespread distribution of lead from vehicle exhaust prove that use of lead as a gasoline additive is potentially injurious to health, consumption of lead as an additive could be curtailed or eliminated in the future. There is a distinct possibility that advances in fuel-cell technology will adversely affect growth in storage battery uses. Long term increase in a dissipative use for lead with concomitant decrease in a nondestructive use will decrease the rate of growth of the scrap pool.

With 2 per cent growth rate in consumption and a growth rate of 1 per cent in the scrap pool, the year 2000 will see a demand for lead of 2.4 million tons per year and a scrap pool of about 0.7 million tons. Presently known domestic reserves will have been exhausted. Unless domestic exploration programs develop large new orebodies, the United States will have to depend entirely on imports or move down the resource scale into lower grade ores. Prospects for major discoveries in the United States are good.

Zinc.

Zinc, like lead with which it is commonly associated, is widely distributed, with major deposits in the United States, Canada Mexico, Argentina, Peru, Finland, West Germany, Italy, Poland, Spain, Sweden, U.S.S.R., Yugoslavia, Japan, Algeria, Morocco, the Congo, Rhodesia, and Australia. In the United States 25 mines produced 81 per cent of domestic output in 1963, with 18 per cent from Tennessee, 12 per cent from Idaho, 10 per cent from New York, 9 per cent from Colorado, and 7 per cent from Utah. About half a million tons of zinc was imported, mainly from Canada, Mexico, and Peru. Zinc is used mainly for alloys, including brass, and galvanizing. The geology of zinc parallels that of lead (p. 309) except that zinc is soluble in the oxidized zone and is separated from lead in the weathering process. This has resulted in formation of deposits of zinc carbonate in oxidized zones. Two-thirds of the known reserves are in the United States, Australia, Canada, Mexico, and the Sino-Soviet Bloc. In addition to ores, large tonnages of zinc are available in slags from previous metallurgical operations to recover other metals. Reserve estimates include these slags. The 1964 world reserve index is slightly in excess of 20 years but probability for discovery of additional reserves is good. The 1964 U. S. reserve index is 20 years for production and 14 years for consumption taking into account 300,000 tons of zinc in the scrap pool. New discoveries of lead-zinc ore in southeastern Missouri will substantially improve the domestic reserve indexes (Weigel, 1965, p. 77) ; there are also very large reserves in the Tennessee district near Knoxville. Demand is forecasted to rise from 1.1 million tons in 1963 to 1.3 million tons in 1970, to 1.6 million tons in 1980—a growth rate of slightly more than 2 per cent (Schroeder, 1965, p. 20). Projected at the same rate to the year 2000, the demand would be 2.4 million tons per year and reserves known as of 1965 would be long since exhausted. The prospects for adding to domestic reserves appear good but the United States will have to continue to make significant new discoveries, move down the resource ladder to lower grade ores, or rely largely or wholly on imports.

Tin.

Tin was the first of the important alloy metals and with copper was used to manufacture bronze—the utility metal of early civilization. With the exception of the large deposits in Bolivia, tin, like tungsten, is, on the basis of present known reserves, an Asiatic metal. Outside of the Soviet Union and China, for which few reserve data are available, world tin reserves are about 4.7 million long tons. Of this total, 3 million are in Burma, Indonesia, Malaysia, and Thailand; 0.75

million are in Africa in the Congo and Nigeria, and 0.20 million in other countries. Potential offshore deposits along the coasts of Indonesia and Thailand are not included in the reserve estimates. Soviet reserves are estimated at about half a million tons. China's reserves, judging by deposits in neighboring Asiatic countries and mineralogical associations, are probably very large. North America appears to be deficient in tin—U. S. reserves are limited to the Lost River, Alaska, district and are negligible; Canadian reserves are only 30,000 to 40,000 tons. South America is more abundantly endowed with tin than North America. Current exploration in Brazil suggests the possibility of large deposits; Bolivian reserves are still substantial. New exploration is in progress in the depleted mines of the famous Cornwall district in England, an historic source of tin since the time of the Phoenicians, and off the Cornish coast. Exploration is also in progress along the Australian and Tasmanian coasts. Significant new discoveries have been made in Tasmania since 1960.

Production of domestic tin ores in the United States has been sporadic with minor production from small deposits in Alaska, California, Colorado, New Mexico, North Carolina, South Dakota, and Texas. About 40,000 long tons of tin per year are imported from Malaysia, Indonesia, the United Kingdom, and Bolivia. It is used for tinplating, solders, bronze and brass manufacture. Because of the small number of large producers, tin is suited to establishment of carteles; currently, the International Tin Agreement is an important factor in tin economics. The present agreement, the second such agreement, involves six producing and fifteen consuming nations. It expires June 30, 1966. Negotiation of a new agreement was in progress at the close of 1965.

Tin, as cassiterite or tin oxide, occurs in vein and disseminated deposits associated with granitic rocks. Because it is hard and resists weathering and abrasion, cassiterite has been weathered from the primary vein and replacement deposits and concentrated in stream and beach placer deposits where it is mined by dredges. The 1964 world reserve index is about 25 years, excluding China. U. S. production and reserves of tin are negligible and the bulk of imports are from the politically unsettled Far East. Supplies are not secure. The major western hemisphere source—Bolivia—has not been able to sustain production in recent years. Congo tin production also has been adversely affected by political unrest. U. S. demand currently is met by imports, stockpile releases, and tin scrap (about 30 per cent of consumption). In the face of this bleak resource picture, the U.S.

TABLE X.3

DEGREE OF CONCENTRATION (GRADE) IN CURRENTLY EXPLOITED MINERAL DEPOSITS,
AVERAGE PRICE OF COMMODITY AS QUOTED IN THE UNITED STATES IN 1964, RANGE
OF AVERAGE PRICE 1960–1964.

Mineral Commodity	Grade of currently exploited deposits[1]	Average Price 1964	Range in Average Price 1960–64
1. Fuels			
Bituminous coal and lignite	[2]	$4.38/ton f.o.b. mines	$4.38 to $4.69
Crude oil	[3]	$2.89/bbl., at wellhead	$2.88 to $2.90
Natural gas	[4]	$0.159/MCF, avg. value at wellhead	$0.140–$0.159
Uranium	Minimum .10% to .20% 2 to 4 lbs./ton	$8.00/lb. U_3O_8 in concentrates that meet specifications, AEC contract price[5]	$8.00
2. Iron ore and Ferro-alloy Metals			
Iron ore	20 to 70% Fe	$10.65 to $11.05/long ton 51.5% Fe, lower lake ports[6]	$10.65–11.05 to $11.45–11.85
Manganese	15 to 55% Mn[7]	$0.72 to $0.77/long ton unit (22 lbs.) contained Mn, c.i.f. U.S. ports, not including duty	$0.72 to $0.90
Chromium	15 to 68% Cr_2O_3[8]	$30.00 to $31.00/long ton, dry basis, 48% to 50% Cr_2O_3, 3 or 3½:1 ratio; lump; f.o.b. cars, Atlantic ports[9]	not published or nominal
Nickel	0.9% plus[10]	$0.79/lb., f.o.b. Port Colborne, Ontario (includes 1¼ cents/lb. duty)	$0.74 to $0.84
Molybdenum	as low as 0.1% to 0.2% Mo (2 to 4 lbs./ton)[11]	$1.55/lb. in concentrates, 95% MoS_2, f.o.b. Climax, Colorado	$1.25 to $1.55
Vanadium	1% to 2% V_2O_5[12]	$0.31/lb. V_2O_5 in ores (f.o.b. mine or mill) nominal quotation[13]	$0.31
Tungsten	0.3 to 1.0% plus in the United States; foreign ores are higher grade	$22.00/short ton unit WO_3, minimum 65%, c.i.f. U.S. ports, duty paid[14] *	$16.63 to $23.86
Cobalt	0.2% to 1.5%[15]	$1.50/lb. f.o.b. New York or Chicago	$1.50 to $1.75

TABLE X.3 (Continued)

Mineral Commodity	Grade of currently exploited deposits[1]	Average Price 1964	Range in Average Price 1960–64
3. Nonferrous Industrial Metals			
Copper	0.5% plus	$0.324/lb., delivered; $0.320 net at Atlantic refineries*	$0.300 to $0.324
Lead	minimum grade about 3.5 to 5% lead[16]	$0.136/lb., f.o.b. New York*	$0.093 to $0.136
Zinc	minimum grade about 5% zinc[17]	$0.135/lb.[18] *	$0.115 to $0.135
Tin	minimum grade about 0.5% in lode ores, lower grade placer deposits can be worked	$1.5772/lb., New York[19] *	$1.0140 to $1.5772
Aluminum	bauxite containing 50% or more of Al_2O_3[20]	$0.238/lb., ingots*	$0.226 to $0.260
4. Precious Metals			
Gold	[21]	$35/troy oz.[22]	$35
Silver	[23]	$1.293/troy oz., average New York price	$0.914 to $1.293[24]
Platinum group metals	[25]	platinum, $88/troy oz.* palladium, $30/troy oz.*	$79 to $82 $23 to $30
5. Minor Metals			
Beryllium	[26]	$253/ton beryl, 10% to 12% BeO at points of export, or about $23/ short ton unit BeO[27]	$253 to $339
Magnesium	[28]	$0.3525/lb.	$0.3525
Mercury	about 5 lbs./ton (as low as 3 lbs./ton in open pits, as low as 8 lbs./ton underground)	$315/flask of 76 lbs., New York[29]	$189.45 to $315.00
Titanium	[30]	$1.27/lb., delivered	$1.27 to $1.60
6. Nonmetallic Industrial Minerals			
Asbestos	lowest grade rock contains 2% to 5% fiber	$100/ton average value[31]	$92 to $100
Fluorspar	minimum grade about 25% CaF_2	$45.57/ton, average mine value[32]	$44.49 to $45.57
Industrial diamonds	[33]	$4.23/carat (value of imports)	$4.16 to $4.82

TABLE X.3 (Continued)

DEGREE OF CONCENTRATION (GRADE) IN CURRENTLY EXPLOITED MINERAL DEPOSITS,
AVERAGE PRICE OF COMMODITY AS QUOTED IN THE UNITED STATES IN 1964, RANGE
OF AVERAGE PRICE 1960–1964

Mineral Commodity	Grade of Currently exploited deposits[1]	Average Price 1964	Range in Average Price 1960–64
6. Nonmetallic Industrial Minerals (Continued)			
Mica	[34]	1. Strategic, imported, duty paid, $1.50 to $25/lb. 2. Nonstrategic, imported, duty paid (a) $0.015 to $0.12/lb. for scrap and punch; (b) $2 to $5/lb. for uncut sheet 3. Scrap mica, North Carolina, $30 to $40/ ton	
Phosphate rock	15% P_2O_5[35]	$7.00/ton f.o.b. plant, average all grades. Florida land pebble*	$5.95 to $7.00
Potash	minimum 14% K_2O in beds at least 4 feet thick at depths less than 4,000 feet (United States)[36]	$0.39/short ton unit K_2O, standard, 60% muriate, f.o.b. Carlsbad, N. Mex.	$0.35 to $0.39
Sulfur	[37]	$23.50/long ton, f.o.b. mine*	$23.50[38]

[1] Figures on grades of currently exploited deposits are for general comparisons only. The grade of a deposit being exploited under the prevailing economic structure and with known technology depends on the size of the deposit, the scale of the operation, the location of the deposit, and prevailing costs and prices. Lower grade ores can be worked more profitably in large tonnage operations than in small operations and in more accessible areas than in remote areas. Domestic ores are more readily exploitable because of their location and such import duties as may prevail; they may be less exploitable due to high labor costs and high taxes.

[2] The entire body of coal is mined; marketability depends on composition (fixed carbon, volatile matter, moisture), physical nature (hard, soft), heating value (in BTU's), and utility as a raw material for manufacture of coke. Estimates of reserves based on minability under current economic conditions and with known technology are controlled by thickness of coal beds, depth beneath surface or nature and amount of overburden, and minimum tonnage recoverable. For bituminous coal and lignite, reserves generally do not include beds less than 2 feet thick but depth of mining and thickness of beds economically minable depend on mining methods.

[3] All recoverable fluids in reservoir are extracted and oil is separated from gas, water, sludge. Economic value of the petroleum accumulation depends on total recoverable crude oil, rate of recovery, gravity and composition of the oil, location, transportation facilities, capital investment, and other economic factors. In some areas, for example, a 1-million-barrel field might be economically exploitable while in other areas the same accumulation might be uneconomic.

[4] Value depends on chemical composition and heating value. Producer beneficiates raw gas to a more or less uniform product for transmission. Gas as bought by consumer has a heating value of 900 to 1000 BTU per cubic foot, less than 20 grains total sulfur and less than 1 grain hydrogen sulfide per thousand cubic feet.

[5] AEC contracts specify a price of $8 per pound of U_3O_8 in specification-grade concentrates through 1968; thereafter, the price will be 85 per cent of allowable production cost per pound plus $1.60, subject to maximum price of $6.70. Prior to 1962, price was based on U_3O_8 content of ores with price ranging from $1.50 per pound for grades of 0.10 per cent to $3.50

consumes 59,000 long tons of new tin per year (plus 23,000 tons of scrap) and demand is rising. The U.S. will have to protect its import sources, hoard its stockpiles, promote western hemisphere exploration, and develop substitutes. Fortunately, in its principal use, tin plate, alternative materials can be used.

Aluminum and bauxite.

The production of aluminum metal depends on reduction and refining capacity, which is a function of electric power-generating

per pound for grades of 0.25 per cent. Premiums were paid on grades higher than 0.25 per cent and a development allowance was also paid. Since 1962, average price paid by mills for ore of 0.25 per cent grade has been $4.05 per pound.

[6] Price also controlled by specifications as to impurities, principally phosphorus, and physical character; pellets are quoted at $0.252 per long ton unit Fe (22 lbs.).

[7] Most reserve estimates do not include material below 30 per cent manganese.

[8] Does not include potential laterite deposits containing 1 to 4 per cent chromium. Ores containing less than 44 per cent Cr_2O_3 must be concentrated. Low grade domestic ores containing 15 to 30 per cent Cr_2O_3 are not now being produced.

[9] For metallurgical purposes a ratio of 3 or 3½ to 1, chromium over iron, is preferred; prices are lower for lower ratios. Price of lower grade (44% Cr_2O_3) Transvaal ores is quoted at $17.50 to $19.00 per ton. Lump ores are preferred over friable ores and concentrates for metallurgical purposes and prices of concentrates may be lower. Friable ores and concentrates are preferable for chemical uses. Low silica content is necessary for both purposes. Ores sold for refractories contain 30 per cent Cr_2O_3 and are high in alumina.

[10] Minimum concentration depends on whether nickel is the only recoverable metal in the ore or whether there are other co-product and by-product metals such as copper or cobalt.

[11] According to American Metal Climax, Inc., Annual Report, 1964, the Climax mine in 1964 produced 13.7 million tons of ore and 47 million pounds of molybdenum. If all of the 47 million pounds was produced from ore mined in 1964, the average grade was about 3.5 pounds per ton.

[12] Vanadium is a by-product or co-product of other mining operations; very large domestic reserves of phosphate rock and titaniferous magnetite ores contain 0.1 to 0.3, and 0.4 to 0.45 per cent V_2O_5, respectively.

[13] Price per pound of V_2O_5 at the shipping point ranged from a high of $1.38 per pound in 1960 to a current low of $0.80 per pound.

[14] Short ton unit, 20 pounds, of WO_3, contains 15.862 pounds of tungsten.

[15] Cobalt is a by-product metal produced mostly in copper and nickel mining operations. In the past high-grade cobalt ores contained up to 5 per cent cobalt. There are large reserves containing 0.07 to 0.1 per cent cobalt.

[16] In most operations lead is one of several metals recovered. U.S. ores average slightly more than 4 per cent combined lead and zinc, and less than 1 ounce of silver. Major foreign producers are working ores containing 10 to 30 per cent combined lead and zinc and 5 to 7 ounces in silver.

[17] In most operations zinc is one of several metals recovered. U.S. ores average slightly more than 4 per cent combined lead and zinc, and less than 1 ounce of silver. Major foreign producers are working ores containing 10 to 30 per cent combined lead and zinc and 5 to 7 ounces in silver.

[18] Weighted price to include all grades. Quotation generally is given as Prime Western, East St. Louis or Prime Western, Delivered, with the Delivered quotation $0.005 higher.

[19] Prices controlled by International Tin Agreement.

[20] Resources containing as little as 30% Al_2O_3 are potential ores.

[21] Gold recovered from placer mining, lode mining, and as by-product of base metal mining. Domestic placers average about 30 cents per cubic yard in gold. Gold is recovered from copper ores at Bingham, Utah, where it averages 35 cents per ton. The lowest grade lode ores now minable in underground mines contain about 0.4 to 0.5 ounces per ton. In a new open pit gold mine in Nevada (Mining Engineering, 1965, p. 139) average grade of 11 million ton orebody is 0.32 ounces and cut-off grade is 0.06 ounces.

capability. At the present time, the principal raw material is bauxite. In a sense, aluminum is to bauxite what steel is to iron ore. Bauxite, however, is not the only raw material that can be used to manufacture aluminum; recently, pilot plants have utilized high-alumina clays to make aluminum on a competitive basis. High-alumina igneous rocks

---

[22] U.S. price fixed in 1934 by Presidential proclamation.

[23] About two-thirds of domestic production is as a by-product of base metal mining. In large scale porphyry-copper mining operations, silver is recovered from ores containing as little as 0.02 to 0.11 ounces per ton. Most silver-bearing lead ores contain more silver than these copper ores. Silver content ranges from a few ounces to more than 20 ounces per ton in some high-grade deposits. Straight silver ores currently mined contain a minimum of about 10 ounces per ton.

[24] U.S. Treasury buying price fixed at $0.905 from July 1946 to May 1963 when buying ceased.

[25] Produced from platinum placers and as a by-product of nickel mining operations. Canadian nickel ores contain 0.03 to 0.06 ounces of platinum. Platinum placers containing an average of about 0.01 ounce per cubic yard can be worked in large volumes.

[26] Small tonnages in pegmatite deposits must contain 0.5 to 1 percent beryl and a minimum of 100 tons. Beryl may be one of several mineral products. Minimum amount of beryl that can be economically recovered also depends on size of beryl crystals. Crystals less than one inch long cannot be efficiently recovered by hand cobbing. Reserves in potentially commercial non-pegmatite deposits are estimated on the basis of a minimum of 0.5 percent BeO.

[27] Domestic prices concealed but substantially higher.

[28] Sea water contains about 0.13 per cent magnesium. Rock sources including dolomite, magnesite, dunite, and brucite contain from 20 per cent to 69 per cent MgO.

[29] Price increased sharply in 1965 to $700–$725 per flask at mid-year; stockpile mercury sold at $685 per flask.

[30] Ilmenite and rutile concentrates are produced as principal products, co-products, or by-products, from heavy mineral sands containing as low as 3 to 4 percent heavy minerals. Ilmenite concentrates contain about 60 per cent TiO_2; rutile concentrates 94 to 96 per cent TiO_2. Rock deposits of ilmenite contain 35 to 55 per cent TiO_2 but concentrates are made from lower grade magnetite-ilmenite ores containing 15 to 20 per cent TiO_2 Titanium slags average about 70 per cent TiO_2.

[31] Price depends on quality and length of fiber, ranging from $1,400 to $1,500 per short ton for the longest, best quality crude fibers to $40 per short ton for the shortest fibers.

[32] Acid grade (97% CaF_2), average mine value per ton, $49.42; metallurgical grade (60 to 72½% CaF_2), average mine value per ton, $26.23.

[33] Currently mined diamond pipe ores average about one part diamond to 15 million parts of waste. South-West African placer deposits are lower in grade but the ratio of gems to industrial diamonds is much higher and mining costs are lower.

[34] Mica "books" are recovered from pegmatites where they generally occur in irregular zones in small tonnages; commonly one or more other saleable minerals are produced in the mining operation. Depending on quality of mica, and depending on other mineral products, a minable mica-bearing pegmatite zone may contain from about 0.5 to 10 per cent or more mica, depending on quality, mining methods and processing techniques. Recoveries by hand sorting are 25 to 40 per cent of contained mica (Page et al., 1953, pp. 35–36).

[35] Concentrated to meet specifications; minimum 31 per cent P_2O_5 for acid grade rock, minimum 24 per cent P_2O_5 for furnace grade rock.

[36] Bedded deposits averaging 5 to 10 percent K_2O are or have been worked in Europe. Brine deposits from which potash salts are recovered along with other salts contain 2 to 3 per cent K_2O.

[37] Sulfur-bearing rock in currently exploited salt dome caps commonly contains 15 to 40 per cent sulfur and may be 25 to 300 feet thick. Sedimentary deposits in Poland are in beds 15 to 80 feet thick containing an average of 20 to 30 per cent sulfur with overburden ranging from 30 to 550 feet thick. Sicilian lenticular deposits average 25 per cent sulfur. The mineral pyrite contains 53.4 per cent sulfur. The mineral anhydrite contains 58.8 per cent SO_3, or about 24 per cent sulfur. Natural gas (sour gas) from which sulfur is recovered contains from less than 1 to almost 50 per cent H_2S. Coals in the United States contain 2 to 3 per cent sulfur.

[38] Posted price, discounted during 1960–64 period of oversupply.

° Prices higher in mid-1965.

TABLE X.4

RESERVES AND POTENTIAL RESERVES OF BAUXITE[1]

(Williams, 1965a, Table 2, p. 7).

(Million Tons)

Country	Reserves[2]	Potential
North America:		
United States	50	300
Jamaica	600	400
Dominican Republic and Haiti	85	40
Costa Rica and Panama	—	80
Total	735	820
South America:		
British Guiana	150	1,000
Surinam	250	150
French Guiana	—	70
Brazil and Venezuela	40	300
Total	440	1,520
Europe:		
France	70	190
Italy	25	—
Yugoslavia	290	—
Greece	85	—
Hungary	300	100
U.S.S.R.	100	—
Rumania, Austria, Spain, and Norway	30	30
Total	900	320
Africa:		
Republic of Guinea	1,100	2,400
Ghana	250	—
Cameroon	—	980
Nyasaland	—	60
Malagasy Republic, Mozambique, Morocco, Angola, and Rhodesia	—	60
Total	1,350	3,500
Asia:		
China (mainland)	150	1,000
India	60	200
Indonesia	25	10
Malaya	10	40
Philippines, Sarawak, Iran, and Turkey	25	120
Total	270	1,370
Oceania:		
Australia	2,060	1,190
Fiji Islands, New Zealand, and Palau Islands	5	20
Total	2,065	1,210
Grand total	5,760	8,740

[1] Most of the estimates are in metric or long tons, dry basis; however, some estimates did not designate size of ton, wet or dry.

[2] Mostly measured and indicated reserves that could be used under economic and technologic conditions existing in 1963.

such as nepheline syenite, andalusite–sillimanite–rich metamorphic rocks, or aluminum sulfates, are also potential sources. Thus, the principal aluminum-producing countries (Table X.2) are industrialized countries with power-generating capacity sufficient to operate reduction plants and refineries. Bauxite flows from various parts of the world to the refining centers. These centers are mostly in the United States, Canada, France, West Germany, Japan, Norway, and the Soviet Union. Availability of power from hydroelectric, natural gas, or coal and lignite fueled facilities is the controlling factor in plant location. It takes about four tons of bauxite to make two tons of alumina, which in turn yields one ton of aluminum metal.

The United States leads the world in aluminum production. The industry is composed of 23 plants operated by seven companies; the three largest firms account for 84 per cent of the production. The industry is well spread with 27 per cent in northwestern states, 27 per cent in Gulf Coast states, 19 per cent in southern states, and 27 per cent in northern states. Imports and exports are more or less balanced. Aluminum is consumed by the building industry, transportation industry, consumer durable goods, and electrical industry. World production is currently slightly less than world production capacity (Table X.2).

Bauxite, the aluminum raw material now used almost exclusively by the industry, is the product of tropical or semi-tropical weathering of aluminum-bearing rocks. It has formed on a wide variety of rocks including syenite, basalt, limestone, and schist. Major deposits occur in all continents. The large deposits in North America are in the Caribbean region in Costa Rica, Dominican Republic, Haiti, Jamaica, Panama, and in the United States. In South America, large reserves are in Surinam, Brazil, the Guianas, and Venezuela. European reserves include deposits in Austria, France, Greece, Hungary, Rumania, Spain, U.S.S.R., and Yugoslavia. Asian reserves are large and are mostly in China, Malaysia, India, Indonesia, Pakistan, and Sarawak. Deposits also occur in Iran and Turkey. In Africa, Cameroon, Ghana, Guinea, and Nyasaland contain most of the reserves. Australian reserves are large. The domestic industry in 1964 consisted of six companies operating 12 mines, with 97 per cent of production from Arkansas. About 93 per cent of production was for production of alumina; the balance went to the abrasives industry. In addition to domestic production of 1,600,000 long tons, the United States imported 10,400,000 long tons from Jamaica, Surinam, Dominican Republic, and Haiti. The 1964 world reserve index is 160 years. A comparison between reserves and potential reserves of bauxite is shown in Table X.4. In the future, other materials will substitute for bauxite in times of political disruptions in international trade or when improved technology gives local materials, such as high-alumina clay, an economic advantage in transportation costs. Although domestic reserves of bauxite (Table X.4) are only sufficient to support a 1964 U. S. reserve-consumption index of 4 years, major import sources (Jamaica, Surinam) are for the most part politically secure and located within the Caribbean area. Moreover, technology which will permit the use of high alumina clays to substitute for bauxite is well advanced and domestic reserves are enormous. Thus from a national security viewpoint, aluminum sources are not in jeopardy. Demand for bauxite (with over 90 per cent used as an ore of aluminum) is currently growing at 7 to 8 per cent per year. U. S. Bureau of Mines predicted a bauxite consumption of 40 million tons per year by 1980 with the increase in demand satisfied largely by increases in imports from Jamaica (Williams, 1965a, p. 11). If this 7 per cent rate of increase were to continue to the year 2000, demand would be 156 million tons per year and the cumulative production required to sustain it over the 35-year period 1965-2000 would be 1.7 billion tons. This is three times Jamaica's current reserves of 600 million tons. It seems clear that if the growth rate is sustained at such a high level, alternate lower-grade aluminum sources will be exploited well before the turn of the century. The aluminum scrap pool should grow substantially in the next two decades, decreasing the demand for new metal. Although there is a trend to build aluminum facilities near bauxite deposits in response to rising demand by raw-material-producing countries for the economic benefits of beneficiating and refining plants, aluminum refining requires large amounts of electric power not everywhere available. Investment of large sums of money in such facilities also demands a guarantee of economic responsibility and political stability. Thus, although the bauxite consumption of the U. S. might be somewhat reduced by construction of aluminum complexes in the bauxite producing countries, U. S. energy resources, availability of domestic low-grade sources, and the big U. S. market for aluminum will maintain a favorable domestic climate for an expanding industry.

PRECIOUS METALS

Gold.

It is not certain whether gold or copper was the first metal used by man—probably the honor belongs to gold which is found more commonly in the native state than copper. In any case, since prehistoric times gold has been searched for and collected by man. In nearly all cultures it has had value—that is, it could be exchanged for goods and services. As an internationally recognized standard of value, a large part of the world's gold supply is held by governments and central banks to provide stability for paper currency and as a medium for settling international trade balances (see section on Money and Minerals, pp. 210–218). A substantial part of the world's gold supply is used in the arts and crafts industries, particularly for manufacture of jewelry, and a substantial part is held privately as an inflation-proof investment.

Geologically, gold occurs in a wide variety of environments and deposits. Generally, however, it is associated with igneous intrusions of a granitic composition. Contact metamorphic and vein deposits are common. Gold, either as a native metal or in combinations with other ore minerals, occurs as cavity fillings, replacements, and disseminated deposits. Because it is chemically inert and very heavy, gold weathered free from primary deposits is commonly concentrated in placer deposits. Man, in his first seekings after gold, harvested the placer accumulations of many millenia and then turned to mining of lode deposits.

In the United States about 40 per cent of gold production is a byproduct of base-metal mining. About 57 per cent of production is supplied by two companies, 15 companies supply 35 per cent, and the remaining firms supply 8 per cent. There are more than 500 domestic producers. Production is from South Dakota (Homestake mine), Utah, Alaska, Arizona, California, Nevada, and Washington. Industrial use in 1964 was distributed as follows: jewelry and arts, 70 per cent; dental, 9 per cent; space and defense, 8 per cent; other industrial use, 13 per cent. From 1960 to 1963, the United States imported gold, mostly from Canada, Columbia, Philippines, and Nicaragua; the large part was in refined bullion in settlement of trade balances. Over the 4-year period, quantities ranged from more than 9 million ounces in 1960 to slightly over 1 million in 1963; imports were less than 1 million ounces in 1964. The greater part of the world's known gold reserves are in the Republic of South Africa, Soviet Union, Canada, Australia, and the United States (Table X.2). According to Ryan (1965, pp. 5-6), the world reserve of recoverable gold may approximate 1 billion ounces with 75 per cent in lode ores and placers and 25 per cent in base metal deposits. In the United States, the reserve of 20 million troy ounces occurs as 1 million ounces in placer deposits, 5 million ounces in lodes, and 14 million ounces in base metal ores—mostly large low-grade copper deposits. Minute amounts of gold are dissolved in sea water but no economical method of extraction is known. Gold reserves held in the various countries of the world and the International Monetary Fund are reported by Triffin (1964, Table 8) (see p. 218, Table VIII.2), and Ryan (1965, pp. 5-6). World reserve index as of 1964 is about 20 years. A reserve index for gold does not have the same significance as indexes of other metals consumed by and essential to industry in large quantities. Only a very small part of gold production is used by space and defense industries. Whether or not gold is essential to back up and stabilize currencies is a question in debate (p. 210). The conservative view is that gold is necessary for fiscal solvency and economic strength and therefore of great strategic importance. The U. S. reserve-production index is about 14 years. On the basis of 1963 *industrial* consumption only, about 3 million ounces, the domestic reserve-consumption index is 7 years. Gold scrap recovered from in-use metal amounts to about 0.9 to 1 million ounces per year. If 1 million ounces of the 3 million ounce industrial consumption is scrap, the reserve-consumption index (industrial consumption) is 10 years. As discussed in Chapter VIII, however, gold moves around the world on the tides of economic prosperity, flowing from countries with international deficits to countries with international credits. Thus, without increasing mine production of gold, or importing gold as such, a nation can augment its gold supplies simply by selling more than it buys—just as long as gold is used to settle trade balances. If the price of gold is maintained as 35 dollars per troy ounce by the U.S. Treasury, it is probable that domestic production will decline in the face of rising costs despite new low-cost open-pit production of about 1 million ounces from Nevada. In any case, it seems certain that all gold that can be economically produced at the present fixed price will find a ready market as monetary gold, arts and crafts gold, or industrial gold. Monetary stocks have increased at a rate of 1.3 per cent per year over the last 15 years in the face of strong and sustained private demand. Consumption will thus be determined by world production capabilities rather than by market limitations. One school of thought holds that gold production is and will be inadequate to expand monetary stocks to meet trade requirements (liquidity) and that major monetary system revisions are in order (p. 217). If there is an increase in the price of gold or a dollar devaluation, new properties will be opened and production will increase.

Silver.

Silver is a metal which in 1965 was suffering from a split personality. Expansion of its traditional uses for coinage on the one hand and for industrial purposes on the other have put a severe strain on production capacity and reserves. World production of some 250 million ounces per year plus accumulated stocks is not adequate to satisfy the predicted demand for coinage and for industrial uses such as photographic materials, silverware, electrical and electronic equipment, and alloys. There are 700 producing firms in the United States, but eight of them supply 60 per cent of production and the next 17 producers supply 24 per cent. Two-thirds of domestic production is as a by-product of base metal mine production. Principal producing states are Idaho, Utah, Arizona, Montana, and Colorado. In 1964, in addition to domestic production of more than 36 million ounces, the United States imported 48 million ounces for purposes other than coinage. Imports were mainly from Canada, Mexico, and Peru.

Silver is commonly associated with lead, copper, and zinc. Most silver occurs in fissure vein deposits where silver-bearing minerals fill cavities and replace parts of the host rock. The Western Hemisphere and Australia seem to be more richly endowed with silver than other parts of the world. Africa produces little silver. The Western Hemisphere is estimated to have produced about 80 per cent of the world's silver supply. Currently, North and South America and Australia account for about 75 per cent of world production. Most of the known reserves are in Canada, the United States, Mexico, Peru, and Australia; little information is available on reserves in the Sino-Soviet Bloc (Table X.2). By drawing analogies with other metals, Merrill et al. (1965, p. 17) estimated the world reserve index for silver at about 23 years and the United States reserve-production index as 16 years. In 1963, the U. S. Treasury consumed 111 million ounces for coinage (from Treasury stocks) and industrial consumption was 110 million ounces. The silver scrap pool provides 1.0 to 1.2 million ounces per year. Based on industrial consumption alone, the domestic reserve-consumption index is about 6 years. Industrial demand has been increasing at rates of about 2 per cent per year. Up until mid-1965, demand for coinage was increasing at 9 per cent per year and it was expected that over 300 million ounces per year would be required by 1967.

Merrill et al. (1965, Table 1, Figs. 1, 2) estimated a silver deficit of some 600 million ounces for the United States and the rest of the Free World between 1965 and 1967. United States demand in 1967

TABLE X.5
SILVER—SUPPLY AND DEMAND (MERRILL ET AL., 1965, TABLE 1)
(Million Troy Ounces)

	1955	1956	1957	1958	1959	1960	1961	1962	1963[1]	1964	1965	1966	1967	1968	1969	1970	Total 1965-70
United States:																	
Supply:																	
Mine production	37.2	38.9	38.2	34.1	31.2	30.8	34.8	36.8	35.2	37.0	38.0	39.0	40.0	40.0	41.0	41.0	239.0
Secondary production[2]	7.4	10.0	12.8	12.0	14.8	22.5	30.0	15.2	9.4	11.4	8.5	9.0	10.0	10.5	11.0	12.0	61.0
Imports[3]	67.7	68.0	60.4	73.9	63.7	56.1	48.9	76.4	59.1	48.0	60.0	60.0	62.0	64.0	66.0	68.0	380.0
Total	112.3	116.9	111.4	120.0	109.7	109.4	113.7	128.4	103.7	96.4	106.5	108.0	112.0	114.5	118.0	121.0	680.0
Requirements:																	
Industrial consumption	101.4	100.0	95.4	85.5	101.0	102.0	105.5	110.4	110.0	111.5	112.3	114.5	116.8	118.0	119.0	121.0	701.6
Coinage	8.2	31.2	52.0	38.2	41.4	46.0	55.9	77.4	111.3	202.5	235.0	267.0	315.0	———	———	———	817.0
Exports	4.8	5.5	10.3	2.7	9.2	26.6	39.8	13.1	31.5	94.0	55.0	50.0	45.0	45.0	45.0	30.0	270.0
Total	114.4	136.7	157.7	126.4	151.6	174.6	201.2	200.9	252.8	408.0	402.3	431.5	476.8	163.0	164.0	151.0	1,788.6
Supply deficit	2.1	19.8	46.3	6.4	41.9	65.2	87.5	72.5	149.1	311.6	295.8	323.5	364.8	48.5	46.0	30.0	1,108.6
Treasury stock[4]	1,929.5	1,980.6	2,014.2	2,106.2	2,059.9	1,992.2	1,862.3	1,766.7	1,584.3	1,217.9	692.5[5]	368.5	3.7	———	———	———	
Free world:																	
Supply:																	
Mine production	191.2	192.7	197.8	205.4	189.2	207.7	203.7	207.7	216.6	220.0	224.0	228.0	233.0	238.0	243.0	248.0	1,414.0
Requirements:																	
Industrial consumption	192.8	210.2	212.6	190.5	212.9	224.6	239.5	247.8	247.0	255.0	264.0	272.0	280.0	288.0	293.0	299.0	1,696.0
Coinage	52.6	56.5	84.2	79.5	86.4	103.9	187.1	136.4	172.2	260.0	295.0	300.0	335.0	———	———	———	930.0
Total	245.4	266.7	296.8	270.0	299.3	328.5	376.6	384.2	419.2	515.0	559.0	572.0	615.0	288.0	293.0	299.0	2,626.0
Supply deficit	54.2	74.0	99.0	64.6	110.1	120.8	172.9	176.5	202.6	295.0	335.0	344.0	382.0	50.0	50.0	51.0	1,212.0

[1] Estimated beyond 1963.
[2] Source—Handy & Harman, 1959–64.
[3] Excludes lend-lease returns.
[4] After withdrawals for coinage and commercial use, 1959–65.
[5] After deducting supply deficit only.

was estimated at about 475 million ounces; other Free World demand
in 1967 was estimated at 615 million ounces. According to the projections made by Merrill et al. (1965, Table 1), silver would not be
consumed by coinage after 1967. However, the United States acted
faster than anticipated and, in mid-1965, to avoid the threatening

FIGURE X.3

Free world silver production and consumption 1955–63 with projections to 1967
(not including the United States) (Merrill et al., 1965, p. 10, Fig. 2).

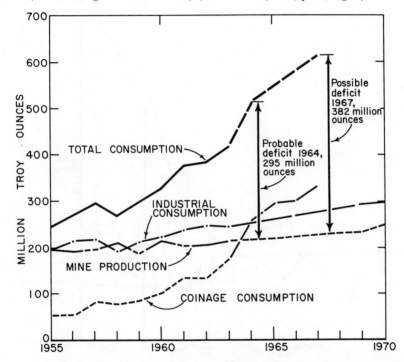

shortage, the U. S. virtually abandoned silver as a monetary metal,
eliminating or reducing silver in U.S. coinage (p. 214), and thereby
reducing the U.S. Bureau of the Mint's silver consumption from a predicted 300+ million ounces to a predicted 30 million ounces per
year—an effective cut of 90 per cent. But even with such an expected
reduction in consumption, world demand as of 1970 was predicted
as about 300 million ounces by Merrill et al. (1965, Table 1). This
forecast did not include any demand for coinage. A prediction by
Handy and Harman was higher and included 360 million ounces for

FIGURE X.4

U.S. silver production and consumption 1955–63 with projections to 1967
(Merrill et al., 1965, p. 6, Fig. 1).

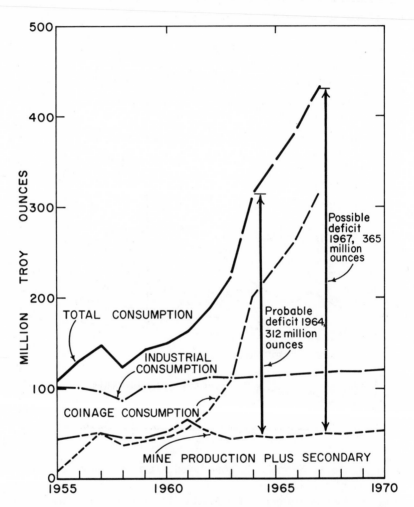

industrial purposes plus 60 million ounces for coinage (Chemical
Week, August 21, 1965, p. 26). Based on 1963 world production, the
predicted increase is at a rate of 9 per cent. World mine production
circa 1970 is expected to total 290 to 300 million ounces. The supply,
together with secondary sources of perhaps 20 to 30 million ounces,
will not succeed in meeting the demand. It seems clear that either

an intensified exploration program will turn up large new sources of the metal or some traditional but nonessential uses for silver will be abandoned (p. 384).

Platinum group metals.

The platinum group of metals, including platinum, palladium, iridium, osmium, rhodium, and ruthenium, are rather rare metals found in placer deposits and in primary deposits associated with the ultrabasic igneous rocks. In the past the principal use for such metals was in jewelry, but more recently chemical and electrical industry demand has increased. World production of about 2 million ounces per year comes from the Soviet Union, Republic of South Africa, Canada, and Colombia. United States production from placer mines in Alaska and from gold and copper refineries is small. About 1.2 million ounces were imported in 1964. Sources for imports in 1960-64 were United Kingdom, Soviet Union, Canada, and Switzerland, but not all of these areas contain platinum mines—platinum was recovered in metallurgical operations. Known reserves are in U.S.S.R., Republic of South Africa, Canada, and Colombia (Table X.2). World reserves on the order of 40 million ounces indicate a reserve index (1964) of 20 years. U. S. reserves are small. Total domestic production, including mine production and refinery production in 1963 (the most recent year for which firm statistics are available) is about 250,000 ounces, of which 117,000 ounces was secondary metal from old scrap. Imports were 1.3 million ounces in 1963. Total consumption (excluding exports and stocks) was about 1 million ounces. Although the high price of platinum discourages large volume use, approximately 75 per cent of consumption is for industrial uses (electrical, chemical). Substitutes, commonly less efficient, could be used in times of shortage for some uses, such as platinum catalysts. As long as platinum is available in world markets, U. S. industrial demand will increase.

MINOR METALS

There are a large number of metals classed as minor metals because they are used in small quantities or in limited industrial applications. Many, however, are vital in certain industries. In addition to those discussed hereafter the list includes antimony, bismuth, cadmium, cesium and cerium, columbium and tantalum, germanium, lithium, rare-earth metals, rhenium, selenium, strontium, tellurium, thorium, zirconium, and hafnium.

Beryllium.

Although beryllium became commercially important in the 1920s as an alloying metal to make special bronzes, it was not until after World War II that its special properties including high-melting point, lightness, and high strength, together with high neutron absorption, aroused industrial interest and sharply increased the demand and the price. Until the present decade, the only ore mineral of beryllium was beryl which was mined from pegmatites—coarsely and irregularly crystalline dike-like bodies associated with granitic intrusions. Distribution of beryl in pegmatites is extremely erratic so that estimates of reserves have been uncertain. Pegmatites occur throughout the world, but tonnages of beryl are small and the deposits do not lend themselves to large-scale mining operations. Recent exploration has revealed the existence of beryllium concentrations in volcanic tuff, igneous rocks, and in contact metamorphic deposits in western states, Labrador, and Mexico—mostly in the minerals bertrandite, phenacite, and barylite. Reserves outside of the United States are unknown.

United States production currently is small. Sporadic small operations during the period 1953-62 produced about 4,500 tons of beryl from South Dakota, Colorado, New Mexico, Maine, New Hampshire, Connecticut, Georgia, Arizona, Wyoming, North Carolina, Maryland, New York, Idaho, and Virginia, ranked in order of production. In 1964, about 6,000 tons of beryl were imported, mostly from Brazil, Argentina, Uganda, and India. Some 22 foreign countries produce beryl in varying amounts—principal producers are Brazil, Argentina, Mozambique, Soviet Union, Uganda, Malagasy Republic, Southern Rhodesia, and India. Due to lack of data on reserves, it is not possible to estimate a reserve index.

The special properties of beryllium promise a bright space-age future in special industrial applications if consumers can be assured of adequacy of supplies over the long term. Pegmatite deposits alone cannot give this assurance. The future of beryllium depends on discovery and successful exploration of low-grade nonpegmatite deposits of significant tonnage. Knowledge of such deposits is still sketchy, so no convincing forecasts of the likelihood of development of sufficient tonnages to guarantee an expanded market can be made. Evaluation

of nonpegmatite deposits in Utah is encouraging and indicates reserves on the order of several million tons of ore containing at least
1 per cent of beryllium oxide. Abundant supplies of other metals
which can substitute for beryllium in many applications—magnesium, zirconium, aluminum, and stainless steel—suggest that beryllium will not develop a large market as a structural metal.

Magnesium.

Sources of magnesium are plentiful the world over. The metal can
be economically extracted from sea water, which is the principal raw
material utilized in the United States. The prime factor in utilization
of sea water is electric power capacity at tidewater and availability of
calcium hydroxide as a precipitating agent. Other sources are brines
and the minerals magnesite (magnesium carbonate), brucite (magnesium hydroxide), dolomite (calcium-magnesium carbonate), and
olivine (magnesium silicate). Large scale desalination of sea water
will produce magnesium-rich effluent brines which will add materially
to brine resources (p. 373). Large deposits of magnesite occur in
Austria, Australia, Brazil, Greece, India, Italy, Manchuria, Soviet
Union, United States, Venezuela, and Yugoslavia; brucite deposits occur in Austria, Canada, and Scotland. Dolomite is plentiful but little
is know of the reserves of magnesium-rich rock. Large olivine deposits
are known in Canada, Germany, New Zealand, Norway, and United
States.

The United States is the world's largest producer of magnesium
(Table X.2) and an exporter of primary metal as well as scrap and
semi-fabricated forms. Domestic production was concentrated in three
companies and four plants. Domestic production is used mainly as
structural metal or in alloys with aluminum. Abundant sources make
a reserve index meaningless. Magnesium compounds are used as refractories and in chemical and manufacturing industries. Current
world production is about 50,000 tons per year less than world producing capacity, with all producers reporting excess capacity. Over
the past 5 years demand for magnesium metal and magnesium compounds (including refractories) has been increasing at an annual
rate of 5 to 6 per cent. According to the U. S. Bureau of Mines
(Williams, 1965b, p. 13) total consumption of magnesium can be
expected to grow at a rate of 7 to 8 per cent per year, requiring 85,000
short tons in 1970 and 170,000 in 1980. The chief competitor of magnesium metal is aluminum; success in this contest will depend on

relative successes in lowering costs and prices in the two industries. Demand for basic refractories will increase at a high rate with increase in steel production and general acceptance of high purity MgO as a superior basic refractory. In the long-term future, magnesium enjoys a large advantage because of the enormous and commonly occurring supplies of raw materials.

Mercury.

Mercury or quicksilver, the only metal stable in the liquid state within the ordinary range of temperatures prevailing on the earth's surface, is just as lively in the market place as it is in droplets rolling about on a smooth surface. The price has ranged from about 80 dollars a flask in 1948 to the 1965 high of about 700 dollars per flask, with ups and downs over the period. The most recent price rise began in 1963 at about 150 dollars per flask, ·climbed to 1965s all-time high of about 700 dollars, and fell to a mid-1966 price of 350 dollars. European transactions were reported as high as 800-900 dollars per flask during the 1965 peak (Wall Street Journal, July 6, 1965, p. 20). The erratic price history is summarized in Figure X.5. Substantial quantities were sold from the United States stockpile in 1965. Without this stabilizing influence, prices would have risen higher.

Although mercury minerals are widespread over the world, large deposits are rare. Significant deposits occur in Europe, the Americas, and Asia. Africa and Australia are mercury-poor. Italy and Spain are the world's principal producers. The bulk of Spanish production is from one mine—the Almadén—which has produced for more than 2,000 years (p. 98). Italian production is from two large mines in the Monte Amiata area. Other major producers include China, Japan, Mexico, Philippines, Soviet Union, United States, and Yugoslavia (Table X.2). The domestic industry is small, with most mercury coming from California and Nevada and sporadic production from Alaska, Arizona, Arkansas, Idaho, Oregon, Texas, Utah, and Washington. There are about 50 operations which recover mercury at the mines but three producers supplied 82 per cent of 1964 production, two companies accounted for 11 per cent, and the remaining 7 per cent was distributed among some 45 companies. Although 1964 production was about 15,000 flasks, the United States also imported about 45,000 flasks, mostly from Spain, Italy, Mexico, and Yugoslavia. Principal uses are in electrical apparatus, electrolytic chlorine and caustic soda plants, special paints, and industrial and agricultural chemicals. It is difficult to find substitutes for mercury.

FIGURE X.5

The price history of mercury (E & MJ Market Guide, January 25, 1965).

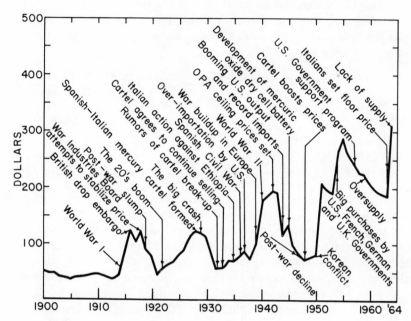

Geologically, mercury occurs mostly in shallow sulfide concentrations in volcanic regions. The main ore mineral—cinnabar—fills cracks, fissures, and breccia zones and is disseminated in host rocks such as limestone, sandstone, shale, or volcanic rock. For the most part, mineralization is erratic, with abrupt changes in grade of ore.

About half of the world's known reserves are in Spain and Italy (Table X.2) with the other half distributed in China, Yugoslavia, Soviet Union, Mexico, United States, Japan, Turkey, Philippines, and Czechoslovakia. The 1964 world reserve index is about 14 years. However, at the time of this writing (1965), demand exceeds supply, the price is at an all-time high, and marginal districts are being brought back into production. Based on consumption of 70,000 flasks per year, U. S. reserve index as of 1964 is only one year—mercury reserves known in the United States are only equal to about one year's demand, and of course domestic mines are not engineered with the capacity to mine and furnace all reserves in one year. About 10,000 flasks of secondary mercury were available in 1963; the amount fluctuates from year to year, but secondary metal provides a significant part of U. S. consumption. The United States is dependent on foreign sources, and to a large extent on European sources (Bailey and Smith, 1964, pp. 3-4). The known reserves of the Americas are not sufficient to supply U. S. demand for more than a few years. The discovery and successful development of new deposits is therefore a matter of great concern from a strategic point of view. Recent U. S. consumption was as follows (Shelton, 1965, p. 6):

1954-58 (avg.)	= 51,926 flasks
1959	= 54,895 flasks
1960	= 51,167 flasks
1961	= 55,763 flasks
1962	= 65,301 flasks
1963	= 77,963 flasks
1964	= 70,000 flasks

Inspection of these data shows that although demand was irregular with increases in consumption coming in surges and reflecting for the most part the requirement of new chlorine-caustic soda facilities, overall consumption in the 5-year period 1958-1963 grew at a rate of 8 to 9 per cent. If increases in demand continue at half of this rate, even the large quantities of mercury in U. S. stockpiles—about 200,000 flasks (p. 197)—cannot continue for very many years to make up the deficit between amounts available (from mine production and secondary sources) and the demand. Either production will have to expand at an equivalent rate or use of mercury will have to be curtailed (p. 385). New exploration programs will probably meet with success and add to the known reserves, but whether they will be successful enough to support an expansion of production of 5 per cent per year or more over a long term is dubious.

Titanium.

Titanium, the wonder metal of the 1950s and voted most likely to succeed by most experts, has lagged in the market place because of formidable technological problems. As a light, strong, corrosion-resistant metal, it comes close to combining the most desirable properties of steel and aluminum; it is an abundant element but costs of reducing and refining it have been high. The principal ore minerals are ilmenite and rutile; titanium-rich slags from smelting of titanium-rich iron ores are also a source. Rutile and ilmenite deposits are widespread and occur in Australia, Canada, Finland, India, Norway,

Malaysia, Sierra Leone, Republic of South Africa, and the United States. No information is availible on Chinese and Soviet deposits. Ilmenite is recovered by dredging of black sands and by hard-rock mining; rutile is recovered entirely by dredging of heavy mineral sands. In Brazil, ilmenite concentrates containing more than 1.3 per cent monazite (0.08 per cent thorium oxide) cannot be used legally as a TiO_2 source because of their potential as a thorium source. At this time, the principal market for ilmenite is in manufacture of titanium dioxide—a white pigment—rather than for metal reduction. Rutile also has other markets in welding rod coatings.

The United States is the principal consumer of titanium minerals and the largest producer of titanium metal and pigments (Table X.2). It produces some 900,000 tons of ilmenite concentrates per year (1963-64) and imports about 160,000 tons (including slags) from Canada and Australia. Domestic production of rutile is only 12,000 tons of concentrate; about 90,000 tons are imported from Australia and the Republic of South Africa. Titanium resources of the world are estimated at about 2 billion tons (TiO_2 content about 250 million tons) with 25 per cent of the total TiO_2 in the United States and 25 per cent in Canada (Stamper, 1965, p. 10). Rock deposits, usually with ilmenite in association with magnetite and basic igneous rocks such as anorthosite and gabbro, contain a much larger fraction of the reserves than beach sand deposits. Domestic resources consist of rock deposits in New York and Virginia and beach sand deposits in Florida, Georgia, and New Jersey. Based on present consumption of rutile and ilmenite concentrates, world reserve index as of 1964 is about 150 years. The U.S. 1964 reserve-consumption index based on an annual consumption of 600,000 tons of TiO_2 (ilmenite, slag and rutile) and reserves of 60 million tons of TiO_2 (ilmenite and rutile, but not including slags), is 100 years (Stamper, 1965, p. 10). Inclusion of slags and low-grade resources will extend this comfortable index substantially. There is yet no titanium scrap pool of any magnitude. The rate of increase in demand for titanium in its various forms, however, indicates that the reserve index will decline rapidly. U.S. demand for TiO_2 pigments is rising at about 5 per cent per year. Demand for rutile for welding rod coatings is growing at 4 to 5 per cent. Demand for titanium metal increased by an annual rate of 20 per cent between 1959 and 1963; it is expected to continue to grow at rates of 10 to 15 per cent per year. Consumption forecast by the U.S. Bureau of Mines (Stamper, 1965, pp. 12–13, 18), with modifications, is as follows:

1963	1970	1980
TiO$_2$ Pigment (TiO$_2$ in raw materials—ilmenite, rutile, slags; short tons)		
567,000 (not including rutile)	850,000	1,200,000
TiO$_2$ Welding Rod Coatings (mostly rutile, short tons)		
16,465	23,000	35,000
Titanium Sponge Metal (short tons)		
8,865	17,000	70,000

At these growth rates, the turn of the century will see a demand for nearly 5 million tons per year of TiO$_2$ for pigments (and other uses) and 0.5 million tons of titanium sponge metal.

SELECTED NONMETALLIC INDUSTRIAL MINERALS

The following discussion touches only on a few of the great variety of nonmetallic industrial rocks and minerals used in construction, chemicals, fertilizers, ceramics, refractories and fluxes, abrasives, insulants, pigments and fillers, and as gems and decorative materials. For a complete discussion of industrial rocks and minerals, see Industrial Minerals and Rocks, 3rd Edition, 1960, and U.S. Bureau of Mines Mineral Facts and Problems, 1965 Edition.

Asbestos.

Asbestos has many important industrial uses including friction materials, insulation, building products, plastics, and filters. Substitutes are possible in many applications but are not now economically attractive. Like some metals, asbestos, while widespread in a mineralogical sense, is rare in large commercially exploitable deposits. Most of the world's known reserves are in Canada, Soviet Union, and Republic of South Africa (Table X.2). The United States consumes nearly 25 per cent of the world's production but has only small domestic reserves of quality fiber in Vermont (1 million tons) and in the Copperopolis area of California (1 million tons) ; a large deposit of matted short-fiber asbestos occurs near Coalinga, California. Domestic production of about 100,000 short tons of fiber will probably increase as the new California deposits increase production. The United States imports about 700,000 tons of fiber, mostly from Canada (92 per cent) and Republic of South Africa (6 per cent).

Geologically, asbestos deposits occur as veinlets in massive serpentine (Canada, Vermont), in altered limestone (Arizona), and in metamorphosed banded ironstones (South Africa). Mineralogically, there are two varieties—serpentine asbestos and amphibole asbestos; value depends on length and softness of fiber, with a very wide range between long spinning fibers (up to 1,500 dollars per ton) and the short fibers (40 dollars per ton).

Although 93 per cent of the world's known reserves are in the major producing countries of Canada, Soviet Union, and Africa, many other countries produce small amounts, including Australia, China, Cyprus, Finland, France, Italy, Japan, Southern Rhodesia, Swaziland, and the United States. According to May (1965, p. 4), world reserve index is 25 to 30 years. U.S. reserves, as of 1964, of about 4 million tons of fiber could support U.S. consumption of some 800,000 tons of fiber per year for about 5 years, but these general figures do not separate demand for various grades of fiber, and are thus misleading. U.S. demands for high quality spinning fiber are met largely by imports from Canada. Although the domestic reserve index is low, location of large reserves and producing facilities in nearby Canada solves problems of supplies for strategic purposes. U.S. demand for asbestos is expected to increase at 3 to 5 per cent per year through 1975 with about 10 per cent of consumption satisfied by domestic production of low value short fiber asbestos. The trend could be changed by successful synthesis of asbestos; from an economic point of view it would be very attractive to develop a synthetic long spinning fiber. Exploration for natural deposits is at a high level; production facilities have been substantially expanded in recent years. During the last decade, world productive capacity has increased from about 1.6 million tons per year to 3.2 million tons. The forecast suggests that world demand will increase to 4 to 5 million tons by 1975 (May, 1965, p. 8).

Fluorine.

Fluorine, as fluorspar (CaF_2), as hydrofluoric acid (HF), and as synthetic cryolite ($3\ NaF \cdot AlF_3$), is essential in modern industry. In addition to its important use as a flux in metallurgical operations, fluorspar is the raw material from which hydrofluoric acid and synthetic cryolite are manufactured. The acid has many industrial uses; synthetic cryolite is necessary in the electrolytic process of aluminum production. The United States imports nearly 700,000 tons of fluorspar per year, mainly from Mexico, Italy, and Spain, and has domestic production of about 200,000 tons per year. Although domestic reserves are substantial, domestic production has been cut back because of failure to compete economically with foreign imports. In 1964, about 94 per cent of domestic production came from four companies in Illinois and Kentucky. Domestic reserves are in Colorado, Kentucky, Illinois, Montana, Nevada, and Utah. World reserves (Table X.2) are mainly in Mexico, the United States, and the Sino-Soviet Bloc. Other significant deposits occur in Canada, France, Italy, Spain, United Kingdom, West Germany, North Africa, and South Africa.

Geologically, fluorspar occurs as vein and replacement deposits in a wide variety of geological environments; residual concentrations due to weathering of vein deposits have been important in Illinois and Kentucky.

Based on 1964 production and known reserves, the world reserve index is about 35 years. However, this figure must be considered in terms of alternate sources of fluorine. The fluorine content of phosphate rock in the United States is estimated as equal to about 900 million tons of fluorspar (Ambrose, 1965b, p. 6). When it becomes economically attractive through price increases or technological improvements, fluorine can be recovered in the process of manufacturing phosphate fertilizers from phosphate rock. The only naturally occurring deposit of cryolite in Greenland has limited reserves (p. 146). U.S. reserves are sufficient to satisfy 1964 domestic demand (metallurgical and acid grade) for about 20 years and, due to a low level of domestic production and a high level of imports, the domestic reserve-consumption index is not declining very rapidly. The domestic reserve-production index is about 90 years. In view of large deposits in Mexico and Canada, substantial domestic reserves, and alternate sources of fluorine in phosphate rock, the strategic outlook is good.

Demand for fluorine will increase with expansion of the steel and aluminum industries and the fast growing demand for fluorine chemicals. The basic oxygen process for making steel—also gaining ground —consumes about 5 times as much fluorspar per ton of steel as the basic open-hearth process (see also Manganese, p. 295). Since 1958 the rate of increase in U.S. consumption has been at about 10 per cent per year. This very high rate of growth probably will not be sustained over the long term. A growth rate of 6 per cent if maintained until 2000 will result in U.S. demand for about 7 million tons of fluorspar per year. Secondary recovery of fluorine compounds is minor; there are no practical substitutes. As a result of the strong demand in the U.S. and in other industrial and industrializing nations, it seems likely that alternate sources of fluorine, namely phosphate rock, will contribute substantially to the market before the turn of the century. This possibility is heightened by the great growth in demand for phosphate (p. 342).

Industrial diamonds.

Except for minor production from South America, Soviet Union, India, Borneo, and Australia, diamonds are an African mineral. The largest production from other than Africa is an estimated Soviet production in 1963 and 1964 of about 2.7 million carats. Africa accounts for 90 per cent of world production, Soviet Union 9 per cent, and South America 1 per cent. African production was divided between the Congo (66 per cent), Ghana (7 per cent), Republic of South Africa (9 per cent), Sierra Leone (3 per cent), and seven other countries. The United States has no domestic production or reserves; nearly 12 million carats per year are imported from various sources, nearly all of which had an original African origin. Industrial diamonds are used in grinding wheels, drill bits, cutting tools, and dies.

Geologically, diamonds occur in kimberlite pipes, dikes, and sills and in placer deposits derived from erosion of primary sources. Kimberlite, a basic igneous rock, does not everywhere carry diamonds—16 out of 150 kimberlite bodies in South Africa contain diamonds and 11 have commercially exploitable concentrations.

The largest reserves are in the Congo in the Bakwanga area; the estimated 500 million carats is about 85 per cent of the known reserves outside of U.S.S.R. (Ambrose, 1965a, p. 5). Another large reserve of some 100 million carats occurs in placers off the coast of South-West Africa. Other countries with diamond deposits, excluding the Soviet Union, include Angola, Central African Republic, Ghana, Guinea, Ivory Coast, Liberia, Sierra Leone, Republic of South Africa, Tanzania, Brazil, British Guiana, Venezuela, Australia, Borneo, and India. The 1964 world reserve index is about 20 years. Diamonds were first synthesized in 1955 and production in the United States is at the rate of 5 to 6 million carats per year. About 50 per cent of

U.S. consumption of 14 million carats per year is now met by manufactured diamonds (5–6 million carats) and secondarily recovered stones (2 million carats). However, the U.S. remains dependent on foreign sources for larger stones (plus 20 mesh) which have not yet been successfully manufactured. U.S. demand for industrial diamonds is growing at a rate "greatly in excess of" the Gross National Product rate of 3.6 per cent (Ambrose, 1965a, p. 8). The demand appears sufficient and stable enough to support both an expanding world diamond mining industry and a growing diamond manufacturing industry for at least several decades. In case of interruption in foreign supplies, the existing manufacturing capacity and stockpiled supplies appear adequate until manufacturing capacity could be expanded to satisfy the entire demand. Because diamonds are low in bulk, emergency long-distance shipments by air are feasible and indeed took place during World War II. Strategic position is good.

Mica.

Mica is classed as 'strategic' and 'nonstrategic.' The term strategic is a left-over from World War II when grades of mica suitable for electronic applications were termed strategic, thus strategic mica is in sheets large enough and clear enough (free from structural flaws and mineralogical impurities) for electronic applications such as tube spacers, capacitor dielectrics, and insulators. Nonstrategic mica is used in sheets for electrical insulation and ground for fillers and coatings. There is no appreciable domestic production of the higher grade strategic mica; between 5 and 6 thousand tons are imported, mainly from India and Brazil. Domestic production of nonstrategic mica is slightly more than 100,000 tons per year, mainly from North Carolina but also from Alabama, Georgia, and from other pegmatite districts in New England, the Black Hills of South Dakota, and the Rocky Mountain states of Colorado, Idaho, and New Mexico. All sheet mica is recovered from mining of pegmatites—dike-like bodies of coarsely to irregularly crystalline rock mainly associated with granitic intrusions. Pegmatite scrap mica which does not meet sheet mica specifications is marketed as ground mica. Fine-grained mica suitable for grinding is also recovered from some mica schist deposits.

Domestic reserves of strategic mica are small; most of the known reserves of both strategic and nonstrategic mica are in India, Brazil, and the Sino-Soviet Bloc, mainly the Soviet Union (Table X.2). These countries are also the major producers. Other producers and areas with reserves include Canada, Malagasy Republic, Republic of South Africa, Argentina, Southern Rhodesia, Australia, Ceylon, and Mexico. Lacking quantitative information on reserves, a reserve index cannot be calculated. Because the United States cannot satisfy its requirements from domestic sources, a great deal of research has been done on synthesis of mica, building of sheets from splittings, and reconstitution of mica by deposition of fine flakes in a continuous mat. These products have successfully substituted for natural sheets in some applications. World supplies are probably sufficient to meet demands for several decades while research on substitutes and improved synthesis continues. Demand for mica by the electric and electronic industries probably will continue to grow with those industries but they are actively pushing into new ground and experimenting with new materials, so abrupt changes are possible. Success in synthesis and manufacture of built-up mica will, of course, affect demand for the natural mineral.

Phosphate rock.

Phosphate rock is the raw material for phosphorus used in agricultural and industrial applications. In the United States, 60 per cent of production went for agricultural purposes (fertilizer manufacture), 19 per cent was used industrially in manufacture of phosphoric acid and elemental phosphorus, and 21 per cent was exported. There are minor imports of low-fluorine phosphate into the United States, mostly for use as an animal food additive. These are mostly from guano deposits in the Caribbean region, Mexico, and the Pacific Islands. Domestic reserves of phosphate rock are very large and the United States is by far the world's largest producer—over 20 million long tons of phosphate rock in 1964. Production is distributed as follows: Florida, 74 per cent; Idaho, Montana, Utah, and Wyoming, 14 per cent; and Tennessee, 12 per cent. Known reserves are in these areas and in North Carolina where new reserves on the order of 2 billion tons have been discovered. Concern about food supplies for rapidly expanding populations have focused attention on agricultural productivity and the use of fertilizers. Phosphate is one of the prime crop nutrients. As a result countries throughout the world have expanded exploration for and production of phosphate rock. There is an economic advantage in locating deposits close to nitrate, potash, and acid supplies—the basic elements of a fertilizer manufacturing complex—and close to prime market areas.

TABLE X.6

PHOSPHATE ROCK—WORLD PRODUCTIVE CAPACITY, 1960–63
(*Chemical Week,* October 24, 1964, p. 115)

Country	Mine location	Owners, operators	TOTAL EST. MARKETABLE PRODUCTION (thousand long tons)			
			1960	1961	1962	1963
United States	(see Table X.7)	(see Table X.7)	17,500	18,600	19,400	19,800
Morocco	Khouribga; Youssoufia	Office Cherifien des Phosphates	7,400	7,900	8,500	8,700
U.S.S.R.	East Siberia; Kola Peninsula; Murmansk	Government agencies	6,500*	7,600*	7,600*	8,400*
Oceania	Angaur Island Australia	………… …………	1,870	2,000	2,200	2,300
	Makatea Island	French Government				
	Nauru Island Ocean Island	British Phosphate Commissioners				
Tunisia	Gafsa	Cie. de Phosphates et de Chemin	2,000	2,000	2,000	2,300
	Metlaouri-Refeyf; Kalaa-Djerda	Soc. Tunisienne d'Exploitation des Phosphatieres				
	Djebel M'Dilla	Cie. Nouvelle des Phosphates du Djebel M'Dilla				
	Ainkerma	Soc. Tunisienne d'Exploitation (Production due late 1964)				
Brazil	Recife	Fosforita Olina, SA Serrana SA de Mineracao Mineracao de Ruberia	860*	640*	550*	550*
United Arab Republic (Egypt)	Sefaga; Hamra-wein; Mine-Kosseir Esna-Eifu, Nile Valley (Sebaiya), Sinai Peninsula, Eastern Desert	Soc. Egiziana per l'Estrazione ed il Commercia de Fosfati (50% Gov't.-50% Italian-owned) Gov't.-owned	560	625	620	650

TABLE X.6 (Continued)

China (Mainland)	Yuman; Szechwan; Hupen; Kieweichow; Hunan; Kwangtung; Auhivei; Kiangsu; New Hailieh; Kanen; Anshan	Gov't.-owned	600	500	600	700
North Vietnam	Loakay	…………	530*	620*	700*	790*
Christmas Islands	Guano-derived rock (Exports)	British Phosphate Commissioners	500	700	500	650
Jordan	Ruseifa	Jordan Phosphate Mines Transjordan Phosphate Mines, Ltd.	350	400	450	480
Senegal	Theis	Cia. Senegalaise des Phosphates de Taiba	100	400	450	550
Algeria	Tebessa Djebel Onk	………… Soc. du Dejebel Onk	(Scheduled 560	for full 400	operation 400	1965) 250
Togo Republic	Hahotoe Akoumape, Lome	Cia. Togolaise des Mines du Benin	…………	50	200	570
Israel	Oron Eyn Yahav; Hameishar; Hor Hahar	Chemical and Phosphates, Ltd. American-Israel Phosphates Co. (Exploring)	220	220	220	300

[1] Other rock-producing areas of the world include: Republic of South Africa, South-West Africa (guano), France, Poland, Belgium, India (apatite).
* Production includes rock and apatite.

Phosphate rock or phosphorite (calcium fluorophosphate) is, for the most part, phosphate-rich sedimentary rock in which calcium phosphate occurs as nodules, pellets, or pebbles. Concentration occurs as the result of primary marine sedimentary processes and through subsequent weathering. In some countries, veins and igneous rocks rich in apatite are exploited. Residual deposits, guano, and phosphatized rock derived from leaching of overlying guano deposits are also commercial sources.

Major producers ranked in order of production include United States, Morocco, Soviet Union, Oceania, Tunisia, Brazil, United Arab Republic, China, North Vietnam, Christmas Islands, Jordan, Senegal, Algeria, Togo Republic, and Israel; minor producers include Republic of South Africa, South-West Africa, France, Poland, Belgium, and India. Large deposits have recently been discovered in Peru, Spain, and the Spanish Sahara. The bulk of the known reserves—more than 70 per cent—are in the United States and Morocco. At the 1964 world production rate of about 53 million long tons of phosphate rock, the world reserve index is 2,500 years so that even drastic increases in demand for crop nutrients will not result in shortages in any absolute sense. Large tonnages of phosphorite in the form of nodules on parts of the continental shelves constitute a big potential reserve. According to Mero (1965, p. 73), if only 10 per cent can be mined economically, the world supply will be increased by some 30 billion tons. This would increase the world reserve index by 500 years. He further estimated that, based on costs of delivered phosphate rock in California, deposits off the California coast can be mined competitively (Mero, 1965, p. 72).

In the United States, marketable production plus imports minus exports gives an apparent consumption of nearly 17 million long tons of phosphate rock in 1964. Domestic reserves are 14,500 million tons of P_2O_5 (Table X.2). Lewis (1965a, Table 1, p. 6) presented reserve data as 7,100 million tons of rock containing 2,100 million tons of P_2O_5 and 49,000 million tons of rock containing 12,000 million tons of P_2O_5; reserves contain an average of 30 per cent P_2O_5, potential reserves contain an average of 24 per cent P_2O_5. Based on 1964 apparent rock consumption, and reserves of 56,000 million tons of rock, U.S. reserve-consumption index is about 3,000 years. The U.S. is currently a major exporter of phosphate rock, exporting about 20 per cent of its production. The domestic reserve-production index is 2,800 years, based on 1964 production of 20+ million tons of rock. Demand for U.S. phosphate rock, both as a crop nutrient and as a result of industrial demand for phosphorus chemicals, has over the last 7 years grown at a rate of about 5 per cent per year, sufficient to double demand every 14 years. It appears probable that growth will continue at this rate, or a slightly greater rate, in the U.S. while world demand grows more rapidly. Lewis (1965a, p. 11) predicted a U.S. demand in 1980 of 12 million tons of P_2O_5 (about 40,000 million tons of phosphate rock). This means that between 1965 and 2000, with a 5 per cent growth rate, the U.S. will use up 2 billion tons of phosphate rock out of the 56 billion ton reserve; by 2015, in half a century, at the same rate of growth, over 4 billion tons, nearly 8 per cent, of the now known reserves will be consumed. If world demand is at a significantly higher rate, sea-floor phosphate nodules

TABLE X.7

PHOSPHATE ROCK IN THE UNITED STATES—PRODUCTIVE CAPACITY IN 1965
(Chemical Week, October 24, 1964, p. 119)

Company	Mines	Estimated 1965 total company rock production* (long tons)	Average P_2O_5 content, percent
FLORIDA			
American Agricultural Chemical (Continental Oil)	Palmetto	3,000,000	32
American Cyanamid	Boyette Orange Park Sidney	1,900,000	32–35
Davison Chemical (W. R. Grace)	Bonny Lake	1,550,000	32–35
International Minerals & Chemical	Achan Noralyn	5,000,000	31–35
Smith-Douglas	Teneroc	850,000	32–35
Swift	Watson Silver City	1,550,000	32–35
Virginia-Carolina Chemical (Mobil)	Clear Springs Homeland Peace River	2,850,000	31–36
Kibler-Camp Phosphate	Dunnellon	100,000	36
Camp Phosphate	Dunnellon		
Kellogg Co.	Kellogg		
Loncala Phosphate	Mona Minehead	Total soft-rock 35,000	
Soil Builders	Mincoll		
Sun Phosphate	Dunnellon		
Superior Phosphate	Dunnellon		

TABLE X.7—Continued

TENNESSEE			
Armour Agricultural Chemical	Columbia	90,000	25–26
Hooker Chemical	Columbia	750,000	25–26
International Minerals & Chemical	(Discontinued Tennessee mining)		
Monsanto	Columbia	1,000,000	25–26
Presnell Phosphate	Columbia	700,000	23–24
Tennessee Valley Authority	Knob Creek Franklin	200,000	23–24
Victor Chemical (Stauffer)	Mt. Pleasant	600,000	23–24
Virginia-Carolina Chemical	Mt. Pleasant	200,000	23–24
IDAHO			
Central Farmers (El Paso Natural Gas)	Georgetown	400,000	24–32
Monsanto	Ballard	500,000	24
	Hot Springs	(Not producing)	
San Francisco Chemical (Stauffer-Mountain Copper)	Montpelier	200,000	24
J. R. Simplot	Fort Hall Soda Springs	1,600,000	24
MONTANA			
George Relyea	Garrison	100,000	24
Montana Phosphate Products (Consolidated Mining and Smelting Co., Canada)	Garrison Phillipsburg	1,050,000	31–32
Victor Chemical (Stauffer)	Melrose	600,000	25
UTAH			
San Francisco Chemical (Stauffer-Mountain Copper)	Cherokee Vernal	600,000	31–32
WYOMING			
San Francisco Chemical (Stauffer-Mountain Copper)	Leefe	300,000	31–32

* Captively consumed or marketed.

will probably be exploited on a commercial basis in certain areas remote from other sources where economics are most favorable well before the turn of the century. Much depends on (1) whether the land-based producing capacities are expanded so as to prevent shortages, and (2) whether worldwide free trade continues without political interruptions. Davan and Houseman (1965) undertook a "plant food minerals forecast to 1980" and concluded that a new 10–12 per cent fertilizer growth rate has been established as a trend. They showed that the individual ingredients phosphate and potash have broken out and above the statistical growth trend established between 1947 and 1962, and predicted a 7.1 per cent world growth for phosphate between 1964 and 1970 and a 6 per cent rate between 1970 and 1980.

Potash.

Potash, like phosphate, is a basic crop nutrient and a necessary raw material for fertilizer manufacture. It is estimated that crops remove 5 million tons per year of K_2O from soils (Lewis, 1965b, p. 10). The need to increase world food resources has focused attention on potash deposits and set off a wave of exploration and development. The major producing countries are the United States, West Germany, East Germany, U.S.S.R., Canada, France, Spain, and Italy. About 92 per cent of domestic production comes from New Mexico; California, Utah, Michigan, and Maryland supply the remaining 8 per cent. Imports and exports are in near balance. Imports are mostly from Canada, France, West Germany, and Spain, a change from earlier years when France and West Germany were the principal sources. Some 94 per cent of domestic production is used to make fertilizer and the remainder is consumed by the chemical industry.

Geologically, potassium is a major constituent of some common rocks and also is widely dispersed as a dissolved salt in waters of lakes, rivers, and oceans. The principal deposits of soluble potassium salts occur as stratiform bodies covering wide areas in the great evaporite basins of the world. In the United States, the New Mexico production is from such deposits in the Permian basin. A large new mine in Utah exploiting deposits in the Paradox basin should increase Utah's share of the domestic market in coming years. Commercially important concentrations of potash salts also occur in brine deposits, such as the deposits at Searles Lake, California. The Maryland production is a by-product of cement plant operations. Other potential sources include potassium-rich volcanic tuff, glauconite, and alunite-bearing rocks.

The largest known reserves of potash are in the Soviet Union, Canada, East Germany, West Germany, Israel and Jordan, United States, France, and Spain. These include both bedded deposits and brines. Domestic reserves are about 120 million tons of K_2O in brine and 340 million tons in bedded salt deposits. The world reserve index is more than 5,000 years. Even a drastic increase in demand for fertilizer would not result in shortages on a worldwide basis. However, disruptions in free trade could cause serious problems in potash-deficient regions such as Asia, Africa, and South America. These are the areas with the fastest growing populations and have the most acute food problems. They constitute the great potential fertilizer market of the world. Forecast is for the present world production of 12.6 million tons of K_2O per year to increase to 20 million tons by 1980 (Lewis, 1965, p. 11). Growth rate, according to this prediction, is about 3 per cent per year. This rate will increase as developing nations modernize their agriculture. The U.S. consumes about 3 million tons per year of K_2O, with imports and exports more or less in balance. Domestic reserves are sufficient to satisfy the 1964 consumption for 150 years. Domestic demand has been increasing at a rate of about 5 per cent annually over the last 6 years, 2 per cent per year over the world rate. Davan and Houseman (1965, p. 86) predicted a higher world growth rate of 7 per cent between 1964 and 1970, and a rate of 6.3 per cent between 1970 and 1980 as a result of a projected fertilizer growth rate of 10 to 12 per cent. There appears to be little justification for consideration as a potential resource of the vast amounts of potassium locked up in insoluble silicate minerals such as granite. Desalination of saline water will produce potassium-rich brines and probably the greatest potential for change in the potash industry lies in the great predicted expansion in desalination and utilization of the waste effluent brines. These brines will be commercial sources of potassium well before insoluble silicate minerals (p. 373).

Sulfur.

Sulfur is a basic industrial mineral which well illustrates the difficulty in maintaining balance between supply and demand of mineral raw materials. In 1950, in the face of an impending shortage of sulfur, exploration was increased and new deposits were brought into production (Mexico). At the same time, new plants were constructed to recover sulfur from sour gas (Canada, France). The resulting success in increasing productive capacity caused a worldwide sulfur glut. Large stocks accumulated and prices fell. It was not until 1964 that rising world demand caught up to productive capacity, decreased inventories, and firmed the price.

Sulfur can be obtained from a number of different natural sources. Native or elemental sulfur deposits associated with salt domes occur around the Gulf Coast in Louisiana, Texas, and Mexico. These deposits are mined by the Frasch process—sulfur is melted by superheated water forced down a well bore and the molten sulfur is pumped to the surface. Some natural gas contains a high percentage of sulfur in the form of hydrogen sulfide. Plants for recovery of sulfur from such gases account for a large percentage of current world production. Another source is pyrite deposits where sulfur is recovered from massive deposits of iron sulfides. Large deposits of calcium sulfate (anhydrite and gypsum) are potential sources. They are only economically attractive now in areas lacking native sulfur and sour gas deposits. England, India, Austria, Pakistan, and Turkey are utilizing or investigating use of calcium sulfate resources. Sedimentary and volcanic deposits have been important in the past and are still exploited in some areas but, in general, the low-grade sedimentary deposits and small, erratic volcanic deposits are not commercially important under present economic conditions. Sulfur is also recovered from various industrial gases and wastes; more sulfur will be recovered from this source in the future as air pollution laws become more strict. It has been estimated that industrial gases contribute about 21 million tons of SO_2 a year to the atmosphere—if half of it could be recovered and converted to elemental sulfur, it would add 5 million tons per year to the world's supply (Chemical Week, December 12, 1964, p. 64). Another potential source for the future are sulfates in effluent brines from large saline water desalination plants (p. 373).

The United States is the world's largest producer of sulfur. Production is mostly from Texas and Louisiana where four Frasch producers supplied 76 per cent of the total production from 11 mines. The remaining 24 per cent came from companies recovering sulfur from sour gas, pyrite deposits, smelter products, and native sulfur mines. Some 85 per cent of production was used to make sulfuric acid for a variety of industrial purposes. The balance was used in manufacture of sulfurous acid for sulfite pulp, carbon bisulfide, and other chemical products. Large volumes of acid are used in treatment of phosphate rock to make superphosphate—about 1,900 pounds of sulfur is required to make one ton of phosphate plant nutrient (P_2O_5). About 40 per cent of total domestic sulfur demand is accounted for by the fertilizer industry. A major innovation in the industry has been the transportation and marketing of sulfur in molten form. The United States produced nearly 7 million long tons of sulfur in 1964, imported about 1½ million tons (from Mexico and Canada), and exported nearly 2 million tons. Major producers of native or elemental sulfur include the United States, Mexico, Sino-Soviet Bloc, Japan, and Italy.

Sulfur recovered from natural gas is produced mainly by Canada, France, the United States, Sino-Soviet Bloc, West Germany, and Mexico. Total 1964 world production of nearly 21 million tons of sulfur from all sources shown in Table X.8 is substantially higher than that shown in U.S. Bureau of Mines compilation of about 15 million tons of mined and recovered sulfur (Table X.2). Information on world reserves of the various sulfur raw materials is not available. United States sulfur reserves are summarized as follows (Ambrose, 1965c, p. 9):

	Millions of long tons
Salt dome deposits	200
Surface deposits	10–30
Sulfide ores	100–150
Coal	5,000
Petroleum	45
Natural gas	7[1]
Shale oil	50
Anhydrite and gypsum	enormous
Sea water	enormous

As Frasch deposits are depleted, dependence will fall more on sour gas sources, pyrite deposits, low-grade sedimentary deposits including gypsum and anhydrite, and perhaps brines. More sulfur will be recovered from industrial processes. Although over the long term, price increases are likely, economics will probably not change drastically because by-products or co-products are produced in utilizing some low-grade sources. Recovered sulfur refers to both the sulfur obtained

---

[1] Probably a low estimate due to the conservative method of reporting natural gas reserves.

TABLE X.8

PRODUCTION AND SHIPMENTS OF SULFUR IN 1963 AND 1964 (EXCLUDING SINO-SOVIET BLOC)

(Chemical Week Report—Sulfur—September 12, 1964)

Elemental	1964		1963	
	Ship-ments	Pro-duction	Ship-ments	Pro-duction
Frasch—				
United States	5,590	5,225	5,050	4,925
Mexico	1,850	1,750	1,534	1,466
Totals	7,440	6,975	6,584	6,391
Other elemental—				
United States	1,050	1,000	975	1,000
Western Canada	1,520	1,520	1,112	1,282
France	1,450	1,450	1,450	1,386
Other countries	1,050	1,050	1,125	1,050
Totals	5,070	5,020	4,662	4,718
Total elemental	12,510	11,995	11,246	11,109

Nonelemental	1964		1963	
	Ship-ments	Pro-duction	Ship-ments	Pro-duction
Pyrites—				
United States	350	350	350	350
Other countries	5,500	5,450	5,450	5,400
Smelter gases, other sources—				
United States	450	450	450	450
Other countries	2,600	2,600	2,500	2,500
Totals	8,900	8,850	8,750	8,700
Total sulfur all forms	21,410	20,845	19,996	19,809

as a by-product of natural gas production and from industrial processes.

World consumption of sulfur in 1965 (excluding the Sino-Soviet Bloc) rose sharply. Inventories were reduced as consumption exceeded production by more than 1 million tons. But although 1965 demand increased slightly more than 8 per cent over 1964, U.S. and world demand for sulfur is expected to grow at 3 to 5 per cent per year. At a 3 per cent growth rate over the 35 year term until the turn of the century, demand in 2000 will be nearly 60 million tons per year; at the higher 5 per cent rate demand will be 115 million tons per year. Unless there are unforeseen interruptions in world industrialization, demand at the turn of the century will probably be between these two figures. Frasch sulfur will supply a declining percentage of total sulfur consumed and the alternate sources discussed will be increasingly utilized. With an average 4 per cent growth rate, U.S. demand will be about 30 million tons per year at the turn of the century. The 200 million ton reserve of salt dome sulfur (Frasch deposits) known as of 1964 will have been exhausted by about 1990 if the current 5 million ton per year production grows at the 5 per cent rate. Of course, unless new salt dome deposits are discovered, the Frasch sulfur production growth rate will lag behind the growth in demand. As deposits are exhausted, production rates decline before production finally ceases altogether. The favorable prospective area for finding new salt dome deposits in the United States is limited to the offshore area of the Gulf of Mexico, more precisely the central and western Gulf. Chances of finding new on-shore domes is poor because the area has been thoroughly explored by geophysical methods. With continuing strong demand, conservation measures forcing clean-up of sulfurous wastes will become steadily more palatable.

OTHER MINERAL COMMODITIES

A number of mineral commodities and products—metals and non-metals—have not been discussed in the foregoing section. They include: antimony, arsenic, asphalt, barite, bismuth, boron, bromine, cadmium, carbon black, carbon dioxide (natural), cement, cesium and rubidium, clays, anthracite coal, columbium and tantalum, corundum (including emery), diatomite, feldspar, garnet, gemstones, germanium, graphite, gypsum, helium, iodine, kyanite and related minerals, lime, lithium minerals, natural gas, natural gas liquids, nitrogen compounds (natural), peat, perlite, pumice, quartz crystal, radium, rare earths, rhenium, salt, sand and gravel, selenium, sodium carbonate (natural), sodium sulfate (natural), stone (crushed stone and dimension stone), strontium, talc (including soapstone and pyrophyllite), tellurium, thorium, vermiculite, zirconium and hafnium. These can be grouped according to the value of domestic production as follows:

Group I (less than $10 million per year)	Group II ($10 to $100 million per year)
barite	antimony
carbon dioxide (natural) *	asphalt
corundum and emery*	boron
feldspar	bromine
garnet	cadmium
gemstones	diatomite
germanium	gypsum
peat	helium
perlite	sodium carbonate
pumice	
selenium	
sodium sulfate	
talc	
tellurium	
vermiculite	

Group III ($100 to $1000 million per year)	Group IV (more than $1 billion per year)
carbon black[1]	cement
clays	natural gas
coal—anthracite	stone (crushed and dimension)
lime	
natural gas liquids	
salt	
sand and gravel	

Value of arsenic, bismuth, cesium and rubidium, graphite, iodine, kyanite (and related minerals), lithium, rare earths, rhenium, and zirconium-hafnium is concealed because of a limited number of domestic producers. Domestic production of columbium-tantalum, *natural* nitrogen compounds, quartz crystal, radium, strontium, and thorium is negligible or nonexistent.

---

* Less than $1 million per year.
[1] Uses natural gas as a feedstock.

Students interested in pursuing studies of mineral statistics are referred to (1) U.S. Bureau of Mines Minerals Yearbook, four volumes dealing with Metals and Nonmetals, Fuels, Domestic Area reports, and International area reports, (2) U.S. Bureau of Mines Mineral Facts and Problems, (3) various materials surveys of the U.S. Bureau of Mines, and (4) annual review issues of the mining and mineral trade publications such as Engineering and Mining Journal, Mining Engineering, Oil and Gas Journal, Mining Congress Journal, etc.

CONCLUSION.

The various mineral commodities discussed in this chapter all present their own special problems of distribution, production, and marketing. Some illustrate better than others a particular geologic, engineering, economic, political, or legal factor.

Chromium, nickel, and tin illustrate the problems of few sources and world reserves under the control of two or three nations. Iron ore is an example of a large-bulk commodity that moves far in trade and which depends on an efficient transportation network. Manganese, from the United States point of view, is a war-sensitive metal; it is an essential metallurgical element and the United States, a major steel producer, has only low grade domestic sources. Mercury perhaps presents the best example of producer-consumer difficulties engendered by wildly fluctuating demand and prices. Lead-silver, uranium-vanadium, and copper-molybdenum illustrate the by-product relationship where production of the by-product is geared to the principal product and bears no relation to demand. Lead provides a good example of the role of scrap in the overall market for the metal. Tin is the cartel metal. Carteles, either private or government-sponsored, can only succeed where sources are controlled by a few producers.

Thorium is a good example of an element whose future depends on technology. Titanium is another such metal. Uranium is the element most closely controlled by government. Aluminum is an example of a metal whose production is controlled by cheap electric power rather than raw material location; it also illustrates how a new metal creates a market by substituting for other metals in their previously established uses. Magnesium is a metal where raw material supplies are not a problem—electric power and market control its production. Beryllium is a very useful metal which has remained limited in applications because short supplies give no guarantee of continued production.

Sulfur illustrates market changes brought about by multiple competing sources, and by cyclic shortage and glut. Limestone shows the importance of 'place value' in development of low unit value commodities. Petroleum provides an example of the problems of balancing imports against domestic production. The coal industry, more than any other mineral industry, is facing changes due to pollution control and reclamation legislation. Phosphate and potash are food-producing minerals responding strongly to runaway population growth. Industrial diamonds are a mineral commodity faced with competition from a synthetic product.

Demand for silver threatens to outrun world supplies and non-essential uses will probably be cut back. Gold is a metal closely tied to politics and monetary theory, and under the most rigid price control.

REFERENCES

Ambrose, P. M. (1965a) Diamond-industrial, *in* Mineral facts and problems: U.S. Bur. Mines Bull. 630, 9 pp.

———— (1965b) Fluorine, *in* Mineral facts and problems: U.S. Bur. Mines Bull. 630, 11 pp.

———— (1965c) Sulfur and pyrites, *in* Mineral facts and problems: U.S. Bur. Mines Bull. 630, 17 pp.

Bailey, E. H., and Smith, R. M. (1964) Mercury—its occurrence and economic trends: U.S. Geol. Survey Circ. 496, 11 pp.

Baroch, C. T. (1965a) Thorium, *in* Mineral facts and problems: U.S. Bur. Mines Bull. 630, 13 pp.

———— (1965b) Uranium, *in* Mineral facts and problems: U.S. Bur. Mines Bull. 630, 31 pp.

Chemical Week (1964a) C W report—sulfur: Chemical Week, September 12, 1964, pp. 71–94.

————(1964b) Sulfur on the spot: Chemical Week, December 12, 1964, pp. 63–66.

Davan, C. F., and Houseman, C. T. (1965) Plant food minerals: a forecast to 1980: Mining Eng., vol. 17, no. 12, pp. 85–88.

Dehuff, G. L. (1965a) Manganese, *in* Mineral facts and problems: U.S. Bur. Mines Bull. 630, 20 pp.

———— (1965b) Vanadium, *in* Mineral facts and problems: U.S. Bur. Mines Bull. 630, 8 pp.

E & MJ Metal and Mineral Markets (1965) Mercury—market guide: E&MJ Metal and Mineral Markets, January 25, 1965, pp. 5–20.

Engineering and Mining Journal (1965) Canada becomes a major moly area as B.C.'s Endako goes onstream: Engineering and Mining Journal, vol. 166, no. 7, pp. 80–83

Fuller, Varden (1959) Natural and human resources, *in* Natural resources, edited by Martin R. Huberty: McGraw-Hill, New York, pp. 1–28.

Hardy, R. M., Jr. (1964) The status of silver production: Address to the Northwest Mining Association, Spokane, Washington, December 4, 1964.

Harris, J. C. O. (1960) Steel, *in* Mineral facts and problems: U.S. Bur. Mines Bull. 585, 26 pp.

Holliday, R. W. (1965a) Chromium, *in* Mineral facts and problems: U.S. Bur. Mines Bull. 630, 15 pp.

——— (1965b) Molybdenum, *in* Mineral facts and problems: U.S. Bur. Mines Bull. 630, 12 pp.

Hubbert, M. K. (1962) Energy resources—a report to the Committee on Natural Resources of the National Academy of Sciences—National Research Council: NAR-NRC Pub. 1000-D, 141 pp.

(1960) Industrial minerals and rocks, 3rd ed.: American Institute of Mining and Metallurgical Engineers, New York, 934 pp.

Lewis, R. W. (1965a) Phosphate rock, *in* Mineral facts and problems: U.S. Bur. Mines Bull. 630, 12 pp.

——— (1965b) Potassium, *in* Mineral facts and problems: U.S. Bur. Mines Bull. 630, 11 pp.

May, T. C. (1965) Asbestos, *in* Mineral facts and problems: U.S. Bur. Mines Bull. 630, 10 pp.

Mero, J. C. (1965) The mineral resources of the sea: Elsevier, New York, 312 pp.

Merrill, C. W., McKnight, E. T., Kiilsgaard, T. H., and Ryan, J. P. (1965) Silver: facts, estimates, and projections: U.S. Bur. Mines Inf. Circ. 8257, 22 pp.

Mining Engineering (1965) Newmont brings in Nevada gold—the modern way: Mining Eng., vol. 17, no. 7, pp. 138–141.

Moulds, D. E. (1965) Lead, *in* Mineral facts and problems: U.S. Bur. Mines Bull. 630, 21 pp.

O'Brien, R. P. (1964) The economics, use and energy demand of the Southwest coastal area for fossil hydrocarbons, *in* Proceedings of the first intermountain symposium on fossil hydrocarbons: Brigham Young University Center for Continuing Education, Salt Lake City, October 9–10, 1964, pp. 11–37.

Page, L. R., et al. (1953) Pegmatite investigation, 1942–1945, Black Hills, South Dakota: U.S. Geol. Survey Prof. Paper 247, 228 pp.

Reno, H. T. (1965) Iron, *in* Mineral facts and problems: U.S. Bur. Mines Bull. 630, 25 pp.

Roscoe, S. M. (1965) Atomic energy developments and future uranium requirements as envisaged at the Third International United Nations Conference on the peaceful uses of atomic energy, Geneva, September 1964: Geol. Survey of Canada, Paper 65-33, 17 pp.

Ryan, J. P. (1965) Gold, *in* Mineral facts and problems: U.S. Bur. Mines Bull. 630, 11 pp.

Schroeder, H. J. (1965) Zinc, *in* Mineral facts and problems: U.S. Bur. Mines Bull. 630, 21 pp.

Shelton, J. E. (1965) Mercury, *in* Mineral facts and problems: U.S. Bur. Mines Bull. 630, 11 pp.

Stamper, J. W. (1965) Titanium, *in* Mineral facts and problems: U.S. Bur. Mines Bull. 630, 20 pp.

Stevens, R. F., Jr. (1965) Tungsten, *in* Mineral facts and problems: U.S. Bur. Mines Bull. 630, p. 15.

U.S. Bureau of Mines (1960) Mineral facts and problems: U.S. Bur. Mines Bull. 585.

——— (1965) Mineral facts and problems: U.S. Bur. Mines Bull. 630, 1118 pp.

U.S. Department of the Interior (1963) Supplies, costs and uses of the fossil fuels: Energy Policy Staff, February, 1963, 24 pp.

Van Royen, W., and Bowles, Oliver (1952) The mineral resources of the world: Prentice-Hall, Englewood Cliffs, N.J., 181 pp.

Wall Street Journal (1965) Mercury production is being raised in wake of price spurt to high: Wall Street Jour., July 6, 1965, p. 20.

Weeks, L. G. (1965) Industry must look to the continental shelves: Oil and Gas Jour., vol. 63, no. 25, pp. 127–148.

Weigel, W. W. (1965) The inside story of Missouri's exploration boom—Part I: Eng. and Mining Jour., vol. 166, no. 11, pp. 77–86, 170–172.

Wideman, F. L. (1965) Copper, *in* Mineral facts and problems: U.S. Bur. Mines Bull. 630, 34 pp.

Williams, L. R. (1965a) Alumina and bauxite, *in* Mineral facts and problems: U.S. Bur. Mines Bull. 630, 12 pp.

——— (1965b) Magnesium and magnesium compounds, *in* Mineral facts and problems: U.S. Bur. Mines Bull. 630, 15 pp.

Zaffarano, R. F., and Lankford, J. D. (1965) Petroleum and natural gas, *in* Mineral facts and problems: U.S. Bur. Mines Bull. 630, 36 pp.

CHAPTER XI

FUTURE SUPPLIES OF MINERALS

Introduction.

The problem of future supplies of minerals for materials, energy, and nutrients has been 'solved' by some who, proceeding from analyses of sea-water or average granite, triumphantly calculate the enormous quantities of various elements contained in a cubic mile of sea-water or granite. This is a wholly frivolous and misleading approach which contributes only a false sense of well-being and cannot withstand a thoughtful probe of the problem. For many commodities these values are not even quantitatively useful in the sense of an ultimate reference base because of the natural inhomogeneities of the crust, and even of large bodies of sea water (in terms of the less abundant elements) (Mero, 1965, pp. 24–25), and the diverse technologic and economic factors which govern exploitation of the various minerals and elements. To provide any meaningful answers to questions of mineral supply over the next two centuries (at least), the inquiry must proceed on an individual commodity basis and involve inventory of those rocks and fluids wherein the mineral or element is naturally concentrated to some degree. It must concern itself with the technologic problems of separation, extraction, and refinement and with the economics of primary production, substitutions, secondary sources, synthesis, and the urgency of society's need. Considering the breadth of the problems, it should be obvious that studies of future mineral supplies will be effective only if carried out by teams of engineers, economists, and scientists. It is in our best economic interest to search out and develop marginal concentrations before submarginal concentrations, and submarginal concentrations before spending our capital and energy on high-cost systems to extract elements from common-earth materials. The work required to search out the marginal concentration has scarcely begun; extensive geochemical surveys are needed before submarginal and lower concentrations can be located and evaluated (p. 14).

The 1964 reserve indexes, calculated by dividing known reserves by annual production or consumption (Chapter X), range from 14 years for mercury to over 5,000 years for potash. Are such indexes really helpful considering the reservations which must be made in projections of future demand, changes in economics and technology, and new discoveries? Providing that the reservations are kept firmly in mind, reserve indexes are helpful in that they provide a quick measure of known and available world inventories at a particular time—a measure of 'stock on the shelves,' in storekeeper terminology. The 1964 reserve index for mercury does not mean that the mercury shelf will be completely empty in 14 years. However, it does clearly indicate that sources of mercury are rather more of a problem than sources of potash, and that society will move down the resource scale into lower grade ores and unconventional sources much more rapidly for mercury than for potash. The reserve index, then, in one sense, is an index of imminence of change in traditional economic patterns.

The possible sources of future supplies of minerals can be summed up as follows:

1. Discovery of new deposits of much the same character as the ones which have been and are being worked (Table XI.1). These might be termed conventional deposits. They include:
   (a) Deposits which crop out in explored parts of the world but which have escaped discovery.
   (b) Deposits in the explored parts of the world which crop out at the present (or Recent) surface but are concealed by thick soils, vegetation, snow and ice, or relatively thin sediments.

(c) Subjacent deposits in the explored parts of the world which do not crop out because the present surface does not intersect the orebody.

(d) Deposits which crop out in the as yet unexplored parts of the world—the continental shelves and sea floors (see 3, below).

2. Development of deposits containing lower concentrations of elements than are now exploited but similar in character to currently exploited deposits.

3. Development of different kinds of deposits not heretofore exploited (e.g., oil shale and tar sands for petroleum; clay for aluminum; phosphate for fluorine; gypsum for sulfur; sea floor nodules for manganese, nickel, and copper; see 1 (d) above). Also, recognition and development of new kinds of deposits heretofore known (e.g., nonpegmatite beryllium deposits of bertrandite, phenacite and barylite).

4. Increase of scrap and waste recovery for both nondissipative elements recovered in original form (scrap metal in the traditional sense) and for converted elements in solutions and gases (e.g., recovery of sulfur from industrial gases).

5. Synthesis and manufacture.

6. Utilization of minerals or elements not now used by society.

7. Extra-terrestrial sources.

Discovery of new deposits.

'The significant conventional mineral deposits which are exposed at the earth's surface have all been discovered; therefore future exploration efforts must be directed toward finding concealed deposits.' This is a commonly heard assertion that is probably true enough to be valid and which certainly becomes more true with each passing decade. However, in some of the less-well-explored parts of the world, discoveries of significant exposed mineral deposits are still being made. A good example are the huge iron deposits of western Australia's Hamersley Range discovered in the early 1960s and now credited with an estimated 15 billion tons of reserves (Mining Eng., 1964, p. 98).

The search for new conventional deposits which are intersected by the present surface of the earth but concealed by thick soils, vegetation, snow and ice, or thin sediments can be successfully prosecuted by techniques already in the field or in an advanced stage of laboratory development. There are basically two geologic situations for consideration (Table XI.1). The first obtains where the cover is indigenous, the second where the cover is transported.

TABLE XI.1

CLASSIFICATION OF UNDISCOVERED MINERAL DEPOSITS

I. Terrestrial Deposits

    A. Exposed deposits not yet discovered.

    B. Concealed deposits cropping out at the present or Recent surface (Fig. XI.1)

        1. Concealed by in-place cover (indigenous soil, vegetation) derived in part from weathering of the deposit and chemically related to it.

        2. Concealed by a relatively thin unconsolidated transported cover of Recent age (alluvium, glacial outwash, snow and ice), and vegetation; deposit not chemically reflected in the cover except through subsequent migration of ions into the cover or through penetration by deep-rooted vegetation.

    C. Concealed subjacent deposits (Fig. XI.2)

        1. Covered subjacent deposits overlain by relatively thick fluviatile or marine deposits, volcanic deposits, or glacial deposits. These mineral accumulations cropped out in the geologic past. Indications of their presence could exist in covering fluviatile or marine strata in the form of placers or eluvial accumulations derived from the deposit when it was exposed.

           (a) Shallow deposits subject to exploitation by open-pit or conventional underground mining.

           (b) Deep deposits subject to exploitation only by deep wells (deposits which are mobile or can be mobilized).

        2. Pristine subjacent deposits never truncated by the earth's surface.

           (a) Shallow deposits subject to exploitation by open-pit or conventional underground mining.

           (b) Deep deposits subject to exploitation only by deep wells (deposits which are mobile or can be mobilized).

II. Marine Deposits

    A. Continental shelf deposits

        1. Surficial deposits on the shelves.

        2. Subjacent deposits of the shelves (only deposits which are mobile or subject to mobilization are likely to be exploitable).

    B. Sea floor deposits (only surficial accumulations or potentially mobile deep deposits likely to be of commercial interest).

In the first case, the orebody came into the zone of surficial weathering and processes of weathering and soil formation have altered and disguised the outcrop; chemical changes may have either dispersed or concentrated the elements making up the ore deposit (Fig. XI.1a).

Generally more than one exploration technique is applied. First, as in any exploration program, the general geology must be evaluated to assess the likelihood of occurrence of mineral concentrations. Regional geologic maps and sections, studies of the nearest outcrops and projections from them, and reconstruction of the geologic history of the region are necessary to the general evaluation of the possibilities for mineral concentrations. The geologist works by analogy, drawing on knowledge of mineral habitat and associations from elsewhere. For example, the presence in the area of ultrabasic rocks might suggest nickel-chromium or talc-asbestos possibilities; volcanic rocks and shallow intrusive rocks are a favorite habitat of mercury; fluviatile sandstones and channel deposits derived from a crystalline terrane might contain a host of placer minerals. With all of the possibilities suggested by a regional geologic study in mind, a number of different exploration techniques are brought to bear on the problem area which in this case is deeply weathered and covered with jungle, forest, or savannah-type vegetation. Aerial photography is the first step; the concealed ore deposits as a body of rocks different from the surrounding host rocks may present various kinds of *anomalies*. As physically different from the host, it may form a low hill or a swale, depending on its relative resistance to weathering as compared to the country rock. As chemically different, it may have produced a color anomaly detectable in colored aerial photographs. In the case of sulfide mineral concentrations consisting in part of iron sulfides, the oxidized part of the orebody is commonly marked by deep red or brown colors. Such iron oxide concentrations are called *gossans* and have long been recognized as ore indicators. The anomalous chemical character of the concealed deposit might also be reflected in the chemical composition of the soil, plants, and even atmosphere directly over and around the deposit. Detection of these subtle chemical clues is the mission of geochemical exploration wherein careful sampling and analysis is required to delineate a prospect. Concentrations of certain minerals produce a rock mass with electrical, magnetic, seismic velocity, and specific gravity characteristics different from surrounding rocks. These can be measured in a number of ways from the air or on the surface, and utilizing natural or induced electrical and magnetic fields, explosive or impact shocks, and the gravity meter. Infrared sensors which measure small differences in heat flow are useful in detecting areas where exothermic chemical reactions are taking place as well as surficial evidence of subjacent volcanic centers. Field instruments have been developed to detect certain elements by neutron-activation analysis. The product of the various methods selected is a prospect which then must be tested by drilling or by excavations through the concealing soil. The cost of such exploration cannot help but be reflected in the cost of the commodity produced. There are large areas of the earth that are covered by deep in-place soils and heavy vegetation. Mostly they are in warm areas of heavy rainfall—in the equatorial belt. Precipitation is also commonly high on the windward side of coastal mountains and in other temperate areas where prevailing storm patterns, oceanic currents, and topography operate together to create high rain and snowfall, and heavy forest cover.

In the second case, the orebody is covered by a transported material not derived from weathering of the mineral deposit (Fig. XI.1b). This

FIGURE XI.1

Concealed mineral deposits related to the present (or Recent) surface.

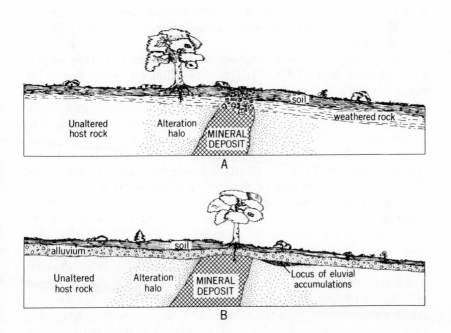

situation prevails in alluviated areas where streams have filled up a valley or built up a wide plain, in areas covered by a thin mantle of glacial deposits, and in areas perpetually covered by ice and snow. The deposit lacks topographic expression unless the mantle of concealing material is very thin. There is no chemical relation between the covering material and the deposit except that migrating fluids might carry chemical traces of the deposit into the concealing material, or deep-rooted vegetation might penetrate through the cover and draw nourishment from the anomalous mineralized material. In general, however, analysis of the covering material or vegetation growing on it gives no clue to the presence of the mineral accumulation. In this kind of deposit, exploration techniques are virtually limited to measurement of physical characteristics marked enough to be detected through the cover. Measurements of magnetic, electrical, and gravitational fields, and sensing of the most volatile substances that might be emitted from the deposit and escape through the cover—such as the mercury ion—are the principal prospecting methods. As in the first case, projections from regional geological analysis should be a part of the geophysical and geochemical program. In the final analysis the targets must be tested by drilling or other excavations. In 1964, near Timmins, Ontario, follow-up of an aero-electromagnetic anomaly disclosed a 60 million ton base metal orebody concealed by only 20 feet of glacial deposits.

From the deposits which crop out at the present or Recent surface but have been covered by relatively thin sediments or ice and snow, it is a short step to those deposits which at one time were exposed but which in the geologic past were covered by relatively thick glacial till, fluviatile and marine deposits, and volcanic deposits including lava flows and tuffs. Geologically, it is perhaps not logical to separate thinly covered deposits beneath a Recent unconformity from thickly covered ones truncated by an older subsurface unconformity. The difference is only a matter of degree. From the point of exploration and exploitation, however, they are two different kinds of concealed deposits—they are herein classified according to the nature of the cover rather than the deposits (Table XI.1; Figs. XI.1, XI.2). (Recent, in the geologic sense, comprises geologic time from the close of the Pleistocene or glacial epoch to the present.) With deposits which cropped out in the geologic past but were subsequently deeply buried can be grouped deposits which have never been exposed at the earth's surface but are the product of internal processes where the environment of mineral accumulation was in a part of the crust not subsequently truncated by erosion. These are together termed *subjacent deposits*. In the first kind of subjacent deposits, covered subjacent deposits (XI.2a) geological estimates of the thickness of the barren cover can be made rather accurately so that target depth to the un-

FIGURE XI.2

Concealed subjacent mineral deposits.

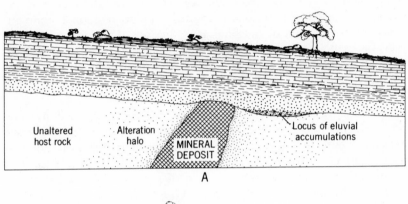

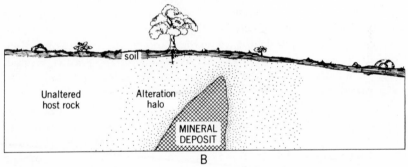

conformity is known. However, the target itself is conceived by geologic analysis and projections from outside the covered area. Indications of the deposit might occur in overlying sedimentary rocks in the form of fossil placers or eluvial accumulations, but probably would not be directly over the deposit. In the second case, pristine subjacent deposits (Fig. XI.2b) the accumulation or the halo of chemical alteration or geophysical anomalies associated with it might lie only a few feet below the surface. A little reflection on the third dimension will surely make clear that the present surface of the earth is a geologically fortuitous plane which, were it a few hundred feet higher or lower, would result in a very different geologic terrane.

An accumulation of minerals is a three-dimensional body. In some districts, the present surface intersects the top of the orebody and its richest parts lie below; in others, only the roots of the orebody are left—the bulk has already been removed by erosion and either recon-centrated as placers or dispersed.

The goal for the future is to find those deposits close enough to the present surface to be economically exploitable. If by chance, for example, a 20,000-foot oil test encounters low-grade copper minerali-zation at the bottom of the hole, it is dubious if the material could ever be exploited by shafts from the surface. The cost of sinking through miles of barren rock would be prohibitive. Only if large amounts of copper could be mobilized and pumped to the surface would the venture have possibilities for exploitation.

Fortunately, many kinds of deposits—the ones emplaced by rela-tively deep-seated internal hot water processes in particular—have associated with them far ranging clues as to their presence. The sur-face might not intersect the mineral body but it may intersect a halo of alteration associated with it, which, if properly interpreted, could lead the probing drills to the target. As previously discussed, clues to the deposits lie in the distortions of regional electrical, magnetic, and gravity fields brought about by the accumulation of minerals, in chemical, radiation, and heat anomalies, and in the creative imagina-tion of the geologist who understands how similar deposits formed. These clues diminish as the depth of the concealed body below the surface increases.

The most fruitful ground for future exploration is in mineralized districts where the nature of the outcropping rocks and controls of mineralization are thoroughly known. Here the third dimension and the subjacent orebody offer hope of major new discoveries. Discoveries outside of known districts will be based on geological analysis fol-lowed by geophysical and geochemical surveys and drilling programs. The procedure involves a progressive narrowing of the exploration area until individual targets are selected.

The geologist exploring for metals could well study the techniques of the petroleum geologist who has from the beginning been con-cerned with subjacent mineral accumulations. In some places he has profited by surface indications such as oil and gas seeps, but for the most part he has sought concealed targets outlined by geologic and geophysical analysis. He has looked not for oil but for geologic con-ditions which elsewhere have been proved productive of oil, and thus his knowledge has grown and been extended on the basis of past success and failure. First he knew only that oil occurred in certain kinds of structures—anticlines and domes. Then he learned about stratigraphic traps and reefs. He found that by building three-dimensional geological models he could find oil, and it is a tribute to his success that he is now probing for blind targets as deep as 25,000 feet below the surface. To build such models he had to understand complex facies relationships and structures within the sedimentary basin being explored, and for this he had to understand the geologic history of the basin. Of course, the petroleum producer enjoys economic advantages over the hard-rock miner in that his exploration system— the well—is also a production system, in that the mineral commodity he seeks is fluid and can be put into motion and brought to hand by effecting pressure differentials, and in that petroleum is the world's prime energy source so that demand is assured and price is relatively stable. It is also true that concealed metalliferous lodes offer smaller targets than oil pools, so the metal finder has a more difficult job. Moreover, he is for the most part dealing with dead or fossil accumulations where current temperature-pressure conditions are different than those in the environment in which the concentration occurred. Many petroleum accumulations are 'live' in the sense that the environment of accumulation was not greatly different than the prevailing geologic environment in the basin and permeability gradients have not changed. The analogy is not completely fair to the explorer for metals. It is true, however, that the metal miner is just now beginning to utilize regional geological concepts and to probe the depths cut by the drills of the petroleum geologist a half-century ago.

Development of deposits containing lower concentrations than are now exploitable.

The working of lower and lower grade ores is a logical consequence of the great volumes of minerals consumed by society, exhaustion of small high-grade concentrations, and improved engineering systems which enlarge capabilities to break rock efficiently and to move it cheaply in large quantities. It is also a dividend of continued mining operations because a fully amortized mine and mill is able to continue operations on a lower profit margin than that required to initiate operations. However, the mining of low-grade ores throughout the world is much more than a gradual slide down the resource scale—it is truly a *resource revolution* which has made available and will make available very large quantities of additional mineral supplies at little or very small cost increments (Table XI.2). Engineering capabilities to work low-grade ores do more than simply permit the operator to

TABLE XI.2

POST-WORLD WAR II REVOLUTION IN MINERALS TECHNOLOGY
(Knoerr, 1964) [1]

I. Mining technology

  A. Drilling, rock breaking, blasting, and explosives
    Improved drills and drilling methods; more cutting and boring, less drilling and blasting. New, cheaper, more efficient explosives and blasting methods.

  B. Shaft sinking, hoisting, loading, haulage
    Multi-machine shaft sinking jumbos, mechanical loaders, automated high-speed hoists. Mechanization of underground loading-hauling; trackless, rubber-tired, diesel-powered loaders. Digging wheels. Bigger payloads in trucks. Bigger shovels, draglines. Pipeline transport of solids. Improved scrapers, dozers, rippers, loaders.

  C. Ground support and stabilization
    Rock bolting, grouting, freezing, sand filling, chemical stabilization, underground use of steel, concrete.

  D. New methods of mining
    Chemical mining, deep sea dredging.

  E. Computers and data-processing
    Production analysis, ore control, ore inventories, operations research, reserves, mining economics.

  F. On-going research
    Rock breaking through application of heavy pressures, nuclear blasting, hydraulic cannon, electro-thermal rock breaking, underground jet-piercing, fuel-cell powered haulage equipment, hovercraft.

II. Mineral processing

  A. Automatic controls instrumentation
    Automatic feeding, analysis, detection, control.

  B. Pyrometallurgy, agglomeration
    Agglomeration, direct reduction, new smelting processes.

  C. Hydrometallurgy and flotation
    New flotation, leaching methods, ion exchange, solvent extraction.

  D. Grinding, screening, sizing, separation
    Autogenous grinding, new classifiers, screens, heavy media techniques, high intensity magnetic separation, electrostatic separation, ultrasonic cleaning.

  E. Crushing, breaking
    Hydroelectric crushing, dielectric breaking, electromechanical breaking, high-frequency shattering, high-pressure hydraulic shattering.

---

[1] For more details on developments, see original source.

chew into the previously marginal parts of known orebodies—they open up exciting new vistas in exploration.

However, the detection of very small quantities of metals in large volumes of rock presents problems in exploration and sampling not faced by prospectors of the past who sought and found higher concentrations visible to the naked eye. It demands sophisticated field techniques backed up by a laboratory capability sufficient to handle large numbers of samples rapidly and efficiently; in some ventures mobile laboratories carrying expensive and complex apparatus are necessary to give the man in the field the information he needs on the exploration site. We have entered an age when the prospector seeks minerals he cannot see. In 1965 Newmont Mining Corporation brought into production an open-pit gold mine near Carlin, Nevada. Possibilities of the area were pointed out in a U. S. Geological Survey report published in 1961. The gold is not visible to the naked eye. The 11-million-ton orebody averages about 0.32 ounces per ton but the company expects to mine rock containing as little as .06 ounces per ton of gold. This involves detection and extraction of an element that makes up less than one-tenth of one per cent of the mineral aggregate—and on a commercial basis!

The great uranium rush of the 1950s perhaps saw the largest numbers of people seeking the smallest concentrations of metal than in any other mineral rushes except the gold and gemstone rushes. The ores contained on the average 2 to 5 pounds of U_3O_8 per ton. But because the ores were radioactive, these small concentrations of metal could be detected by a simple instrument that almost anyone could operate—the geiger counter. Consider then the problem of finding such concentrations that are not radioactive. In the case of beryllium exploration, sensitive chemical tests that can be applied in the field have been developed and an instrument was designed to detect the element by gamma-ray activation and counting of neutrons emitted by the beryllium. This instrument—the berylometer—is not comparable to the simple geiger counter. It is expensive and requires a trained operator. The U. S. Geological Survey recently announced field tests of a 'silver snooper' which also employs the principle of neutron activation analysis. Similar refined sensors will be the rule in the future. Thus, it seems clear that the large low-grade concentrations of tomorrow—volumes of rock containing a few pounds of the desired elements in each ton—will be discovered and developed by teams of specialists backed up by sophisticated laboratories. Exploration for and development of such bodies will require large capital investment and payout period will be long. Revision of mineral law will be necessary to protect the mineral industry and the public. Political and economic instability is not conductive to such mineral enterprise and therefore it will lag in these parts of the world where governments are not stable.

There is also an important environmental consequence of development of large low-grade mineral deposits (p. 255). Most low-grade orebodies, unless the contained element has a very large value, can be economically developed only by surface open-pit methods. Such excavations, involving movement and disposal of large volumes of overburden and the removal and processing of large volumes of rock, scar the landscape, modify terrain and drainage, and present a waste problem in disposal of sediment and, commonly, highly mineralized waters. There is a strong trend in the United States and in other populous countries to make land reclamation a necessary part of mining operations. In Pennsylvania, a Bituminous Coal Open Pit Mining Conservation Act went into effect in 1964. Although tied to the coal industry in Pennsylvania, similar acts will surely follow in other mining states. Reclamation plans will affect mining methods and add to direct mining costs. However, some long-term financial benefits might accrue from such plans. For example, the reclaimed land can be restored for (1) recreation oriented enterprises—hunting, fishing, boating, swimming; (2) agricultural enterprises such as orchards, row crops, and pasture; and (3) for common commercial and residential development. Surface coal mine operators have recently organized a Mined-Land Conservation Conference within the National Coal Association. Coal miners have taken the lead in this area because by far the greater part of their activities are in the more heavily populated part of the country east of the Mississippi. Most of the large open-pit metal mines are in less densely settled land west of the Mississippi. However, modern phosphate miners in Florida and North Carolina must be conservation minded. In North Carolina, Texas Gulf Sulfur carried on extensive ground-water studies in connection with planning of their large open-pit operation south of the Pamlico River near Aurora so as to satisfy the state's Department of Water Resources that no contamination of fresh water would result from the mining operations.

Development of different kinds of deposits.

Through the sciences of mineralogy and geochemistry and accumulation of a large body of information from rock analysis, a good deal is known about the distribution of the various elements and their mineralogical associations. There are large quantities of valuable or

potentially valuable minerals and elements locked up in rocks and
minerals not commonly considered as source rocks or ores. For example, it is known that shale deposits in the Green River Formation
of Colorado, Utah, and Wyoming contain some 2 trillion barrels of
oil equivalent (in the form of a solid kerogen) in rock containing
10 gallons or more per ton; of this about 80 billion barrels is in accessible deposits in rock containing 25 or more gallons per ton judged
to be recoverable in today's economic structure (Duncan and Swanson, 1965, p. 9). Although a great deal of experimentation has been
done and is in progress to develop ways to economically extract this
oil, up until now the industry has utilized conventional sources and
pumped oil from subsurface reservoirs rather than mining and retort-
ing oil-rich rock. Sulfur is currently mined from salt dome deposits
by the Frasch method, recovered from natural sour gas, from deposits
of pyrites, from volcanic deposits, and from sedimentary deposits. The
sulfate mineral anhydrite which contains about 24 per cent sulfur is
not a conventional source of sulfur but is commercially exploited in
a few sulfur-deficient parts of the world. As conventional supplies decrease, plants to recover sulfur from anhydrite with production of
lime as a by-product will become more numerous. Sulfates might also
be recovered from sea water and used as a source of sulfur. The
mineral fluorite (CaF_2) is the world's commercial source of fluorine;
however, it is known that phosphate rock commonly contains 2.5 to
3.5 per cent fluorine. As fluorite reserves are depleted, fluorine will be
recovered from wastes produced in processing of phosphate rock to
make superphosphate fertilizer. High-alumina clays are as yet an unconventional raw material for aluminum manufacture, but successful
pilot plant development in the early 1960s resulted in the decision to
construct a new aluminum refinery in the southeastern United States
in mid-1965. Use of high-alumina clay will increase as bauxite supplies decrease. Sea-floor manganese-nickel-copper nodules and continental shelf phosphorite are new kinds of deposits and thus belong
in this unconventional source category; however, they are also deposits in unexplored areas and are discussed under that heading. In
a sense the sea is an unconventional source of fresh water. The great
assemblage of silicate igneous rocks contain vast quantities of minerals, some in rather high concentrations. Utilization of such rocks is
not now technologically and economically practical. However, in the
future such supplies will be *selectively* utilized. The selection will be
based on extensive exploration and analysis to inventory the highest
natural concentrations of this or that group of elements. The key to

success lies ·in advances in rock breaking, mineral separation, and economic recovery of several elements rather than one or two.

Also in this category are new kinds of deposits not now recognized. For example, it has only recently been recognized that beryllium occurs in concentrations of commercial interest in minerals (bertrandite, phenacite, barylite) other than beryl in pegmatite deposits. Increased knowledge of the geochemistry of other minor and rare elements will probably reveal concentrations in geological environments not now prospected for those elements.

Development of unconventional sources will come slowly in a world of free and open trade where minerals from conventional sources can move to markets; it will come rapidly if free trade is interrupted.

There remains a vast area of the earth—about 71 per cent—covered by water and commonly divided into the submerged continental shelves and the sea-floors. What does this submarine region offer for the future in terms of mineral supplies? And what about the sea itself—a great mineral-charged body of water wherein the minerals are already in solution and mobile? This question has recently (1965) been treated in a book by J. L. Mero entitled "The Mineral Resources of the Sea."

From what is known of the geology of the earth, it is expected that the kinds of mineral deposits found in continental rocks, including the submerged shelves, differ from those in sea-floor rocks. In very general terms, the continents are granitic and the sea-floor rocks are basaltic; according to prevailing theories on the origin of mineral deposits, prospects for mineral discovery are much greater in continental rocks. Unfortunately from an exploration point of view, the continental rocks of the shelves are not only submerged beneath the sea, they are also mantled by sediments. Exploration problems are therefore very formidable. They include all of the problems of finding concealed terrestrial deposits with the added problem of a water cover. Where the rocks of the shelves are sedimentary basin rocks, unaltered and underformed or moderately deformed, their mineral resource potential is largely in terms of oil and gas. Oil and gas exploration on the continental shelves is already well advanced. Weeks (1965, p. 132) estimated their crude oil potential as 700 billion barrels. Nonmetallic industrial minerals customarily found in sedimentary environments are too low in unit value to be exploited in such a difficult terrane except for those minerals which can be mobilized—minerals that can be melted or dissolved from the host and brought to the surface through a well bore (sulfur, potash).

Shelves composed of crystalline rocks rather than sedimentary rocks (or the basement rocks of largely sedimentary shelves) should be mineral-rich and good hunting grounds; along some continental margins they are parts of continent-margin orogenic belts (mountain belts) which have been truncated by erosion and submerged. Over the world such mountain belts have been the locus of extensive igneous activity and mineralization. Exploration for conventional kinds of metalliferous mineral deposits on the shelves—vein and replacement deposits, disseminated deposits—will be practically restricted to those parts of the shelves where the prospectable rocks are not mantled by sedimentary rocks and where they are swept clean of surficial sediments so that they crop out in the hydrosphere. Such exploration will probably start along faulted coastlines where mineralized districts can be projected out to sea; techniques developed in exploring these submarine extensions of continental deposits can be further refined for use in locating new submarine mineral belts. Some rocks of the shelf can be exploited by extension of land-based mines from which workings are run out under the sea. Coal is being extracted from such mines in several countries (England, Japan, Norway, Chile) ; some of the old Cornish tin mines extended beyond the coast.

Placer concentrations occur in the off-shore sediments themselves —either as a result of minerals carried into the sea by rivers or through drowning of previously formed fluviatile and beach placer deposits. Gold, tin, and diamond placers are now being worked or explored along the coasts of western North America, Indonesia, South-West Africa and Tasmania; iron sands are mined off the Japanese coast.

Beach deposits have been worked for many years for both heavy minerals concentrated by beach processes and for silica sand concentrated through removal of other minerals in a high-energy environment. Gold, diamonds, platinum, ilmenite, rutile, magnetite, tin, zircon, and monazite have been mined in beach deposits. The future trend, as these deposits along the strand are exhausted, is to move off shore. Other near-shore but submerged resources include shell reefs dredged as a raw material for manufacture of lime and cement, as an aggregate in stone-deficient areas, and as a road-base material. As existing supplies are depleted, reefs may be 'farmed' in artificially controlled optimum environments. Mero (1965, pp. 73-83) called attention to other continental shelf mineral accumulations including glauconite, barite, and sand and gravel. The growth of coastal urban complexes, exhaustion of nearby terrestrial sand and gravel deposits, and common shortage of hard rock (for crushed stone) in coastal plain areas point toward large-scale exploitation of marine sand and gravel deposits in the near future.

In addition to exploration for conventional deposits in the unexplored submarine realm of the shelf, there are new kinds of deposits which offer a commercial potential. These are manganese and phosphorite nodules which occur in some areas on the shelf and can be exploited by specially designed dredges. Shelf phosphorite reserves are very large (p. 342) but there is no shortage of terrestrial phosphate rock. The shelf deposits will probably be exploited only in areas distant from terrestrial deposits where transportation costs are a large part of the total cost of the mineral material.

Sea-floors present a different problem—deeper water and a geologic environment composed of soft sediments about 1,500 to 2,000 feet thick and underlain by basaltic rocks. The soft sediments include red clays, and siliceous and calcareous oozes. Only low-cost large-scale dredging could put any of these clays or oozes in the category of a mineral resource and the cost of such deep-water dredging is not known. Of considerable interest as a mineral resource, however, are concentrations of manganese nodules containing small amounts of cobalt, nickel, and copper. It is clear that these represent a very large and valuable resource that will be subject to exploitation by new marine technology in the near future. Mero's analysis (1965, p. 272) suggested that estimated costs are already in line with current prices. The sedimentary sequences of the ocean-floor and continental slope are possible petroleum provinces (McKelvey, 1964). The underlying basaltic rocks might contain deposits of metals such as cobalt, nickel, copper, chromium, and platinum, as well as talc, serpentine, and asbestos, but exploration and production problems are so staggering as to put such exploration ground well out of our 20th-century reach. Basaltic rocks are not generally mineral-rich on land.

The development of engineering systems capable of extracting minerals from shelf and sea-floor requires large research and development budgets. When successful systems are designed, and they seem sure to be, the capital costs of building such systems will require long payout periods. Marine mineral exploration, as indeed already demonstrated by off-shore oil exploration, will be carried on by very large and well financed private corporations or government companies. Recently a cooperative venture by the U. S. Bureau of Mines, Lockheed Missiles and Space Company, and International Minerals and Chemical Corporation was initiated to consider the problem of undersea mining and to develop appropriate systems.

In summary, the shelves and sea-floor will be able to supply some of the large quantities of mineral commodities needed in the future but they cannot solve the problem for many essential minerals.

Seawater contains between 3 and 4 per cent of dissolved mineral matter which, because of the tremendous volume of water (more than 300 million cubic miles) constitutes a very large quantity of mineral matter—about 166 million tons per cubic mile (Mero, 1965, p. 24). However, more than 99 per cent of the dissolved matter is composed of nine elements which, expressed in terms of ions, are chloride (54.8 per cent), sodium (30.4 per cent), sulfate (7.5 per cent), magnesium (3.7 per cent), calcium (1.2 per cent), potassium (1.1 per cent), carbonate (0.3 per cent), bromide (0.2 per cent), and borate (0.07 per cent). At the present time only magnesium, bromine, common salt, and fresh water are commercially extracted from seawater, although processes have been proposed to extract iodine, calcium sulfate, potassium, gold, silver, uranium, and deuterium. The future will see a gradual increase in extraction of magnesium and bromine and a very large increase in extraction of potable water. Large-scale desalination of seawater by nuclear-powered facilities designed to produce both electric power and potable water will also make it possible to recover large volumes of sodium, magnesium, potassium, and calcium salts. These potential by-products will ultimately affect conventional mining for salt, potash, gypsum, and sulfur in the same way that recovery of sulfur from sour gas affected the Frasch sulfur mining industry. To be able to produce potable, industrial, and irrigation water at an economically attractive price, such plants will have to produce a minimum of 50 million gallons per day, and probably more than 100 million gallons per day. The largest facility now being contemplated is a nuclear plant capable of producing 620 million gallons per day of water and 1,460 megawatts of electrical energy (Maxwell, 1965, p. 102). Capital costs of such facilities are very large. The smallest economically feasible plant will cost at least 200 million dollars; costs of a 1.5-million-gallon-per-day plant planned for the Los Angeles area are estimated at about 300 million dollars. Estimates of water costs from such plants depend on power sales but range from 20 to 30 cents per thousand gallons. According to one estimate, at least 20 billion gallons per day of desalination capacity will be operational by 1984 (Wall Street Journal, April 29, 1965). The 20 billion gallons of fresh water produced each day will result in production of effluent brines containing large quantities of dissolved mineral matter. The waste disposal problem will be simplified if some of it can be produced as by-product minerals. Dumping the extracted salts back into the sea will cause environmental changes wherever such dumping takes place and unless they are efficiently conveyed away from the plant intake will cause operational problems by increasing the salinity of the raw seawater. In the near future much of the capacity will be in small-capacity high-cost plants where recovery of salts probably cannot be made economically and disposal is not a major problem; however, with construction of very large plants disposal of the salts will present a major problem. Mero (1965, Table III, pp. 43-44) considered the production of salts from treatment of effluent brines from desalination plants and concluded that for the most abundant salts the production would be far in excess of the market. McIlhenny and Ballard (1963) calculated yearly tonnages of various salts available from a "seawater factory" handling 660 billion gallons per year (or about 1.7+ billion gallons per day) as 76.3 million tons of sodium chloride (NaCl), 45 thousand tons of magnesium, nearly 6 million tons of magnesium compounds, 2.5 million tons of sulfur, about 6 million tons of anhydrite ($CaSO_4$), over 2 million tons of potassium chloride, 184 thousand tons of bromine, 76 thousand tons of strontium sulfate, and 113 thousand tons of borax. They concluded that it will not be economical to extract elements with a concentration less than that of boron (4.6 milligrams per liter). Assuming a fresh-water extraction efficiency of 25 per cent, this "factory" would be smaller than the largest facility now contemplated (Maxwell, 1965, p. 102).

Increased recovery from scrap and waste.

The minerals that are extracted from the earth fall into two broad classes— (1) those that are used by society in such a way that they are dissipated and dispersed, and (2) those that are not dissipated but are manufactured or converted into durable products which may be used as a secondary source of mineral materials upon termination of the original product life. Dissipative minerals include the mineral fuels which are converted to energy and mineral raw materials for the metallurgical, chemical, and fertilizer industries which are, for the most part, changed in form and dispersed in a number of chemical processes and products. The burning of coal and petroleum for heat energy destroys the mineral fuel but at the same time results in production of waste products which in themselves may be a secondary source of minerals. Some coal ash, for example, contains concentrations of vanadium and germanium; gases given off in combustion are commonly high in sulfur. The components of mineral fluxes are disassociated and recombined in other forms and thus are not reusable.

Fertilizer minerals are rendered soluble, dispersed in soils, and used by growing plants. Chemical raw materials used to make plastics, solvents, conditioners, additives, catalysts, and electrolytes are either consumed in the industrial process, converted in form, contaminated, or dispersed through marketing, and are rarely recoverable for reuse.

Whether or not a nondissipative mineral material can be reclaimed for secondary or tertiary uses depends on its resistance to chemical and physical breakdown, the quantities of it available in the recoverable unit, the price, and the ease with which it can be extracted from the primary product. For example, a piece of obsolete iron machinery weighing several tons is a profitable secondary source of iron, but a few hundred pounds of reinforcing steel rods in a concrete foundation could not be economically extracted from the containing concrete. The amount of iron in an old barbed wire fence would not pay for the man-hours necessary to collect it. Collection of lead storage batteries provides an economically recoverable source of lead, but the lead in spent bullets or in residential plumbing seals is too small in

TABLE XI.3

SCRAP METAL IN THE UNITED STATES
(compiled from U. S. Bureau of Mines
Mineral Facts and Problems, 1965 Edition)

Metal	Approximate annual recovery from scrap[1]	Remarks
Iron	70 to 85 million tons[2]	Includes both new (about 60%) and old scrap. In the iron cycle from mine to product to recovery, the loss of iron is 16 to 36%. About half the feed for steel furnaces is scrap.
Ferro-alloy		Most special purpose steel scrap containing a high percentage of chromium, cobalt, molybdenum, nickel, tungsten, and vanadium (high temperature alloys, stainless steel, high-strength and high-speed steel) is remelted without separation of the alloy metal. Tungsten is recovered from carbide and metal sludges and recast into carbides. Manganese is recovered by chemical and metallurgical industries from spent MnO_2 oxidizing solutions. About 11,000 tons per year of nickel are recovered from nonferrous scrap. Recovery of molybdenum from nonferrous scrap is small. About 12 million tons per year of manganese-rich open-hearth slags are produced in the U.S. and some 25% of them are re-cycled; these slags contain 5 to 9% manganese and are potential sources. Some slags from re-melting of steel contain up to 12% chromium but these are not currently used as sources.

TABLE XI.3 *(Continued)*

Copper	1 million tons	Secondary copper production from old and new scrap ranges from 900,000 to 1,000,000 tons per year, about half of which is old scrap. Old scrap reserve is estimated at 35 million tons in cartridge cases, pipe, wire, auto radiators, bearings, valves, screening, lithographers' plates.
Lead	0.5 million tons	Estimated reserve is 4 million tons of lead in batteries, cable coverings, railway car bearings, pipe, sheet lead, type metal.
Zinc	0.25 to 0.40 million tons	Zinc recovered from zinc, copper, aluminum, and magnesium-based alloys.
Tin	20,000 to 25,000 long tons	Tin recovered from tin plate and tin-based alloys, 20%; tin recovered from copper- and lead-based alloys, 80%.
Aluminum	0.3 million tons	Because aluminum is a comparatively new metal the old scrap pool is small, but it is growing rapidly.
Precious metals	gold = 1 million ounces silver = 30 million ounces	Precious metals including platinum are recovered from jewelry, watch cases, optical frames, photo labs, chemical plants. Because of the high value, recovery is high.
Mercury	10,520 flasks (1963)	Recovery is high. Nearly all mercury in mercury cells, boilers, instruments, and electrical apparatus is recovered when items are scrapped. Other sources are dental amalgams, battery scrap, oxide and acetate sludges.

[1] Includes old and new scrap. New scrap or "home" scrap is produced in the metallurgical and manufacturing process; old scrap is "in use."

[2] Old and new scrap *consumed* rather than *recovered*.

quantity and too widely dispersed for collection to be economically feasible. Lead used as a gasoline additive as tetraethyl lead is dissipated. Recovery of asbestos fibers from manufactured fireproofing mats is not economically attractive. The lead and titanium in paints is widely dispersed and not recoverable. The zinc in galvanized pipe is also widely dispersed. Only a part of the copper in the myraid small electrical devices manufactured finds its way into scrap. Aluminum pots, pans, and heavy castings can be recovered; aluminum foil used by the housewife is lost. The aluminum scrap pool is growing rapidly but because aluminum is a relatively new metal the accumulated supply is still relatively small compared to other metals. Scrap metal recovery in the United States is shown in Table XI.3. According to McDivitt (1965, p. 76), scrap accounts for about 50 per cent of steel furnace feed (this includes old scrap plus 'home' scrap from steel plant operations), 40 per cent of domestic lead consumption, 25 per cent of domestic copper consumption, and 5 per cent of domestic zinc consumption.

From a dollar-and-cents point of view, secondary recovery of mineral products is virtually restricted to metal scrap and, to a much lesser extent, to used dimension stone and used brick. The growing market for used stone and brick is in the mid-20th century an architectural fad, but through history brick and stone structures have from time to time been robbed to build new structures. Concrete, although durable, cannot be reused (except as fill or riprap) because it is cast in forms and cannot be conveniently disassembled.

The service life of mineral products ranges from less than a year to millenia. The quarried stone blocks of the Egyptian pyramids are in use in the original structure; bronze church bells more than 1,000 years old are still in service in some parts of the world. On the other hand, an automobile may be scrap after a crash during the first day of its use; a lead storage battery may wear out in less than two years. In any industrialized country, particularly those with a long industrial history, scrap iron constitutes an important source of raw material for steel manufacture. The principal charge for electric furnaces is scrap. In the future the scrap pool will grow larger and collection of it more efficient.

It has also become imperative for man to clean up his industrial wastes so as to stop the poisoning of the environment. Conservation laws now being written will force industry to cut down the amount of sulfur and other noxious products spewed into the atmosphere and dumped into streams and rivers. These laws will change the economics of waste treatment and make it economical to recover sulfur and perhaps other pollutants. One of the most important compounds that can be recovered from both gaseous and liquid wastes is pure water for reuse in the industrial process or release into streams and lakes.

Reworking of old mine dumps, mill tailings, and slag piles for sulfur (in pyrite), base metals (in slags), and perhaps manganese, molybdenum, and other ferro-alloys (in slags) is a possibility for the future. The aggregate tonnages of these wastes throughout the mining districts of the world is very large.

Synthesis and substitution.

Dependence on natural sources can be lessened by synthesizing or manufacturing the naturally occurring mineral. The effort at manufacture is directed mostly toward mineral substances that are valuable for their crystal structure (diamond, sapphire, ruby, quartz crystals, mica, zeolites) or mineralogical properties rather than as sources for particular elements. The elements themselves are, of course, used to build the crystalline compound. Efforts to synthesize have naturally been focused on minerals in short supply or those strategic minerals whose major sources lie outside of the United States. Success in synthesis not only removes dependence on natural supplies but also permits quality control. It is logical to include with synthesis the modification of natural minerals to give them a desirable property not inherent in the natural deposits—activation of clays is an example.

Diamonds were first manufactured successfully in the United States in 1955. Now manufactured diamonds are also produced in Ireland, Japan, Republic of South Africa, U.S.S.R., and Sweden. The manufactured stones are nearly all single crystals and thus abrasiveness is more uniform and generally higher than the natural bort which includes broken fragments and slivers. The main problem in diamond manufacture lies in increasing the size of the crystals. Production of manufactured stones is expected to increase steadily. Synthesis of corundum was an early success, and synthetic aluminum oxide for industrial use was introduced as early as 1900. Synthesis of gem grade crystals followed; at the present time crystals of ruby, sapphire, spinel, rutile, and beryl can be successfully and commerically grown. Of these, ruby and sapphire have industrial applications. Use of synthetic stones is increasing. Sythesis of quartz crystals on a commercial basis became a reality in 1958. In several decades, it is likely that the manufactured product will replace natural quartz crystals. The only mica which is synthesized for industrial purposes is a fluorphlogopite mica which is ground and substituted for the natural mineral in glass-bonded mica. No successful process for growing large mica crystals has been discovered so that manufactured mica cannot substitute for strategic mica. Research to produce large crystals of synthetic mica continues.

One of the earliest naturally occurring minerals to be synthesized was sodium carbonate or *trona*. The Solvay process, invented in 1863, utilized salt, limestone, and ammonia as basic raw materials. The Solvay process replaced an earlier process—the LeBlanc process invented in 1791—which used salt, limestone, and coal. Sodium carbonate from natural deposits competes with manufactured sodium carbonate; the natural material now accounts for about 25 per cent of domestic production, an increase from 13 per cent in 1958. Sodium sulfate is another mineral product produced in part from natural sources and in part manufactured. Nitrogen affords a classic example of replacement of a natural mineral source by a manufactured mineral product. Until the 1920s, most of the world's nitrate was mined in Chile. Then research on various processes permitted commercial fixation of atmospheric nitrogen which today constitutes the world's principal source. The successful use of clays and zeolites for a number of industrial purposes including catalysts, decolorizing, and filtering agents prompted research on treatment of natural materials to enhance natural properties (activation of clays) and on manufacturing of catalysts and zeolites in large quantities. Manufacture of glass fibers and of mineral wool have resulted in synthetic mineral fibers which in part have eased the demand for natural rock fiber or asbestos. This is really simulation and substitution rather than synthesis because the artificial product is neither chemically nor mineralogically similar to the natural fiber.

The future will see more synthesis, simulation, modification, and improvement in quality of natural mineral products. The factors that control research in this area are (1) shortage of natural supplies, (2) price of natural material, (3) desire for domestic sufficiency, (4) inadequacies or quality defects in natural materials, and (5) possibility of producing marketable by-products in the manufacturing process.

Substitution is, of course, quite different from synthesis. It involves abandonment of a traditional raw material and the substitution for it of another natural mineral material or some manufactured material which does not attempt to duplicate the original. Because of wartime substitutions, substitution carries the connotation of making do—of using a slightly inferior material or of producing a slightly inferior product. Such a connotation is unfortunate because substitution does not necessarily involve a decline in product quality. What makes substitution difficult to achieve except under conditions of extreme shortage is resistance to substantial modifications of the industrial process which utilizes the raw material. Modification not only requires capital investment but also results in interruption of a successfully operating routine and may require retraining of personnel. For this reason, substitutions are usually resisted by operating personnel while supported by the research division which conceived the substitution.

Substitution of more abundant natural materials for less abundant or substitution of a modified abundant mineral for a less abundant are obvious first steps in substitution. The future will bring more drastic substitutions wherein an entire process will be redesigned or replaced to eliminate the need for a particular mineral in short supply. Thus one metal may replace another, or a ceramic, glass, or plastic may replace a metal entirely.

At present nuclear engineers have the capability of changing or transmuting elements by altering the structure of the atomic nucleus. It is not likely that in this process one metal will be transformed to another in large volumes for industrial purposes, such as, for example, lead into gold or into mercury. Although such transmutation is technically possible, the cost with today's technology might be measured in millions of dollars per pound. However, commercial production of certain isotopes for military research and medical purposes is already a reality.

Utilization of minerals or elements not now used by society.

An industrial society through changes and advances has a way of creating resources by creating demand for minerals which previously had no beneficial use and devising a means of economically extracting and refining the minerals or elements. It is difficult to separate demand from capability to supply—both can exist independently but the *resource* is created by action in concert. Figure XI.3 shows the historical rise in the variety of minerals consumed by an evolving industrial society. Mineral resource statistics of 1880 did not include many reported on regularly in modern tabulations. Uranium, beryllium, germanium, and zeolites are well-recognized examples. The trend will no doubt continue so that by the turn of the century industry may be demanding minerals which are not now exploited. Our knowledge of mineralogy and the composition of the crust is of course relatively advanced over what is was in 1880 so that the same rate of increase in variety cannot be expected in the future. Probably

FIGURE XI.3

Increase in the variety of minerals used by society (U.S. Geological Survey
Long Range Plan, 1964, Figure 14).

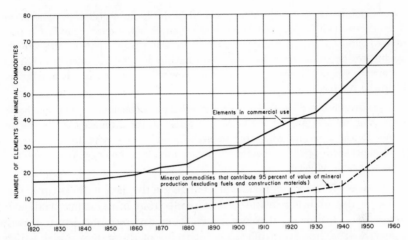

the big advance will come in the modification of natural materials
(p. 379).

Extra-terrestrial sources.

For decades science fiction has portrayed voyages to the asteroids,
planets, and faraway stars to secure cargoes of valuable metals to be
brought home to a depleted earth. Calculations of the amounts of
energy required to transport such cargoes render the entire idea so
fantastic by any conceivable economic standard of today that, up
until recently, no engineer or economist would dare to suggest the
kind of economics or technology that might make such extra-terrestrial mining a reality for fear of being laughed out of the profession.
How provocative it was, therefore, to read the following captions in
two of the most reputable and conservative mining journals—"USBM
Studies Moon Mining Under Research Grant" in the Engineering
and Mining Journal for July, 1965, p. 24, and "Hard Rock Tunnel
Driving . . . On the Moon?" in Mining Engineering for July, 1965,
p. 147. The first reference is here quoted:

Interior's Bureau of Mines has begun looking into the problems that may be
encountered in mining on the moon. The project is being conducted with a
$300,000 grant from the National Aeronautical & Space Administration. The

program isn't aimed at finding new sources of metals and minerals for use on earth, but at opening up sources of supply for the time when man begins to inhabit the moon and will need local resources to survive, return to earth and build a 'space base' for further exploration.

USBM points out that fuel might be found in the form of acetylene some scientists believe might be trapped in ancient volcanoes. Explorers might find it possible to build shelters from sulphur. Subsurface water pools, some scientists think, might provide fresh water. Besides supplying life-demanding water, water from moon mines could theoretically be broken down into oxygen for breathing and hydrogen for fuel.

Experts are enthused by the project but concede moon mining may not be so easy as it sounds. Walter E. Lewis, Director of the Minneapolis Bureau of Mines Research Center where the program is under way, says 'the extremes of environment will probably require an all new mining technology. Mere modifications will be insufficient.'

Because of the acceleration of change in the last half-century, this writer is not inclined to state categorically that mineral materials will never be transported through space from an extra-terrestrial source to earth. It is, however, difficult to conceive of the system under which such an enterprise could take place. Mining of local materials around extra-terrestrial bases, however, is something entirely different and makes good sense. The pioneers on earth found that where transportation facilities were nonexistent or where they were prohibitively expensive, they had to make do with local materials. Space pioneers will be in the same situation. Use of local minerals for sources of oxygen, for energy, and for materials will undoubtedly be more economical than large-scale transport from earth. Thus although extra-terrestrial minerals are not likely to be a source for augmenting earth supplies, they are a source which will reduce by minute amounts the export of earth minerals.

Imminent problems—silver and mercury.

On the current world scene (1965), two metals, silver and mercury, seem to offer an immediate example of the shortage which will come later for other more important industrial metals. There are others, such as copper which could become scarce as a result of changes in the current political situation, gold which is approaching shortage, and uranium which could become scarce in a short time if exploration continues to lag. It is profitable therefore to review silver and mercury and prospects for alleviating the shortage.

The demand for silver currently exceeds production and has since 1959. The world reserve index is 23 years; United States reserve index based on production is 16 years. Based on consumption, the domestic index is 6 years (p. 323). One reason for the strong demand is increased demand for coinage and rising demand for silver for industrial purposes and for the arts. A world supply deficit of several million ounces is anticipated over the next few years (p. 324). The U. S. part of this deficit will be made up from accumulated supplies, largely U. S. Treasury stocks.

One obvious response to shortage is to increase production—in this case, a world production of 256 million ounces per year—and usually increases in production are effected automatically through higher prices for silver. In this case, however, ordinary market conditions do not apply because the United States, through redemption of its silver certificates, sells silver at the monetary value of 1.293 dollars per ounce and as long as large quantities can be bought at this price, there is an effective, albeit temporary, ceiling. But even as this ceiling is recognized as temporary, there are no really large known reserves of marginal 'straight silver' ores that can be exploited as the price rises. Most of the known reserves are as components of base metal ores whose economics are not the economics of silver alone, but are geared to general industrial demand. Increased scrap recovery does not offer a solution because silver is already efficiently recovered from scrap and from industrial processes; some improvement in recovery from photographic wastes is possible. In November of 1965, the U. S. Bureau of Mines announced success with a technique using steel wool to recover silver from spent film-fixer solutions, which could perhaps result in savings of several million ounces of silver per year.

New discoveries and unconventional sources present the best hope for increasing silver production. If, however, projected discoveries are to overcome the deficit, there will have to be large-scale worldwide exploration successes. The high silver-bearing base metal orebody recently discovered near Timmins, Ontario, and called the 'find of the century' will, on the basis of known size and grade, contribute about 300 million ounces over the life of the mining operation—probably on the order of 25 or 30 years. With an initial production capacity of 2 million tons of ore per year, this large new discovery will add about 10 million ounces per year of new silver production—far short of the deficit. The government is attempting to stimulate exploration for silver by increasing the money available for silver-exploration loans and by developing new techniques such as infrared prospecting. Research by the U.S. Geological Survey has this year turned up a potential new silver source mineral—black calcite which in some districts at least contains substantial amounts of silver.

The other obvious approach to the problem is to reduce demand. Silver consumption can be reduced slightly by using substitutes in some alloys and solders but there are no practical substitutes for most industrial uses. Platinum can be substituted for silver, but of course the price differential is in favor of silver so substitution is not economically practical. The major governmental action taken to reduce silver demand has been to reduce sharply the amount of silver used in coinage by eliminating silver from dimes and quarters and reducing the content in half dollars.

Whether the measures taken to increase production and decrease demand will balance production and demand and ease the shortage over the long term remains to be seen. Of course, substantial price increases also increase production and decrease demand. If the silver price rises to 2 or 3 dollars an ounce, some marginal ores will come into production and there will be increased silver recovery through refinements in metallurgical practice. Silver jewelry, plate, and tableware will become higher priced and demand will decrease. But such drastic price increases are to be avoided, if possible, because they will initiate changes in the economics of silver-using industries and price increases for their products. In any industrial crisis brought about by inadequate silver supplies, particularly in view of cold-war pressures, government allocations are a certainty. If society is forced to choose between silver for the chemical and photographic industries and silver for tableware, silver will be made available to industry at the expense of the arts, crafts, and jewelry. Silverware will probably be replaced by stainless steel.

The demand for mercury is industrial demand mostly reflecting the increase for chlorine and caustic soda. In the process of manufacture, a mercury cell with capacity of 1 to 2 tons of chlorine per day requires an initial charge of about 85 flasks of mercury and about 0.5 pound of mercury is 'used up' in making a ton of chlorine. Chlorine and caustic soda can be manufactured (more expensively) by processes which do not require mercury, thus the demand could be cut substantially by a radical change in the industry. The 1965 world reserve index is 14 years (p. 331). The greater part of the known reserves are in Spain and Italy. The price has soared as quantities of mercury offered in world markets decreased—the only stabilizing influence has been major sales from the U.S. stockpile. Unlike silver, there is no large Treasury stock of mercury; nor is there a large pool of the metal in nonessential luxury items such as silverware, silverplate, and jewelry. In 1963 about 10,000 flasks were recovered from secondary sources (Table XI.3). For most uses of mercury there are no adequate substitutes.

There are some indications that the current shortage is the result of attempts by the major producers to control the market and increase the price, but even if the current scarcity is a 'managed shortage,' the ability of the few major producers to manage the market successfully points clearly to long-term inadequacy of reserves and productive capacity (Bailey and Smith, 1964, p. 3).

With industrial demand rising, prospects for substitutes dim, secondary recovery already operating efficiently, and known reserves limited, from where will come the supplies of the future? The only source is new discoveries and lower-grade deposits than have hithertofore been exploited. To achieve this goal, new techniques for sensing small amounts of mercury in gases, soils, and rocks have been developed and prospectors soon will be exploring for mercury *halos* —abnormal concentrations of the volatile mercury ion which may indicate the presence of subjacent deposits.

In view of the long-term outlook, it is likely that mercury will be one of the first metals to come under some kind of governmental allocation system. When there is not enough of a particular commodity to satisfy all of the demand, the various users will have to bid in open market and there will be resulting industrial disruptions due either to a greatly increased price for the commodity in the case of the rich or to lack of the commodity in the case of the poor. The alternative is establishment of an authority, such as that which prevailed during World War II, with responsibilities for establishing industrial priorities and allocating the inadequate supplies according to the priority scale. In future decades, various metals will probably come under an allocation system, at least during times of acute shortages. This will serve to lessen demand by regulating it. Distribution of resources by a central authority causes many undesirable social and political repercussions. It is, however, part of the price which must be paid for a fast-growing industrial world.

Conclusion.

The preceding analysis of future sources of minerals indicates a future of challenge. This is not an average or compromise between gloom and rosy optimism, but a real challenge of our society's ability to solve its problems. Basic to success is whether or not we can bring some order to accelerating changes in population and environment. Runaway populations must be brought under control in a beneficial way rather than by catastrophic and tragic natural forces. Pollutants must be handled so that the industrial capabilities which make possible society do not eventually destroy it. At the same time, as industrial society grows more complex and its elements more interdependent, the degrees of freedom in the production-consumption system will be reduced and government will exercise more authority over production and consumption of natural resources including mineral resources. If the system is to work, and work efficiently, its managers must be informed about the earth and its resources.

REFERENCES

Bailey, E. H., and Smith, R. M. (1964) Mercury—its occurrence and economic trends: U.S. Geol. Survey Circ. 496, 11 pp.

Duncan, D. C., and Swanson, V. E. (1965) Organic-rich shale of the United States and world land areas: U.S. Geol. Survey Circ. 523, 30 pp.

Knoerr, A. W. (1964) The technological revolution in mining: Address to National Western Mining Conference, Denver, Colorado, February 6–8, 1964, with Mining Factbook Supplement.

Maxwell, J. C. (1965) Will there be enough water?: Amer. Scientist, vol. 53, no. 1, pp. 97–103.

McDivitt, J. F. (1965) Minerals and men: Resources for the Future, Inc., Johns Hopkins Press, Baltimore, 157 pp.

McIlhenny, W. F., and Ballard, D. A. (1963) The sea as a source of dissolved chemicals: in Symposium on economic importance of chemicals from the sea: Amer. Chem. Soc., Div. Chem. Marketing Econ., Washington, pp. 122–131.

McKelvey, V. E. (1964) Changes in patterns of energy consumption and their bearing on exploration: Paper presented at meeting of the Society of Economic Geologists in connection with the XXII International Geological Congress, New Delhi, India, December 19, 1964.

Mero, J. L. (1965) The mineral resources of the sea: Elsevier, New York, 312 pp.

Merrill, C. W., McKnight, E. T., Kiilsgaard, T. H., and Ryan, J. P. (1965) Silver: facts, estimates, and projections: U.S. Bur. Mines Inf. Circ. 8257, 22 pp.

Mining Engineering (1964) Australian iron ore prospects budding: Mining Eng., vol. 16, no. 10, pp. 95–101.

Netschert, B. C., and Lansberg, H. H. (1961) The future supplies of the major metals: Resources for the Future, Inc., Washington, 65 pp.

Wall Street Journal (1965) Water from the sea: Wall Street Jour., April 29, 1965.

Weeks, L. G. (1965) Industry must look to the continental shelves: Oil and Gas Jour., vol. 63, no. 25, pp. 127–148.

INDEX

Abraham, Herbert: 94, 96
Abyssinia: 91
accession system, mineral ownership: 152
Accord of Montevideo: 227
Acquired Lands Act of 1947: 152
Adams, Brooks: 122
Adelaide. *See* Australia.
ad valorem property taxes: 204
Afghanistan: 103
Africa: 140
   Algeria, iron and base metal deposits:
     140
   Bushveldt complex, chromite: 141
     platinum: 141
   Congo, Shinkolobwe uranium depos-
     its: 141
   Gold Coast, bauxite deposits: 141
   Johannesburg: 141
   Katanga, copper deposits: 141
   Kimberly, diamond deposits: 140
   mineral history: 140–141
   Morocco, iron and base metal depos-
     its: 140
   N'Suta, manganese deposits: 141
   Orange River, diamond deposits: 140
   Rhodesia asbestos deposits: 141
   coal deposits: 141
   copper deposits: 141
   Great Dyke, chromite deposits: 141
     platinum deposits: 141

Africa—*Continued*
   Rhodesia—*Continued*
     Northern Rhodesia copper belt: 229
     Zambia, copper: 229
   South Africa, asbestos deposits: 141
     Bushveldt complex, chromite depos-
      its, platinum deposits: 141
     coal deposits: 141
     manganese deposits: 141
   Southwest Africa, Tsumeb mine, cop-
     per-lead-zinc ores: 141
   Tunisia, iron and base metal deposits:
     140
   Witwatersrand district, gold deposits:
     141
African mineral boom: 128
Agatharchides: 80
Age of Metals: 74
Agricola, Georgius: 40, 113, 114, 116, 157
agricultural acts: 164
Ahearn, V. P., Jr.: 240
Alabama: 173
Alaska, Purchase of: 161
Alberta. *See* Canada.
alchemists: 40
Algeria. *See* Africa.
Allen, S. W.: 184
Allentown. *See* Pennsylvania.
Alliance for Progress: 227, 228
alloying: 75

Allsman, P. T.: 187
Almaden quicksilver deposit: 139
aluminum: 136, 199, 280, 314, 316, 317, 319, 320, 329, 352, 369
amalgamation: 123, 124, 125, 138
Ambrose, P. M.: 336, 337, 338
American Association of Petroleum Geologists: 135
American Institute of Mining & Metallurgical Engineers: 135
Amstutz, G. C.: 42
Anaconda Company: 255
Anguar Island, phosphate: 146
antimony: 145, 351
Antwerp. See Belgium
apex law of mining: 167
applied ecology: 252
Arabia, crude oil reserves: 145
Archimedes: 116
  screw: 116
Arctic Archipelago: 136
Argentina. See South America.
Aristotle: 95, 96, 113
Arizona: 174
  Pima: 255
  San Manuel copper mine: 253
  Twin Buttes area: 255
Arps, J. J.: 28, 29
arsenic: 351
Arthur's Excalibur: 107
asbestos: 49, 135, 141, 283, 314, 334, 335
Asia, Central, copper deposits: 140
asphalt: 90, 138, 351
assaying: 116
assessment, boards of: 35
  work: 175
Atai. See U.S.S.R.
Athens: 94, 151, 152
Atomic Age: 74
Atomic Energy Act of 1946: 171
  of 1954: 171
Atomic Energy Commission: 195, 292
Aurora. See North Carolina.
Australia: 141, 142, 203
  gold rush: 158
  mineral history: 141–143
  Newcastle, blast furnace: 142
  New South Wales, Ballarat, Victoria, gold deposits: 142
    Bathurst, gold deposits: 142
    Bendigo, Victoria, gold deposits: 142
    Broken Hill, silver-lead-zinc deposit: 142
    Ophir, gold: 142

Australia—Continued
  Northern Territory, Darwin, gold deposits: 142
  uranium: 143
  Perth: 143
  Rum Jungle, uranium: 143
  Queensland, bauxite: 143
    Mount Isa, copper-silver-lead-zinc ores: 142
    Mount Morgan, gold: 142
  South Australia:
    Adelaide, lead: 142
    Burra mine, copper: 142
    Glen Ozmond, lead: 142
    Iron Knob, iron: 143
    Iron Monarch range, iron deposits: 143
    Middleback range, iron deposits: 143
    Moonta mine, copper: 142
    Walleroo mine, copper: 142
  Tasmania, Mount Lyell, gold: 142
  Western Australia:
    Coolgardie gold deposits: 142
    Hamersley Range, iron deposits: 143, 358
    Kalgoolie, gold: 142
    Kapunda mine, copper: 142
Austria: 220

Babylon: 92
bacteria: 45, 47
Bailey, C. C.: 205
Bailey, E. H.: 332, 385
Bailly, P. A.: 23, 28, 29, 159, 256
Bain, H. F.: 102, 103
Baja California. See Mexico.
Balkans: 92, 129, 139
  mineral history: 139–140
  oil supplies: 271
Ballard, D. A.: 374
Ballarat. See Australia.
Ball, S. A.: 85, 93, 99
Banking Act of 1933: 215
Baraboo (Lake Superior region) : 131
barite: 59, 351
Bartolome de Medina: 123
base metals: 57, 135, 136, 138, 140
Bateman, A. M.: 43, 66, 130
  classification of minerals: 65
    of nonmetals: 68
Bates, R. L.: 58, 59
Bathurst, New South Wales. See Australia.

Bathurst-Newcastle area, New Brunswick. *See* Canada.
bauxite: 138, 139, 141, 143, 145, 316, 317, 319, 320
Bawdin mine. *See* Burma.
Becker, G. F.: 98, 123
Belgium: 119
 Antwerp: 113
Bendigo. *See* Australia.
beneficiation: 31
beryllium: 129, 281, 314, 328, 329, 352, 370
beach deposits: 371
Bethlehem Steel Corp.: 138
Bihar. *See* India.
Bingham Canyon. *See* Utah.
bismuth: 351
Bituminous Coal Open Pit Mining Conservation Act: 368
black beach sands. *See* sands.
Black Lake, Quebec. *See* Canada.
Blainey, Geoffrey: 142
Blind River, Ontario. *See* Canada.
Blondel, F.: 10, 11
Boarman, P. M.: 216
Boericke, W. F.: 205
Bohemia: 113
Bolivia. *See* South America.
Bomi Hills iron deposits. *See* Liberia.
Bonanza Creek: 133
Bonini, W. E.: 235
Borden, G. S.: 204
boron: 351
Bowles, Oliver: 266
Braden copper deposit, Chile. *See* South America.
brass: 93
Brazil. *See* South America.
breeder reactor: 292
breeding process: 20
brickmaking: 91
brines: 7, 46, 48
Britain: 96, 124. *See also* England.
British Parliament's Gold Standard Act of 1816: 215
British Columbia. *See* Canada.
Broken Hill, New South Wales. *See* Australia.
bromine: 351
bronze: 89, 123
 vs. copper: 74
Bronze Age: 74
Brown, Harrison: 104
Brown, J. C.: 143, 144
Buck, W. K.: 235

Building Stone Act of 1892: 170, 171
Burma, Bawdin mine, silver-lead-zinc-copper ores: 144
 Katha district, rubies: 144
 mineral history, 143–145
 Mogok Valley, rubies: 144
 Shan States of, Bawdin mine: 144
 tin: 144
 tungsten mining: 144
 Yenangyuang oil field: 144
Burma Ruby Mines, Ltd.: 145
Burmah Oil Company: 144
Burra mine, South Australia. *See* Australia.
Bushveldt complex. *See* Africa.
Butte. *See* Montana.
 district. *See* Montana.

cadmium: 351
California: 165
 gold rush: 128, 166
 Huntington Beach: 241
 Los Angeles: 241
 Searles Lake: 303, 345
 State Water Project: 237
 Water Plan: 237
Callaway, H. M.: 36
Canada: 135, 136, 203, 205, 209
 Alberta tar sands: 136
 aluminum: 136
 British Columbia:
  Copper Mountain, base metals, gold, silver: 136
  Kootenay, base metals, gold, silver: 136
  Rossland: base metals, gold, silver: 136
  Sullivan, lead-zinc: 135
 gas, natural: 136
 law, mineral: 178–179
 Manitoba:
  Flin Flon, copper-zinc-silver-gold: 136
  Sherrit-Gordon, copper-zinc-silver-gold: 136
  Thompson mine, nickel: 136
 mineral history: 135–137
 New Brunswick, Bathurst-Newcastle area, base metals: 136
 Northwest Territories:
  Great Bear Lake, uranium: 136
  Great Slave Lake, base metals: 136
  Yellowknife, gold: 136

Canada—*Continued*
  Nova Scotia, gold: 135
  Ontario:
    Blind River, uranium: 136
    Cobalt, silver-cobalt-nickel: 136
    Falconbridge mine, copper-nickel: 136
    Kirkland Lake, gold, copper: 136
    Porcupine, gold, copper: 136
    Steep Rock Lake, iron: 136
    Sudbury, copper-nickel: 136
    Timmins, base metals: 136
  Quebec:
    Black Lake, asbestos: 135
    Noranda, gold, copper: 136
    Thetford, asbestos: 135
  Saskatchewan, gas fields: 136
    helium reserves: 136
    potash: 136
  Yukon Territory, gold: 136
Canadian shield: 135
Cananea. *See* Mexico.
Cane Creek. *See* Utah.
capital costs: 34
carbon black: 351
carbon dioxide: 260, 351
Carlin. *See* Nevada.
carteles: 352
cast iron. *See* iron.
Caucauses. *See* U.S.S.R.
cement: 128, 351. *See also* portland cement; pozzolanic cement.
ceramic materials: 57. *See also* clays.
Cerro Bolivar, Venezuela. *See* South America.
Cerro de Pasco, Bolivia. *See* South America.
cesium: 351
Ceylon: 103
  gems: 144
Chaldeans: 86
Chapman, W. M.: 150
charcoal: 76
Charles III, King of Spain: 121, 158
chemical and biological processes: 45
chemical materials: 57
Chihuahua. *See* Mexico.
Chile. *See* South America.
China: 100, 102, 103, 145
  Great Wall of: 103
  Hunan, lead, zinc: 145
  Manchuria, coal deposits: 145
  mineral history: 101, 102
  Shansi iron industry: 102
  Yunnan, copper, tin: 145

Christmas Islands, phosphate: 146
chromite: 141, 145, 297, 298, 299
chromium: 144, 146, 276, 297, 313, 352
Chuquicamata copper deposit, Chile. *See* South America.
city: 235
civil codes, Roman: 158
  law: 154
Clarke, F. W.: 13
classifications of minerals. *See* minerals.
Clawson, Marion: 235
clays: 59, 67, 351. *See also* ceramic materials.
  high alumina: 369
Cleveland. *See* Ohio.
Coahuila. *See* Mexico.
coal: 53, 95, 96, 103, 119, 124, 125, 136, 139, 141, 142, 143, 144, 145, 170, 273, 274, 285, 286, 287, 291, 313
  anthracite: 351
  bituminous: 273
  hydrogenation of: 139
  lignite: 273
Coal Age: 74
Coal Act of 1873: 170, 171
cobalt: 136, 278, 303, 305, 313
Cobalt, Ontario. *See* Canada.
Coeur d'Alene. *See* Idaho.
coinage: 121, 154
coke: 124
Collins, W. F.: 101, 102
Colorado, Fremont Pass, molybdenum: 133
  Leadville, lead: 133
Colorado Plateau: 134
Colombia. *See* South America.
columbium: 351
Columbus expedition: 122
Commodity Credit Corporation: 195, 199
commodity stabilization: 200
common law. *See* law.
Common Varieties Act of 1955: 170, 171
Comstock lode: 131. *See also* Virginia City, Nevada.
  silver camp: 131
concentration, beneficiation, and refining, ecological effects of: 259
concentration clarkes: 21
Confucius: 102
Congo. *See* Africa.
conservation: 183, 184
  laws: 34, 255
Consolidated Diamond Mines of South-West Africa: 224
construction materials: 57, 236, 238

Continental Congress: 160
continental rocks: 370
   shelves: 149
Cook, Captain James: 141
Coolgardie, Western Australia. See Australia.
copper: 18, 45, 46, 83, 86, 89, 128, 130, 133, 136, 137, 138, 140, 141, 142, 144, 145, 199, 272, 278, 306, 307, 308, 309, 314, 352, 369
   porphyry copper: 133
   pyrite deposit: 139
Copper Mountain, British Columbia. See Canada.
Copper Range Company: 205
coppice woods: 124
Cornwall: 93, 107, 108, 154. See also England.
corundum: 351
cost concept: 18
   depletion: 206
costs, capital: 34
   transportation: 34
Crusades: 104
crushing and grinding: 32
cryolite: 146
Crystal Falls (Lake Superior region): 131
Ctesibius: 116
Cuba, lateritic ores, nickel from: 146
   manganese ores: 146
   nickel ores: 146
cultural stages: 74
currency: 100, 213
custom mills: 32
Cuyuna (Lake Superior region): 131
Cyprus: 86, 87, 92
Czechoslovakia: 118, 119
   Joachimstahl: 113
   uranium: 139

Damascus: 103
Damastium: 93
Daniel, G. E.: 74
Dapples, E. C.: 4
Dark Ages: 103, 104, 154
Darwin, Northern Territories. See Australia.
Daubrée: 130
Davan, C. F.: 345, 346
Davies, Oliver: 100, 129
Dawson Act: 163
Dawson City: 133
Declaration of Punta del Este: 227

Defense Production Administration: 199
Defense Production Act Inventory: 195
   of 1950: 195
Dehuff, G. L.: 305, 306
De Launay, Louis: 130
Delius: 40
depletion allowances: 208
   cost: 8, 206
   discovery value: 206
   percentage: 8, 205–206
deposits, conventional: 357
   subjacent: 358
depreciation: 206
Derbyshire: 107, 108, 154, 166. See also England.
De Re Metallica: 40, 113
desalination: 373, 374
Descartes: 40
developing nations: 218
development, factors controlling: 220
Devonshire: 107, 108, 154. See also England.
Dey, A. K.: 143, 145
diagenesis: 47, 53
diamond drill: 132
diamonds: 64, 95, 138, 140, 144, 337, 338
   industrial: 284, 314, 337, 353
   synthetic: 378
diatomite: 351
direct shipping ores: 31
discovery, probabilities of success: 28
discovery-value depletion: 206
dominal theory: 121
Donetz Basin. See U.S.S.R.
DPA Inventory or Stockpile: 195. See also Defense Production Act Inventory.
Drake, Colonel: 131
dragline: 30
dredging: 30, 253, 257. See also mining.
Duncan, D. C.: 369

Eastern Mediterranean region: 92–93
East Texas oil field, Texas: 135
Eckel, E. C.: 91
Egypt: 86–92, 150, 271
   manganese deposits: 141
   resources of: 91
Egyptian screw: 116
Elba: 98
electrical field: 362, 364
electrical separators: 32
Élie de Beaumont, Leonce: 130
El Pao, Venezuela. See South America.

El Romeral, Chile. *See* South America.
El Tofo, Chile. *See* South America.
Ely, Northcutt: 121, 151, 153, 158, 178, 180
emeralds: 138
emery: 351
eminent domain: 149, 240
Emmons, S. F.: 130
Emperor Justinian: 152. *See also* Justinian Code.
endogenous: 52
energy, geothermal: 20
    nuclear: 20
    reserves: 291
    solar: 20
    tidal: 20
Engineering and Mining Journal: 352
England: 107, 108, 119, 125, 154, 166. *See also* Britain; Cornwall; Derbyshire; Devonshire.
Eolithic man: 83
epigenetic: 49, 51
epigeneticists: 41
equalization, boards of: 35
Erzegebirge: 107, 113
Ethiopia: 90
Eureka. *See* Nevada.
Europe, mineral history: 139–140
    Northern: 124
Evans, J. B.: 36
evaporation process: 46
exogenous: 52
exploration architecture: 23
    probabilities of success: 28
    stages in: 22
    techniques: 360
extralateral rights: 176
    mining: 165, 166
extra-terrestrial sources: 381

Faggioli, R. E.: 192, 243
Faja de Oro oil field. *See* Mexico.
Falconbridge mine, Ontario. *See* Canada.
Far East: 100–103
    mineral history: 145
Federal register of mining claims: 176
Federal Reserve Banks: 213
    notes: 213
    Water Power Act of 1920: 172
feldspar: 351
ferroalloy metals: 55
fertilizer growth rate: 345
    materials: 57
feudalism: 154

Fifth Circuit Court of Appeals: 8
Finland: 220
    Kokkola: 139
    Petsamo: 139, 271
Finlay, J. K.: 35
fire setting: 80, 118
First Geneva Conference of 1958: 149
Fisher, W. L.: 32, 59, 60
Flin Flon, Manitoba. *See* Canada.
Florence (Lake Superior region) : 131
Florida: 173
    phosphate: 135
        field: 134
flotation cells: 32
fluorspar: 203, 283, 314, 335, 336, 337
fluorine: 335, 369
flux: 116, 119
Forbes, R. J.: 75, 76, 83, 85, 89, 90, 91, 93, 94, 96, 98, 99, 100, 103, 105, 129, 152, 153
formation of mineral deposits, classification of processes: 52
    chemical and biological processes: 45
    internal deposits: 42
        processes: 48
    physical (mechanical) processes: 43
    surficial deposits: 42, 43
        processes: 43
Fortescue, J.: 23
Fouqué: 130
France: 119, 125, 129, 160
    Lacq sour gas field: 140
    Lorraine: 139
Francisco Xavier de Gamboa: 158
Frasch process, sulfur mining: 134
Freiberg: 113, 130
    Mining Academy: 41
Fremont Pass. *See* Colorado.
Fuller, Varden: 294
fumaroles: 46, 48

Gabon: 233
Gadsden Purchase: 161
Gale, H. S.: 6
Gambler's Ruin: 29
gamma-ray activation: 367
garnet: 351
gas: 136, 143, 170
    natural: 129, 136, 140, 275, 289, 290, 313, 348, 351
        liquids: 351
gem mines: 93, 99
gems: 144
gemstones: 57, 351

General Services Administration: 195
Geneva Conference, First, 1958: 149
  Second, 1960: 149
Geological Society of America: 135
geological surveys: 234
  costs of: 234
Georgia. See U.S.S.R.
Georgius Agricola. See Agricola, Georgius.
Gerhard: 40
germanium: 351
Germany: 107, 108, 113, 125, 157, 166, 271
  Kupferschiefer copper deposits: 139
  Stassfurt potash deposit: 139
Gilmour, Pa... 61
Glacier Bay...
glass: 91
Glen Ozmor...
  tralia...
GNP: 245. ...
  Prod...
Gogebic (L...
gold: 83, 8...
  138,
  210,
  314,
  exchange...
  limited...
  reserve:...
  rush, A...
    Califo...
  standar...
Gold Coa...
Gold Res...
  Standard Act of 1816, Britain: 215
  of 1920, United States: 215
Golden Fleece: 95
Goldschmidt, V. M.: 13
Gondwana coal measure. See India.
granite: 59
graphite: 351
gravity concentration: 43
gravitational field: 362, 364
Gray, W. Howard: 178
Great Bear Lake, Northwest Territories. See Canada.
Great Dyke, Rhodesia. See Africa.
Great Salt Lake. See Utah.
Great Slave Lake, Northwest Territories. See Canada.
Great Wall of China. See China.
Greece: 93, 94
Greenland, cryolite: 146
Green River Formation: 48

Gross National Product: 219, 245. See also GNP.
ground water deposits: 7
growth rates, significance of: 265
Guadalupe Hidalgo, Treaty of: 161, 162
Guam: 162
Guanajuato. See Mexico.
Guianas. See South America.
guano: 146. See also phosphate.
Gulf Coast salt-dome sulfur deposits: 134. See also sulfur.
gypsum: 137, 351, 373

hafnium: 351
Hahl, D. C.: 6
H... and Norcross mine. See Nevada.
... 92
...ange. See Australia.
...exander: 161
...g: 32
...ies: 216
...O.: 296
...A.: 241
...108, 157
... tanks: 32
...: 74
...Saskatchewan: 136
...T. A.: 16
...40, 90
...e Mexico.
...T. C.: 207
...s area: 8
...onservation district: 8
Holliday, R. W.: 298, 301
Homestead Act, Stock Raising: 164
Homestead Law: 161
  gold and silver: 166
Hoover, H. C.: 35, 76, 77, 78, 80, 81, 90, 91, 93, 95, 98, 113, 116, 124, 155
Hoover Commission: 174
Hoskold formula: 35
hot springs: 46, 48
Houseman, C. T.: 345, 346
Hubbert, M. K.: 15, 286
Huntington Beach. See California.
Huntington Beach Company: 241
Hutton, James: 41, 117
hydration: 45
hydrologic cycle: 45
hydrothermal solutions: 52
  theory: 48

Iceland: 220
Idaho, Coeur d'Alene, lead-silver: 133
Idria. *See* Italy.
ilmenite: 283
Incas: 137
income taxes: 204
India: 100, 103
  Bihar, coal deposits: 144
    mica pegmatites: 144
  gems: 144
  Gondwana coal measure: 143
  mineral history: 143–145
  Mysore, Kolar gold field: 144
  Orissa, coal deposits: 144
  Raniganj coal field: 143, 144
  Singhbhum copper workings: 144
  Travancore, black beach sands: 144
Indian lands: 171
Indonesia, bauxite deposits: 145
  iron deposits: 145
  tin mining: 145
industrialization: 220
industrial materials: 57
Inter-American Development Bank: 227
internal processes: 52
Internal Revenue Code: 4, 177, 205, 207
International Bank for Reconstruction
    and Development: 227, 232
  Cooperation, White House conference
    on: 150
  Development Association: 227
  Finance Corporation: 227
  Monetary Fund: 216, 217
  Minerals and Chemical Corporation:
    372
  Tin Agreement: 312
international liquidity: 217
investment capital: 220
iodine: 351
Ionian philosophy: 40
Iran: 86, 93
  crude oil reserves: 145
Iraq, crude oil reserves: 145
iron: 55, 57, 89, 90, 92, 98, 102, 119, 125,
    128, 130, 131, 136, 138, 140, 141,
    143, 145, 272, 293, 294, 295, 306
  cast: 125
  formations, Precambrian: 294
  industry, Shansi, China: 102
  Lake Superior region: 131
  meteoric: 89
  ore: 137, 275, 313, 352
    blast furnace: 142
    minette: 139
  wrought: 90

Iron Age: 74
Iron Knob, South Australia. *See* Australia.
Iron Monarch range, South Australia.
    See Australia.
iron ranges: 131
Iron River: 131
Israel: 221
  phosphate deposits: 146
Isthmus of Tehuantepec. *See* Mexico.
Italy: 119
  Idria, quicksilver: 139
  Monte Amiata, quicksilver: 139

jade: 103
Jamaica: 205
Japan: 103, 119, 145, 221
jigs: 32, 43
Joachimsthal. *See* Czechoslovakia.
Johannesburg. *See* Africa.
Jordan, phosphate deposits: 146
Just, Evan: 36
Justinian Code: 99, 158

Kalgoolie, Western Australia. *See* Australia.
Kapunda mine, South Australia. *See* Australia.
Katanga. *See* Africa.
Katha district. *See* Burma.
Kazakstan. *See* U.S.S.R.
Kemp, J. F.: 130
Kennecott Copper Corporation, Utah
    Copper Division: 255
Kennedy, President John F.: 128
kerogen: 48
Keweenaw Point. *See* Michigan.
Keynes, Lord: 215
kiln treatment: 32
kimberlite: 64
Kimberly. *See* Africa.
King Solomon: 92
  copper mines: 92
Kirkland Lake, Ontario. *See* Canada.
Kiruna. *See* Lapland.
Klondike: 133
Knoerr, A. W.: 178
Kokkola, *See* Finland.
Kolar gold field, Mysore. *See* India.
Kootenay district, British Columbia. *See* Canada.
Korea, South, Sangdong tungsten mine: 145

Krivoi Rog iron deposits. *See* U.S.S.R.
Kupferschiefer. *See* Germany.
Kuwait, crude oil reserves: 145
Kuznetsk Basin. *See* U.S.S.R.
kyanite: 351

labor laws: 34
Lacq sour gas field. *See* France.
Ladendorff, G. H.: 175
Lake Superior copper district: 130
  region: 131
Land Act of 1796: 162
land grants, railroad: 163
  school: 162
  swamp: 164
Land Ordinance of 1785: 161
Langdon, J. C.: 192
Langford, R. H.: 6
Lapland, Kiruna iron deposit: 140
Lasky, S. G.: 10, 11
Lassius: 40
lateritic ores, nickel from: 146
Laurium: 80, 93, 94, 151
law, civil: 154
  common: 154
    English: 154, 157
  conservation: 34, 149, 255
  labor: 34
  mineral: 178, 179
  Roman: 152. *See also* civil codes.
  zoning: 149
leaching tanks: 32
lead: 46, 52, 93, 98, 132, 133, 135, 142,
    144, 145, 203, 272, 279, 309, 310,
    314, 352, 367
Leadville. *See* Colorado.
Lebanon: 92
legal systems: 119
Leith, C. K.: 188, 194
lessee system of mining: 152
Levy, Walter J.: 202
Lewis, R. W.: 342, 345, 346
Liberia, Bomi Hills iron deposits: 141
light metals: 57
lignite: 273, 313
lime: 351
limestone: 67, 353
limited gold bullion standard: 215
Lincoln Sand and Gravel Company: 241
Lindgren, Waldemar: 64, 66, 130
  classification of minerals: 63
liquidity: 217
  international: 217
lithium: 129, 351

Lockheed Missiles and Space Company:
    372
lode claims, minerals: 168, 169
London: 261. *See also* England; Britain.
  urban area: 251
Lopez, R. S.: 115
Lorraine. *See* France.
Los Angeles. *See* California.
Louisiana: 173
Louisiana Purchase: 161
Lovering, T. S.: 89, 119, 201
Lucretius: 74

MacDiarmid, R. A.: 59, 117
Macdonell, Harry: 178
machinery, mining: 116
magnesium: 282, 299, 314, 329, 330, 352
magnetic field: 362, 364
  permeability: 32
  separators: 32
McKatea Island, phosphate: 146
Malaya, bauxite deposits: 145
  iron deposits: 145
  tin mining: 145
Manchuria. *See* China.
manganese: 138, 140, 141, 144, 145, 295,
    296, 297, 313, 352
  nodules: 47, 149, 369, 372
  ores: 146
Manheim, F. T.: 7
Manitoba. *See* Canada.
manorial system: 107
manufacturing: 31
  materials: 57
marketability test: 178
Marquette (Lake Superior region) : 130
Marvin Shurbet et ux. vs. *U.S. Internal
    Revenue Department:* 8
Marx, Karl: 215
Mason, Brian: 13
Massachusetts Colony: 160
materials, chemical: 57
  ceramic: 57
  construction: 57
  fertilizer: 57
  industrial: 57
  manufacturing: 57
  metallurgical: 57
  refractory: 57
Materials Reserve Inventory: 199
  Stockpile Act of 1965: 199
Mato Grosso, Brazil. *See* South America.
Mauritania: 233
Maxwell, J. C.: 374

May, T. C.: 335
McCracken, P. W.: 221
McDivitt, J. F.: 55, 56, 232
McIlhenny, W. F.: 374
McKelvey, V. E.: 11, 187, 372
mechanical tables: 43
meer. *See* head meer; regular meer.
megalopolis: 235
Menominee: 131
Mercer County. *See* Pennsylvania.
mercury: 19, 98, 125, 195, 272, 282, 314,
    330, 331, 332, 352, 357, 382, 384,
    385. *See also* quicksilver.
Mero, J. L.: 47, 356, 370, 371, 373, 374
Merrill, C. W.: 103, 243, 323, 324, 325,
    326
Mesabi (Lake Superior region) : 131
Mesopotamia: 86
metallurgical materials: 57
metals: 55
    Age of: 74
    base: 57, 135, 140
    ferroalloy: 55
    iron: 55, 57
    light: 57
    minor: 55, 327
    nonferrous: 55
    precious: 55, 57
    rare: 57
metamorphism: 49
meteoric iron: 76, 89
    water: 52
Mexico: 121, 122, 123, 203
    Baja California, phosphate: 137
    Cananea, copper: 137
    Chihuahua, silver: 137
    Coahuila, coal, phosphate: 137
    coal: 137
    Faja de Oro oil field: 137
    Fresnillo, silver: 137
    Guanajuato, silver: 137
    gypsum: 137
    Hidalgo, silver: 137
    iron ores: 137
    Isthmus of Tehuantepec, oil, sulfur:
        137
    mineral history: 137
    Moncloya, steel: 137
    Monterrey, steel: 137
    Nacozari, copper: 137
    Oaxaca, silver: 123
    Pachuca, silver: 137
    Panuco-Ebano oil field: 137
    Parral, silver: 137
    Poza Rica, oil: 137

Mexico—*Continued*
    Sabinas Basin, coal: 137
    San Francisco del Oro, silver: 137
    San Luis Potosi, gypsum: 137
    Santa Eulalia, silver: 137
    Sonora, copper: 137
    sulfur: 137
    Tampico, oil: 137
    Vera Cruz, oil: 137
    Zacatecas, phosphate, silver: 137
Mexico City: 261
mica: 59, 315, 339
    nonstrategic: 284, 338
    strategic: 283, 338
mica pegmatites: 144
Michel-Lévy: 130
Michigan: 35, 130, 161, 204
    mining taxes: 204
    state mine valuation: 35
Middle Ages: 157
Middleback Range, South Australia. *See*
    Australia.
Middle East: 145
military reservations: 171
Minas Gerais, Brazil. *See* South America.
Mined-Land Conservation Conference:
    368
mineral deposits: 4
    classification: 59
    concealed: 358, 359
    continental shelf: 359
    conventional: 358
    descriptive classifications: 59
    exposed: 359
    formation of: 39
        classification of processes: 52
        internal deposits: 42
            processes: 48
        physical (mechanical) processes: 43
        surficial deposits: 42, 43
            processes: 43
    genetic classifications: 59
    growth of: 7
    marine: 359
    processes of formation: 50
    sea floor: 359
    subjacent, concealed: 359
        pristine: 359
    terrestrial: 359
    undiscovered, classification of: 359
    valuation: 33
mineral estate: 6
mineral exploration, costs of: 24
    methods of: 24
mineral fuels: 57

mineral history, Africa: 140–141
  Australia, 141–143
  Burma: 143–145
  Canada: 135–137
  China: 101, 102
  Europe, Scandinavia, U.S.S.R., and the Balkans: 139–140
  Far East: 145
  India and Burma: 143–145
  Mexico: 137
  South America: 137
  United States: 130–135
mineral industry, United States, employment: 244
  freight: 244
  investments: 244
  national income: 244
  salaries and wages: 244
  value of production: 244
mineral law, Canada: 178
  United States: 174
  U.S.S.R.: 180
mineral ownership: 150
  accession system: 152
mineral policy, United States: 203
mineral production, United States, value of: 244
  world, distribution of: 267
mineral property, appraisal of: 35
mineral resources, consumption in the United States: 128
  cost concept: 17
  orebody concept: 17
  urban areas: 235
mineral rights: 5
mineral statistics: 243, 264
mineral water: 8
Mineral Leasing Act for Acquired Lands, 1947: 171
  of 1920: 170, 171
Mineral Location Act of 1872: 167, 169, 170, 171
minerals, classifications of: 54, 55
  common varieties: 6
  definition of: 1, 2, 3, 4
  extraction of: 30
  food producing: 20
  future supplies of: 356
  lode claims: 168, 169
  placer claims: 168
minerals technology: 366
minerals and other natural resources, consumption of: 246
mine surveying: 81
minette iron ores: 139

mining, apex law of: 167
mining claims, federal register: 176
mining codes: 153
Mining Congress Journal: 352
mining, dredging: 253, 257. See also dredging.
  ecological effects of: 253
  extralateral rights: 165, 166
  machinery: 116
  methods: 30
  open pit: 253
  taxes: 204
  underground: 253
Mining Engineering (Journal of) : 352
mining law, apex: 167
  Canada: 179
  legislation, federal, 1866, 1870, 1872: 166
  lessee system of: 152
  usufruct system: 153
Mining Laws of 1866 and 1870: 171
Minnesota: 35, 205
  mining taxes: 205
  state mine valuation: 35
minor metals: 55, 327
Mint Act of 1792: 215
Mississippi: 173
Missouri, southeastern, lead: 132
Mitke, C. A.: 31
Moab. See Utah.
Mogok Valley. See Burma.
molybdenum: 128, 133, 277, 300, 301, 302, 313, 352
Monclova. See Mexico.
money: 210, 211, 212
  intrinsic value: 212
  token value: 212
Montana, Butte, copper: 132
  district: 7
Monte Amiata. See Italy.
Monterrey. See Mexico.
Moonta mine, South Australia. See Australia.
Morocco. See Africa.
Moulds, D. E.: 310
Mount Isa, Queensland. See Australia.
Mount McKinley National Park: 172
Mount Lyell, Tasmania. See Australia.
Mount Morgan, Queensland. See Australia.
Muir, John: 194
Multiple Mineral Development Act of 1954: 171
  Surface Use Act of 1954: 176

multiple use: 185
  sequential: 185
  simultaneous: 185
Multiple Use Acts of 1954 and 1955: 170
Munitions Board: 199
Murray, G. W.: 81, 97
Mysore, Kolar gold field. See India.

Nacozari. See Mexico.
Napoleonic Code: 121, 159
National Coal Association: 368
National forests: 172
National Materials Reserve: 201
National parks and monuments: 171
National Security Resources Board, 199
National stockpile: 199
National Wilderness Preservation System: 173
natural gas. See gas, natural.
natural resource ethic: 194
Nauru Island, phosphate: 146
Neolithic flint mines: 85
  man: 84
  Period: 83
Nevada: 174
  Carlin, gold: 367
  Eureka, silver-lead: 132
  Hale and Norcross mine: 131
  Virginia City: 131
New Brunswick. See Canada.
New Caledonia, chromium ores: 146
  nickel ores: 146
Newcastle. See Australia.
New Guinea, gold deposits: 142
New Mexico: 170, 190
  potash deposits: 134
New Mexico Oil Conservation Commission: 190
Newmont Mining Corporation: 367
New South Wales. See Australia.
New World: 121
New York: 160
New Zealand: 220
  gold deposits: 142
nickel: 136, 139, 146, 276, 299, 300, 313, 352, 369
Niggli, Paul: 64
  classification of minerals: 62
Nikopol, Ukraine. See U.S.S.R.
Nineveh: 92
nitrate: 138
nitrogen: 379
  compounds, natural: 351
nitrum: 95

nonferrous metals: 55
nonmetals: 55, 57, 59
Noranda, Quebec. See Canada.
North American Conservation Conference: 184
  Water and Power Alliance: 237
North Carolina, Aurora: 368
  Beaufort County: 135
  phosphate: 133, 134
North, F. J.: 91
North Sea: 149
Northern Rhodesian copper belt. See Africa.
Norway: 118
Northwest Compromise: 161
Northwest Territories. See Canada.
Nova Scotia. See Canada.
N'Suta. See Africa.
Nubia: 86, 91
Nuclear Age: 74
nuclear explosives: 31
  fuel: 20, 291
nutrients, crop: 20

Oaxaca. See Mexico.
O'Brien, R. P.: 291
O'Callaghan, J. A.: 166
occupation taxes: 204
Ocean Island, phosphate: 146
Office of Defense Mobilization: 199
  Emergency Planning: 201
Ogallala Formation: 7
Ohio, Cleveland: 254
oil: 135, 136, 137, 143, 144, 145, 170, 202.
  See also petroleum.
  and gas: 127, 145, 291
  crude: 313
    reserves: 145
  fields: 135, 137, 140
Oil Age: 74
Oil and Gas Journal: 352
Oil Placer Act of 1897: 170, 171
oil shale: 170, 291, 369
Omnibus Stockpile Bill: 199
Ontario. See Canada.
open pit methods: 30
  mining: 253
Ophir (probably Arabia) : 92
Ophir, New South Wales. See Australia.
Orange River. See Africa.
ore, definition of: 11
  indicated: 10
  inferred: 11
  measured: 10

ore, definition of—*Continued*
  possible: 10
  probable: 10
  proved: 10
orebody concept: 18
ores, direct shipping: 31
  washing of: 80
Organ Pipe Cactus National Monument: 172
Orissa. *See* India.
Ostia: 153
Outer Continental Shelf Lands Act of 1953: 170, 171, 173
Outokumpu process, conversion of pyrites: 139
Owen, E. W.: 15
Owens Lake: 6
oxidation: 45
oyster shell: 190

Pachuca. *See* Mexico.
Paleolithic man: 83
Panuco-Ebano oil field. *See* Mexico.
Pardee, F. G.: 35
Park, C. F., Jr.: 117
Parral. *See* Mexico.
Parsons, A. B.: 253, 256
Paschall, R. A.: 35
patented claims: 168
  townsites: 172
patio process: 123, 124
peat: 351
Pedis Possessio: 168
pegmatite mining operations: 32
pegmatites, mica: 144
Penn, William: 160
Pennsylvania: 130, 131, 160, 368
  Allentown: 134
  Mercer County: 130
  Pittsburgh coal seam: 131
  Scranton: 254
percentage depletion: 8, 205, 206
Peripatetic school: 96
perlite: 351
Perth. *See* Australia.
Peru. *See* South America.
Petrie, W. M. F.: 82, 87, 88, 89
petroleum: 128, 129, 135, 138, 139, 140, 202, 272, 287, 288, 289, 313, 353. *See also* oil.
  crude: 274
  formation of: 46
  policy: 15
  resource estimates: 16

Philippine Islands: 162
  chromite deposits: 145
  gold deposits: 145
  iron deposits: 145
  manganese deposits: 145
Phillips, William B.: 164
Phoenicians: 92, 93
phosphate: 127, 129, 134, 137, 140, 145, 146, 170, 306, 315, 337, 353
  Florida: 134, 135
  North Carolina: 133, 134
  South Carolina: 134
  rock: 284, 339, 341, 342, 343
Phosphoria Formation: 135
phosphorite: 342, 369
  nodules: 372
Pickett Act of 1910: 172
pigments: 103
Pima. *See* Arizona.
pipeline stockpile: 195
pitch lake, Trinidad: 138
pit control: 32
Pitman, Frank: 178
Pittsburgh coal seam: 131. *See also* Pennsylvania.
place value: 353
Placer Act of 1870: 166
placer claims: 168
  deposits: 371
  minerals: 44
plaster and mortar: 91
platinum: 141, 281, 314, 327
Playfair, John: 117
Pliny: 96, 98, 100, 117
point of no return: 104
population: 222
  growth: 17, 220
Porcupine, Ontario. *See* Canada.
portland cement: 134, 144, 226. *See also* cement.
Portugal: 158
Posěpný: 130
potash: 127, 129, 134, 136, 139, 170, 190, 255, 272, 285, 315, 345, 346, 353, 357, 370, 373
potassium: 170
Potosi, Bolivia. *See* South America.
  Peru. *See* South America.
Powell, John Wesley: 194
Power Act Reservations: 172
Poza Rica. *See* Mexico.
pozzolanic cement: 96. *See also* cement.
precious metals: 55, 57
Pre-emption Act of 1841: 161, 162
preservation vs. conservation: 185

President's Materials Policy Commission: 187
processing: 31
production taxes: 204
profitability test: 178
prudent man test: 169, 178
Przibam: 130
Public Law Land Review Commission: 174
Public Law 250, 1953: 171
Puerto Rico: 162, 205
pumice: 351
pyramids: 90
pyrites, conversion of, Outokumpu process: 139

quartz crystals: 351
Quebec. See Canada.
Queensland. See Australia.
quicksilver: 95, 123, 138, 139, 330

Radioactive Minerals Age: 74
radioactive wastes: 260
radium: 351
Raniganj. See India.
rare earths: 351
rare metals: 57
Raymond, I. W.: 115
Raymond, L. C.: 36
reclamation withdrawals: 172
Red Sea: 87
Redwood, Boverton: 94, 103
reduction of ores: 75
refining: 31
refractory materials: 57
regalian system: 150
    theory: 121
redistribution of minerals, ecological effects of: 261
regular meer: 108
Renaissance: 107, 112, 157
Reno, H. T.: 294
reserve index: 271, 272
    —consumption index: 271, 272
    —production index: 271, 272
reserves, classification of: 10
    definition of: 9, 10
    indicated: 10, 14
    inferred: 11, 14
    measured: 10, 14
    probable: 10
    possible: 10

reserves, classification of—Continued
    potential: 11
    proved: 10, 14
resource base: 13, 14
resources, definition of: 9
Resources for the Future, Inc.: 245
rhenium: 351
Rhodesia. See Africa.
Rickard, T. A.: 74, 75, 76, 80, 89, 91, 92, 95, 96, 99, 100, 103, 108, 113, 123, 151, 152, 153, 158, 213
Rio Tinto. See Spain.
    mine. See Spain.
Roberts, W. A.: 35, 204
rock, average composition: 14
rocks, continental: 370
    sea floor: 370
Roman civil codes: 158
    civil law: 152
    empire: 96
Rome: 96–100, 153, 158
Romney, M. P.: 245
Roosa Plan: 217
Roosa, Robert V.: 217
Roscoe, S. M.: 292
Rossland district, British Columbia. See Canada.
royalty: 108, 121
rubidium: 351
rubies: 144
Rumania, oil fields: 140
Rum Jungle, Northern Territory. See Australia.
Russia: 119. See also U.S.S.R.; Soviet Union.
rutile: 283
Ryan, J. P.: 321, 322

Sabinas Basin. See Mexico.
Saline Placer Act of 1901: 170, 171
salt: 46, 95, 96, 153, 351, 373
salt lakes: 46
saltpeter: 95
Salton Sea: 7
    wells: 7
salt wars: 82
sand and gravel: 35, 351
sands, black beach: 144
San Francisco del Oro. See Mexico.
Sangdong tungsten mine, South Korea. See Korea.
San Luis Potosi. See Mexico.
San Manuel copper mine. See Arizona.
Santa Eulalia. See Mexico.

sapphires: 144
Saskatchewan. *See* Canada.
Saxony: 107, 113
Scandinavia: 129, 139
  mineral history: 139–140
Schemnitz: 80, 118
Schneeberg: 113
Schneiderhöhn, Hans: 64, 66
  classification of ore deposits: 64
Schroeder, H. J.: 311
Schubert, H. R.: 124
scrap: 358
  and waste: 374
  metal: 375
scrubbing: 32
sea floor, ownership of: 149
  rocks: 370
Searles Lake. *See* California.
seawater: 373
Second Geneva Conference of 1960: 149
Secretary of the Interior: 170
sedimentary processes: 44
selective deposition: 45
  leaching: 45
selenium: 351
self-sufficiency index: 272
separators, magnetic and electrical: 32
Serro do Novio, Brazil. *See* South America.
severance taxes: 204
shaking tables: 32
Shan States of Burma. *See* Burma.
shale oil: 48
Shalowitz, A. L.: 173
Shansi iron industry. *See* China.
shell reefs: 47
Sherlock, R. L.: 251, 261
Sherrit-Gordon, Manitoba. *See* Canada.
Shinkolobwe, Congo. *See* Africa.
Shoemaker, R. P.: 36
Siete Partidas: 158
silver: 19, 46, 86, 94, 122, 123, 131, 132,
  133, 135, 136, 137, 138, 142, 144,
  189, 210, 211, 213, 214, 281, 314,
  323, 324, 325, 326, 327, 352, 353,
  367, 382, 383, 384
  certificates: 213, 214
Silesia: 113
simulation: 379
Sinair Peninsula: 86, 91
Singhbhum copper workings. *See* India.
sintering: 32
Siphnos: 93
Smith, C. S.: 93
Smith, R. M.: 332, 385

Society of Economic Geologists: 130, 135
sodium: 170
  carbonate: 351, 379
  sulfate: 351
solubility: 32
Solvay process: 379
Sonora. *See* Mexico.
South Africa. *See* Africa.
South America, amalgamation: 138
  Argentina, petroleum: 139
  Bolivia, gold and silver: 137
    Cerro de Pasco, silver and base
      metals: 138
    Potosi, silver: 137
    tin: 138
  Brazil: 122
    coal: 139
    diamonds: 138
    gold: 138
    iron: 138
    Mato Grosso, manganese: 138
    Minas Gerais, iron: 138
    Serro do Navio, manganese: 138
  Chile: 233
    copper deposits: 138
      Braden: 138
      Chuquicamata: 138
    gold and silver: 137
    iron: 138
      El Romeral: 138
      El Tofo: 138
    nitrate: 138
  Colombia, emeralds: 138
    gold and silver: 137
    petroleum: 139
  gold and silver: 137
  Guianas, bauxite: 138
    highlands, gold: 138
  mineral history: 137
  Peru, gold and silver: 137
    silver, base metals: 138
  Venezuela:
    Cerro Bolivar, iron: 138
    El Pao, iron: 138
    petroleum: 139
South Australia. *See* Australia.
South Carolina, phosphate: 134
South Korea. *See* Korea.
Soviet Union: 129, 221. *See also* Russia;
  U.S.S.R.
Spain: 107, 121, 122, 158, 221
  Charles III, King of: 121
  Rio Tinto mine, copper pyrite deposit: 139
  U.S. treaty with: 161

specific conductance: 32
  gravity: 32
Spindletop oil field, Texas: 135
spirals: 43
stamper, J. W.: 333
stamp mills: 116
Stassfurt potash deposit. *See* potash;
  Germany.
State mine valuation, Michigan: 35
  Minnesota: 35
steel: 93, 98, 103, 125, 131
steam: 46, 48
steam engine, Savery: 118
Steep Rock Lake, Ontario. *See* Canada.
Steno, Nicolaus: 40, 113
Stevens, R. F., Jr.: 303
stockpile: 20, 273
  as an economic stabilizer: 200
Stock Raising Homestead Act: 164
stone, crushed and dimension: 351
Stone Age: 74
strip mine reclamation: 257
strontium: 351
stopes, classification of: 31
stoping method: 30
Strabo: 99
Strategic Materials Act: 195
  Stockpile: 195
subsidies: 34
substitution: 379
Sudbury, Ontario. *See* Canada.
sulfur: 91, 99, 103, 128, 129, 136, 137,
  139, 140, 284, 315, 346, 347, 348,
  349, 350, 353, 369, 370, 373
  Gulf Coast salt dome deposits: 134
  mining, Frasch process: 134
Sullivan lead-zinc mine, British Columbia. *See* Canada.
Supplemental Stockpile: 195
surface chemistry: 32
  estate: 6
  processes: 52
Surface Resources Act of 1947: 170, 171
surface rights: 5
Swanson, V. E.: 369
Sword of Roland: 107
syngenetic: 51
syngeneticists: 41
synthesis: 379
  and manufacture: 358
Syria: 86

Taconite Amendment: 205
taconite ores: 138

talc: 59, 67, 351
Tampico. *See* Mexico.
tantalum: 351
tariffs: 34
tar sands: 136, 291
taxation: 204
taxes, *ad valorem* property: 204
  income: 204
  mining: 204
  occupation: 204
  production: 204
  severance: 204
Taylor Grazing Act of 1934: 172
Tchiaturi, Georgia. *See* U.S.S.R.
tellurium: 351
Texas: 164, 173, 191
  East Texas oil field: 135
  Republic of: 161
  Parks and Wildlife Commission: 190
  Railroad Commission: 255
  Spindletop oil field: 135
Texas and Pacific Railroad: 164
Texas Gulf Sulfur Company: 132, 368
Thales: 40
Thasos: 93
Themistocles: 94
Theophilus: 99
Theophrastus: 95, 96, 113, 116
Therring, Hans: 118
Thetford, Quebec. *See* Canada.
Thomsen, Christian J.: 74
Thompson mine, Manitoba. *See* Canada.
thorium: 292, 351, 352
Thrace: 94
tidelands: 148
Timmins, Ontario. *See* Canada.
tin: 19, 93, 97, 98, 107, 138, 144, 145,
  279, 282, 311, 312, 314, 316, 352
  mining: 145
titanium: 314, 332, 333, 352
Toledo blades: 125
touchstone: 116
Transbaikal. *See* U.S.S.R.
transmutation: 380
transportation costs: 34
Travancore. *See* India.
Treaty of Guadalupe Hidalgo: 161, 162
  of Tordesillas: 122
  with Spain: 161
Triffin, Robert: 214, 216, 217
Trinidad pitch lake: 138
Tri-State district: 52
trona: 379
Tsumeb mine, Southwest Africa. *See*
  Africa.

tungsten: 144, 145, 277, 302, 303, 313
Tunisia. See Africa.
Turin Papyrus: 87
Turkey: 86, 90
  chromium deposits: 146
Twin Buttes area. See Arizona.

Udall, Stewart: 183
underground mining: 253
United Arab Republic: 271
United Nations: 223, 233, 235
  Conferences on Law of the Sea: 149
United States: 119, 130
  mineral history: 130–135
  mineral industry, employment: 244
    freight: 244
    investments: 244
    national income: 244
    salaries and wages: 244
    value of production: 244
  mineral law: 174
  mineral policy: 203
  mineral production, value of: 244
uranium: 51, 127, 129, 134, 136, 139,
    141, 143, 176, 275, 290, 292, 352
Urals. See U.S.S.R.
U.S. Bureau of Land Management: 168,
    171, 177
  Bureau of Mines: 16, 21, 372
    Mineral Facts and Problems: 351
    Minerals Yearbook: 352
  District Court, Northern District of
    Texas: 3
  Forest Service: 177
  Geological Survey: 16, 21, 135
  gold reserves: 216
U.S.S.R.: 139, 140, 221. See also Russia;
    Soviet Union.
  Atai, gold deposits: 140
  Caucauses, copper deposits: 140
  Donetz Basin, coal: 140
    iron deposits: 140
  Georgia, Tchiaturi, manganese depos-
    its: 140
  Kazakstan, copper deposits: 140
  Krivoi Rog iron deposits: 140
  Kuznetsk Basin, coal: 140
  mineral history: 139–140
  mineral law: 180
  Transbaikal, gold deposits: 140
  Ukraine, Nikopol, manganese depos-
    its: 140
  Urals, copper deposits: 140
    gold deposits: 140

Urals, copper deposits—Continued
    iron deposits: 140
    platinum deposits: 140
  Vorkuta Field, iron deposits: 140
U.S. Steel Corporation: 138
U.S. Treasury: 214
usufruct: 99, 153
Utah, Bingham Canyon, copper: 133,
    255
  Cane Creek potash mine: 132
  Great Salt Lake: 6
  Moab, potash: 134
Utah Copper Division, Kennecott Cop-
    per Corporation. See Kennecott
    Copper Corporation.

valuation: 34
  procedures, state mine: 35
value series: 59
vanadium: 129, 278, 305, 306, 313, 352
Van Hise, C. R.: 130, 194
Van Royen, W.: 266
Vasco de Gama: 122
vein, apex of: 169, 176
Venezuela. See South America.
Vera Cruz. See Mexico.
vermiculite: 351
Vermillion: 131
Victoria, New South Wales. See Aus-
    tralia.
Virginia Charter: 160
Virginia City, Nevada. See also Com-
    stock lode; Nevada.
Virgin Islands: 162
vitriol: 95
Vitruvius: 116
Vogt, J. H. L.: 130
volcanic gases: 48
  vents: 46
volcanoes: 48
Von Cotta: 130
Vorkuta Field. See U.S.S.R.

Walleroo mine, South Australia. See
    Australia.
washing and screening: 32
Washington, H. S.: 13
washing of ores: 80
waste recovery: 358
water: 7, 8, 9, 20, 57, 236
water resource projects, ecological ef-
    fects of: 258
Weaton, G. F., Jr.: 35

Weed, W. H.: 7, 130
Weeks, L. G.: 370
Weigel, W. W.: 310, 311
Werner, Abraham Gottlob: 41, 117
Wertime, T. A.: 74, 76, 78, 79, 84, 86, 87, 91, 92, 93, 102
Western Australia. *See* Australia.
White, D. E.: 7
White, G. F.: 185
White House Conference on International Cooperation: 150
White Pine project: 205
Wideman, F. L.: 307, 308
Wilderness Act, Public Law 88-577: 173
William and Mary: 154
Williams, L. R.: 320, 329
Wilson, J. T.: 145
Witwatersrand district. *See* Africa.
Wolfe, J. A.: 255
Wonnacott, Paul: 217

World Bank: 227, 232
wrought iron. *See* iron.

Yellowknife, Northwest Territories. *See* Canada.
Yenangyaung oil field. *See* Burma.
Yukon Territory. *See* Canada.
Yunnan. *See* China.

Zacatecas. *See* Mexico.
Zambia. *See* Africa.
Zapp, A. D.: 15
Zechstein series: 139
zeolites: 379
zinc: 46, 52, 93, 132, 135, 136, 142, 144, 145, 203, 279, 310, 311, 314
zirconium: 351
zoning: 240

PRINTED IN U.S.A.